IN THE GUTTER...
LOOKING
AT THE STARS

IN THE GUTTER...
LOOKING
AT THE STARS

A LITERARY ADVENTURE THROUGH KINGS CROSS

EDITED BY

MANDY SAYER + LOUIS NOWRA

RANDOM HOUSE AUSTRALIA

Random House Australia Pty Ltd
20 Alfred Street, Milsons Point, NSW 2061
http://www.randomhouse.com.au

Sydney   New York   Toronto
London   Auckland   Johannesburg

This Random House Australia edition first published 2000

National Library of Australia
Cataloguing-in-Publication Entry

In the gutter . . . looking at the stars: a literary adventure through Kings Cross

Bibliography

ISBN 1 74051 012 7.

1. Short stories, Australian—New South Wales—Kings Cross. 2. Australian poetry—New
South Wales—Kings Cross. 3. Authors, Australian—Homes and haunts—New South Wales—
Kings Cross. 4. Kings Cross (N.S.W.)—Social life and customs. I. Nowra, Louis, 1950– .
II. Sayer, Mandy, 1963–

A820.80329441

Cover design by Greendot Design
Internal design by Greendot Design
Typeset in Goudy Old Style by Midland Typesetters
Printed and bound by Griffin Press, Netley, South Australia

10 9 8 7 6 5 4 3 2 1

*In memory of Kenneth Slessor
and his long literary love affair
with the Cross*

We are all in the gutter,
but some of us are
looking at the stars.

—*Oscar Wilde*

Contents

The Forties 91

Literary Locations of Kings Cross

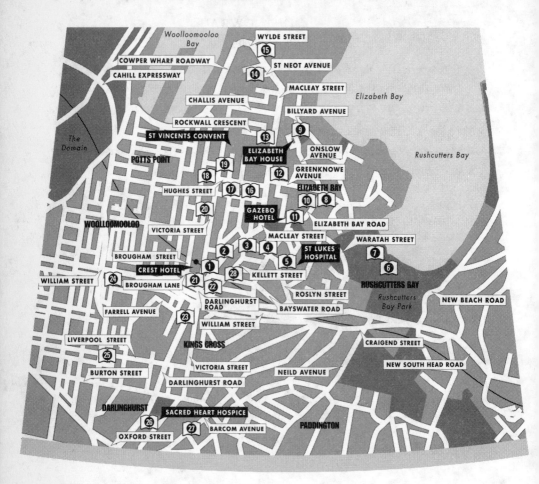

Key

1. **Kings Cross Station, Darlinghurst Road** (site of the childhood home of Robin Dalton *Aunts Up the Cross*)

2. **38 Darlinghurst Road**—The Pink Pussycat (setting of 'Messages' by Yusef Komunyakaa)

3. **Corner of Darlinghurst Road and Roslyn Street** (setting of 'John Says' by Yusef Komunyakaa)

4. **6 Roslyn Street**—Piccolo Bar (setting of 'Living the Piccolo Mondo' as told to Gina Lennox and Frances Rush by Vittorio Bianchi; 'The Piccolo' by Yusef Komunyakaa; 'At the Piccolo' by John Tranter)

Map xiii

5. **73 Roslyn Street**—formerly Lulworth (setting of *Voss*, former home of Patrick White)
6. **Rushcutters Bay Park** (setting of Bruce Beaver's 'Angel's Weather')
7. **Rushcutters Bay Park** (setting of Kate Grenville's extract from *Lilian's Story*)
8. **Elizabeth Bay Road** (setting of Frank Moorhouse's 'The American, Paul Jonson')
9. **18 Billyard Avenue** (former home of Kenneth Slessor)
10. **Elizabeth Bay Road** (setting of Sumner Locke Elliott's novel *Fairyland*, and Kenneth 'Seaforth' Mackenzie's novel *The Refuge*)
11. **Gazebo Hotel** (setting of Barry Humphries' 'Don't Wake Me For Cocktails')
12. **Greenknowe Avenue** (former home of Bob Herbert and setting of his play *No Names...No Pack Drill*)
13. **Rockwall Crescent** (former home of Lydia Gill and setting of her extract 'Kings Cross')
14. **1 St Neot Avenue** (former home of Ronald McCuaig, where he self-published *Vaudeville*, a collection of his poetry)
15. **Wylde Street** (setting of 'The Gala Drag and Drain Party' from Jon Rose's *At the Cross*)
16. **18 Orwell Street** (where Dymphna Cusack and Florence James wrote *Come In Spinner*)
17. **22 Orwell Street** (former home of M. Barnard Eldershaw)
18. **115 Victoria Street** (setting of Mandy Sayer's chapter 'The Heiress' from her novel *The Cross* and also one of Sayer's childhood homes)
19. **Victoria Street** (setting of Roberta Sykes' chapter from *Snake Dancing*)
20. **Brougham Street** (setting of Inez Baranay's 'The Great Rite: Sex Magick' from her novel *Pagan*)
21. **Corner of Brougham and William Streets** (the former jazz club, El Rocco, setting of John Clare's chapter from *Bodgie Dada & the Cult of Cool*)
22. **Corner of William Street and Darlinghurst Road** (setting of John Tranter's poems 'Leaving the Sixties' and 'Storm Over Sydney')
23. **1 Farrell Avenue** (former home of Dulcie Deamer)
24. **William Street** (setting of Graeme Aitken's chapter from *Vanity Fierce*)
25. **303–307 Liverpool Street** (former home of Jack Lindsay)
26. **170 Darlinghurst Road**—Sacred Heart Hospice (setting of Lorenzo Montesini's chapter from *My Life and Other Misdemeanours*)
27. **Barcom Avenue** (setting of Peter Doyle's chapter from *Get Rich Quick*)
28. **Corner of Bayswater Road and Kellett Street**—Mansions Hotel (setting of chapter from Louis Nowra's *Red Nights*)

INTRODUCTION

Kings Cross is both a real place and a state of mind. Throughout the twentieth century, scores of Australian writers either lived in Kings Cross, or wrote about it in novels, stories, poems, plays and memoirs. So much so, that it could be said that the history of Kings Cross can also be read as a history of Australian literature. Like its other inhabitants, writers of the Cross have been fascinated and sometimes even repulsed by the way the area encompasses both the glamorous and the tawdry, the corrupt and the innocent, and by how the immoral, the eccentric and the everyday co-exist, as if the Cross is an island, separate from the rest of Australia.

Some people liken its bohemian atmosphere to Soho or Montmartre; to others it is an inferno of depravity, or as one North Shore woman remarked to the cartoonist George Sprod, it's a place of 'thieves, muggers, whores, drug addicts, all-night discos [and] sexual deviants'. For Jon Rose the reality was more complex and interesting: 'The Cross-ites were the sharpest, maddest, cruellest and warmest people in the world.' In the novel *When the Man in the Gold Mustang met the Girl from the Pink Pussycat*, James Cockington describes the Cross '. . . as two dimensional as a movie set propped up with balsa struts'. In the 1960s, rock musician Billy Thorpe fondly remembers Kings Cross as a roll call of restaurants and hotels: 'Surf City, the Chevron Hotel,

xvi   IN THE GUTTER...LOOKING AT THE STARS

the Rex, the Mansions, the Hampton Court, the Mayfair, the Pink Pussycat, the Paradise, Angelo's Spaghetti Bar, the Kellet Club, Les Girls, Italian Hungarian, Thai and Indian food and the best bloody schnitzels on the planet.' During the same decade the famous chronicler of the Cross, poet and journalist Kenneth Slessor, tried to sum it up as:

... 100,000 human beings, cats, dogs and budgerigars packed into a square mile of hilltop in the heart of Sydney, and is one of the most thickly populated focal points of white men's habitation on the face of the earth. Layer upon layer of humanity lives, loves, suffers, exults, despairs or dies at every moment in the great antheap of its brick and concrete. The streets are perpetually crowded day and night, 1 a.m. or 1 p.m., not only with residents but with equally vast swarms of 'foreigners', visitors, tourists, adventurers, merrymakers, gourmandisers, businessmen, tradesmen, conmen, longhairs, shorthairs, beatniks, honey-mooners, housewives, de facto wives, policemen, firemen, ambulance-men, sailors, millionaires, crackpots and deadbeats.

The poet Judith Wright, writing about Kings Cross of the late 1930s, says it 'was regarded as a hot bed of political radicalism infested with pros-titution and drink'. In order to quell her family's fear of the place she gave her address as Elizabeth Bay. One didn't even have to visit the Cross to feel its insidious influence. In the pulp novel *Vice Trap, Kings Cross* the narrator comments: 'There was some connection, something unwhole-some that could reach out from the neon-glittering sophisticated night of Kings Cross and wreck the well ordered, narrow suburban lives of people . . .'

In 1887 the area was named Queens Cross but in 1905 its name was changed to Kings Cross in honour of Edward VII. But where was it exactly? No one quite knew. It both existed and did not exist. The place, Kings Cross, had no postal boundaries. Some thought it was merely the convergence of William and Victoria Streets and Darlinghurst and Bayswater Roads; others thought it included Woolloomooloo, East Sydney and the far reaches of Darlinghurst. It was not until 1965 that Kings Cross was officially recognised as a postal address but by that time the popular concept of Kings Cross had become something geographically larger than the official version, so that it has ended up encompassing sections of Potts Point, Elizabeth Bay and Rushcutters Bay.

During the nineteenth century the area was for the wealthy and was dotted with mansions and sprawling gardens, but the Depression of the 1890s and several more credit squeezes during the next two decades meant that the wealthy had to sell their properties or transform their mansions into flats. After the First World War the Cross became a cheap place to live and had the added virtue of being only a twenty-minute walk into the city. Dulcie Deamer says that she was attracted to the Cross because of the low rents, but she stayed because it suited her bohemian temperament. The Cross of the 1920s was different from the rest of Australia. Here the wealthy, the raffish, the damned and the desperate existed side by side. Unlike today, brothels were tucked discreetly away from sight. There was a huge underground sly grog trade. Cocaine was the drug of choice for prostitutes and the bright young things of the flapper era (infamous supplier Harry Newman was dubbed the Cocaine King) and coffee houses stayed open after eleven at night.

There has always been a sense that the Cross is a village unto itself, a place where everyone knows each other, where the natives seemed to operate outside of the rest of society's rules. Despite the growing vice and drug trade Kings Cross still had not lost its charm well into the 1960s, as Nick Pounder relates:

When I recall my first impressions of the Cross—cake shops, delicatessens, the rich pure smell of coffee, florists, gaudy signs, the lurid club facades strange in the daylight; the smells of grilled meat, cigar smoke, people at their open windows, the curtains blowing above the street for three floors; faces peering down on the moving scene below where everything seemed to be happening at once. I suppose more than anything else it appeared like a village in that so many were visibly living right in the middle of it. It looked as though as much opened at five as shut, and there was an extroverted feeling about the place— something less purposeful than one would encounter in another busy part of the city. The only thing I could liken it to was the English seaside—the piers and arcades of a holiday at high season.

Given the mind-numbing conformity of suburban Australia between World Wars and into the 1950s it was no wonder that artists and writers flocked to the Cross. It was probably one of the few havens for like-minded souls, and if they didn't like it up the Cross, then the next step was to flee Australia entirely, as did such writers as Christina Stead and Patrick White. For decades the Cross was a spiritual refuge for many artists including John Olsen, Russell Drysdale, William Dobell, Robert Klippel, Donald Friend, Martin Sharpe and the Yellow House artists. Film makers have also used the Cross and its environs as subject matter. *Sunshine Sally* (1922) dramatised the love affair between a working-class girl of Wool-loomooloo and a wealthy Potts Point boy, to indicate the steep class divide between neighbouring suburbs. *The Killing of Angel Street* (1981) and *Heatwave* (1982) both dramatised the Green bans and disappearance of heiress and activist Juanita Nielsen. In 1999 the film *Two Hands* depicted the seamier world of the gangsters and clubs of Kings Cross.

But it is the writers who have articulated the attractions, distractions and appeal of Kings Cross better than anyone else. Before the First World War American author Jack London wrote about the Rushcutters Bay Stadium when reporting on the famous World Heavyweight title fight between Tommy Burns and the black American Jack Johnson (as a fore-runner of the Cross's infatuation with transvestism, London's wife had to disguise herself as a man to see the fight). However, even though Australian writers drifted into the Cross during the 1920s they seldom wrote about it except later on in memoirs, such as Jack Lindsay's delightful *The Roaring Twenties*. Dulcie Deamer, Christopher Brennan and others may have enjoyed the bohemian atmosphere and its freedom from conventional morality, but they gazed inwards when writing and their literature is populated by fauns, sirens, the classical gods and pagan mysticism. Of course the very notion of bohemianism meant that one did not even have to write. According to Peter Kirkpatrick's study of this era, *The Seacoast of Bohemia*, the production of art was far less important than the living of one's life as art and the elevation of style and recreation to an art form.

If anyone finally saw Kings Cross as authentic subject matter it is the hero of this anthology, Kenneth Slessor. It is valid to say that Australian modernist poetry was born out of Slessor's big-city journalism and his

Smith's Weekly job writing light poetry about the Cross in *Darlinghurst Nights*. Reacting against the obsession of Australian poetry with the bush, he used Kings Cross as his muse and, like Baudelaire before him, knew that it was the city and not some sterile pastoral fantasy that was at the heart of modern culture.

If anything was to galvanise authors into writing about the Cross, rather than just living there, it was the Second World War. Even though it was feared that the Japanese would invade Australia, the Cross seemed to be involved in one long party. Operating as a safety valve it became a carnivalesque oasis of randy soldiers, good-time girls, drag parties, boozing, fornicating and a celebration of the triumph of life over death.

One cannot underestimate the potent impact of two generations of American soldiers on the Cross, both in the Second World War and during the R&R period of the late 1960s. One also has to acknowledge the pervasive influence of 'foreigners' who, from the late 1930s, brought to the Cross such things as the espresso machine, ethnic foods and a European love of the arts and culture. While the Cross embraced the change and new sensations these refugees and immigrants brought with them, the rest of Australia sneered at the cosmopolitan attitude of the Cross. A 1962 *Bulletin* article on Kings Cross reported: 'Radio comedians in national shows could always be sure of an interstate laugh with that standard line "Hey, what do you think happened to me at Kings Cross last night? Somebody said goodnight to me—in English!"'

From the Second World War onwards, Kings Cross became a household name in Australia and the mere mention of it conjured up visions of deviants, bohemians, crooks, sin and vice. Yet for the non-conformist outsiders—those different young people who could not express themselves or their deepest artistic cravings in suburbia—the Cross became an alluring siren call promising release from the shackles of a drab world. Jon Rose imagined the Cross was 'The Paris of the Southern Hemisphere'. For the small town fifteen-year-old girl in *Flat 4 Kings Cross*, who had heard and read about the area, 'it seemed to me to be the most fabulous place in the world. Well, perhaps not fabulous like Hollywood, or New York . . . but I couldn't see myself getting to the other places, so I was determined to get to Sydney'.

Numerous Australian stories and novels begin with the narrator's desire to escape his or her dreary surroundings and flee to Kings Cross. Sometimes it is even more fabulous and wonderful than they could have hoped, as in Jon Rose's *At the Cross*. For those who were sexually different—such as Sumner Locke Elliott and the transsexual Carlotta—it was paradise. It was not only the night life and the freedom from puritan values but the enormous relief in finding others of similar artistic or sexual sensibilities after years of believing they were alone. Other grand discoveries were a coffee house, restaurant, nightclub or bar that you could call your own and meet like-minded people. In articles and memoirs and poems such places are recalled with an almost feverish nostalgia as in Les Murray's 'Tanka: The Coffee Shops' where he reminisces about such legendary places as Vadims.

The Aquatic Club was another favourite haunt for creative and theatrical types. Actor Peter Finch drank there regularly and fellow actor Chips Rafferty managed to die on the path outside. For playwright Steve J. Spears the Aquatic Club became 'my office, my refuge, my luncheonette, my bank. It's where my friends are. It's my Moulin Rouge'. For others such enclaves as the jazz club El Rocco or the Bottoms Up bar in the Rex Hotel became a home away from home.

Of course, with this nostalgia came the mythologising of the Cross. Dorothy Hewett saluted the bohemian paradise of the Cross in her play *Pandora's Cross*, and Billy Thorpe's memoir *Sex and Thugs and Rock 'n' Roll: A Year in Kings Cross, 1963–1964* became another prime example of this impulse. The local newspaper *The Kings Cross Whisper* (1960s-1970s) reinforced the naughty, risqué reputation of the Cross while the pulp paperbacks of the 1960s glorified its sordid notoriety in such titles as *The Kings Cross Caper, Vice Trap Kings Cross, Twisted Echoes* (about a manic killer stalking Kings Cross), *The Kings Cross Racket, Kings Cross Hooker, 96 Kings Cross* and *The Dirty Half Mile* so that for Australians who had not visited the Cross it became hard to disentangle fact from fiction. Reading these titles now the world they describe is almost quaint. They are titillating stories of topless bars, marijuana (many writers confusing it with heroin), cosy brothels and gloomy beatniks philosophising in dingy coffee bars. Even now the murky nocturnal world of the Cross is still used as a convenient shorthand for moral dissolution by such thriller writers as Gabrielle Lord, Dave Warner and Susan Geason.

If pre-1950s literature portrayed a serene, happy Kings Cross, there evolved another strand of writing that was darker and more grimly reflective. In W.A. Harbinson's *Running Man* (1967), the alcoholic writer arrives in the Cross expecting it to be 'fabulous', but he finds no such thing. Later it is his Aboriginal mate Collins who tells him a few home truths:

> Behind every neon light in the Cross there's a fella like you—a small, scared, defeated thing crying that he doesn't belong, that he's just passing through. Believe me, if the tourists knew they'd shiver. Well, in a sense it's true. They often *do* just pass through—but they come in like half baked humans and they leave like wet spaghetti.

Once hard drugs appeared, the writers described the phenomenon in such books as *The Cure* by Kevin MacKay, *Jodie's Story* by Jeanette Grant-Thomson, and Luke Davies' *Candy* where there is no such thing as redemption, only the desperate desire to know where the next fix is coming from. Such a bleak outlook was to reach its peak in the 1990s with the so-called 'grunge novelists' whose descriptions of the Cross represent a hell on earth. And for journalists like John Birmingham, who spent a week on the streets of the Cross researching an article for *Rolling Stone* (it later appeared as a chapter in his book *Leviathan)* the Cross is simply a corrupt, joyless place of hookers, junkies and bent cops.

However, other writers have avoided nostalgia, bohemian vapidity or bargain basement pessimism and discovered that the Cross has allowed them to tackle issues that the rest of society avoided. The 1969 novel *The Worshipful Company* by Jan Smith describes in unsentimental detail an interracial love affair. Inez Baranay fictionalises the Kings Cross witch Rosaleen Norton and her casual destruction of the career of the composer/conductor Sir Eugene Goossens. Writers such as Jon Rose, Frank Moorhouse, Sumner Locke Elliott, Carmen, Carlotta, Graeme Aitken and Roberta Perkins describe, unflinchingly, the world of gays and crosses and trannies.

The list of authors who have written about the Cross seems endless and, besides the ones whose extracts are in this book, includes writers such as Nancy Phelan, Kylie Tennant, Christopher Koch, Matt Condon, Janette Turner Hospital, Frank Clune, Anne Summers, Gaby Naher, Jessica

Anderson, Adam Aitken, Rosie Scott, Justine Ettler and Peter Robb. In fact, the editors had an enormous bulk of material to draw from—memoirs, fiction, plays, poetry and oral history. Our criteria were to present writing of quality that not only gave a vivid picture of Kings Cross and its people but avoided the journalists' cliché of 'the dirty-half mile'. We decided to divide the selections into decades. Although this may seem arbitrary, the more we read the more we became convinced that every decade did seem to have its own spirit and defining moments. With each decade a new influx of writers, artists and free spirits thought they were reinventing sex, drugs and social non-conformity. Essentially the Cross remained the same, but one just has to notice the progression from cocaine to heroin, from discreet brothels to zonked-out hookers on the main street, from tasteful striptease to live sex acts on stage to realise that in the search for new sensations, the Cross has undergone profound changes, while still proudly retaining its identity as the place that exists both in reality and in the imagination.

Because many writers have written about the Cross, we have included their extracts in the decades in which the work is set, as each extract gives a different or nostalgic slant on the period. However, one thing that became obvious in selecting extracts for this anthology was how some more conservative and banal works, not specifically about the Cross, found a vigour and a potency when the narrative shifted to the Cross and its people, as if the 'difference' of the Cross had energised the author. Novels and plays such as *Come in Spinner*, *Tomorrow and Tomorrow and Tomorrow* and Patrick White's *Shepherd on the Rocks* are vivid examples of this. But let's leave the last word to M. Barnard Eldershaw's *Tomorrow and Tomorrow and Tomorrow* where Sydney burns to the ground in an apocalyptic inferno:

As the Cross had lived, so it burned, with greater gusto than any other part of the city, as if it were more inflammable, as if the very stones and concrete of its material body from a constant contact with life had lost their hard inanimate surface and become friable. Once the fire had taken hold it was up and away with banners, out of control.

✳

The genesis of this project was at a small dinner party at the author Linda Jaivin's apartment in Elizabeth Bay Road. The three of us talked about how much we loved Kings Cross and its literature and how wonderful it would be to edit an anthology about it. Unlike most ideas that have been hatched over dinner and wine this one actually got underway, but Linda had to drop out, due to other commitments.

People who helped during the editing were Nicholas Pounder; Veronica Kelly; Bill Harding (who provided a copy of the gorgeous *At the Cross*); Tom Thompson, whose book on Kings Cross, co-written with Elizabeth Butel, was a constant inspiration; Barry Humphries and Robert Gray with many suggestions; the staff at Kings Cross library; Cornstalk Bookshop whose pulp fiction about Kings Cross is unrivalled; and Doug Nelson of Ex Libris Bookshop. Lastly, the title owes everything to Oscar Wilde.

There were the usual limitations of space, money and time so some work that deserved inclusion did not make it. The co-editors, both of whom live in the Cross, had their first meetings at Moran's restaurant/café before it closed down in late 1999. The atmospheric Sebel Hotel, and its deliciously claustrophobic bar, was scheduled for demolition during the editing of this book, reinforcing the hunger for change that is so much a part of the Cross. In the spirit of exploration and experience typified by many extracts in this volume, the co-editors mulled over the contents of this anthology as they trolled through many a Kings Cross bar and restaurant, from the starry eleventh-floor heights of The International to the gutter-level squalor of the Goldfish Bowl, developing the dubious reputation of always being the last to leave, until their livers and credit cards almost ran out.

Mandy Sayer and Louis Nowra
Kings Cross, 2000

The Nineteenth Century

'. . . the night, close and sultry as savage
flesh, distant and dilating as stars,
would prevail by natural law.'

—*Patrick White*

Typically, the early days of the area that would become Kings Cross were defined by dramatic events. In 1788, a party of convicts was cutting reeds in the swamp that would later become Rushcutters Bay Park. The Sydney Cove settlement was expanding, and the reeds were needed to thatch the roofs of the colony's huts in Woolloomooloo. While working in the swamp, six of the convicts raped five Aboriginal women who were camping by the bay. Upon the party's next visit to the swamp, two of the convicts were speared to death in an act of revenge. It was the first time in the short history of the colony that whites had been killed by Aborigines. The rapes and murders could be viewed as the first crimes of Kings Cross.

Originally, the area known as the Cross, Darlinghurst, and Elizabeth Bay was Australia's first Aboriginal reserve, first known as Blacktown, then Henrietta Town. In the eighteenth century, windmills stood on the rise of Bayswater Road, their arms slicing through the breeze rising up from a luminous harbour. Soon, Henrietta Town was renamed Queen's Cross as a tribute to Queen Victoria during her Diamond Jubilee.

One of the people responsible for the current geography of the area was Colonial Secretary Alexander Macleay, who was granted 54 acres by Governor Darling in 1826. Apart from building the State Library, the Museum, and creating the Botanic Gardens, Macleay also built Elizabeth Bay House in 1835, which has remained a landmark of the district throughout the decades. Macleay's large estate, landscaped with lush gardens and paths, extended entirely around Elizabeth Bay and along Macleay Street, the main entrance of which was where the El Alamein Fountain stands today. In 1857, Macleay's nephew, William, moved into Elizabeth Bay House with his bride. Obsessed with natural history, botany, and zoology, William was an avid collector of specimens, most of which were contributed to the fledgling collection of the Australian Museum.

William and his wife were also ebullient hosts, and their Sunday night whisky parties became a regular occasion for intellectual exchange and conviviality. In 1875, however, most of the garden was subdivided and sold, after which many of the narrow and serpentine streets of the Cross were constructed. Macleay's widow lived in Elizabeth Bay House until her death in 1903.

The late nineteenth century is considered the golden age of the area. Garden parties, high tea, croquet, and tennis were favourite pastimes for the more cultured residents of the Cross. Groomed horses and ornate carriages transported people between stately homes and newly-built villas. In his chapter from *Voss*, Patrick White precisely details the elegance and austere beauty of Potts Point in the nineteenth century, most of which is set in the garden of White's former family home on Roslyn Street, now the site of St. Luke's Hospital. In terms of Australian literature, with the creation of the character Laura Trevelyan and her illegitimate child, White also inadvertently gives us the first fallen woman of Kings Cross.

In nearby Woolloomooloo (the 'loo), however, the nineteenth century was quite a different experience. In contrast to the serene and gracious lifestyle associated with Elizabeth Bay House and other mansions of the Cross, by the middle of the century, rows of cheap terraces were constructed in the 'loo for the lower classes, quickly creating a slum. The 'loo soon became a popular seaport, characterised by rough hotels, brothels, and criminal activity. Prostitutes and standover men populated the area, as did the razor gangs—or Pushes—most of whom wielded blades and terrorised local residents.

Towards the end of the century, the golden age of the Cross was beginning to fade. The thugs, prostitutes, and razor gangs of Woolloomooloo began to drift up into the genteel environs of Potts Point, possibly due to the construction of the McElhone Steps, which replaced the primitive wooden ladder that ran between the wharves and the bottom end of Victoria Street. At the same time, more and more stately homes were subdivided to house the growing working classes. Electric trams replaced hansom cabs as the main form of transportation. Many of the better terraces became sumptuous brothels, opening their doors to well-heeled businessmen on their way home from city offices.

PATRICK WHITE

from *Voss*

By that hour, before the tea-things were brought in, the lamplight, which in the beginning had been a solid, engrossed yellow, was suffused with the palpitating rose colours. The petals that had fallen on mahogany were reflected upward. The big, no longer perfect roses were bursting with scent and sticky stamens. And it was rather warm.

Partly for that reason Laura Trevelyan had gone out through the moths to the terrace where the stone urns were, and where somebody had been crushing geranium, but the heavy air of darkness was, if anything, more distasteful to her than that of the rapt, cloying room. As she strolled she was still attended by the light from lamps. This, however, could not be stretched much farther, and she did hesitate. It was now possible that the usually solid house, and all that it contained, that the whole civil history of those parts was presumptuous, and that the night, close and sultry as savage flesh, distant and dilating as stars, would prevail by natural law.

Drifting in that nihilistic darkness with agreeable resignation, the young woman bumped against some hard body and immediately recovered her own.

'I beg your pardon, Miss Trevelyan,' said Voss. 'You also have come out in search of refreshment.'

'I?' said Laura. 'Yes, it was stuffy. The first hot nights of the season are difficult. But so deceptive. Dangerous, even. A wind may spring up in half an hour from now, and we shall be shivering.'

She was already, despite the fact that they were swathed in a woollen darkness. Down there, round the bay, there was still a rushy marsh, from which a young man who had recently gone in search of mussels had contracted a fever, it was told, and died.

But Voss was not at that moment interested in climatic peculiarities.

To what extent is this girl dishonest? he wondered.

Unaccustomed to recognize his own dishonesties, he was rather sensitive to them in others.

It is disgraceful, of course, Laura realized; I have come out here for no convincing reason. She was defenceless. Perhaps even guilty.

'I try to visualize your life in this house,' said Voss, facing the honeycomb of windows, in some of which dark figures burrowed for a moment before drowning in the honey-coloured light. 'Do you count the linen?'

He was truly interested, now that it did seem to affect him in some way not yet accounted for.

'Do you make pastry? Hem sheets? Or are you reading novels in these rooms, and receiving morning calls from acquaintances, ladies with small waists and affectations?'

'We indulge in a little of each,' Laura admitted, 'but in no event are we insects, Mr Voss.'

'I have not intended to suggest,' he laughed. 'It is my habit of approach.'

'Is it so difficult then, for a man, to imagine the lives of poor domesticated women? How very extraordinary! Or is it that you are an extraordinary man?'

'I have not entered into the minds of other men, so that I cannot honestly say with any degree of accuracy.'

But he would keep his private conviction.

'I think that I can enter into the minds of most men,' said the young woman, softly. 'At times. An advantage we insect-women enjoy is that we have endless opportunity to indulge the imagination as we go backwards and forwards in the hive.'

'And in my instance, what does your imagination find?'

He was laughing, of course, at the absurdity of that which he expected to be told. But he would have liked to hear practically anything.

'Shall we go a little?' he invited.

'Walking in this darkness is full of dangers.'

'It is not really dark. When you are accustomed to it.'

Which was true. The thick night was growing luminous. At least, it was possible almost to see, while remaining almost hidden.

The man and woman were walking over grass that was still kindly beneath their feet. Smooth, almost cold leaves soothed their faces and the backs of their hands.

'These are the camellia bushes Uncle planted when he first came here as a young man,' Laura Trevelyan said. 'There are fifteen varieties, as well as sports. This one here is the largest,' she said, shaking it as if it had been an inanimate object; it was so familiar to her, and now so necessary. 'It is a white, but there is one branch that bears those marbled flowers, you know, like the edges of a ledger.'

'Interesting,' he said.

But it was an obscure reply, of a piece with the spongy darkness that surrounded them.

'Then you are not going to answer my question?' he asked.

'Oh,' she said, 'that silly claim I made! Although, to a certain extent, it is true.'

'Tell me, then.'

'Everyone is offended by the truth, and you will not be an exception.'

That it would take place, they both knew now.

Consequently, when she did speak, the sense of inevitability that they shared made her sound as if she were reading from a notebook, only this one was her head, in which her memorandum had been written, in invisible ink, that the night had breathed upon; and as she read, or spoke, it became obvious to both that she had begun to compile her record from the first moment of their becoming acquainted.

'You are so vast and ugly,' Laura Trevelyan was repeating the words; 'I can imagine some desert, with rocks, rocks of prejudice, and, yes, even hatred. You are so isolated. That is why you are fascinated by the prospect of desert places, in which you will find your own situation taken for granted, or more than that, exalted. You sometimes scatter kind words or bits of poetry to people, who soon realize the extent of their illusion.

Everything is for yourself. Human emotions, when you have them, are quite flattering to you. If those emotions strike sparks from others, that also is flattering. But most flattering, I think, when you experience it, is the hatred, or even the mere irritation of weaker characters.'

'Do you hate me, perhaps?' asked Voss, in darkness.

'I am fascinated by you,' laughed Laura Trevelyan, with such candour that her admission did not seem immodest. '*You* are *my* desert!'

Once or twice their arms brushed, and he was conscious of some extreme agitation or exhilaration in her.

'I am glad that I do not need your good opinion,' he said.

'No,' she said. 'Nobody's opinion!'

He was surprised at the vehemence of feeling in this young girl. In such circumstances, repentance, he felt, might have been a luxury. But he did not propose to enjoy any such softness. Besides, faith in his own stature had not been destroyed.

He began to bite his nails in the darkness.

'You are upset,' he said, 'because you would like to pity me, and you cannot.'

'If that were the case, I would certainly have cause to be upset,' she blurted most wildly.

'You would like to mention me in your prayers.'

By this time Laura Trevelyan had become lost somewhere in the dark of the garden. But I, too, am self-sufficient, she remembered, with some lingering repugnance for her dead prayers.

'I do not pray,' she answered, miserably.

'*Ach*,' he pounced, 'you are not *atheistisch?*'

'I do not know,' she said.

She had begun to tear a cluster of the white camellias from that biggest bush. In passing, she had snapped the hot flowers, which were now poor lumps of things. She was tearing them across, as if they had not been flesh, but some passive stuff, like blotting-paper.

'Atheists are atheists usually for mean reasons,' Voss was saying. 'The meanest of these is that they themselves are so lacking in magnificence they cannot conceive the idea of a Divine Power.'

He was glittering coldly. The wind that the young woman had promised had sprung up, she realized dully. The stars were trembling. Leaves were slashing at one another.

'Their reasons,' said Laura, 'are simple, honest, personal ones. As far as I can tell. For such steps are usually taken in privacy. Certainly after considerable anguish of thought.'

The darkness was becoming furious.

'But the God they have abandoned is of mean conception,' Voss pursued. 'Easily destroyed, because in their own image. Pitiful because such destruction does not prove the destroyer's power. *Atheismus* is self-murder. Do you not understand?'

'I am to understand that I have destroyed myself. But you, Mr Voss,' Laura cried, 'it is for you I am concerned. To watch the same fate approaching someone else is far, far worse.'

In the passion of their relationship, she had encountered his wrist. She held his bones. All their gestures had ugliness, convulsiveness in common. They stood with their legs apart inside their innocent clothes, the better to grip the reeling earth.

'I am aware of no similarity between us,' Voss replied.

He was again cold, but still arrested. Her hands had eaten into his wrist.

'It is for our pride that each of us is probably damned,' Laura said.

Then he shook her off, and the whole situation of an hysterical young woman. He was wiping his lips, which had begun to twitch, though in anger, certainly, not from weakness. He breathed deeply. He drank from the great arid skies of fluctuating stars. The woman beside him had begun to suggest the presence of something soft and defenceless.

Indeed, Laura Trevelyan did not feel she would attempt anything further, whatever might be revealed to her.

'For some reason of intellectual vanity, you decided to do away with God,' Voss was saying; she knew he would be smiling. 'But the consequences are yours alone. I assure you.'

It was true; he made her know.

'I feel you may still suspect me,' he continued. 'But I do believe, you must realize. Even though I worship with pride. Ah, the humility, the humility! This is what I find so particularly loathsome. My God, besides, is above humility.'

'Ah,' she said. 'Now I understand.'

It was clear. She saw him standing in the glare of his own brilliant desert. Of course, He was Himself indestructible.

And she did then begin to pity him. She no longer pitied herself, as she had for many weeks in the house of her uncle, whose unfailingly benevolent materialism encouraged the practice of self-pity. Love seemed to return to her with humility. Her weakness was delectable.

'I shall think of you with alarm,' she said. 'To maintain such standards of pride, in the face of what you must experience on this journey, is truly alarming.'

'I am not in the habit of setting myself limits.'

'Then I will learn to pray for you.'

'Oh dear, I have caught you out doubly,' he laughed. 'You are an Apostle of Love masquerading as an atheist for some inquisitorial purpose of your own. My poor Miss Trevelyan I shall be followed through the continent of Australia by your prayers, like little pieces of white paper. I can see them, torn-up paper, fluttering, now that I know for certain you are one of those who pray.'

'I have failed to be. But I will learn.'

These simple ideas were surrounded with such difficulties they would scarcely issue out of her inadequate mind.

Then he was touching her, his hand was upon her shoulder-blades, and they realized they had returned into their bodies.

'Is it not really very cold?' she said at once, shivering.

'People will come to look for you. You are lost in the garden.'

'They are too agreeably occupied.'

'I have been hateful to you this evening,' confessed the German, as if it had just occurred to him, but she did not resent it; in her state of recovered conviction his defects were even welcome.

'We were unwise,' he said, 'to flounder into each other's private beings.'

She smiled.

'I know you are smiling,' he said. 'Why?' he asked, and laughed.

'It is our *beings* that pleases me,' she replied.

'Is it not expressive, then?'

'Oh, it is expressive, I dare say, in its clumsiness.'

The beautiful, but rather tentative young girl of that evening, in her smouldering, peacock dress, and the passionate but bewildered soul of the woman that had flapped and struggled in the dark garden in its attempt to rescue (let us not say: subdue) were being dispossessed by a clumsy contentment of the flesh.

'I have long given up trying to express myself,' she sighed warmly.

The man yawned.

He knew that he did enjoy the company of this young woman, who was exhausted, and standing as naturally in her shoes as her careful upbringing would allow.

'When I was younger,' said this girl, as if it had been a long time ago, 'I kept a diary. Oh, I wrote down everything, everything. I could not express too much. And how proud I was to read it. Then I no longer could. I would stare at a blank page, and that would appear far more expressive than my own emptiness.'

The man yawned again. He was not bored, however, but very happy. He, too, was rather exhausted by what had happened, but his physical exhaustion was sealing up the memory of it.

'While I am engaged on this expedition,' he said, 'I will, of course, keep a journal, that you will read afterwards, and follow me step by step.'

Even his pride had grown tired and childlike.

'The official journal of the expedition,' murmured the young woman, not ironically, to the tired child.

'Yes. The official journal,' he repeated, in grave agreement.

It was obvious that she would read it with that interest women took in the achievements of men.

Ah, I must pray for him, she said, for he will be in need of it.

He was inexplicably flattered by her no longer communicative presence in the darkness, and very contented.

Then Mrs Bonner had emerged from the square light, and was puckering up her face at darkness, and trying to read its mind.

She called:

'Laura! Laura, dear, where are you? Laur-*a*.'

So that her niece felt it her duty to approach. In leaving, she barely touched Voss upon the hand. He was not sure whether he was intended to go or stay, but followed immediately.

They came out into the light almost together. Almost as if they had been sleep-walking, Aunt Emmy feared.

'My dear child, you will be frozen,' she began to complain, and frowned.

But as if she did not see Voss.

'In this treacherous wind.'

With that wretched man.

She half-arranged an invisible shawl as a protection against her own distress in such a situation.

'Miss Hollier particularly wants to hear you play the Field nocturne, the one with the pretty tune towards the end, you know, that I so much like.'

They went into the rosy room, where Uncle had built his hands into a gable, and was explaining to Mr Palfreyman, whose eyeballs had grit behind them, the dangerous hold the sectarians, not to say Roman Catholics, already had upon the Colony. It was strange that things spiritual should make Mr Bonner's flesh swell.

Laura Trevelyan immediately sat down at the piano, and gave rather a flat rendering of the Field nocturne.

The German, who had followed the ladies into the room, stood biting his lips, unconscious of the awkward, even embarrassing attitude of his body, listening, or so it appeared, as if the music propounded some idea above the level of its agreeable mediocrity. Then he went and flung himself down, boorishly, Miss Hollier remarked afterwards to a friend, flung himself upon an upright sofa that did not respond to him. He sat or sprawled there, passing his hand intermittently over his forehead and his closed eyes, and remained more or less oblivious after Laura had left the piano.

So he spent what remained of the evening. He himself could not have told exactly of what he was thinking. He would have liked to give, what he was not sure, if he had been able, if he had not destroyed this himself with deliberate ruthlessness in the beginning. In its absence there remained, in the lit room, a shimmering of music, and of the immense distances towards which he already trudged.

The Twenties

'Verses in beer on the counter . . .'
— *Jack Lindsay*

By the 1920s, the genteel reputation of Kings Cross was further muddied by a growing criminal element and a sluggish economy. The well-heeled residents of the golden age purchased the first automobiles and moved out to suburban bungalows. The population of the Cross was increasing, however, and the mansions and grand homes that the former residents left behind were converted to private hotels and boarding houses. The rows of terraces along Darlinghurst Road were renovated into grocery stores and fruit shops.

Meanwhile, razor gangs continued to dominate Darlinghurst and Wool-loomooloo. Gang members carried cut-throat razors and harassed people on the streets. The pattern of violence and intimidation, however, was part of a more complex web of corruption spreading throughout the area. In 1916, the government had passed a law enforcing six o'clock closing for all public hotels. Thus, throughout the 1920s, sly grog shops flourished in the back streets of the Cross, selling gin and homemade whisky. The district quickly became an oasis for thirsty Sydneysiders who needed more than an evening tipple.

The sly grog racket was closely linked with other criminal activities such as prostitution, most of which were controlled by three powerful women. Kate Leigh was an infamous underworld figure of the time, who used to push a wheelbarrow up William Street, peddling alcohol in quart bottles. Leigh supplied many of the sly grog shops in Kellett Street and Kings Cross Road. Her notorious rival for underworld Queendom was Tilly Devine, who ran a brothel on Palmer Street. All-in-all, Devine accumu-lated 204 charges of prostitution and assault throughout her life. It was rumoured that she collected many of her working girls from the nearby Crown Street Women's Hospital, which was a haunt for young women from the bush who wished to bear illegitimate children in secret. The third player in this boisterous, tawdry drama was prostitute Nellie

Cameron. Endowed with a crown of blonde hair and almost classical features, Cameron earned over ten times the average wage of most men. Over the years, she lived with several Kings Cross mobsters, including Normie Brutin, Frankie Green, and razor thug Guido Calletti, whom she married in 1933. The macabre irony is that every man Cameron lived with ended up being shot dead.

By the end of the 1920s, the local community and the press were agitating for protection. Shootings and razor slashings were common, often instigated by underworld figures like Scarface Divine and Melbourne criminal Squizzy Taylor. The Darlinghurst Push centred around the Tradesman's Arms Hotel, which allowed immediate access to the city's red-light district. But by the end of the decade, sly grog and prostitution weren't the only games in town. In the 1920s, Sydneysiders had discovered cocaine, and the drug had become increasingly popular with the mob element. There was, however, a stigma attached it. Cocaine use was considered an older person's habit; the youth of the Cross boasted that they didn't need the extra stimulation.

During this decade anyone could purchase a bottle of gin after dark, but few people could buy a hot meal. Thus, Charlie the Pieman made a small fortune hollering up and down Victoria Street each night, selling homemade pies to hungry workers. On the weekends, residents flocked to see films at the local theatres. Episodes of *The Perils of Pauline* and *Tarzan of the Apes* were screened weekly, during which an organist led the crowds in singing songs like *My Canary has Circles Under his Eyes* and *The Prisoner's Love Song*. At the same time, Woolloomooloo became the location for some of Australia's first motion pictures, due to its colourful and dangerous atmosphere, and its proximity to the Rushcutters Bay film studio, which was completed in 1912.

Gangsters, prostitutes, blue collar workers, filmmakers, and poorer families were tangled in a bawdy struggle for survival throughout the decade. Even though the Cross was a risky place in which to live in the 1920s, it was the only place in Australia that tolerated outsiders, misfits, and those who dared to be different. It was probably the one area of the country where a homosexual could relax. And if a man and a woman were going to live together without being married, Kings Cross was the only district that would have accepted the couple.

Given the liberal attitudes that wove through the tree-lined streets, it is little wonder that Kings Cross also began to attract certain artists and writers. Frank and Thelma Clune purchased a property on the corner of Macleay Street and Challis Avenue in the 1920s, which would soon become home to some of Australia's most recognised painters: Russell Drysdale, John Passmore, and John Olsen. As the following excerpts reveal, the Cross also became a refuge for writers escaping more traditional institutions. When writer and classical scholar Christopher Brennan was dismissed from his prestigious university position, he came up to the Cross and he got down in the gutter with his daughter, Anna. He drank in dives along William Street, and took to writing verses in beer on the counters of bars. Writer Dulcie Deamer escaped the confines of her marriage and moved into a room in a Kings Cross terrace because it was vibrant and lively, and only cost one pound per week.

JACK LINDSAY

from *The Roaring Twenties*

Amendola's, Ray says, will always remain in his mind as the place where he first saw 'that fabulous beautiful bitch Annie Brennan. I will never forget how, one Saturday afternoon, she came in drunk and danced among the bottles and glasses on the table. It was an old stunt of hers, but to my goggled still-adolescent eyes it was the most spectacular event I had ever seen. I whispered to Hugh Brayden, 'Who is she?' 'Annie Brennan,' he said. 'How beautiful,' I sighed. 'You should have seen her a couple of years ago,' he replied, bored. I was horrified at such blasphemy. But that bitch. How she dominated all that crowd in those days. Leon Gellert was inspired to write *The Isle of San* by the thought of her downfall. Everybody was in love with her, even Gruner, although everybody knew what a slut she was. I always think it was a sad waste that her particular choice piece of feminine bitchery has never been immortalized in paint, so many artists were in love with her. But I do not know of any who would have had the ability to record her unique charms. He would have had to possess the bravura of an Augustus John, the sentimental sensitivity of a Greuze, and the bitch-insight of a Toulouse-Lautrec. But her beauty, vivid as it still is to me, was very subtle. Her small delicate features with the Germanic colouring inherited from her mother, her slow smile, the soft

cadence of her voice, her grace of movement, were all factors that went to
disguise the Queen of All Bitches.

'At that time she had a flat in Victoria Street, on the other side of Kings
Cross, not far from the Fire Station. I went back with her there that night
after I first met her, and I sat there entranced, just gazing raptly upon her
beauty, my bladder near bursting point with cheap wine, but too coy to ask
where to go and ease it. I'll never forget my relief when I got outside against
the wall of St John's Church. I used often to go up to her flat in the mornings
and sit there bemused and dumbfounded as I watched her dressing and titi-
vating herself after a night's debauchery in expectation of another to come.
But the idea of doing more than gaze never crossed my worshipping mind.'

At this time Phil too often went to her flat in the mornings and tidied
it up, just for the pleasure of gazing at the goddess. I confess that I never
felt quite this magic in Anna. I found her a notable spectacle, but one that
moved me only at a certain distance, as if I were watching her on the films.
But one more anecdote of Ray's is worth giving as an example of the way
Anna could spell people with her queenly Teutonic presence, which in
repose seemed often to have an air of nobility and virtue.

'Despite all her bitchery, her selfishness, her utter unscrupulousness, she
retained an extraordinary and uncanny ability to arouse love. As an
example of this, I remember sharply an incident of some years later. One
Saturday night I went to an Italian café, the Roma, then popular with us
all, accompanied by a girl I was getting around with in those days. To my
surprise, there was Anne seated alone at a table, looking very tired and ill.
I had not seen her for some time; I believe she had been in Melbourne. As
we passed her, I wished her good evening and she replied with that slow,
grave, sweet smile of hers. When my girl and I were seated, she excitedly
asked who Annie was. I told her and she exclaimed how beautiful she was.
'You should have seen her a couple of years ago,' I replied, unconsciously
quoting Hugh's remark to me when I first saw Anne. But my girl could not
take her eyes off Anne and said that I must introduce them as she wished
to kiss her! (My girl was perfectly normal, let me say.) I was horrified and
told her not to be silly, not to dream even of doing such a thing as Annie
was by that time rotten with T.B. and God only knows what else.
However, when we had finished our meal and were leaving the table, she
rushed over to Anne, introduced herself, and asked if she might kiss her. I

looked on, stricken but entranced. Annie, with all the dignity and grace of a princess, gave that irresistible, beautiful smile of hers and accepted the kiss as her rightful homage. I never saw her again.'

Anna Brennan like the others came now and then. And suddenly one night her father Christopher arrived. We had all assumed there was no contact between the two since Anna left home to live on her considerable wits and her ample charms. I had not met Brennan before, though he was a close friend of Lionel's. Norman did not think much of his poems and for this reason I had not read them closely after an initial attraction. Someone whose word I trusted had told me that one night over his cups C.B. had talked about Anna in the days before her flight and had expressed the most ferocious jealousy. C.B. declared that he waited up at nights behind the door to leap out on her when she came home late, smelling too warmly of kisses and wine and dance music; he was determined, he said, to stop her before she went to the bad. From this account I felt sure that his too-heated anxieties had played a strong part in driving her into the extreme step she took, and that he was an example of the domineering father unconscious of the roots of his jealous furies. Anna herself told Ray of her girlhood at Newport: how C.B., when in liquor, used to force her into a corner and abuse her intolerably.

There was certainly between Anna and her father both a sharp antagonism and a deep bond. And clearly the bond had become twisted and lost inside the antagonism. What happened at Betsy's, though in part obscure, showed both the irritated attraction and the inability to live in any sort of lasting accord. C.B. installed himself at Betsy's, in a little room in a courtyard at the back, and drank steadily. He was rather heavily turned in on himself, silent, but not unfriendly to us others, only rarely coming out with one of his ripely opinionated comments, saying that the piano didn't disturb him, music being no more than a vague background for entangled bodies and minds or a stimulant for those too poor in purse or spirit to buy liquor, tolerable anyhow if bad enough and not played too loudly. 'Every night,' says Ray, 'he used to appear in the room upstairs which was reserved for Betsy's more intimate customers. He would seat himself quietly in a corner with his own bottle of beer and appeared to take little interest in the drunken cavortings around him. Actually he was a shy man, did not mix easily with other people, and had no small talk.' He was sunk in a prolonged and unrelenting crisis. He had given in. No longer could he bear a life of domestic respectability and university boredom. (I have been told that he had given up marking exam-papers, let them accumulate and lie on his table, then at long last ordered them to be taken out and burnt; the students he allotted places according to what he knew of their ability.) He wanted to get down into the gutter where Anna had taken refuge. She had proved stronger than everything else in his life, and with morose determination he tossed his prestige, his scholarship, his peace of mind and his assured income into her wide and insatiable lap. But Anna won only because she had as her ally his poetry, the pressure on his mind of the poetry he had once written and didn't want to understand, the poetry which accused his society, his civilization, of a total dereliction from the human path, the human dream. His poetry, devilishly nestling between Anna's breasts, proved stronger than all his rationalizations about it, all his studies in so many languages of verse, all his hopes of a definitive edition of Aeschylus. (Only a few scraps found at his death: 'It's all here,' he said, tapping his brow.) Anna and his poetry became one, the defiant whore and the song that would accept nothing less than Eden in a world of money and the fragmentation of men, the reduction of men to things.

Brennan was the only genuine *symboliste* poet in the English language, deriving in large part from the work of his master Mallarmé, but owning the rages of Rimbaud and the vision of the city of alienation that was Baudelaire's. The overpowering vastness and the ancient bones of desolation that litter his inner landscape have however their Australian basis; and A *Burden of Tyre* brings out fully this Australian rebirth of *symbolisme* in his work, its relation to our national development and the crisis of imperialism: for Australia the decisive changes linked with the Boer War, Federation, and the movement into modern nationhood.

It is one of the great regrets of my life that I did not even try to say one intelligent word to him as he sat brooding with his quick eyes dulled, sucking at his great curved pipe and bending over his beer-mug with his magnificent beak of a nose and his mane of rusty black hair brushed back. A strange predatory image, a defeated eagle, too lost even to wave his pipe argumentatively. When he stood up, he stooped more than ever, his more-than-six-feet broken. Anna too, very hard up, was taken in by Betsy; and she and C.B. drank together and quarrelled bitterly. Whatever brief emotion had flared up in the gutter-meeting was dissipated in the chafing animosities of a pair whose love had irreparably become envenomed. To save the fallen woman, to go down and become part of her, purging guilt by a deeper guilt, repudiating the burden of a consciousness hopelessly divided against itself . . . Anna, already suffering badly from T.B., hammering on his door and demanding money for her medicine, shouting foul things; Brennan slumped inside his clothes, opening his mouth to speak and unable to speak.

But after a while he was joined by a woman from New Zealand, Violet Bird, of pleasant but not striking looks. They were fond of one another; perhaps the bond went deeper than one thought. Once or twice, seeing him glance at her with a half-smile, I felt that we were underrating her, that I was prejudiced in my youthful down-at-heel scorn for their ageing seediness. Underneath she had had a sweet bright light careless quality; and I had the conviction that with his feeling of a foundered world and the confused anguish of his hell-descent after Anna he had become emotionally dependent on her. Their relationship had begun before he took the Avernian Road to Betsy's. They used to drink, Ray says, in winebars and pubs around the University, and C.B. was warned not to make a show of himself in full view of the students. In any event, she turned up at Betsy's soon after the collapse of the reunion with Anna. Then one night, after she had been on a visit up the coast to Mick Paul's place near Narrabeen, she thought the last tram had gone; it crashed round a bend and knocked her down, killing her. Brennan was badly hit. I saw him in his crushed misery; but what could I, who had never known him, say? Then he faded from Betsy's and I did not see him again.

I have cited the story that I think was most prevalent about Violet's end. But my faith in the folklore and scandal of pubs was somewhat shaken when I consulted Ray. 'Brennan had returned,' he said, 'temporarily to Newport where he had lived for many years. Newport is on the seaside, about twenty miles from Sydney. Today you can travel there in comfort in modern double-decker buses direct from the city at Wynyard Square and over the Harbour Bridge. But in those days you had to take the ferry to

Manly, a tram to Narrabeen, and then an antiquated bus to Newport. Well, somewhere on that stretch between Manly and Narrabeen, poor Vi (drunk of course) was hit by a tram one night and killed. Chris went into great poetic attitudes of drama at his mistress being thus killed while on her way to see him. His beery eyes becoming more and more goldfish-like and distended at the thought. However, my approach to the drama became rather cynical when I heard Mick Paul, who lived at Dee Why, about halfway between Manly and Narrabeen, bewail, with tears in his one eye, how Vi had been so tragically killed while on her way to see him. Then a drunken Scottish architect named Armstrong who lived at Manly (several years later he jumped off Manly ferry in a state of alcoholic ecstasy), told me, with his bloodshot eyes more bloodshot than usual, that on that awful night Vi had been on her way to visit him.'

Perhaps it was out of a rage against her father that Anna acted perfidiously towards Betsy. She brought in a couple of police pimps and had the place raided. Betsy managed to survive this, but a second raid put her out of business. She was already in difficulties through another piece of duplicity. She took in out of the kindness of her heart a White Russian named Theo, who, after living in the house for some time and paying nothing, opened up a rival café at the corner of Campbell and Pitt Streets. 'I remember,' says Ray, 'how Betsy used to limp round her place and screech in that awful voice of hers, "That bastard Theo! The skunk only made up to me to learn how I cooked spaghetti, and now he's trying to put me out of business."'

As for Brennan, he had entered irretrievably on the broken life he kept up till his death in 1932. Forced to resign his associate professorship in 1925, he survived on contributions from various friends (including Anna after her marriage). It seems to me that he was himself unable to face the complex of emotions that had driven him into his pitiable revolt. The events I have narrated have been hidden away, but there are many accounts of his later picturesque career as a fallen giant. However, I give Ray's memories of those failing years. 'He was certainly a complex and frustrated figure. I remember him well up to the time he died, when he had become quite a figure around King's Cross. He was always amiable enough, but quite lacking in personal charm, with his watery bulbous eyes, great beak of a nose, and a characterless mouth disappearing into chinlessness. He was usually very dirty, smelling like a stale brewery, given to wearing black shirts, which in those days were usually worn only by engine-drivers, hob-nailed boots, and quaintly shaped hats, the brims of which were always so twisted as to remind one of Robin Hood. He was not a good conversationalist and was only at ease when he could pontificate in a Johnsonian manner. After his collapse at the University he had a rather tough time and used to drink in the lowlier pubs at the bottom of William Street. But as conditions improved slightly with him, he moved gradually up until he reached the heights of the Mansions Hotel at Kings Cross. There he used to hold court, seated in the saloon bar; and he could be quite entertaining with an audience, quoting bawdy passages from the classics. You could approach the Presence as long as you bought him a schooner of beer; and after an afternoon's homage from admiring university students, or others like myself who knew him so well, the old boy would be left at closing time with more beer than he could drink . . . Poor old Chris Brennan, at least I had the privilege of literally being sick on his head when recuperating, drunk, one night at Betsy's.'

Is it worth while bringing up all these details about Brennan? I myself hold to the simple faith that the truth is always worth telling and that if there is any spiritual depth, any positive value, in a man, it will come out in spite of and because of the pangs, ordeals and shames to which he is brought by his inner conflicts. Brennan, if not a fully great poet, had many elements of greatness; he represents the most complex and penetrating point of poetic vision in Australian culture up to the present. For this reason all the significant details of his life are of the utmost interest. He is big enough to need and to demand the most searching light on all his deeds; and his collapse is integrally related to the conflicts defined in his poems, his social and his poetic insights, his grasp of the divided and alienated nature of man in the post-Baudelairean world of the cash-nexus and the city-desert. His relations to Anna help to reveal what he is really getting at in his poems, and to distinguish its genuine *symboliste* vision from its vague and emptily idealistic elements. And so Anna too has her meaning in this world of the 1920s, when the conflicts that Brennan grasped or intuited were coming to a new head, baffling us and yet driving us forwards. Rightly enough she keeps on reappearing in this book, an emblem both of desecrated life and of the beauty that survives desecration and stirs our hearts against the desecrating forces.

∗

The earlier bottle-throwing that week had occurred in Anna B.'s flat, or rather the flat of the man with whom she was living in Forbes Street. She had taken up with ex-pug turned sporting-journalist, a squat man with flattened nose and cabbage-ears. He still hadn't got over the excitement of seeing his name printed as commentator on the sports page where he used to read the reports of his own matches; and he felt the need to confer, overflowing in friendliness, with a fellow-author, someone who ought to be able to appreciate his pride at rising into the intellectual world. 'Jack,' he kept saying as he took my arm and pressed it, 'us authors have got to stick together.' He took out a batch of cuttings and made me read them. 'Now what do you think of that? I know I've got to polish up a bit, but I don't mind saying I've got the knack of it. If you'd told me a year ago, I wouldn't have believed you.' He retrieved the cuttings and read out choice phrases. 'Now what do you think of that?' He was anxious to find if I had any enemies so that he could bash them for me. We had a drink in a quiet pub and he showed me what progress he had made in yodelling. Some of the customers looked round with an intention of saying rude things, but after a glance at his battered face they thought again. 'Jack,' he told me, clutching my arm again and fixing me with a look of ferocious sincerity, 'it's good to meet a bloke that takes writing as serious as what I do.'

Ray was present on the afternoon he met Anna. 'He was a real larrikin, and, with his bullet head cocked on one side, in Pelligrini's bar, he suddenly said to Anna: "I bet I'll have you in a fortnight."' The term used was rather stronger than that. Will had been impressed by Anna's majestic deportment and tickled by her bawdy complacence of language. To possess her appeared both impossible and easy, necessary and fabulous. 'The extreme bluntness of this attack did not at all move the imperturbable Anna; she merely gave him her sweet composed smile and said, "I don't think you will." Of course he did, if not that night, probably the next; and he continued to do so for some time, anywhere and at any time.'

Anna had been originally seduced by an Italian waster, who was said, as a connoisseur of female plumpness, to have a bed specially made with boards for mattress. But she continued to hanker after him. All the while she was steadily going downhill; but her affair with the ex-pug marked a definite point of degradation. He liked to take his friends home to show her off, being as proud of keeping such a woman as he was of being a writer with his name printed in large type (plus a photo-smear of his glowering bull face). The night he took me home she was in a bad temper and he wanted to put her through her paces for my benefit. That started the trouble. She didn't want to be put through any paces, she wanted to sulk comfortably and drink. Also I think she was ashamed at my seeing her installed in Will's lair. Not that she cared for me or my opinion, but I did represent in some sort of way her father's world, and she didn't like to feel degraded before that world. To the end she nourished an idea of writing and being a not-unworthy daughter of Christopher the Poet.

Will couldn't see that she was getting angry. He kept on telling me what a bonzer girl she was, how different she was from the usual pack of blinkblankblonk, and how suited he and she were. So at last she said, 'Hell to all that, go and buy me a bottle of brandy.' He said the local pubs didn't know him yet. 'You go to so-and-so's,' she replied, 'and mention my name. If they don't know you, they know me.' He said he wouldn't wait on no dashdash woman and she said he dashdash might as well get used to it, so start as soon as possible. 'You don't get me as cheap as you'd like to.' They began shouting at one another; and by the time they had really got going, the respectably-nurtured Anna was easily a match for Will, who glared at her in a daze, with a punch-drunk sway.

'Give us a yodel,' I suggested with ill-advised humour.

'That dashdash of a woman don't appreciate art, Jack,' he dolefully answered me. 'Not like you and me do. Shut up,' he roared at her. 'You're worse than a roof-full of tomcats. If only you were a man I'd put my fist through your dashdash guts,' etcetera, etcetera.

'You're not dashdash man enough,' etcetera, etcetera.

'Don't be so dashdash sure of that, you're not dashdash dead, though you soon will be,' and so on.

'Listen to him, Jack, listen to the funny sod, I'll tell you a few things about him.' She told them.

'Listen to me, Jack, you don't know what that woman'll descend to. I'll tell you.' He told me.

He was annoyed when she appealed to me, standing against the wall with her hands on her broad hips, her face rosily lighted with her anger, her eyes flashing with their cornflower blue, her bright hair tossed about her thrownback head. So he started appealing to me too. I felt the danger of the position and tried to mumble words of placation. But they were both at me, insistent that I speak up and agree. I sympathized with Anna; but if I had to choose, I feared Will's large fist more than her tongue. Besides, I was flattered by his liking for me, though it was really only a liking for his own name in print.

She threw the first bottle. There was a number of beer and milk bottles standing on a box by the kitchen door. She threw the bottle slowly, calmly, but without aim. It smashed on the wall some six feet away from Will. He said, 'Cri, I won't stand for that from a woman.' So he threw a milk jug. The milk splashed over me, flecked her big bosom and gleaming face. 'So you would, would you?' she remarked. They spoke without shouting now, in a tense angry coldness. Anna threw the second bottle. He threw a soup-plate. They were not many feet apart and could easily have hit one another, but their careful lobs and throws became a sort of ritual of destruction, not intended to damage anything but the walls. I was cut off from the door, seated against the dresser, and didn't know what to do. Someone from another flat yelled below. Anna and Will went on throwing things at one another (at the wall), uttering stereotyped insults in cold harsh voices.

The peltings seem to have been a nightly practice; for Ray records that when he visited the flat, the same thing happened. 'It was their custom to whip themselves up into a frenzy of lust. On this particular night they hurled practically every ornament and piece of crockery at each other, together with such delightful and imaginative insults as . . . (censored). I remember also, at Pelligrini's, Margot R., wiping alcoholic tears of amusement from her eyes and giving a detailed account of the previous night when the loving couple, having been flung out of the flat by their landlord for the noises they made, arrived at her room, pushed her out of her own bed, and installed themselves there. Margot added, in her philosophic manner, that as she herself now had nowhere to sleep, she filled in the time by washing Annie's one and only pair of pants (although, if I remember rightly, bloomers were then usually worn because of the shortness of skirts). After the affair ended, Will returned to his lawful wife, an enormous arrogant woman with cross eyes, and continued his successful career.'

Anna, I mentioned, tried now and then to write. A few times she told me that she'd like to write a novel, though what she had in mind was a piece of self-vindication. She never forgot her father, as he for his part had been unable to forget her; she wanted to show him that despite everything she had some of his creative fire. She had listened intently to his talk and repeated many of his ideas. Thus, he had a low opinion of psychoanalysis, which he liked to describe as a modern conjuration of devils. In April 1924 Anna contributed an article to the *Bulletin* Red Page, in which, writing in an easy forcible style, she denounces the works of Freud as a 'prostitution of science,' a device for peopling the undermind with 'foul-smelling ghosts' and 'unsavoury fantasies'. She attacks the interpretation of dreams about teeth falling out as showing 'tendencies towards sex-perversion'. (One wonders what analyst ever said that, since the normal interpretation of such dreams would be that they showed a fear of impotence or castration, probably linked with masturbation, which did not possess any special intensity unless linked with other symptoms.) She goes on:

> Freud himself tells of a girl of eighteen suffering from those ordinary 'nerve' symptoms which frequently follow shock or prolonged strain—fear of crossing the street, of being in a room alone with the door shut, irritation at the ticking of a clock, excessive fidgetiness as to the placing of things. He works out by a train of reasoning which is screamingly funny or very nauseating, according to the reader's type of mind, that the girl is obsessed by a peculiar and revolting sex-passion; and, in spite of continuous and sustained denials, by persistent pressure he breaks her down to acquiesce. That is to say, he finds her a nervous girl, he leaves her a sex-pervert.

This prim and disgusted statement is made by the girl whom we have met at Betsy's and in the ex-pug's flat. Freud, I think, would have smiled benevolently if he had been given her essay. He would hardly have needed a dossier to diagnose that its author was suffering from a very bad father-obsession which was doubtless working out in odd ways. He would have noted the obvious resistances to bringing up into consciousness the hidden structure of motivation. As for us, knowing what we do, it is hard not to see in the fantasy of Freud who 'finds her a nervous girl, leaves her a sex-pervert', the father-image towards which she had such an ambivalent attitude.

Her yearning for escape, her repeated wish to get away to the clean sea, the wind of God, the healing earth, was real enough, and embraced memories of her earlier years at Newport. Here too there was an echo of her father's views. Rose in her Notes on Brennan's conversation at Spring-wood mentions that he talked 'of his home life, his wife's excellent cooking, his love of sleeping naked between blankets, summer and winter, because on hot nights they mopped up the sweat, and in cold they warmed the blood. To sit on a blanket, eat a potato baked in its jacket, and drink red wine at his seaside cottage, was all that he wished for his old age.' That seaside cottage with its simple life haunted Anna too. After her marriage she tried to inhabit it; but her husband was taken by a shark on one of the beaches and she died soon after.

DULCIE DEAMER

from *The Queen of Bohemia:*
The Autobiography of Dulcie Deamer

By this time I knew, in a general way, that such a handy to town location as Kings Cross existed, and that impecunious people holed-up there. Therefore, it must be cheap as well as handy.

I prospected, saw a 'Vacancies' card in the window of an old, grey-stone, three-storeyed terrace house on the main thoroughfare where the trams ran, and rang the bell. (That sombre residential, one of a quadruplet, is still there. I often glance at it.)

So on that long-ago day I moved into a small 'first-floor back', with a gas ring, one window overlooking a back alley, but the other offering—oh, joy! for I love trees—a close-up view of a jacaranda in a neighbour's backyard. The small room's rent was a pound a week. I could have got something cheaper if I hadn't been so new at the game.

Today's Sydneysiders and the perpetual waves of tourist visitors who head for our now widely known night-life centre, our Montmartre, assume that the Cross has always been like that. Even the journalists who've interviewed me over and over again, ad nauseam, on the subject seem to have the same idea fixed immovably in their heads. During the last ten years or so, if a paper's short of copy, somebody hotfoots up to me to enquire breathlessly concerning sin-spangled nights at the top of

William Street thirty or forty years back.

I keep on telling them that around their birthdate sin-spangled nights were not more prevalent at the top of William Street than anywhere else, and that striptease shows were not imported until after the Second World War.

Truth is stranger than fiction, and often much duller. They depart frustrated.

Well, not always. Sometimes a young journalist's natural desire to keep his job prompts him to employ his imagination. As in a rather sleazy publication dealing with the Cross's 'history' wherein I was reported to have stated that I had been present at 'a thousand parties' in that rather circumscribed locality. If they had said 'a dozen', even that would probably have been stretching things, and only small get-togethers, anyhow, for the *real* parties I *did* attend over years were all downtown. The ridiculous statement attributed to me was on a par with the leopard skin legend. I suppose we must have our myths.

I've got used, over the years, to popping up in the Press as 'the Queen of Kings Cross'. It sounds all right, doesn't it?

Only that there isn't any substance in it! My stamping ground, complete with 'coronation', was very much somewhere else.

There are other apocryphal stories concerning me and the Cross, one, which really annoyed me, retailing how I and other associates propelled an unfortunate horse into a flat and locked it in there, as a reprisal against a landlord who had evicted one of us. I'm very fond of horses, as of all animals—except some journalists—and would rather be hung, drawn and quartered than aid and abet such a beastly proceeding. Excuse me for getting hot under the collar.

To return to 1923—what *was* Kings Cross like when I rented my first cheap room there?

It was wholly innocent of its present honky-tonk, razzle-dazzle facade. No girly striptease or imitation-girly homosexual joints. No displays of coloured neon lights. No restaurants tricked-out with various stage properties to persuade you that you're dining in Sweden, Czechoslovakia or Japan. No murderous traffic tangle. No steel and plate glass skyscrapers as characterless as giant biscuit tins. Oh, yes, I freely confess that I liked it very, very much better as it was in the 'earlies'.

Originally, as all historians of Old Sydney know, the Cross was a select, out-of-town hilltop area, where the wealthy, behind wrought-iron carriage drive gates, occupied tree-shadowed stone mansions. On the main highway through it, and spilling over into adjacent side streets, were the usually three-storeyed terrace houses of the not so affluent; and in one such, a long time later, I was to rent a room.

With the coming of the motor car the wealthy moved further out, and as population pressure increased, neat but more modest terrace houses, all with wrought-iron balconies and a tiny strip of front garden, spilled downhill towards Rushcutters Bay.

In the matter of 'vice': when I took up residence in the locality there were two or three discreet brothels in Woolcott Street—now become Kings Cross Road—and that steep, narrow thoroughfare was jocularly known as 'the dirty half mile'. But I was to inhabit two addresses there a little later, and never saw or heard anything that could have raised a blush on anyone. The poor old dirty half mile was very demure and very quiet. Sorry to keep on disappointing the eager journalists, but one must tell the truth.

Wealth, when its carriages were transformed to cars, had moved farther afield before I became a Cross-ite. Some of the mansions, derelict, were then human rabbit warrens; the hard-up cooked and quarrelled and loved where plywood partitions divided dignified rooms, and washing hung on strings across tall and stately window openings.

Economics bred the rabbit warrens, and also persuaded the occupiers of the terrace-dwelling to sublet rooms, as population pressure and soaring city values forced the small-earner up the slope of William Street to find diggings from which, if necessary, one could walk to one's job in town in twenty minutes.

Thanks to being acquainted with a bright-brained family who were down on their luck, I became intimate with a draggled dowager, a one-time duchess among mansions, who gave me the perfect picture of how-are-the-mighty-fallen. It's permanently imprinted on memory and I treasure it with delight.

A pair of stone lions guarded a massive feudal portal—you couldn't simply call it a front door. The entrance hall was floored with black and white marble, and from heavy gilt frames aldermanic gentlemen with heavy faces, funereally painted to start with, and age-darkened on top of it, regarded you. Also regarded empty soft drink bottles, a bicycle, a rubber tyre, a toy pram and a toddler's damaged stroller.

Why hadn't the depressing ancestors been removed? Was the family simply sick of them? But the frames were worth something; I wouldn't have minded having a couple of them to dispose of to a second-hand dealer. Why hadn't some extra hard-up rabbitwarrener snitched them at dead of night and done just that? One of those questions that are never answered. It has always bothered me. But the ridiculous effect of those solemn, self-important faces, under the circumstances, was joyful. Of *course* they'd been left behind; nobody wanted them. Nobody could.

Marble mantelpieces in dignified rooms divided down the middle by a makeshift partition, and therefore occupied by two families, supported milk bottles, cheap alarm clocks and shaving apparatus. Washing hung everywhere, as did small meat safes wherever there was a draught. Broken-nosed classic statues rose from weed plots that had been flower beds in the once-upon-a-time ostentatious garden expanse at the mansion's rear, where a rusted, cast-out gas stove leaned against a magnolia tree.

Oh, yes, there were drunkenly hanging wrought-iron gates at the driveway entrance.

Everything was so incredibly shouldn't-ought-to-be that it had a comic fairytale quality. And gramophones tinkled, and somebody had, tragically, dropped a bottle of cheap wine in the entrance hall, and children shouted as they played cricket between the damaged statues.

I saw quite a lot of that draggled dowager of a mansion for a while. It remains with me as a treasured symbol of the not-much-money, happy-go-lucky Cross before the razzle-dazzle era.

When you disembarked at the top of the steep approach up William Street from that forgotten traffic-carrier, a semi-toastrack tram—goodness, how they exposed one to the weather!—what was the hub of Kings Cross like, forty-five years ago?

I must draw an outline of its portrait, not only because I've been asked so many blankly uninformed questions about it, but it was part of the offstage—yes, quite offstage—background of the Golden Decade.

Wipe out the polyglot pavement crowds of the present moment, the espresso coffee lounges at every second step, the mushroom crop of cafes down every side street, where you eat in Hungarian, Italian, Hindustani,

German, and half a dozen other languages; obliterate also the tourist boutiques vending koalas, boomerangs and souvenir postcards, the high-priced dress salons and the beanstalk-high blocks of flats. It's an effort of imagination, isn't it, but you'll have to make it.

The scene at the top of William Street in 1923 was certainly not crowded, and there was nothing eye-arresting about it. Two solid and very respectable pubs and a large Chinese cafe dominated it. They are still there. Nobody pays attention to them now, but they were revered landmarks in 1923. So—at least to me—were a pair of green griffins above the facade of the Kings Cross Picture Theatre. For long and long they watched us, a charming bit of the Cross's skyline, and I'd loved them since, just after renting that first room, and within sight of the griffins, I bought ambiguous rissoles at a ham-and-beef shop opposite the tram stop. I had purchased the rissoles not because I liked them, but because, like sawdust, which they rather resembled, they were filling, and only a few pence each. I caught the eye of the griffins as I came out of the shop, and experienced a lifting of the heart. Why didn't they find some skyline place for them when the picture theatre became a dance hall for teenagers full of pep pills, and then a skyscraper?

Reverting to cheap eats at the Cross in those far off days, unpretentious little places were discoverable where one could have three courses for half a crown, and if one trekked down the slope of William Street there were rough-and-ready eateries where Irish stew or sausage-and-mashed would only set you back eighteenpence. Thus chancy earners, like myself and many others, could manage a change from the rissoles and the fried egg on the gas ring.

We could also dress as cheaply as we could eat, thanks to the proliferation of second-hand clothing shops, referred to as 'wardrobe shops'. The area was sprinkled with these discreet, small premises. They fascinated me. And they were even more important to me than to most, for an attempt in childhood to teach me to sew had to be abandoned; I not only loathed it, but had as little aptitude as the lowest grade of the mentally retarded. I can replace a button, but that is all.

One could pick up a gay, if slightly tarnished, party frock for ten shillings. For a pound—oh dear, that was a week's rent—something quite striking might be obtained.

Apart from my weekly contributions to the *Woman's Mirror* throughout the whole of its existence—stories, articles, verse under heaven knows how many pen-names—I also contributed, wherever I could find or force an opening, to a lot of other publications. And whenever an extra cheque arrived I would hotfoot it—you bet—to a wardrobe shop. (No, I've never been on a paper's staff throughout the whole of my career; always a lily-white freelance.)

Right at the Cross, past a pawn shop and down a narrow side street, was a dingy little place vending an extraordinary variety of junk, suggesting the pickings from rubbish dumps—odds and ends of metalware, crockery oddments, goodness knows what. But quite passable shoes sometimes turned up there, and quite useable handbags. Such fossickings were adventurous, could be rewarding, and lent colour to life.

Cataloguing these basic facts—lodging, food, and clothing—I've endeavoured to convey a low-earner's stamping ground of the twenties. For Kings Cross was just that. But it had an 'atmosphere'. Almost indefinable, yet sensed immediately; tension-relaxing; a sort of 'So what? Smile, damn you' feeling. And an inner conviction that it was always sunny thereabouts—even if it was raining.

Was it the few hundred feet lift into hilltop ozone? An 'out of the city, so do as you please' laissez faire? Telepathy seeping from the personal attitudes of a sub-population—half-broke, sanguine, visionary—of artists, sculptors, poet-scribblers, holed-up in basements, third-storey attics, any living-crevice that was really cheap?

Was it due to a fusion of all these intangibles? The result was warm, casual; an impulse towards Lawsonian matey-ness, but rather more sophisticated.

For one thing, no one at the Cross seemed to notice how you dressed. Probably because they were inured to the can't-be-helped, odd ensembles of the impecunious artistic sub-population. But the bearded, long-haired, barefoot, and sometimes unbathed young beatniks of today were not only unknown then, but would have had everybody—including the would-be painters and poets—gawping out of the toastrack trams at them, and surging out of pubs to stare and guffaw and shout ribaldry.

You see, there were neither poseurs nor 'rebels' in those days. If you were shabby or makeshift you grinned and bore it, and your pals gave you anything they could spare, and bought you a drink.

Neither, despite the locality's easygoing aura, did we ignore the basic fitness of things. If stretch pants, the most disastrous giveaways of the deficiencies of the female shape ever invented, had been current in 1923 I can positively assure you that no very, very pregnant young woman would have paraded them, minus even a half-length jacket, as she chatted to friends on the most central corner. (She was the first I observed; there were others, equally convex, perpetrating this imbecility, this scaling down to zero of one's physical image.) I am not easily surprised, I've seen much more than most, but this might make even a 'bus baulk if it had artistic sensibilities. The spectacle was much more astonishing than the common-or-garden striptease. And one didn't have to pay anything to see it. No wonder the Cross is a sightseer's Mecca these days.

On the edge of Decade doings—a lot of us got to know him—drifted a radical bohemian, a really far-out one. I bring him into the picture not only because he was truly a 'character', but because, through him, I was involved on a never-to-be-forgotten occasion with one of our literary 'greats'—even though, poor man, a 'great' in eclipse.

Shortish, thinnish, fairish, with a sharp, intelligent face, Geoffrey Cumine was grubby, shabby, and claimed descent from Sir Walter Raleigh. He had an acute, sardonic, intellect, a wide knowledge of literature, and wrote real poetry. If I ever knew I've forgotten how he managed to scrounge a bed and a crust. But he was never sorry for himself. And his contempt for such a multitude of things was such that 'What bloody rot!' was his most frequent expression. After a course of this, when I had known him for some time, I got fed up and gave him 'What bloody rot!' back. It shook him, because I never used anything stronger than 'damn', regarding bad language as a confession of vocabulary inadequacy. He became, at least with me, more constrained when voicing contrary opinions. As one would expect, he scorned the Noble Order—which, among ourselves, we often spoke of as I Felici—referring to it as the 'Evil Itchy'.

Often unwashed and frequently drunk, Geoff was a personality one always remembers—which is more than I can say for not a few 'well known people' I've encountered. And I came to have a sort of exasperated affection for him; possibly partly because he had a genuine affection for me.

Geoff, with his keen feeling for literature, describing my *Devil's Saint* as 'a tapestry of words', gratified me very much. For, as they say, he 'knew his onions'. Mentioning onions brings to mind a thick and exotic species of pea soup (there were onions in it) which he occasionally carried up to my bug-ridden top-floor bed-sitting room in a billy. So much did my now-and-then guest appreciate these pea soup sessions that he dashed off a couple of verses, the title being 'Dulcie Deamer'. I have them among scraps and clippings I've preserved. Here they are:

We travel many paths, and most are rough:
Back-swinging twigs strike us across the eyes,
Sad, slimy patches cease to cause surprise
And just to find a track is task enough.
But always there's a light, could we but find it—
To show the whimsy oddity behind it.

I've seen it pretty glum and fairly tough,
And God's a goat, and all their teaching lies.
Learning is nothing—charity is wise
Because she cuts out analytic stuff.
And yours the wisdom and the wit behind it—
Mine the good fortune in my pain to find it.

'My pain' wasn't figurative. Through more than half the time I knew him Geoff was in constant pain. All his own doing. Full of grog, he'd borrowed without permission a friend's motorbike, which he hadn't learnt to ride—and went smack into a telephone pole, smashed the bike, and injured his left arm so critically that from then on it hung useless, causing racking nerve spasms.

His gratitude for the occasional conversations over shared pea soup was extravagant. But he was also a liability. Coming home one evening I found him sprawled on the stairs halfway to my landing, collapsed from drink and pain. Somehow he had to be levered up and got home. I semi-supported him halfway down William Street to his lodging. Thanks to the mind-your-own-business Kings Cross creed, nobody took any notice.

This was nothing compared to the night he visited me—sober—and told me that he was going home to commit suicide: the pain was too much, and it was the only sensible thing to do.

I had encountered would-be suicides before, emotional cases, and talked them out of it. That night there was simply nothing I could say. Geoff's life, and his angle on it, left one with no argument.

After he'd gone a violent storm broke. My door banged open. I sat up in bed as if I'd been shot. He'd done it—and was letting me know!

In excuse I must remind the scornful of my years in a very haunted house. They'd left an indelible impress that I'd much rather have been without.

Next day I saw him in the street. He greeted me with a twisted grin. 'I felt too sick last night to kill myself.'

How's that for an anticlimax?

After a spell in an inebriates' home, and grogging on again as usual, Geoff discovered, in the lowlier type of pub, a poet's idol to worship. Chris Brennan.

Christopher Brennan, one of our 'greats' in scholarship and poetry, had fallen on evil times. Never mind the rights and wrongs. I had heard often enough of that towering figure in our literature, but had never met him. Now he was down, as not a few of his compeers have been, to gutter-level. Unkempt, seedy, alcoholic, and the respectable—literary or otherwise— kept to one side of the street if he was on the other.

The pubs where Geoff had encountered him gave him the mateship of half-broke, would-be scribblers, and Geoff was now enthusing to me of his discussions with the Master, as he called him, and who, he said, wrote verses in beer on the bar counter.

Came Christmas. (No, I can't give the exact date, but I was still in my bug-ridden living-place in Victoria Street, and it may have been 1928.) Geoff, very eager and half apologetic, asked might he bring Christopher Brennan up my three flights of stairs for Christmas dinner.

It appeared that nobody at all wanted the fallen poet-scholar at this goodwill season; and he was lonely and hungry.

I said Yes.

When I told Cecily what was about to happen she, a poetry enthusiast, offered at once to come along and 'bring something'. It was she who provided the tinned Christmas pudding, which was a real help, me being short of cash as usual. The 'turkey' had to be a delicatessen baked rabbit reheated; they were very cheap in those days. I couldn't afford two rabbits, and as one wouldn't be quite enough I added some sausages, and I think Cecily brought a tin of peas.

The circular, green baize covered table, not very steady on its antique, single central leg, would just about seat four. Cecily was very excited. She'd never met Brennan, either.

I hadn't realised how big he was—in build as in literary reputation. Wearing a voluminous, black-caped raincoat, as Byronic as it was seedy, he seemed to fill the room and almost bump the ceiling. His long, black, rather greasy hair brushed his collar. A pale, heavy, rather unusual face; courtly manners; a deep, measured, cultured voice, quoting scraps from the classics. At this stage he was mellow and not 'shot'.

Introduced to my offsider with the red-gold curls, he said, 'Cecily—oh, no. That means "the little blind girl".' Then dipped a finger in the wine— they had brought some—and drew a cross on her forehead, telling her, 'I baptise thee Sicily'. Then described to us how extremely beautiful the island was.

Charming. I wish I could recall some of the other things he said. The scholar-poet. And I had a little image of the Madonna on a shelf; he spoke warmly of how its opened arms were a symbol of universal refuge for 'all poor sinners, even the worst'.

The do-it-as-well-as-you-can Christmas dinner seemed to be appreciated. But the guests had brought rum as well as the wine, and when they got onto *that*—Cecily and I didn't touch it—'the scene changed', as an old-style novel would have put it.

Our famous guest waxed increasingly drunk, and endeavoured insistently to make love to Cecily; and when someone of his height and bulk seems intent on a classical saturnalia type of amour, and there are no open spaces to which the quarry can flee, the situation becomes more than awkward.

Geoff could have usefully intervened—if he hadn't got properly stuck into the rum, to which he was rather addicted, and had collapsed, only semi-sensible, on a decrepit cane chaise longue under the window. Later, as explanation and apology, he was to confess that he had downed what remained in the rum bottle so that the principal guest shouldn't have it and become too difficult.

Things were difficult enough, goodness knows! Fortunately I usually knew what to say and how to say it. And when I'm really determined have always felt that I can move mountains; in this case a very large and inebriated poet. Somehow Cecily and I got Chris Brennan and the dazed and mumbling Geoff out onto the landing.

And locked the door. I felt at the time that *that* was a major miracle. It left us shattered.

Anyway, our scholar-poet *did* have a Christmas dinner, which he really needed.

Geoff was so upset by the outcome of that evening that he cancelled his discipleship. It was the end of his bar-worship of Chris Brennan. He told me, 'I had a little garden that was precious to me. I invited a friend to share the privilege of seeing it, and he trampled the flowers.' I didn't view the matter quite like that; and if he hadn't brought along that bottle of rum proceedings might have remained at a fairly easy level to handle.

Years later, when Brennan was dead—and therefore unembarrassing— speakers at a gathering of the Fellowship of Australian Writers were eulogising him as an immortal. Remembering shabby Lawson cadging beer, and ostracised Brennan in need of a dinner, I stood up and told the praisers of the safely dead about the baked rabbit and the hungry social leper. I think it jarred them. But one sincere and truly charitable woman thanked me warmly afterwards for what I'd said.

Poor, often unwashed, self-crippled Geoff, with his arm, his binges, and his scorn of most things and people, became more and more eccentric. To one ear he attached a large imitation pink pearl ear-stud. On his forehead he had 'To Let' tattooed; this was to announce that his brains were available for any sort of hiring. Understandably he was presently in a mental institution; where, until his demise, he at least had food and care. A pity his carelessly scattered, short, polished poems were never collected, for he *was* a poet.

*

Meanwhile Kings Cross was changing.

It was on the edge of the incoming Depression that the Cross became, quite suddenly, a hang-out of the underworld. Not that you'd have known it from casual day-to-day observation. This enclave where, from 1923 onward, I lived and worked, and still do, presented, as the Depression crept in, its usual easy, cheery, mind-your-own-business face. But almost overnight the papers were full of razor gang vendettas and back lane dope peddlers, the locale of the lawlessness being always the area around the top of William Street. I never could figure out *why* there was that sudden irruption. Though admittedly the Cross has a network of narrow side streets ideal for sly-grog handouts and other offstage activities.

All sorts of people kept asking me wasn't I 'afraid' to live there. I wasn't. Unless you were dumb enough to blunder into the sort of company from which gang associates were recruited, or disoriented enough to sneak down side alleys to traffic with cocaine vendors (it was cocaine in those days, not LSD 'trips'), you wouldn't have a clue as to what was happening offstage. You only read about it in the Press.

It was a phase that provided headlines, flourished, and then was scotched.

The Thirties

"You find this ugly; I find it lovely . . ."

—*Kenneth Slessor*

By the 1930s, the gangs that had claimed the streets of the Cross were slowly diminishing. Urban development was partly responsible—many of the large homes on the early land grants were demolished, replaced by art deco apartment blocks such as Cahors, Birtley Towers, Franconia, and the Macleay Regis. The more prestigious buildings boasted bellboys, porters, and even their own restaurants. As Lydia Gill reveals in her following excerpt, smaller homes were divided into bed-sitters, attracting more working-class people and struggling artists, all of whom could live well on very little money.

The gang members who still roughed it around the pubs of Kings Cross began to coexist with a new breed of Cross-ites—the bohemians. In 1929, American Dick McGowan opened the California Cafe, which quickly became the epicentre for Sydney's cafe society, and also became a model for many subsequent coffee shops in Kings Cross like The Willow and The Arabian Cafe. In the California, coffee was sixpence a cup, musicians performed impromptu recitals, and paintings of the comic artist and Cross resident Emile Mercier lined the walls.

It was during this decade that eighteen-year old Rosaleen Norton left her North Shore home and moved into a stone stable in Roslyn Gardens, beginning her extraordinary career as notorious Kings Cross witch and artist. The humorist Lennie Lower, who wrote the popular comic novel *Here's Luck*, owned five houses in Woolloomooloo during the 1930s, all of which were furnished with a typewriter. Publisher and artist Sydney Ure Smith resided in Manar, on Macleay Street, while Dulcie Deamer packed up her infamous leopard skin dress and moved over to Farrell Avenue. At twilight each evening, pianist Dot Mendoza walked her chihuahua through the Cross. Actor Peter Finch shifted from Brougham Street to Wylde Street and then to Elizabeth Bay Road. Author Steele Rudd lived in a bedsitter on Roslyn Street. In the early 1930s, Christopher Brennan was still lurching out of the Mansions; poet Mary Gilmore nested in her flat on the corner of Darlinghurst Road and Roslyn Street; and the eccentric Bea Miles crawled out of dozens of taxis at the intersection of Kings Cross without paying the fares. As Kenneth Slessor notes in his chapter on the Cross, even the royal biographer, Hector Bolitho, assumed a bohemian mantle, and often strolled up Macleay Street wearing a bowler hat and lavender gloves. In the meantime, Ronald McCuaig printed a limited edition of his groundbreaking volume of poetry, *Vaudeville*, in the bedroom of his St Neot Avenue flat.

The artists and bohemians who filled the cafes of Kings Cross did so amidst Sydney's sly grog racketeers. As Sumner Locke Elliott points out in the extract from his novel, *Fairyland*, the six o'clock ban on alcohol was an inconvenience for the night animals who populated the area. Since it was comprised of a network of shadowy and obscure lanes, the Cross was the perfect location for the sale of illegal alcohol at black market prices, and for the procurement of cocaine.

Phil 'the Jew' Jeffes was the most feared man in the Cross throughout this decade. Jeffes worked as a bouncer in various sly grog shops, including the 50-50 Club, and the 400 Club, and regularly extorted money from prostitutes and illegal bookies. Kate Leigh, however, still reigned as the Sly Grog Queen. Her Majesty even managed to shoot Snowy Pendergast after he brandished a gun inside her illegal club. Whenever a member of the underworld was wounded, all he or she had to do was appear on the doorstep of Cross resident Dr Jim Eakin, who was affectionately known as 'the gun doc'. Eakin treated gangsters without asking questions or passing judgment. The following excerpt from *Aunts Up the Cross*, by Robin Dalton (who was Eakin's daughter), details the peculiar ways in which the various subcultures of the Cross embraced one another while she was growing up in a house on Darlinghurst Road, which once stood on the site of today's Kings Cross train station.

In the 1930s, the streets were crammed with cars, trams, bohemians, prostitutes, gangsters, artists, cabs, and even the odd horse. By the end of the decade, Kings Cross was the most densely populated area in Australia. At dusk, high-rise apartments created ornate silhouettes against the sky, and many of those all-night soirees laced with sly grog and cocaine would become send-off parties for soldiers drafted for the impending war.

ROBIN DALTON

from *Aunts Up The Cross*

Our house was the only private residence in Kings Cross, the city's 'European' quarter—the 'Montmartre' of Sydney, people call it, with flattery and nostalgia. Actually, it is fairly hideous; like all of urban Sydney being a dusty hodge-podge of low-built buildings, all in need of a coat of paint—the upper halves flats and residential rooms and the lower halves shops, offices and cinemas. Between the two, cutting off the dirty stucco and dingy brickwork from the glaring neon signs, are the ubiquitous iron or concrete awnings, the most characteristic features of Sydney's dim architecture.

'Maramanah' stood at the end of Darlinghurst Road, our street, only two blocks away, but already on the corner of a far smarter one, which led down to the harbour's edge. At the other end, Darlinghurst Road joined a smaller, steeper and dustier street known, because of the preponderance of pimps and prostitutes among its inhabitants, as the Dirty Half Mile. My grandmother referred to the girls as 'Soiled Doves'.

In front of our house was the only tree in the Cross, a broad and dusty-leaved plane-tree and, together with the house, it formed a small oasis of incongruous suburbia amid the glare and noise of the flashing signs, the foreign voices, the juke boxes and the cinema crowds. As a child, I drifted to sleep at the front of the house, immune to the noise ten feet below my window.

The house itself was really very small, I now realise, for the life it contained. It was a wonderful child's house, full of dark corners, hidden cupboards, unnecessary doors, delicious shiny round banisters, and two of those areas of waste space but endless possibility, the 'light areas'. There was both a flat roof, for laundry and sun-bathing and dolls' houses, and a sloping tiled one over the front half of the house for perilous climbs. There was a sheer drop of about sixty feet to be bridged when leaping to the fire escape of the block of flats next door with the odious little red-haired boy who lived in them, and there was, surprisingly enough, no supervision or restriction on these activities. It can only be that my father was busy, my mother playing bridge, and the current servants about their own business during these danger-fraught forays, for I can certainly remember no admonitions or warnings except my grandmother's with which I fought a bitter and unceasing war, sure of paternal backing for any amount of defiance.

Nevertheless, when these battles were over and I had climbed down from roof, drainpipe or banister, it was always to her drawing-room I went for the private, secret place which a child needs away from adult household life. It was a long, low, dark, cool room, whose windows looked out onto the feet of passers-by, and like everything else touched by my grandmother and Juliet in their seemingly constant and shared state of bereavement, its colour scheme was in varying shades of what they called 'heliotrope'. They both started wearing this as half-mourning very early in their death-bespattered lives. My grandmother carried it into her furnishings with a certain amount of relief in the way of pale background chintzes and a grey cushion here and there. Juliet's bedroom was, on the contrary, a stretch of unbroken purple. Her heavy mahogany furniture, combined with this funereal grandeur, did indeed give added weight to the mausoleum-like effect created by the many photographs of the departed.

As may be surmised, ours was a house in which the feeling of being 'lived in' flourished to the exclusion of all else. I suppose it must have been fairly shabby but one didn't notice this amid the crush of people, the cigarette smoke, and the constant preparation or eating of food. My mother smoked nearly 100 cigarettes per day—there was not a piece of furniture which had not been scarred by her butts, and, not in the least house-proud, all her enormous energy and creativeness, she focused on her kitchen. She never cooked until the war, and then when we were reduced to Rosa, increasingly cranky and growing older, and one maid, she attacked the business of cooking with gusto and joy. She was a natural chef—inventive and lavish. She was indifferent to her own comfort; the sofa would, and often did, do as well as her bed. She and my father shared a large dressing-room which was always littered with his clothes, and the only place in the house to which she could retire in an attempt at privacy was the unlockable bathroom. 'My idea of luxury,' she would say, 'is to be allowed to go to the lavatory by myself.' This seldom happened, as my grandmother hated to be shut out, and thought it was an unnatural and unfilial act.

There was nothing in the house forbidden to me. I was allowed to choose my own wallpaper and paint my own bedroom. One year, when I was about nine, I chose a bright, sick, pink, and the next year an even brighter hospital green. Half-way round the skirting board, with only the fronts done of my chest of drawers and wardrobe, I would tire, and the painter would be called in to finish the job, but not until I had painted the lavatory seat in the year's favourite shade.

These twin themes dominating the house, of death and lack of privacy, merged and culminated in the unhappy event of my mother killing the plumber. At one end of the upper hall was the back door, normally left open for sun and air. One summer morning the servants were busy else-where, the house was for once empty, and my mother emerged naked from her dressing-room en route to take a bath. At that moment the plumber (he was a new one) came up the back stairs and met her on the landing. He promptly had a heart attack from which he never recovered. My mother always felt that the fact that death was not instantaneous detracted from the impact of her nudity and the dramatic possibilities of the story.

Although I was a solitary child in a house full of adults, the house was undeniably always full, and this variety of characters I knew intimately at an early age was a rich fund of entertainment. I remember Tony McGill, our 'Starting-price' bookmaker, who ate a pound of raw tripe every morning for breakfast. Off-course bookmaking was illegal in New South Wales at that time and starting-price bookmakers like Tony found that the most accurate method of making a book was through research in the pubs of the city, checking on the odds being offered and laying off if the book became too heavy. This work needed a practitioner with a physique like Tony's.

Thursday was 'settling' day. Every Thursday night, Tony McGill came round to finalise the previous Saturday's betting. Tony had a special line in patter, which he had learnt from the then famous Fitzpatrick Travelogues. Something about the rich, resonant tones of Mr. Fitzpatrick's voice and his choice of exotic sounding places impressed Tony. As he left with the week's takings he would wave to assembled company and call out in his ringing bookmaker's voice:

'Farewell to Calabadad, Land of Mysterious Women!'

Occasionally, if his visit was later than usual, my mother asked him to stay to dinner, but even in such an easy-going household as ours this was a risky move and apt to create tension. Flushed with whisky and bent on entertaining the party, Tony would go through his repertoire of Fitzpatrickisms and once having exhausted these, would feel that something more spectacular was expected of him. Another regular visitor was a genteel and aged governess of my mother's, Sally Thornton, who one night had the misfortune to sit next to Tony, casting around for fresh topics. When all else failed, his own body never ceased to fascinate him. He leapt to his feet, pushed back his chair, and, whipping his shirt out of his trousers, thrust his bare and hairy chest close to Sally's face.

'How's that?', he roared. 'Go on—have a feel—as hard as a rock and in the pink of condition.'

Sally leant across this offering and addressing herself, quivering with gentility, to Tony's other neighbour. 'Don't you feel, Mr. Blackman', she said, 'that Gilbert and Sullivan were antipathetic?'

Poor Tony could never understand the rebuff.

As frequent a visitor as Tony was Siddie Jacobs, a dim-witted car park attendant to whom my father would lend £5 to be repaid at the rate of sixpence a week over the years: he was once caught chasing little girls and my father guaranteed his good behaviour to the police. Siddie was about five feet high. He lisped badly and wore a long white coat flapping around his ankles. When my father felt particularly mischievous he would say to Siddie on his visits to the surgery.

'Go upstairs, Sid, and say hello to Mrs. Eakin. She's not doing anything.'

As my mother invariably was doing something, and, once up, Siddie was not easy to get down, this was not a popular move.

There was always a current 'lame dog' of my mother's in the house. There was the girl behind the cash desk at the butcher's shop opposite who suffered from a painful and recalcitrant boil on her behind. It was too far for her to travel to her home each day for the prescribed treatment and so she came at lunchtime and sat patiently in a bowl of boiling water and boracic on our bathroom floor while my mother served her delicious luncheons on a tray.

More disrupting were the resident visitors. During really full periods, my mother sometimes never slept in a bed for weeks at a stretch. One fruity-voiced gentleman my parents met on a cruise—he lived with us for two years before disappearing with all the whisky and leaving behind a pile of unpaid bills. Shortly after his departure, my mother came home with a loathsome Viennese from her bridge club: I was turned out of my bedroom for him, and was incensed still further by the large framed photograph of himself kept on my bureau and the coronets embroidered on his under-pants. It took nine months for us to convince my mother that, despite his excellence at the bridge table, he must go.

Not all our house guests, eating or sleeping, were mistakes. One English theatrical producer whom my father invited to dinner remained in close harmony and affection—nightly—for seventeen years. Next to racing, the dominant influence in our lives was the theatre. The theatre in Sydney today is a very barren field compared to the richness with which it flour-ished when I was a child. There are now two legitimate theatres (and one of them boringly inaccessible—too far by public transport and too difficult to park by one's own) compared to the many of my youth, and, although there is beginning to be a vigorous stirring of Australian playwrights, the best of Australian talent leaves home in search of wider scope and a more appreciative audience. But thirty years ago, we had Her Majesty's, the Criterion, the Theatre Royal, the Tivoli—we had whole visiting compa-nies from England and America and Opera companies from Italy—and my father had them all as patients. He was the official theatre doctor to all the companies, and so a great deal of my time was spent behind the wings, chasing through the corridors and dressing rooms, whilst he was attending one of the company.

My father's patients were all part of our lives, in those days of close family doctor and patient relationships. There were the Pierce boys, a family of rugged fishermen and keen amateur yachtsmen whose favourite family joke was that my father had circumcised one of the younger boys 'crooked'. Twice a week my father drove to the fish market in the early morning and came home with a car load of fresh Pierce fish, a sack of oysters which I was taught to open at a very early age, and two or three live lobsters romping around in the back of the car and waving their antennae through the windows at startled passers-by.

We all mourned when one of his old ladies died, for she whiled away the last of her senile and bed-ridden days composing couplets to be recited at the doctor's visit. These fitted the ailment of the day. When her nightdress was lifted to bare her abdomen, she shrilled:

'Pull down my shirt,
I'm Fanny the Flirt.'
and for an abscessed breast brought forth:
'Isn't it a pity—
That I've got a titty.'

On mornings when I was not at school I frequently accompanied my father on his rounds, sometimes visiting the patient and sometimes waiting in the car outside. If he left me in a doubtful slum area, he always admonished me, 'Now if anyone speaks to you just make a noise like a five-year-old girl' at whatever age was appropriate at the time. When he emerged he would sometimes tell me about the case. I remember some of our family intimates only through their ailments which, if they were startling enough, my father could not resist recounting. Thus, one plump and coyly coquettish lady was embedded in my consciousness since a tic had 'crawled up her'. My father felt her charms were forever damned because, as he put it, 'when I got to the poor brute, it had died'.

Actually, for me, all Sydney was an extension of the security of the house. My days never had an even, but always an assured, tenor, and certain events brought their certain flavour.

The flavour of illness was an exciting one, not only the patients' illnesses, but my own. Then my mother swamped me with presents: I lay in feverish anticipation every time she left the house for she never went out, even for half-an-hour, without returning with armfuls of treasures. When my appendix came out a whole room of the hospital was hung by my mother in pink brocade, and every day a new lace or satin pillow cover arrived with a pillow spray of flowers in the appropriate colours, to pin beside my face.

My tonsils and adenoids came out in my father's surgery, suitably draped in sterile sheets, and I, aged four, attended by three doctors. I am told that I sat up on the table as the anaesthetic wore off and lisped at them:

'You three damned doctors get to hell out of here.'

No recollections of luxury attend the occasion on which I swallowed a shilling: that was my mother's adventure. I was standing in a queue at the greengrocer's waiting to buy an ice-cream, and, undecided as to flavour, was tapping my teeth reflectively with the shilling. In a flash it was gone: I flew home, thoroughly alarmed. The radiologist was a gambling crony of my mother's—as they waited for the X-ray of my lungs to be developed, my mother laid bets with him as to whether heads or tails would show. The shilling emerged side on.

KENNETH SLESSOR

'My King's Cross', 'Choker's Lane', 'Ticket in Tatts!',
'Up in Mabel's Room', 'William Street',
'King's Cross Gardens', 'Nocturne'

My King's Cross

When I say 'my' King's Cross, I don't wish to give the impression that I ever owned King's Cross or even felt that it belonged to me after a couple of drinks on a Saturday. I mean 'my' in a sense of time and not of property. The time I mean was my (and the century's) twenties, which is the right age for appreciating indigestible food, dubious drinks, prehensile women, exhausting conversation, hair-raising gymnastics and about two hours' sleep a night. At this time, however, I considered the food and drink as exciting as the conversation and I could still bounce like a golf ball after walking five or six miles and sleeping two hours.

Today my King's Cross is somebody else's King's Cross. It seems to have vanished utterly. So, of course, has my youth, and it seems only fair to take into account the possibility that one depended on the other. There are still swarms of young human beings eating, drinking, talking and making love in what passes for King's Cross today, and no doubt they are enjoying it as intensely as I did. But, looking at it from the aguish plateau of my (and the century's) sixties, the place just doesn't seem the same.

I don't know whether my King's Cross was any better than today's—or any worse. For, whatever happens to its landscape, King's Cross will always be a tract apart from the rest of Sydney, still contemptuous of the rules, still defiantly unlike any other part of any other city in Australia. And, though its skyline keeps on changing in an unpredictable and bewildering way, its essence of individuality does not change, its flavour, noises, sights and smells remain the same immutably. For this reason I find as much pleasure in contemplating it today as I did when I looked out of a Woolcott Street window in 1922—indeed, with its unending flux of lights and colours, its gaudiness and reticence, its sunsets and midnights, it seems (to me) a good deal more beautiful than the highly advertised stones and sand of Central Australia. To me, the Chevron Hilton hotel, with its glittering windows and huge verticals, is as awe-striking as Ayers Rock.

Where is King's Cross, or what is it? Literally, I suppose, the Cross is where the five streets cross at the top of William Street. But, in the geography of the post office, letters addressed to King's Cross may go to Darlinghurst, Elizabeth Bay, Potts Point, Woolloomooloo or even the fringes of Rushcutters Bay. It is a term rather than a place. Its boundaries are flexible. People who 'go to the Cross' or 'live at the Cross' may mean anywhere from Taylor Square to Wylde Street. This doesn't matter. They are expressing a state of mind, just as the Cross itself is perpetually expressing a state of mind.

With the exception of some vexing intervals in places like Melbourne, Bugbug, Port Tewfik and Tidworth (Wilts.), I have lived in or on the margin of King's Cross for more than forty years. The Harbour has never been out of my window. During that time I have watched hundreds of houses decay and vanish, streets change their names as well as their geometry, rows of buildings topple and become holes in the ground, and other buildings rise almost instantly like the mango-trees of Oriental conjurers. I have seen the swishing trolley-buses come and go and I have watched horses change to station-wagons. I have watched the pushes give way to the bodgies and the bodgies to the hippies (or whatever is the newest name for flash young men in search of adventure). I have watched the old William Street eating-places (21 meal-tickets for £1) turn into bistros, niteries, wine-and-dine cafés, steak houses, spaghetti-bars and espresso lounges.

Through all these transformation-scenes, the Cross has managed to cling defiantly to the tatters of its unconformity. Its streets today are just as crowded with eccentric, extroverted or fantastic people, but instead of the ripe Australian idiom of the C.J. Dennis period most of them issue torrents of Italian, Hungarian, Slavic, Dutch and German and Greek. The skysigns still blossom as brilliantly as ever in the electric gardens overhead, but their alphabets are fluorescent now where they used to be spelt out with clusters of naked globes. The buildings are higher, straighter, airier, lighter and more antiseptic, but the extraordinary old contrast between mansion and slum (a grimy two-floor tenement huddled next to a tower of 'luxury' apartments) has practically gone.

In spite of its vestigial flamboyance, for all the survivals of its native sauciness, King's Cross is not the King's Cross I remember from the '20s and '30s. Its people, certainly, are noisy, irreverent, crackpot and emotional, but they are not the kind of people who used to charm and horrify and puzzle me when I lived in Old Hampton Court. Where have they gone? Where has my digestion gone? Where has my hair gone?

Last week I dug up an old book of jingles which I wrote about 'Darlinghurst' over 30 years ago. In those days, Darlinghurst meant nothing but King's Cross—

> Where the stars are lit by Neon,
>   Where the fried potato fumes,
> And the ghost of Mr Villon
>   Still inhabits single rooms,
> And the girls lean out from heaven
>   Over lightwells, thumping mops,
> While the gent in 57
>   Cooks his pound of mutton chops . . .

and also:

> Where the Black Marias clatter
>   And peculiar ladies nod,
> And the flats are rather flatter
>   And the lodgers rather odd,
> Where the night is full of dangers
>   And the darkness full of fear,
> And eleven hundred strangers
>   Live on aspirin and beer.

The fried potato has given way to deep freeze or instant food, all mutton has become 'lamb' (just as all fowls have become 'chicken'), the Black Maria seems to have disappeared with its nickname, and the 1100 strangers living on aspirin and beer have proliferated into 11,000 strangers living on aspirin and beer and also on smoked eel, metwurst, goulash, salami, Vienna schnitzels, benzedrine and tranquillizers.

No doubt the strangers and lodgers are still odd enough, but they no longer charm or horrify me. Nor—possibly because I have since acquired fixed ideas about the hours at which I rise or retire—do I seem to see, as I used to, unshaven gentlemen in boiled shirts and the remains of black ties tottering about at 7 a.m. as if the daylight hurt their eyes. Nor do I see blondes in nightgowns or pyjamas clip-clopping in and out of delicatessen shops at high noon, a spectacle which aroused little or no comment in the 1930s.

As for the food, it has been said that the postwar influx of Europeans has widened our taste and improved our cooking. This strikes me as boloney in the full sense of the Bologna sausage. It is true that King's Cross is crowded today with restaurants and cafés of a dozen nationalities— Dutch, Hungarian, German, Russian, Indian, Italian, Swedish, Indonesian and others—but this is no evidence of better food. Since the only two great cuisines of the world are French and Chinese, both of which flourished superbly in Sydney before the war, the new tides of Slavs and Balts and middle or southern Europeans have merely imposed the exigencies of their sparse national larders on the Australian menu. They have contributed a number of sausages as well as a number of ways of disguising veal. But anybody who believes they have improved Australian eating is clearly ignorant of the state of Sydney's restaurants in the first quarter of the century. The claim is preposterous to anyone who remembers the glories of Monsieur Lievain's Paris House, Stewart Dawson's Ambassadors, the first Romano's, Pearson's fish-café and Watson's Paragon, the Cavalier in King Street, the Cafe Francais in George Street, Petty's Hotel and a dozen more dining-rooms, all now vanished. I find little compensation today in walking through King's Cross and looking at the spaghetti-bars, the hamburger-counters and the lines of electrically 'barbecued' chickens rotating in their glass coffins.

Perhaps something a little too calculating, a little too prudent, a little too commercial has corroded the *joie de vivre*. There were few inhibitions of cost, respectability or the need for publicity in the King's Cross I remember. I never saw the spirit of the Cross more charmingly demonstrated than one night before the war when I was living in a balcony-flat directly over the waters of Elizabeth Bay. I had come home late from the theatre and stepped on to the balcony to enjoy the silence of the Harbour, glittering with reflected lights. Suddenly I became aware of a regular plopping noise, followed by soft thuds and hisses. Gazing up, I was delighted to find that someone on a balcony above me was engaged in sailing large white dinner-plates into the moonlit air. They soared out into the night, glimmered for a moment and splashed into the water below. But what was the hissing noise? Peering farther up, I was even more delighted to observe that someone on another balcony was taking advantage of these targets from Heaven by firing an airgun at them.

Perhaps there was some of the same spirit in the disc-smashing parties which were popular in the '30s, before long-playing and almost indestructible records were invented. The host would provide piles of old played-out records, those which bored him most, and the guests would shatter them over each other's heads until they were ankle-deep in vulcanite. I recall, too, a 'house cooling' party, given the day before the entire apartment-building was due to be demolished, at which the guests were invited to lend a hand by sawing doors in halves, pulling up wainscoting and ripping the wallpaper down in strips.

Perhaps, indeed, the inhabitants of King's Cross have changed in 30 years. At any time I can shut my eyes and see them again—'Hop Harry', the amiable retired welterweight who became an 'interior decorator' (i.e. bootlegger); Chris Brennan shambling to his lonely bed-sitting-room in Rockwall Crescent; Bea Miles, then like Lil Abner's girl, shapely and brown in shorts far ahead of their time; Arthur Allen, the rich solicitor, floating past in his transparent electric buggy; Mary Gilmore gazing out from her flat in Darlinghurst Road; Will Dalley, delicately wheeling a game-pie home in a borrowed perambulator; Hector Bolitho, the Royal biographer, darting along Macleay Street in lavender gloves and a bowler hat; 'Bad Bill' Quinn, self-appointed guide to the underworld; Dulcie Deamer, inextinguishably vivacious in a leopardskin after the Artists' Ball; Geoffrey Cumine with his blue beret, pea-green shirt and brass ear-rings and a butterfly tattooed on his face; Driff, the black and white artist who hired a taxi-driver to take his old white cockatoo for a ride around Centennial Park—hundreds more in the procession.

But even the streets have altered. Woolcott Street has become respectable and changed its name to King's Cross Road. The old mansions have been pulled down. William Street itself, with its broad double lanes and flowery centrepiece, has been transformed completely since the days when I walked its length coming back from the Stadium. Then it was less than half its present width, a narrow and somewhat sinister street lined on one side with frowsy terraces and dimly-lit shops. It was the original 'Dirty Half-Mile', a title afterwards transferred to Woolcott Street and now without a claimant.

This was my King's Cross. Whether it was any better or worse than today's King's Cross I wouldn't know. But I loved every inch of it.

Choker's Lane

In Choker's Lane, the doors appear
  Like black and shining coffin-lids,
Whose fill of flesh, long buried here,
  Familiar visiting forbids.

But sometimes, when their bells are twirled,
  They'll show, like Hades, through the chink,
The green and watery gaslight world
  Where girls have faces white as zinc.

And sometimes thieves go smoothly past,
  Or pad by moonlight home again,
For even thieves come home at last,
  Even the thieves of Choker's Lane.

And sometimes you can feel the breath
  Of beasts decaying in their den—
The soft, unhurrying teeth of Death
  With leather jaws come tasting men.

Then sunlight comes, the tradesmen nod,
  The pavement rings with careless feet,
And Choker's Lane—how very odd!—
  Is just an ordinary street.

Ticket in Tatts!

Ride a Blue Cab to the top of King's Cross,
Don't mind the money, don't think of the loss,
   Three cheers for Flemington,
   Bah to the Remington,
Farewell to Pitman, good-bye to the boss,
No more dictation and no more comptometers,
Blow up the office and burn the chronometers,
Buy a few diamonds and price a few hats,
Flaunt a few furs and inspect a few flats,
   No more economy,
   Here's to gastronomy,
Daisy's won—how much?
FIVE
   THOUSAND
      IN TATTS!

Farewell finances that wrinkle the brow,
Good-bye to trams, we use Cadillacs now,
   Hickory, dickory,
   Gas-rings and chicory,
Watch us drink nothing but Moët—and how!
Bring out your truffles, we'll dine upon venison,
Smile at Sir Samuel, hobnob with Denison,
Flirt with George Cohen in ten-guinea hats,
Fox-trot with no one who doesn't wear spats—
   In a kind of paralysis,
   Picturing palaces,
Daisy dreams on,
WITH A
   TICKET IN
      TATTS!

Up in Mabel's Room

The stairs are dark, the steps are high—
    Too dark and high for YOU—
Where Mabel's living in the sky
    And feeding on the view;
Five stories down, a fiery hedge,
    The lights of Sydney loom,
But the stars burn on the window-ledge
    Up in Mabel's room.

A burning sword, a blazing spear,
    Go floating down the night,
And flagons of electric beer
    And alphabets of light—
The moon and stars of Choker's Lane,
    Like planets lost in fume,
They roost upon the window-pane
    Up in Mabel's room.

And you with fifty-shilling pride
    Might scorn the top-floor back,
But, flaming on the walls outside,
    Behold a golden track!
Oh, bed and board you well may hire
    To save the weary hoof,
But not the men of dancing fire
    Up on Mabel's roof.

There Mr Neon's nebulae
    Are constantly on view,
The starlight falls entirely free,
    The moon is always blue,
The clouds are full of shining wings,
    The flowers of carbon bloom—
But you—YOU'LL never see these things
    Up in Mabel's room.

William Street

The red globes of light, the liquor-green,
The pulsing arrows and the running fire
Spilt on the stones, go deeper than a stream;
You find this ugly, I find it lovely.

Ghosts' trousers, like the dangle of hung men,
In pawnshop-windows, bumping knee by knee,
But none inside to suffer or condemn;
You find this ugly, I find it lovely.

Smells rich and rasping, smoke and fat and fish
And puffs of paraffin that crimp the nose,
Or grease that blesses onions with a hiss;
You find it ugly, I find it lovely.

The dips and molls, with flip and shiny gaze
(Death at their elbows, hunger at their heels)
Ranging the pavements of their pasturage;
You find it ugly, I find it lovely.

King's Cross Gardens

Where the flats are crowded flatter,
    She was floating down the street—
There was music in her chatter,
    There was magic on her feet,
But I hadn't got a notion,
    Till she hastened to convey,
With a flutter of emotion—
    She was 'gardening' to-day.

Then I said: 'I beg your pardon,
    There's a thing I'd like to know—
If you've really got a garden,
    Where the devil does it grow?
Though we lunch upon a lotus,
    Not a blossom ever falls,
And the only beds I notice
    Are the beds that fold in walls.'

But she took a sudden turning,
    Paused a while to pluck a rose,
And the window blurred with yearning
    Where she pressed her pretty nose,
And she smelt a bunch of crocus,
    Pulled a lily from its moss,
And the shop flew out of focus—
    There were gardens at the Cross!

Nocturne

The Daily Telegraph Pictorial *and the* Sun *have been printing vile slurs on our Australian girlhood—allowing them to be called, without exception, 'clandestine prostitutes'.*

Darkness; a cloud of lace;
  Shines in the quiet air
Barbara's pale and lovely face
  In a rain of yellow hair.
Moonlight smoking below . . .
  Barbara lazily blinks—
Barbara, evening papers know,
  Is a shameless minx.

Smear her! Slime her!
  Cover her with scum!
Shrilly from the toadstools
  the little voices hum.

Night like a golden dust
  Trembles upon the trees;
Caught in a strayed September gust,
  Marjory hugs her knees.
Silence across the bay . . .
  Only the cry of a gull . . .
Marjory, evening papers say,
  Is a brazen trull.

Daub her! Foul her!
  Dirty her with mud!
Shrilly from the quagmire
  the little voices flood.

Under a sleeping tree,
    Water and stars and night,
Dorothy looks at the running sea;
    Eyes that are crystal bright;
Fingers that fairies kiss,
    Powder and puff to dab—
Dorothy, evening papers hiss,
    Is a heartless drab.

Smirch her! Soil her!
    Drag her in the gutter
Shrilly from the midden
    the little voices mutter.

LYDIA GILL

'Kings Cross' from *My Town—Sydney in the 1930s*

In the early thirties, Kings Cross was a dream of a place—cosmopolitan, exciting, clean, cosy and friendly. At that time, many people lived in flats, simply for the convenience of being close to the city, concerts and the shops. Visiting friends in some of the high-rise blocks of flats was always a pleasure, since so many had glorious views of the Harbour and surrounds. At the end of Macleay Street, however, Potts Point suddenly turned into Woolloomooloo, much to the disgust of some of the bordering houses: Woolloomooloo was definitely not smart.

When I was sixteen I had a flat in Rockwall Crescent, which I know sounds very grand, but actually it was a huge bedsitter with a tiny kitchenette, with a dining suite and daybed for furniture. The bathroom was down half a flight of stairs; only in the Cross did one find half a flight of stairs. My landlady, who was English but had a strong American accent, was a gem. She and her husband ruled everybody's comings and goings in the building with a rod of iron. I hadn't been in my flat on the first floor for too long before my landlady asked me whether I would move to another flat which was one floor higher and not quite as large. Rather apologetically, she explained that this was because she could get eighteen shillings and sixpence per week for my place, which was classed as a double flat, and I was only paying fifteen shillings: the extra money would come in very useful. I wasn't too unhappy about that; my smaller flat only cost twelve shillings per week. Money was very tight in the thirties.

The couple in the basement loved giving parties, and usually asked me but because my landlady was protective towards me (I was the youngest in the building) I never seemed to last the distance after about nine o'clock! The moment she heard a risque song or joke, she flew to my side and said: 'Come on, Lyddy, say goodnight. Time for us to go and have a cuppa.'

Every morning, I was awakened by the sound of piano practice: the good sisters in nearby St Vincent's College or the advanced students played scales early. I was hungry for music, so they were a constant joy.

And meeting people in the flats was also a joy. One of the other tenants, a woman who was probably in her late thirties (and therefore aged to a sixteen-year-old!) had what I thought was a fascinating job. She spent a lot of time cutting out the coloured advertisements from the American magazine *The Saturday Evening Post* in jigsaw patterns, especially the ads showing exotic birds and scenery. Then she glued them to an ordinary china plate and lacquered and baked the result in a kiln. The results were extraordinary; I'm sure the plates sold very well. This woman had a beautiful soprano voice and had trained with 'Our Glad', Gladys Moncrieff. She had a favourite nephew whom she often took to the theatre, always in a box seat (my pals and I felt very lucky if we made the two-and-sixpenny hangovers, or the gods). This nephew was named Sumner Locke Elliott, and he grew up to be a well known novelist and playwright. A little further down the street, on the opposite side of the road, lived Dame Mary Gilmore; I'd love to have met her.

The Cross always had more than its share of odd bods. Most of them were happy and friendly, though I remember that one night I listened to a gramophone next door playing, over and over, the latest hit 'Have You Ever Been Lonely, Have You Ever Been Blue?' Too right we had, but who was going to admit it?

Sometimes, usually on Friday nights (Friday was payday) my mad girlfriend would come and stay the night with me. I would go back to her place on Saturday after work, go to the club dance in the evening, and stay at her place until Sunday. On Fridays, whether we were window shopping or had just emerged from a five o'clock movie, we would take the tram to the Cross and walk slowly along Darlinghurst Road, past Springfield Avenue and the large Kookaburra cake shop. Little food shops were everywhere; for a time there was a Woolworths in Darlinghurst Road, with a cafeteria dining room at the top, accessible even when the store was closed. Just before the corner into Macleay Street, there was a ham and beef shop and mixed business. One could leave a dish or plate in the morning on the way to work and collect it on the way home: on the plate would be an inviting salad of tomato, lettuce, spring onion, radish, a piece of cheese and a slice or two of hard-boiled egg, all for sixpence. In cooler weather one left an enamel dish, preferably with a lid, and collected a generous serve of something hot.

Shopping at the Cross was fun, even if we did have to count every penny. We could buy quarter-pound packets of tea, tiny tins of jam or soup, a quarter of a pound of butter. My mad girlfriend actually asked for a quarter of a pound of peas, and the shopkeeper didn't turn a hair. Sydney didn't know about coffee then, though milk coffee, made with coffee essence, was always popular, especially at Sargent's. Then Repins cafes introduced their black coffee with the tiny jar of cream—and the second cup was free, which was wonderful. The Repins chain of cafes were mainly in the city, but we also knew the White Rose cafes, specialising in cheap mostly Greek food, which was superb. We had a favourite in William Street, just down from the Cross; their bread and butter custard was only bettered by that of my little Irish grandmother.

If we happened to be going home at night, we wouldn't walk near the gutter; 'the girls' were starting to do a lot of business in and with passing cars. The Kings Cross pros, who were not quite as young as they are today, kept very much to themselves. I'll never forget one night, as I walked down Macleay Street with my girlfriend, a big, black expensive car pulled into the kerb, a girl pushed the passenger door open, climbed out, then slammed it with all her strength. Turning to us, she said, 'What did he expect for two and six?' after which she turned and walked away.

When a friend of mine suddenly lost her father, she asked me to share with her and her now-widowed mother (also a great pal of mine) in Clovelly and later in Bronte. I stayed there until I went to Melbourne for two years to help my aunt; when I returned to Sydney I stayed with my girlfriend and her mother again, as by this time they were almost family, and we came to the Cross. This time we moved to Royston Square, actually a very charming crescent, and this time we had a proper flat, though it was very small. The block was owned by a peace-loving Irishman and his wife, and if a party in a neighbouring block was too noisy, he put the Vice Squad onto them. But I remember one nice, kind gentleman, a retired bookmaker whose name I think was Lemon, who came down every night to feed the stray cats in the area.

But the war clouds were beginning to gather, and the parties in the Cross were becoming sendoffs. The Cross was changing: at about this time, many different people came to live there, not as migrants, but as refugees. Strange and sometimes overpowering cooking odours wafted out of many kitchens in Royston Square. Some of these refugees were arrogant, treating Australians as slightly inferior beings, but many others were happy to be in a safe country.

One night, I was coming home with my girlfriend and her mother and through an open window we saw a family group. Across the square we heard the 'Maori's Farewell', with its poignant lyrics: 'Now is the hour, when we must say goodbye', and saw two lads in uniform. As though the singers had been showing too much sentiment, they changed to 'Wish Me Luck as You Wave Me Goodbye'. We heard this song and the 'Maori's Farewell' so often in the next little while.

That night, as we turned into the front door of our own block of flats, we saw our peace-loving Irishman watching the sendoff too. Pulling out a large handkerchief, he blew his nose, said, 'Must be getting a cold, good-night, ladies,' and disappeared into his flat.

Underneath all its glitter, tawdriness and perhaps shame, the spirit of the Cross may still be there today, but greater skill than mine is needed to find it. I can speak only of the Cross I knew and loved in the thirties, that part of the Cross of which I can say, 'I was there.'

When I lost my pal, best friend, sharer of thoughts of books, sports, music and life generally, so loving and so loved husband, I received, with so many others a letter of sympathy from a friend we had not seen for years but who had shared the ups and downs and the happiness of the thirties with us both. He wrote of the 'wonderfully happy days of the thirties' and this really set me thinking, also. One has little time to look back, but when the family is busy starting on their own families and one is alone, thoughts wander. So much of what I have remembered should be shared, so this is my excuse for these pages. I know we were hungry sometimes, and we cut pieces of cardboard to put in holey shoes and walked miles to save a penny fare, but if we could save from lunch, the perfume of that sweet scented brown boronia, bought instead of lunch, was truly compensation.

Sydney was a great town in the 1930s. It was my Sydney in the 1930s. I wish you had been there with me. Perhaps you were.

RONALD McCUAIG

'The Razor', 'The Letter', 'Pretty Kid',
'They Also Serve Who Only Stand and Wait',
'Music in the Air'

The Razor

Edged with incuriosity
Whom it cuts, or if, or why,
Her beauty is a lazy razor
Drawn across the brain that has her:
Death so alive is mere illusion;
So is her beauty, which, being gone,
Stays as a razor, cold and jagged,
Lazily over the brain is dragg'd.

The Letter

Dear, as I write and think of you,
And several other people too,
The flooring of the flat above,
Creaking with aged, illicit love,
Reminds me, when I was trying to write
These very words the other night,
He spoke from three till half past four
Merely repeating she was a whore.
The boy below has just begun
To find it not precisely fun;
The trouble is, as he explained
The Thursday evening when it rained
To a judicial prig of a friend
(I thought their talk would never end),
The girl is really not the kind
Of girl he really had in mind.
But still he keeps her on, for fear
Of hurting her. And now I hear
The lovely girl who loves to dwell,
And dwells to love, across the well,
Saying, since he is married, he
Should be considerate, in that she
Is taking risks. As for the rent,
She fears, it has been otherwise spent.
The opposite flat is dark and dumb,
Yet I feel certain he will come
Home to his love as drunk as ever
And, in a slowly rising fever,
Noting the whisky bottle gone,
Will trip and curse and stumble on
Into the bathroom, pull the chain,
Fumble the cabinet, curse again;
Will ask the slut where she has hid
His toothbrush; blunder back to bed,

Find his pyjamas tied in knots
And give her, as he puts it, what's
Coming to her. She won't escape
Her deeply meditated rape.
But I must write of love, and all
That once was high, and had a fall,
And how I burn; and I confess
It gives me little happiness:
Encompassed so, my rooms become
A kind of lovers' vacuum,
Dear, as I write, and ache for you,
And dream of all that we could do
If these delights thy mind might move
To live with me and be my love.

Pretty Kid

Framed by a plate of postered glass
She sits and sees the people pass
Through eyes that, great and golden-brown,
Roll into joy the visible town;
But her young breasts comprise her main
Business asset; of these you gain
A private view when, bending bare
Of any restrictive underwear,
She fiddles about and hesitates
Deep in her piles of cigarettes:
And lonely smokers, blowing rings,
Dream that they see those exquisite things
Dangling desire from wavering wreaths,
Which soon more sage reflection breathes
Away with hope: that base erotion
Ever should trade on sales-promotion
No good customer dares expect;
One feels it would not seem correct;
Besides, her husband might object.

They Also Serve Who Only Stand and Wait

In flats, on streets, behind the bar,
Her eyes are neither near nor far.
They are as quiet, calm and cool
As a beslimed, stagnating pool
Charged to a dense putridity
With things a lady shouldn't see.
Her days, bruised to the neutral squalor
That stains her body's natural pallor,
Are sometimes brightened up in streaks,
Like her red, poster-painted cheeks,
With haemorrhage of brains unbarred
And roses charming wives discard:
The labourer, the artisan,
The guzzle-gutted business man,
Find her a cheap, convenient sewer
For any good turn they care to do her;
Sometimes abuse her, sometimes pet her,
And, having used her well, forget her.

Music in the Air

There was music in the air
And the moon shone bright
When Jack had his girl
On Friday night.

He closed his desk
At the close of day.
As he passed the counter
They gave him his pay:
  There was music in the air
  And the moon shone bright
  As he walked down town
  On Friday night:

She was a typist
Down at the bank.
Her mother was religious.
Her father drank:
  There was music in the air
  And the moon shone bright
  As they drank and prayed
  On Friday night:

Her boss was a beast;
He kept her late.
Jack got a headache,
Having to wait:
  There was music in the air
  And the moon shone bright
  When she came at last
  On Friday night:

They went to a café.
The soup was cold.
The beef was scraggy,
The prunes full of mould:
　　There was music in the air
　　And the moon shone bright
　　As they ate their dinner
　　On Friday night:

They sat very still
In the rattle and hum.
Jack said, 'Mary,
I want to go home':
　　There was music in the air
　　And the moon shone bright
　　When he spoke her name
　　On Friday night:

'I want to go home
And go to bed;
Besides, you remember
What you said':
　　There was music in the air
　　And the moon shone bright
　　When Mary remembered
　　On Friday night:

She picked up her bag,
Made no reply;
She pushed back her chair
With a quiet sigh:
　　There was music in the air
　　And the moon shone bright
　　When they left the café
　　On Friday night:

He took her arm
Through a traffic jam.
They stood on the corner
To wait for a tram:
    There was music in the air
    And the moon shone bright
    As they stood on the corner
    On Friday night:

Their faces were pale
In the crimson spite
Of the shop-sign's whorish
Beckoning light:
    There was music in the air
    And the moon shone bright
    When the tram crawled by
    On Friday night:

They got in the tram.
It jolted them down
To the end of the section
On the edge of town:
    There was music in the air
    And the moon shone bright
    As they crossed the road
    On Friday night:

Jack had a room
On the second floor.
They climbed the stairs
And opened the door:
    There was music in the air
    And the moon shone bright
    Through the open door
    On Friday night:

They closed the door.
Mary hung
Lax in his arms.
His fierce lips stung:
   There was music in the air
   And the moon shone bright
   When they closed the door
   On Friday night:

His fierce lips stung
At her throat like a bee;
Like a snake, like a sleek
Little leopard was he:
   There was music in the air
   And the moon shone bright
   When his fierce lips stung
   On Friday night:

Like a leopard, and she
Was placid prey;
She'd dreamed it for months
All night and day:
   There was music in the air
   And the moon shone bright
   When her dreams came true
   On Friday night:

He loosened her blouse
And mad waist-bands;
She tried to help
His clumsy hands:
   There was music in the air
   And the moon shone bright
   When he loosened her blouse
   On Friday night:

She loved his hands.
She said, 'Oh, mind;
I'll do it myself.'
He drew the blind:
 There was music in the air
 And the moon shone bright
 When he drew the blind
 On Friday night:

The whore next door
Had a radiolet,
And she was seeing
What she could get:
 There was music in the air
 And the moon shone bright
 As she screwed at the dial
 On Friday night:

A loud voice sang
From heaven above
With a screeching scratch
Of the joys of love:
 There was music in the air
 And the moon shone bright
 As the loud voice sang
 On Friday night:

Of the joys of love:
Pale in the gloom,
She was deaf to the world
In her wild blood's boom:
 There was music in the air
 And the moon shone bright
 Through her booming blood
 On Friday night:

Like the boom of trams
Outside, and the squeal
Of nerves on the curves
Of shrieking steel:
  There was music in the air
  And the moon shone bright
  In curving nerves
  On Friday night:

Like shrieking steel
In his shaking embrace
Through a slit in the blind
Light streamed on her face:
  There was music in the air
  And the moon shone bright
  Through a slit in the blind
  On Friday night:

On her anguished face
And tight-shut eyes:
Jack won't forget it
Until he dies:
  There was music in the air
  And the moon shone bright
  When Jack had his girl
  On Friday night.

SUMNER LOCKE ELLIOTT

from *Fairyland*

'Listen,' Buck was theatrically casual, 'what're you doing tomorrow arvo, like to take a Sunday walk?' Oh *yes*, he said, all too eager, all sparkle. Elizabeth Bay then, did he know it? Down by the boatshed in the little park by the harbor. About four-ish?

He dressed shakily with disgraceful care, best shirt and tie and the application of a great deal of greasy stuff named Pomade de Soir without which no Arncliffe boy would be seen dead socially even though the girls protested in horror at the gooey stuff and kept their hands from wandering to the boys' necks. Sheepish, he lied to Essie, saying his date was 'one of the girls in the show' and regretting his biggish nose in the mirror, recombed his hair for the fifth time, wetting down a dog's hind leg. The pitiful disguise for all this primping and readying himself only exacerbated an involuntary disgust at his willingness, this headlong rush to be seduced by possibilities that had the weight of probability and more than a whiff of the counterfeit about them. All the way into town on the train he was assaulted with a conviction that the ultimate was meant to come about.

The awe in which he found himself, not sacred and yet not wholly profane, merely voluptuous, thickened his tongue from the moment Buck emerged from behind the boathouse wearing a weathered Harris tweed jacket in smoky colors and they began what seemed a purposeless walk. Yes, he murmured, he had seen this and that film, no he had not yet been to enjoy the delightful Alice Delysia at the Grand Opera House. Fancy, he said to everything as they trudged disinterestedly by the big white Cali- fornian-Spanish mansion of the Albert family built, Buck informed, from the millions earned by sheet music and 'Boomerang' mouth organs.

Heartsick as the day waned, he began to accept the appalling possibility that this was all it was intended to be, a *walk*. He had become predisposed to a foregone conclusion, surrendered, and now it was corrupted with anti- climax. Now they trudged on joylessly through Billyard Avenue past buildings of uninteresting flats and with flatter conversation. How would it end? and was Byron Hall so bored or else so unbelievably obtuse that he didn't know how to end it?

But then quite apocalyptically rain began, quite heavily, and Buck said, 'Turn up your collar and we'll run, I'm only a few blocks up the hill from here,' and they ran up Elizabeth Bay Road and turned a corner and came up panting in front of a severe-looking old brick building of flats with 'Ashburn Court' in frosted glass over the entrance of dirty white marble steps that led into a dim lobby of unused cracked leather furniture and steel engravings. Buck lived in the ground floor apartment, which had been converted into 'roomette' flats consisting of one large room and a corner into which a sink and tiny gas range had been inserted; the bathroom and lavatory were down the hall.

'Take off your wet jacket,' Buck said and took off his. There was nothing in the least presupposed in the way things happened—Buck's knee just happened to graze Seaton's and the next moment they were in a tight embrace, not entirely realistic. There was no affectionate talk, no murmuring of sweet words as they were somehow precipitated onto the large bed under the window and into undressing in an agreement of pretended surprise. Buck even laughed once or twice, deprecatingly. He was as skin smooth undressed as he was in conversation and assured as a general in battle. But they ventured then into a serious silent agreement during which their eyes never left each other, as though only through their eyes could they maintain a feasibility to the fable in which they'd become involved and some time later (time passing slowly and silently) they achieved it, they arrived together at a supreme junction within seconds of each other and they were marvelously released and, loosening their hold on each other, they sighed and, drooping, they relaxed onto the pillows in a state of astounded joy.

Only then, at long last, did Buck lean over and quickly, light as a moth wing, kiss him on the mouth, but in the glancing touch Seaton felt more emotion and gratification than in the whole orgasmic eruption and then, glancing sideways, saw that Buck had sat up and was absorbed in something across the room, saw that he was looking into the mirror facing the bed and that he was stroking his fallen hair back into place.

Then shortly it became extraordinarily formal, covering their former excesses with towels and finding each other's socks and shoes, the getting into underwear in a prissy precise manner as though they had been at a gymnastic class or had had a medical examination. 'Borrow a comb?' he asked. 'It's stopped raining,' Buck said at the window and then as Seaton combed his hair said kindly, 'Don't put that greasy stuff on your hair, it spoils the nice wave you have, and it's common-looking. Let your hair stay dry and soft.'

Which he was to do for the rest of his life. And remember this late wet afternoon.

'The Tudor Inn,' Buck said, 'for a bite of dinner. What say?' Just up around the corner and expensive, Seaton knew, but it would postpone the inevitable conclusion.

Even though it was the mildest June evening, the antipodean early winter was being observed in the Tudor Inn by a crackling log fire, cheerful flames reflected in hanging copper pans and bedwarmers on the walls. They were immediately given priority seats in the best banquette by the fireplace, Buck obviously being known here, and the Elizabethan-dressed waitresses, whom you were expected to summon by crying 'wench,' bobbing to him. They were handed large menus of parchment scrolls upon which were handwritten in flowing Shakespearean script the list of entrées at hair-raising prices (the sirloin of beef with Yorkshire pudding was seven shillings and sixpence, half of Seaton's weekly wages) and, assuming nonchalance, he ordered the inexpensive tripe and onions.

'Don't be silly,' Buck said teasingly, 'have the half of roast chicken, you silly goose, it's my treat this evening.' You minx, Buck added teasingly as the serving wench departed. 'Minx,' he said again. He seemed to be enjoying his role of *patron*. He squeezed Seaton's hand under the table and said what a shame that in this puritan 'wowser'-ridden country the serving of alcoholic drinks was forbidden after six o'clock, otherwise they could have toasted each other. It wouldn't be the same in dear old England or anywhere else on earth that had a smidgen of intelligence about good living. He added that he intended to shake off the dust of Aussie forever just the minute he had the fare, never to return.

But of course. He meant that he would become a star, there was no doubt of it.

His deeply pure eyes seem to swim with affection; it was as heady as any amount of drinking just being with him.

And exciting, debilitating to the appetite. Seaton barely picked at the delicious roast chicken, said no to a parfait. Outside, now dark and under the streetlight, they parted eventually.

'You know, don't you?' Buck asked. They were shaking hands like business acquaintances.

'What?'

'What I'm thinking about you. Do you?'

'I think I do, Buck.'

'Minx. Good night, minx. Sleep then. Good night, sweet prince.'

Rocking, all the way back to the tram, then train, then walking. Rocking with a new inner sense of secret knowledge and a profound new anxiety. How long would it last? Would it be snatched away from him or might it go on, might they be long-lasting mates? A dreadful word but all they had to describe each other in public. One would never be permitted to say 'this is my lover, my love.'

But the following Sunday there was no artful pretence about taking walks and Buck opened the door in a dressing gown and seemed to be in a hurry, almost irritable, anxious for them not to waste a precious minute on small talk or polite chitchat even though, foolishly, Seaton had been saving up tidbits all week of comic interludes at work, overheard inanities. They were swept by tidal influences onto the rumpled bed, unmade from the night before. This time, more leisurely, it seemed to Seaton astonishingly, that love with Buck had begun to be an extension of Buck's need for admiration and the act to become the physical exercise of self-praise. Again it was performed in churchlike silence and this time there was no afterward kiss, no hand touching. Buck leapt up and into his Chinese green robe and said startlingly, 'I wonder would you hear me my lines, old son.' He had been cast as the king in Shaw's *The Apple Cart* and it contained one uninterrupted speech of nearly six pages. Thus they sat in the pretend world of Shavian witticism in the fading light, after which Buck took a shower but didn't offer the bathroom. Again they went to the Tudor Inn where the wenches bowed them in, but tonight there was no fire either in the fireplace or in their hearts, it seemed. Buck laughed a lot at very little and occasionally glanced at his watch and this time, the treat patently not being his, did nothing to restrain Seaton from the tripe. 'Good night, old son,' Buck said under the streetlight and walked quickly away, running into two actressy-looking friends and greeting and laughing with them boisterously.

The third and last Sunday (there was only one more Saturday then left of the run of *Rose and Thorn*) the intermingling became even more perfunctory and this time Buck said abruptly as though lovemaking had already delayed important business, 'I have exam papers to correct' (he taught first-year French three mornings a week at a girls' private school at Pymble) 'so if you don't mind, kid, we won't dine this evening.' He was already holding open the door to the hall and while Seaton was getting into his overcoat, there were creases of slight impatience around Buck's mouth.

It couldn't—

At the door, helpless but impelled from behind by a wave, Seaton leaned over to kiss Buck and kissed air as their heads bumped in a slapstick evocation of what really was going on. 'Silly billy,' Buck said, laughing, and 'seeyuh.' The door to the flat shut Seaton out.

It couldn't—

It couldn't be that this was the end, could it? That it was all a flash in a pan? Was it only the hunt that aroused Byron Hall? Was it a fact that once the stag had been struck with the arrow there was no further interest?

During the following wondering days, Seaton permitted Buck endless extenuating circumstances. 'Look,' he said aloud to the mirror, 'he has a difficult job and a huge new role to learn, you know.' 'You know,' he told himself, 'men don't appreciate too much tenderness, you were an idiot to want him to kiss you good-bye.'

'Talking to yourself, darl?' asked innocent Essie at the door of the bathroom. He was spending Sundays with that same girl, she had been told. Perhaps one Sunday he'd bring her home for tea in the evening, she'd cook a nice roast of lamb, pet.

There was no manifestation of the slightest interest on the last night of the play, no being seized from behind and held and kissed, no reaching for his hand in the dark as they waited for their curtain calls, but Seaton had stuffed a saved ten shilling note into his shirt pocket in the forlorn hope that he might confront Buck and invite him to last-night supper, but it seemed from voices calling up and down the dressing room hall that bloody awful Mimi Ostral was giving a party at her flat for all the principals and that three taxis were coming to transport them.

As Seaton dressed and hung despairingly near the stage exit in the last lost hope that the loved, the adored might at the last moment—

Might even come to say so long, bye-bye, Fair page. When Betty Jollivet appeared, carrying her makeup case, he grabbed her and said, 'Where are you going? Have supper with me?'

'Aren't you going to Mimi's party?'

'Wasn't asked.'

'Then I won't go either.'

She took his arm firmly. It was positive just walking with her. They went into Cahills where a haughty hostess crammed them into an outside hall table, possibly because they were so young.

'But there are tables in the big room,' Betty protested.

'Reserved.'

'Not after nine P.M. Says on the menu.'

The hostess sighed and led them into the big room. Threw down menus.

'Have a cheese dream,' Seaton said. If you assessed somebody's value by the prices on a menu, then Betty Jollivet was worth a cheese dream. She was looking at him through her cigarette smoke with a mixture of curiosity and perhaps slight *noblesse oblige* because of his callowness. She was aged about thirty-two in her sensibility about things and at other moments, sixteen in her enthusiasms. 'Super duper,' she said as they brought the platter of melted cheese in a forest of asparagus. 'This is so nice, Seaton,' she said and patted his hand. She might never have been asked to supper before and yet had probably danced with all the most eligible young rich men in Sydney. Seaton had not yet danced a step in his life, would not have known how to hold the girl.

First, he was amazed at his own boldness in asking her out and, second, even more astonished to find now that they were like long-acquainted people at ease with each other. Part of the miracle of Betty Jollivet was the accomplished ease with which she managed to balance a relationship between politeness and close intimacy. As the Cahills after-theater crowd diminished, they grew more and more loquacious, at times interrupting each other and 'Sorry, no, *you* go on,' they said. 'Superb,' she said and 'marvelous,' encouraging him with her frank open looks and smiles until he was racing ahead with opinions on this and that, opinions he had had no idea he held, almost as though he were the ventriloquist dummy on the knee of a worldly, highly intelligent grown man of vast experience. Until he struck a rock.

'I would like to be more like Byron Hall' came out of his mouth for some reason.

'Why?'

'Because he knows exactly what he wants all the time and goes after it.'

She was silent, seemed dubious, her chin was poignant with doubt. 'Byron Hall,' she said, wonderingly, trying perhaps to conjure him up. Was he tall? Supreme in any sense?

'Oh,' Betty said, 'but he isn't *real*. I'd want to be like someone much realer than Byron Hall.'

'Sorry, but we're closing now,' said the glacial hostess, descending on them with the bill. They were left with so much to say that they had not noticed they were the last people in the restaurant.

I'll see you into the tram, he had said when she mentioned Darling Point Road, and when the tram trundled up he said, 'Let me see you home,' and got on with her. Because it was chilly they sat inside. Few people were on this late-night tram. Because they were so young and so agreeably captivated by one another they were assumed to be lovers by an amiable drunk.

'G'night, sweet-art, til we meet tomorrer,' sang the drunk. Perhaps in an effort to achieve jauntiness he had clipped a little blue tin butterfly to his tie. 'The saddest butterfly I ever saw,' Betty said.

'Are you sweet-arts?' the drunk inquired. 'Are you? Are you?' In the alcoholic inquisitiveness that knows no quenching, 'You sweet-arts, darlings?'

'Say yes,' Betty said, 'or he'll just keep on and on.'

'Yes,' they said together.

'You sweet darlings, what a darling pair.' The drunk was straphanging directly over them although there were seats in abundance. Rose Bay matrons looked fixedly at their skirts in distress. 'Live together, do you, darlings? Go to bed together, do you?'

'Yes,' Seaton said eventually.

'Listen,' the drunk said, swaying all over them, 'don't let the barstards stop you, they'll stop you if they can, the barstards that run this friggin' world, they took away my sweetie and turned her into an ox. I'm married to a flaming ox now, biggest arse you ever saw. Give us a kiss would you, darlings?' Sidestepping the gasoline fumes of alcohol, they slithered past him at Darling Point Road and got off the tram, but the tearful voice followed them across the road.

'Keep on keepin' on, darlings, you sweet little doves, you got the whole fuckin' world, darlings, but it won't last, nothing lasts in this bloody world.'

When they reached Betty's gate, there were steps leading down to lawns seemingly clustered with moonlit black-and-white bushes of great rhododendron. Lights could be seen in the big house and Betty said would he like to come in and meet the family. 'Because in all probability they're still up listening to the test cricket from Lords in England on the shortwave.'

No thanks, he said and then, assisted by the emotion of night and trees, blanched silver flowers, moonlit water, and with the small wavering oval of her face lifted to him in the provocative way she had, all purity but intended to provoke, he leaned down and kissed her on the mouth and, having gone beyond all imaginings, held her closely to him and moved his face up against the sweet softness of her hair and suspended for moments in this fallacy, possessing her only perfunctorily, but momentarily deluded by the similarity to conquest, he continued holding her closely until she moved away and spoke in a voice of quiet certainty.

'Now don't *you* be unreal.'

She unlatched the gate.

'Good night, Seaton dearest.'

So she shook him out of the falsehood. So she knew. She knew about him in the way she had known about Byron and Mimi Ostral being lovers. She knew the way of him and that it was as ancient as sin and as irredeemable. She knew and yet she wisely and lovingly cared. Seaton dearest.

Good night, he said, committed now to loving her for the rest of his life.

Drawn like the murderer back to the scene, drawn in exquisite misery, unable to resist the damnable urge, he hopped on a tram after work up to Kings Cross and walked down to Elizabeth Bay Road and to Ashburn Court for no other reason than to stare uselessly up at Buck's lighted window (the blind was pulled down, perhaps he was marking exam papers, listening to the evening news on the wireless or maybe just sitting disconsolately) and all because—Because, he had told himself aloud for the thirtieth time, he remembered Buck saying it was a nuisance his not being reachable by phone. 'Suppose I suddenly have great need of you. Couldn't you arrange for me to leave a message somewhere in code, like it's your dentist phoning to remind you of your appointment with him this evening?'

All the time drawing imaginary rings around Seaton's navel. 'Why would I be going out with my dentist in the evening?'

'Perhaps you have a thing going with him.' The boisterous laugh.

Or Buck might even come out of the flat and throw his arms around him and exclaim 'oh happy day,' or something of the sort. Say he was feeling blue and lonely, perhaps, how dear of you to turn up just when I needed you.

As the day darkened the streetlights came on. Occasionally a shadow passed across the window blind. How long was he going to stand here rooted to the spot and perhaps attracting curiosity? He walked slowly to the end of the block and slowly back and again took his stand under the window, deriding himself for being such a fool and yet unable to break off from the faint excitement of being physically adjacent to where sweetness was and became so inured to the somber musings it provoked that he was completely unaware of time passing or of lights being put out in windows until he heard, or seemed to hear, his name spoken matter-of-factly and, turning, felt the onrush of a deep red flush through him at being caught, heart beating suddenly with excitement and shame, and Buck said, 'I thought it was you.'

Buck, wearing an ugly tan raincoat, was looking at him sharply, the red dot on his nose seemed larger, and he was with, of all people, Merle Mayhew, the assistant stage manager and 'props' at the Drury Lane. She was a small, pale, tired-looking girl with dull hair, always vanishing into ecru voile dresses, who had little to say and to whom no one said anything much except 'Do you have my sword?' She had thin lips that met almost in a crack and at her best, whatever that was, she was far from personable. Yet this evening she was transformed into sulphurous lightness. She might as well have had on a placard reading WE HAVE BEEN DOING IT; her little mouth was drawn back into a smirk of triumph as she stood with her arm through Buck's, radiant with the joy of being well and truly ravished, hanging on to her handbag as if it were the coronation orb of England. 'Hello, Seaton,' Merle said and grinned as Seaton flusteringly mumbled some blather about having been delivering a book from where he worked which was urgently—

The three stood there in the full knowledge of one another's fraudulence until Buck said, 'We're taking a cab down into town. Can we drop you?'

'No thanks,' Seaton said, backing away and in further foolishness, waving at them.

'Good night, so long.'

He had been dropped already, thank you.

And according to Betty Jollivet by someone who wasn't real.

The Forties

'Meanwhile, all was gorgeous bedlam . . .'

—*Jon Rose*

In the 1940s, Kings Cross was Americanised, due to thousands of World War II servicemen on rest and recreation. Battleships were docked at Garden Island and, night after night, sailors rushed up the Wylde Street hill to the Cross. The marines were loaded with American dollars, but had very little time. Nightclubs and strip joints mushroomed along Darlinghurst Road, prostitution skyrocketed, and black marketeering became a way of life. Prices in the area doubled. Numerous brothels catered exclusively for black American G.I.s, because it was soon discovered that they were more generous with their money. Riots sometimes broke out between blacks and whites over patronage of the same brothels. As suggested in the following excerpts from Australian classics *Come In Spinner*, and Bob Herbert's play *No Names . . . No Pack Drill*, suburban women, both single and married, flocked to the Cross for a fling with a serviceman, causing many of the working girls of the area to nickname the hopeful lasses 'charity molls'. Though, as Sumner Locke Elliott points out in his chapter from *Fairyland*, sometimes the charity moll was a hopeful gay man.

During the 1940s, the Cross also sustained its reputation as a sanctuary for outsiders and misfits, and several of the following extracts illustrate just how broadminded and accepting the local community could be. In her autobiography, Betty Roland finds the colourful red-light district the perfect venue for her new identity as an independent woman following the break-up of her marriage. George Johnston's narrator, Meredith, from the novel *Clean Straw for Nothing*, admits the Cross is the only place in Sydney where he can live happily and easily with his pregnant lover, whilst still being married to his wife. In a chapter from the novel *The Refuge*, Kenneth 'Seaforth' Mackenzie describes the Cross as a haven for Jewish immigrants escaping the perils of the war in Europe:

As the world's most thickly-populated district of comparable size, it had long ago become a refuge within a refuge. Every foreigner who landed from Sydney harbour or stepped to earth at Mascot aerodrome knew of the Cross already, and went there as though drawn by an irresistible passion, there to fade—if he chose—into a consoling anonymity . . .

In a chapter from *At the Cross*, author Jon Rose represents the district as a different kind of refuge. The excerpt detailing the rambunctious Gala Drag and Drain Party of the early 1940s—replete with feather head-dresses and sequined lights, at which there are eight Carmen Mirandas, a Queen of Sheba, and a singer lurching about dressed as Dame Nellie Melba—is a hilarious account of Sydney's gay culture in the 1940s. The excerpt can be read as a literary precursor to the annual Gay and Lesbian Mardi Gras that would flourish in Darlinghurst three decades later.

But it wasn't all sex, whisky, and swinging jazz. In the 1940s, Kings Cross residents lived with blacked-out windows, and the area's nightly anthem was the shrill cacophony of an air-raid siren. On 31 May 1942, the Cross was transformed once again when a Japanese midget submarine attacked Sydney Harbour. The morning after, a rumour swept through the district, suggesting that the Japanese had infiltrated Garden Island and were ambushed inside buildings along Wylde Street. Suddenly, Macleay Street was jammed with removalists' trucks and people were moving to the suburbs faster than you can say 'sayonara'. From that point, and all through the war, the sumptuous, art deco apartments of Kings Cross, many of which were penthouses with sweeping harbour views, could be rented for a pittance. Needless to say, many of the artists and writers of the area stayed on, moving from cramped bed-sitters into these grand, residential buildings, without having an increase in rent.

Playwright and author Betty Roland lived in Elizabeth Bay throughout the 1940s. Novelist Katherine Susannah Prichard resided in Wool-loomooloo. Actor Chips Rafferty lived in an apartment on Challis Avenue and drank regularly at the Mansions Hotel. Poet Judith Wright lived in the Cross during World War II, while studying and doing secretarial work. Following the break-up of his marriage to Margaret Coen, poet Douglas Stewart also moved to the Cross in 1946. During this decade, Marjorie Barnard and Flora Eldershaw lived in a William Street flat, which would become the setting for their co-authored novel *Tomorrow and Tomorrow and Tomorrow*. Fellow authors Charmian Clift and George Johnston also shifted to the Cross in the 1940s. Kathleen Robinson created Whitehall Productions in the Minerva Theatre on Orwell Street, at which a young Australian actor called Peter Finch performed in the company's radio plays.

JON ROSE

from *At the Cross*

As I had guessed, the news of the big party soon spread, and became the centre of many a conversation. Milly insisted that I should go as Peter Pan, she intended going as Georges Sand—we would make up a party. True to Thelma's word, my invitation arrived. I read it out to Bella. 'You are invited to a Gala Drag and Drain party. Only those in drag and with invitations allowed in.' The price of admission was twelve and sixpence, which included food and drink, cabaret, a show-girl parade, and also a real orchestra. It was to be held in a hall quite near the Cross.

Everybody started to think like mad of what they could make and wear. Preferably something that would wreck and put to shame every other person's costume. And sure enough, as I suspected, everywhere I went people were working away like beavers. Arnold put it around that, after a lot of research, he had discovered that the Queen of Sheba was in fact rather old when at the height of her powers, so beware any other Shebas. Zoe, as she nightly moved around her darkened club, kept up an ominous quiet, but rumour had it that she had something up her sleeve which would rock everyone. As the excitement mounted, rumours ran riot. If Frank Sinatra wasn't actually going to sing, he was at least going to be there. The worlds of the theatre and society were flat out trying to get invitations. Also, an added promised joy was the possibility of Australia's greatest professional female impersonator—Lea Sonia himself, was coming in nothing more than a diamond headdress and four pekingese on leads.

Meanwhile, I did my nightly ignored stint at the Bamboo. One night, after I had finished and was sitting talking to Claude, a little man came up and said 'Excuse me, I'm from Radio Station 2GB.' I looked at him—I had heard that song before. He said 'Would you like to sing on the radio?' Of course I would, so we talked about it for some time. He gave me his phone number and I gave him mine. Then I picked up the material for my Peter Pan costume and left, making my way to a friend's flat, where Milly was waiting for me and the material to finish my costume. The further we got on with the costume, the stranger it looked; it was Peter Pan, but it was so brief and so tight that I began to wonder. Everyone else said it was marvellous, so I stood being jabbed with pins and stitched up. Just as I was getting used to the idea of the costume, a boy who was a hairdresser drifted in with his girl, took one look at me and said 'Ash blond, that's it, ash.' But I felt that this was going too far. Milly said 'Why not? Leon can dye it in the morning, and dye it back the following day.' I didn't agree. Rich mouse I was, and I felt I had better stay that way. During the next few days I thought I had better find another job.

I finally found one which after promising to love, serve and obey the firm, its ideals and directors for ever, seemed as if it might do. The job was selling high-class groceries in a large shop. I felt slightly caged after my other jobs. Whacky as they had been, they had at least been different. It seemed strange turning up and clocking in, having to put on a white uniform and with it take off any personality I had. The rest of the staff were nice, but seemed only half alive after Tim or the café. During the coffee breaks, they would sit, telling one another coy, slightly dirty stories which made me squirm, because though the stories were never actually dirty, they were crammed so full of repressed desires that they seemed to me to be even more indecent. I used to sit, half awake, hearing all about their small worlds of store intrigue, Saturday night hops, and hopes of getting married. When anyone asked me where I lived, I would reply 'Up at the Cross,' and immediately notice their eyes either widen, or often, harden, as they said something like 'Well, of course, I've heard about what goes on up there, I have a cousin who went there a few times . . .'

The selling part of the job was easy, even though I used to turn up to work so tired I could barely see the labels. All the work was just a matter of routine and common sense, but that didn't seem to be enough for the management. To further confusion and sales, every other afternoon we had to go up to the lecture hall, where a bogus posh lady stood waiting to teach us the art of salesmanship. For my money, after watching half a dozen of these so-called demonstrations, if I had been the customer, I would have thrown the goods back. But it didn't worry me, because I hardly saw much of anything. After the first five minutes, during which I realized that nothing new was coming my way, my head would seem to become full of warm winds on which floated beautiful voices that talked to me from far away. I would grow incredibly drowsy, then as the winds and the voices grew louder, my head, feeling as if it was made of warm lead, would slowly tip, nod and sway its way towards the table and a total blackout. I would be hauled up amidst laughter at the beginning, but after they had tried everything, from opening windows to turning up or down the air conditioning, the mood turned to one of annoyance, and hurt dignity on the part of the lady lecturer. The strange thing was, that when I had come to, she would ask me what she had said, I'd tell her, get up, sell a packet of Goo with great charm, then go straight back to the desk and sleep. This happened every day, and caused such chaos that they even got a doctor to see me. He looked at me, I looked at him, but neither of us found anything wrong with me, so I went on sleeping, no one having had the idea of just leaving me below selling away.

The first few days there, and my last nights at the Bamboo, were as different a combination of sensations as, say, the ice-cold cream on top of a boiling hot cup of Viennese coffee is. The change from the organized and fostered feeling of security of the store to the savage individuality of the club excited me.

At last it was Saturday. Nervously I went to Leon's to have my hair dyed. By this time it seemed that I would have been a raving misfit not to have it dyed. I sat bewildered, and rather frightened as layer after layer of frothing stuff fizzed all over my head and in my ears. In the middle of the dyeing Thelma arrived with a suitcase and Alan in tow. We had arranged to meet and then go down to Milly's where we would work out the final arrangements. Finally after several rinses, Leon said 'There.' Thelma took one look at me and yelled 'Hamlet!' I looked into the mirror and got the shock of my life—the image that looked back at me was me, and yet it wasn't. It was as if I had suddenly been slipped into another body, and I didn't like it. Yet even as we sat drinking coffee and I constantly looked at myself in the mirror, I started to get used to it. After I had made Leon swear to re-dye it Sunday afternoon, we left. When we called at my flat on the way down to Milly's, Bella took one long look, and said 'Well, I like it louse, but for God's sake, watch yourself—you know what I mean.' The day wore on, full of double takes and people making pseudo-sexy sounds as we walked up to the pub at lunchtime. By the time I had arrived at the Bamboo I just didn't care. Claude looked and said nothing, and whether it was my new hair or just Saturday night, I don't know, but my songs reduced the place to a stamping, yelling uproar. As I left I felt rather sad saying good-bye to Nedge and Claude, but glad that I would see them in a fortnight's time. Meanwhile I would rehearse a new act with Nedge in the early evenings.

The new ash blond me sped through the Cross and down to Milly's, where all was chaos. Thelma, dressed as Captain Hook, had already knocked over a bottle of wine with the hook, and then caught it in the radiogram. Alan, a very reluctant and ineffectual looking little pirate, was flirting to the point of no return with Leon's friend, a plump girl dressed as Dorothy Lamour. Milly was a rather drunk, top-hatted Georges Sand, complete with a large false book made out of wood and a riding crop. Leon was covered in mirrors and paint, and was supposed to be something from a Salvador Dali painting. Milly and Leon started covering me in gold paint; as soon as it dried I dressed, then Leon combed my hair into a pixie-like shape, and swamped it with lacquer so that it set and felt like cardboard. After a few more drinks and one or two near rows, we set out on our way to the first port of call, which was Arnold's.

Walking along Macleay Street, we passed several clusters of people all going to other places before the party. Outside a café we saw two men with two Amazon sized glittering showgirls, one of whom was trying to explain to a rather stunned taxi-driver that they wanted the such-and-such hall. As we drew level with them, the other befeathered girl said 'Hullo pet, see you?' I looked at the six foot of copper-coloured, diamond flashing body and recognized the voice of Freddy, who worked in a local chemist's shop.

Ringing Arnold's bell, I found myself wondering how the Queen of Sheba would look made out of food, fruit and vegetables. She wasn't, she was covered in gold lamé, veils, and moonstones, the only fruit being a surprising and rather beautiful head-dress made of pomegranates and vine leaves. Cliff and Dennis were dressed as Greek soldiers. Also in the house were ten other people including two Carmen Mirandas, one of whom was frantically trying to turn herself into Dolores del Rio.

Some drinks later we set off in a small fleet of taxis. As we approached the hall, we could see a crowd of at least two hundred gazing with stunned eyes, as group after group of the most exotic and fantastic people passed up the stairs, and in through the main doors. Arnold's Sheba drew an enormous half cheer, after which he turned, and quite loudly thanked them for being such happy peasants. Once inside the hall, the heat, noise and crush was fantastic. It was only midnight, but the ball was well away. A drink and a dance later, I began to sort out friends hidden in or behind lavish costumes. A somewhat surprised but happy orchestra played away below the stage, which was and would be till cabaret and showgirl parade time, curtained.

Meanwhile, all was gorgeous bedlam: half the theatre and radio world seemed to be there, as well as quite a few people who, one would have thought from listening to their usual comments on life and people, would sooner have been found dead in the nearest gutter than be seen at such a degenerate 'do'. Amongst other games was trying to use the lavatories: if I went to the gents' what seemed like a host of hair-arranging girls shrieked all as one, 'try the ladies',' and a lot of gentlemen yelled—wonderful chaos. The hall bashed on: some two hundred dressed up souls danced, fainted, talked and drank away, all waiting for the big moment when the cabaret began and after it, the prize winning showgirl parade. I was sitting on the floor, listening to Thelma's ideas on theatre, when a sudden strange silence almost descended. Some people stood swaying on the spot instead of dancing, others, glasses half way up to their mouths, froze and stood looking towards the main door. Thelma and I couldn't see anything, so we stood up on a windowsill in order to see what was going on.

Once up, we saw the enormous white figure standing in the entrance, its head-dress swaying and glittering. By this time, the crowd had parted, and I recognized Zoe. Then I looked up near the bandstand: Sheba was sitting on a big chair, being fanned by Carmen Miranda, and the now

Dolores del Rio. I looked back at Zoe—three little boys painted black stood around her, each one holding a piece of her vast white feathered cloak, which had floating panels falling away from it. Zoe, now sure of her audience, paused, then pulled a satin cord. As the cloak fell off, a gasp went up. Even the orchestra nearly stopped playing. She walked forward, her tall white head-dress swaying above her glittering, silvered eyelids and white lips. She had long, white feathered pants on, which ran up to her thighs and then stood out at the back like a bird's tail. The rest of her torso was naked and painted white from her loins to the cups of her breasts, the upper parts of which, along with her neck, were her natural glistening black skin. As she turned slightly, I could see loops of pearls and roses beginning at the tops of her legs and running down into a tail-piece. She raised one white-fingernailed hand in acknowledgement to the thundering roar of applause that went up. The orchestra played with renewed vigour, the evening slipped back into gear. The black and white goddess moved forward, accepted a drink, raised it as she tilted her head-dress towards Sheba, and then drank.

Thelma and I danced, but we had so much trouble with the hook that after she had almost unknowingly hooked at least three people's wigs off, she left to find Alan to unstrap it. I found Milly, who was busy trying to find somewhere to put her giant book that she was sick of carrying. She didn't mind the whip, but the book was much too bulky. We dumped it down the back of a seat, and stood watching the dancers. I had never seen such a crowd. A person dressed as Pola Negri danced past us with someone who had come as a candle and was covered in wax. Milly and I counted at least eight Carmen Mirandas, most of whom glared at one another. Only one didn't seem to care and danced round gayly throwing fruit and beads at people, utterly enjoying his or herself. There was a fanfare, and the curtains swung open on the stage, then a microphoned voice said 'Ladies and—er—Gentlemen, it's cabaret time, so could you kindly, and please comfortably, seat yourselves.' There was a loud buzz as people found places to sit either on the floor, or on one another. Slowly, as the bedlam subsided, an expectant hush gradually forced its way over the hall, the compère walked into view, microphone in hand, and stood smiling from the stage.

'Good evening, I hope you are all comfortably settled?'

There were lots of shouts of 'No' after which there were odd complaints like 'How can a birdcage sit down?' or a quite genuinely desperate utterance of 'What can I do with this bustle?'

The compère stood professionally smiling and waiting till everyone was settled. 'As you know, no expense has been spared on tonight's fabulous show, so I won't waste any of your time by going into the lavish account, I'll just present to you our opening number. Ladies and Gentlemen, The Triss Troupe!' With that the orchestra struck up, and on to the stage bounced eight very big-limbed, and over made-up 'lovelies', to the tune of *The Fleet's In.* Four minutes later they kicked their way off with a last raucous 'Hey There Mister, you'd better watch your sister—' to a great roar of applause.

The compère came back on. 'Thank you, thank you, now for the first glamorous act tonight it gives me great pleasure to present none other than the fabulous Miss Lana Turner.' There was a round of applause and Lana swished onto the stage nearly bursting out of her white gown, dripping in jewels, and flailing an enormous feather fan. She walked downstage, looked the audience full in the face, then began singing *Please don't Talk about Me When I've Gone,* and doing things with the fan that made sure people would never stop talking about her, or for ever after look a fan in the face with the same calm as before. She finished and swayed off to an enormous hand.

As the uproar died down, the compère came back on stage, paused for a minute, took on a look of mock respect and announced in a rather awestricken tone of voice that there had been a change in the programme. A change, he hurriedly assured us, which was nothing short of the miraculous. It appeared, that though the lovely 'Dildol Sisters' couldn't be with us, thanks to some smart celestial shuffling the next act we were about to be privileged to witness was none other than Dame Nellie Melba, who would sing some of her favourite arias for us. She would be accompanied at the piano by 'Miss Tilly Trade.' This brought another big hand. During the applause a little old woman walked on to the stage, stood in the centre, curtsied, put a pair of glasses on and sat down at the piano. She then took off eight rings, dropping each one with a bigger clang than the last, and to a bigger laugh. Then she put on another two pairs of glasses, one on top of the other, had another look at the piano keyboard, paused, took out a false breast and began wiping the keyboard and the rest of the piano down with it. When she was satisfied that they were clean enough she stuck it back in behind the beaded bodice, gave us a toothless grin and started to play *Lo, Hear the Gentle Lark*.

As she played, a noise which sounded like a cross between a very old soprano's top note and a banshee, shot out from the wings, and was followed by an enormous Nellie Melba. Nellie, when she finally hove into view, wore an old-fashioned dress with an eight foot train, a frighteningly red wig, and a giant tiara. She also carried an enormous lorgnette, which she used to look the audience over with, or to bop the lady at the piano. When clouted Miss Trade started to cry loud and bitterly and refused to play. Melba did her best to coax her into playing again, but she wouldn't. After Melba had offered her her ear rings and finally practically everything she wore, she threatened to get her pearl handled whip out—at which Miss Trade threw her hands in the air, uttered an ecstatic little cry, and played like mad.

Melba finished the song with the crowd practically cheering: during the applause she fished a bottle of gin out of her vast bosom took a swig, then walked over to the piano and poured some over Miss Trade's hair, which immediately stood right up on end. Tilly got up from the piano and taking her wig off, sloshed Melba with it, wrung it out and put it back on. Melba, who'd looked a bit stunned during this, started fishing around in her bosom again. Finally she pulled out a whip and said 'Back to the keys!' Miss Trade flew back to the piano. Melba adjusted her tiara, saying 'I'll correct this wayward slip of a thing, later . . . !' then with a sideways glance to the pianist, said 'I will now sing the *Jewel Song*.' Tilly started playing and Melba began singing. After we had nearly been blasted off the floor with a series of Wagnerian shrieks, we suddenly noticed that as Melba sang, her already mountainous breasts started to grow bigger and bigger. The further on she went through the song, the larger they grew. Hundreds of eyes popped, waiting for the bang.

It came. Not from Melba up on the stage, but from the back of the audience somewhere near the front entrance. At the same time voices yelled out. The tall windows down either side of the hall opened, and in through them hurtled and dropped what seemed like dozens of policemen. As soon as they hit the floor, bedlam tried to break out and nearly succeeded. Then the main entrance doors opened, and police fanned through them into the hall, making lots of chaos-causing sounds as they did. Some people panicked, but most were too paralysed with shock to utter or move. Melba, who'd nearly strangled on a high note, stood dead centre of the stage, glaring. The leading cop walked down the middle of the hall saying, as he either walked over people, or knocked them flying 'Come on down, you poffta'. Melba put her hand on her hip and said 'Just supposing you come up and get me you big bull.' The copper was furious and started yelling 'I told you to get down off there, you great bastard, I'll bash you black and blue when you do.' Melba wagged her lorgnette saying 'Oh you great big impetuous dream boy, why don't you come up to Momma?' The cop glared and bellowed 'You're no Momma, you'll never even be a Poppa.' Melba flashed back 'Really darling, I know you're upset, but that's no way to speak to a dame—' The copper, still trying to get over bodies, almost shrieked 'Dame! dame? You're no dame you, you big pervert.' Melba yelled back 'And you're no gent, and I'll bet you're bloody lousy in bed as well.' And that second a tremendous gale of screams rent the air, as twenty-five show girls, getting dressed backstage, started to get an inkling of what was happening in front.

Before the screams had died down, everything in the hall went mad: cops started grabbing people, pulling off wigs, having a look, then slamming a wig back on, and hauling the wig's occupant towards the main doors. Then everyone yelled at everyone else, and the leading cop kept trying to climb up onto the stage, which was difficult for him, because he first had to climb over the stunned orchestra who sat not knowing whether to play, drop dead on the spot, or bash him and his helpers with their instruments. Some eight feet up, the stage also seethed with activity. Melba and her little friend let the cops have the lot, everything they could lay their hands on. The head cop and Melba fought it out, he trying to climb up, she bashing him down with her lorgnette. The little pianist threw music, her shoes, her wig, and something that, frightened out of my wits as I was, surprised me when I saw it fly overhead. Coming from nowhere, it was a water melon. It hit a Betty Grable, knocking her out on the spot. Just then Melba, with a triumphant yell, crowned the cop with a pot of flowers. Milly and I sat holding one another, terrified yet excited, trying to see through the general mêlèe if we could spot Thelma and Alan, or see where Cliff and Dennis were. As we looked, two cops grabbed us. One felt me and pulled at my lacquered hair till I yelled. He stopped pulling, looked at me, then at Milly, dropped me and started on two other people nearby.

By this time I was really frightened. What had been a looked forward to gala night, had turned into a savage mess of screaming human beings, wrecked lives, hurriedly arranged blackmail, and a dance floor knee deep in the remains of beautiful costumes. I just sat clutching Milly's arm, and saying to myself 'I'm nearly eighteen, I've done nothing wrong, I'm nearly eighteen.' As I was flat out doing this, I looked up and saw Zoe. She was standing looking towards the main entrance. There, on her way out, was a strangely quiet and dignified Sheba, slowly moving her lamé across the floor, leaving in her own way and time, despite the hysterical cops trying to push and shove her. I thought it looked sad, and so did some of the cops and many of the guests. There was a lull in the racket, then a voice said 'All right, boys, that's it,' and all the police left. Milly and I picked ourselves up and found Thelma and Cliff, but not Dennis or Alan. We began looking for them amongst people who moved around trying to find their bits and pieces in a curious stunned way, rather like people searching for friends and things loved amongst the wreckage of a city after an earthquake. We couldn't find Alan or Dennis and were just about to leave, when three policemen crashed back in. They reached the now deserted orchestra pit, picked up the cop who had fought Melba and carried him out. They passed me quite closely. I peeped at the face of the cop; it looked as if he was quietly sleeping with a slight smile around his lips, but as they went by, I found myself thinking a swift little prayer for Melba's safety.

Outside the hall a large mixed crowd stood watching the black marias drive away. As the door slammed on the last one, it left a piece of orange net hanging out. I thought, as I said at almost the same time, 'I wonder who's on the other end of that piece of net?' We started to walk back to the Cross, sometimes passing other slightly battered groups of people in fancy dress. Once at the Cross proper, the atmosphere was electric. Everybody, from the tramps to the café cleaners seemed to know what had happened to the 'Gala Drag and Drain Ball'. People stood buying papers and eating hot dogs or pies as they checked each band of survivors when they passed through, either in cars, or on weary feet. For one minute I almost laughed as I looked around at the battered ballerinas, historical figures and Carmen Mirandas eating hot pies and talking in outraged voices, to themselves and to anyone who cared to listen, about the bedlam they had been through. Lights started up in many flat windows. People no one even knew came up saying, 'It's a stinking disgrace, why don't they leave the boys alone, and get after the black market gangsters and molls?' Thelma kept muttering between bursts of laughing, 'Just wait, if they haven't carted that bastard of mine off, he'll wish they had after I've finished with him.' None of us mentioned Dennis. Somehow we all knew that as usual, he'd struck while the iron was hot, and most likely was blissfully unaware of the night's chaos, as he told a new pair of eyes how beautiful they were, maybe only a few yards away.

A young couple who had joined our crowd asked us back to their flat, which was just nearby in Darlinghurst Road. There, everyone began speculating as to who would be phoning for bail either now or Sunday. For one moment I really panicked. 'Suppose Leon had the misfortune to be put in the cooler for the weekend leaving me with a head of ash blond hair, stiff as cardboard with lacquer?' After I had aired this doubt someone said they had seen him leaving on foot with his girl friend. The more we talked about the night the clearer it and Melba's last stand became. Later, just as everyone was nearly sick with laughing there was a sharp ring on the doorbell, followed by a voice. Instantly we all froze. The man and woman whose flat we were in stood up as the bell went again—this time followed by bangings. The man went to the door and opened it. As he did, he was nearly knocked flat by what looked like a demented shop window dummy come to life. It flew into the room, spun around, then collapsed into a heap on the floor. We all looked with stunned eyes. Then it spoke, 'For God's sake loves, hand me a drink.' The shock over, we looked again and recognized Lana. His wig hung in lumps and strands. The one shoe still on was smashed, bits of stocking fluttered from his legs like fern fronds, the remains of a corset and dress were covered in blood, as were his face and body. After he had had a quick drink, Lana started to tell us what had happened backstage.

It turned out that no one there had really quite known what was going on in front they were so busy dressing and making up for the big parade, until Melba flew through yelling her head off. Then the awful truth dawned, at which they all lost their heads and started trying to get out before the uniformed ones found their way backstage. The obvious choice of exit for most, including Melba, was the windows. Unfortunately, in the blind rush, there were two things no one realized. The first was that the hall was on the side of a hill and the back windows were in some cases two storeys up; the second, that a dog breeder's kennels was below them. With Melba leading, everyone started dropping out of windows, landing with bone-jarring crashes in the middle of a wire compound and eight rather shattered alsatian dogs. After the 'girls' and the dogs recovered from the shock, the battle between fangs and the heels of shoes really began in earnest. As wigs and costumes started to fly in all directions, someone, Lana thought it was Melba, smashed through the wire gate and started the retreat. Everyone left, dogs and all, via the only escape route that could be seen which was up a pathway stiff with standard roses, and through the nearest doors, which happened to be french windows. They were only open at that moment because the lady of the dog breeder's house was entertaining some friends. She and her startled guests were treated to the sight of an incredible mixture of battered show girls and snarling dogs, screaming and hurtling right through them, the dining-room, the lounge, and out through the front door, from where they all noisily disappeared into what was left of the 'gala' Saturday night.

DYMPHNA CUSACK AND FLORENCE JAMES

'Sunday VI' from *Come In Spinner*

Claire slipped two thick T-bone steaks under the griller and examined the vegetables steaming on the hotplate. Everything was going nicely. She set out cream lace mats on the dark polished gate-legged table and golden-brown wallflowers in a horseshoe centrepiece of translucent green. Nigel had given her the heavy sterling silver spoons and forks with the old crest almost obliterated from generations of use; the two Queen Anne candlesticks were his too, they had been sent out to him from his great-aunt's home in Devon. She straightened the wick of each green candle. Time enough to light them when he came in. She stood back and admired the table. Everything was perfect.

Nigel always said the room, with its thick cream carpet and deep, luxurious green chairs, was a perfect setting for her. He really said the sweetest things. She looked up at the large portrait on the wall; it was quite the best thing the studio had done of him. His sensitive face was strongly highlighted, his beautifully-shaped hand curved round the bowl of his pipe. There was no doubt he was marvellously photogenic; she could never understand why they had not snapped him up for films. Of course local stuff was so crude and they were probably jealous of him, but if only he could get overseas she was sure he would be rushed for the

Esquire type of modelling, and he was simply made for English films.

She turned to the long mirror and looked at her own reflection with satisfaction, admiring again the exotic green housecoat floating around her. It made her look taller than her five feet two, and concealed how skinny she was. She really would have to try and put some weight on, she was getting positively scraggy. But even so, she consoled herself, I am much pleasanter to look at at thirty-seven than I was at twenty-seven . . . well, perhaps not pleasanter . . . but more striking, more distinctive.

She smiled experimentally into the mirror and smoothed the wings of chestnut hair that swept up gleaming from her temples. She did hope Nigel would like her new hair style; he was so proud of her when she looked her best. The light threw faint shadows under her too-prominent cheekbones, caught the clean line of her jaw and showed the droop of her small mouth. She'd have to do something about those lines at the corners, Nigel was so fussy about these little things. She bent forward and examined her lipstick anxiously. Yes, the line was right, it made her lips look fuller and it wasn't overdone. Your mouth really is too small, my girl, she told herself, you should never be seen without lipstick.

She turned away from the mirror. God, she was tired and her veins were giving her hell. That climb up the stairs with all the parcels always finished her. It wasn't that Nigel was thoughtless, but he so hated carrying parcels that she hadn't the heart to ask him to pick up anything on his way home. He wasn't used to that kind of thing.

She turned to the sideboard; she'd have a quick one before he came in. She poured out a glassful of sherry and drank it eagerly. Ah, that was good! Better have a mouthwash; Nigel hated her to smell of drink or cigarette smoke, he was so fastidious.

From the bathroom she went back to the kitchenette to turn the grill, whistling softly to herself; she never felt happier than when she was preparing for an intimate meal with Nigel. They had been terribly lucky to get two adjoining penthouses in 'The Cross'—the whole roof to themselves; you could make a home of it. That was one of the good things that had come from the war. The tenants had fled to some inland hideout when the Pacific War started and luxury flats on the top of any building in the eastern suburbs went for two a penny. Even if you could get flats like this today, you'd have to pay through the nose for them with landlords cashing in on the housing shortage everywhere. Thank God rents were pegged and their old Shark could do nothing about it, no matter how much he grumbled about what he ought to have been making out of the flats while the Yanks were in Sydney.

She wandered out on to the roof. The roar of planes going back to Richmond blotted out the sound of the city traffic and searchlights raked the sky with inquisitive fingers. The sliding pencils of light silvered the planes high up, then glided down the sky to rest, leaving the night darker than before. Below her the city fell away from the foot of Victoria Street to the trough of Woolloomooloo in a sea of twinkling electric lights, and rose again in a glittering wave to the broken skyline beyond Hyde Park. The narrow street below was bright and busy and three slender poplars beside the Minerva Theatre were bathed in silver light from a passing car. The rattle of trams, the tooting of taxis, the grumble of buses and the distant roar of an electric train crossing the Harbour Bridge rose to her in a muffled throbbing.

The sherry had given her a pleasant glow; she was certain they were going to be lucky tonight. With that seventy-five pound win on Storm-cloud to play with, they simply couldn't lose. She rested her arms on the parapet and began to calculate just how much they had to win to get that thousand in the bank . . . 'I wouldn't ask any woman to marry me with less,' Nigel always said, no matter how much she protested that it wasn't necessary. Until they'd got into the Game she couldn't see any way they'd ever land a thousand. Poor darling, he was so honourable, other men wouldn't care. There was no doubt about it, breeding did count. There was nothing crude about Nigel; she adored his clear-cut profile and his tall, slender body. But for all his exquisite delicacy there was nothing effemi-nate about him either, that's why he modelled men's fashions so perfectly. There was an innate refinement about him too. To be married to him would be all her dreams come true. . . .

She heard the outer door open, and turned to go back. 'Hello, darling,' she called gaily.

'God,' Nigel sighed, bending to kiss her. 'I've had a madly exhausting afternoon. My head's simply splitting.'

'You poor darling, you must be terribly tired. Take off your things while I bring your lounge coat. Now sit down and rest, while I get you a sherry. The dinner's practically ready.'

He sank into a deep chair and closed his eyes. She smoothed his fair straight hair with a gentle hand. 'Sure you wouldn't like an APC?'

He shook his head: 'I'll be all right after a drink.'

She took two crystal glasses, filled them with sherry, and sat down close to him on the wide arm of the chair.

'Clever sweet,' he said, holding his glass to the light. 'Where did you get it?'

'My faithful Blue—we're like that.' She held up two fingers tightly crossed. 'Doss gets it for him.'

'That virago!' he shuddered. 'Look out she doesn't tear your eyes out.'

She dropped a kiss on his ear. 'I'll risk it for you, darling. But you haven't told me how your screen test went.'

'It didn't. I waited round simply hours at the studio and then nothing happened. I'm sure it's all a fake.'

'I think that's the limit,' she said indignantly, 'when they promised to call you.'

'My sweet,' he made a gesture of utter fatigue, 'they really don't want men of my type for Australian films. A decent accent is a handicap in this country.'

'Never mind, darling. When we get our thousand we'll go abroad and then you'll get your chance.'

He lifted her hand and pressed it against his cheek. 'Ma petite,' he murmured, 'what would I do without you?'

She scanned his face anxiously. He did look exhausted. The corners of his mouth drooped pathetically and the slight puffiness under his eyes was discoloured. Poor darling, having to rub shoulders with all sorts in this business world was a perpetual torture to him with his background and upbringing. She clinked her glass to his: 'I'm sure it's going to be a lucky night for us, darling. Both our stars say so. Now take your time and I'll serve.'

Nigel uncoiled himself slowly from the big chair when she brought in the dinner.

'Everything looks perfect,' he murmured as he pushed her chair in for her and sat down opposite.

'I hope it's as nice as it looks.' Claire gave a little nervous laugh and looked at his plate with the creamed potatoes between the fresh green peas and grilled tomatoes.

He began to cut the steak and took a mouthful, then looked up at her, drawing his brows together. 'Not so tender as usual.'

She tasted her own. 'Mine seems all right. Would you like to change?'

'Oh, it doesn't matter. Where did you get it?'

'With the meat strike on I had the greatest difficulty in getting any steak at all yesterday. I had to go to five butchers and I was just lucky that Teddy up in Darlinghurst Road had this put away for someone else and gave it to me. I only got it because I passed on to him that Stormcloud tip.'

'Well, you'd better tell him if he wants any more tips like that in future, he'll have to see that we get tender meat.'

Claire's chin quivered and she put down her knife and fork distastefully. Really, she wasn't terribly hungry after all.

The telephone rang as they were drinking their coffee. Claire got up to answer it. 'It's for you, darling,' she handed him the receiver.

When he'd finished, he turned to her. 'That was Coddy. The School moved again last night, they're at Point Piper. He said they'd send a car for us. What do you think?'

'Just as you like, darling. But the big money's at Joe's.'

'That's what I think. Better call him back and say not to bother.'

'Mind you,' Claire dialled as she spoke, 'Coddy's is much nicer if you want a social evening and I must hand it to him, that blonde pick-up of his can put on a supper. We'll go another time; I want to keep in with Cynthia. But if it's real baccarat you're after, you can't beat Joe's, and while our luck's in . . .'

'I feel that way, too. He seems to bring me luck. Besides, you haven't got the threat of being raided constantly hanging over you down there. It's as safe as if you were dining at Government House.'

'Nothing will happen for a few weeks anyway after last night's raid.'

'What's the time?'

'Just on nine.'

'Good.' He stretched out in the lounge. 'I'll have forty winks while you're fixing up. There's no hurry, they never start to warm up till about half past ten at Joe's.'

Claire closed the door of the kitchenette and did the washing-up as quietly as she could, methodically setting out her own breakfast things and a morning tray for Nigel. Oh, she felt happy tonight! The run of luck they'd had last Friday and again at the races yesterday was surely a sign they'd moved into a lucky cycle. If only her veins didn't ache so . . .

She was almost gay as she dressed, putting on the new cocoa-brown suit that she was keeping as a surprise for Nigel. It represented a nice spot of commission from Madame Renoir on the Marie-Antoinette patrons she'd sent round, and when Deb married McFarland she'd put the nips into the old girl again. That introduction would be worth hundreds to any frock shop.

The brown suit was just her cup of tea, she thought, simple and tailored, yet essentially feminine. So was the bit of velvet nonsense—brown and ochre flowers in a mist of tulle—that served as a hat. It was gay and ridiculous. Thank heaven for Cynthia, who could discard hats according to whim without considering either coupons or cash and pass them on to her friends for next to nothing. My God, what a rakeoff she must get from Coddy! Well, she earned it. She'd made his school. They said that whatever school she was at was absolutely safe from the police. How on earth did she do it?

When she'd finished dressing she tip-toed into the lounge where Nigel was still sleeping. She bent and dropped a kiss on the end of his nose. 'Time to go, darling.'

He opened his eyes and blinked at her. 'What a vision,' he murmured, 'I haven't seen that bonnet before—or the suit. Let me look at you.' He scanned the details of her outfit. 'Perfect! You grow lovelier every day. Now turn round. Yes, I couldn't have chosen anything for you myself that I liked better. Give me a kiss before we go.' He sat up and pulled her down beside him.

'Do be careful, darling. You'll ruin my makeup.'

'You'd be just as lovely without.' He pressed his lips gently on to her closed eyelids as she lay still a moment, her head against his shoulder. Then he drew her up. 'Come along,' he said with mock firmness, 'much more of this nonsense and we'll never get to the Game.' He took a wallet out of his inside pocket. Claire whistled at the neatly folded notes: 'Seventy-five lovely smackers!'

'Minus twenty-five pounds,' he corrected as he put it back. 'I simply had to pay the tailor for this suit.'

'Oh Nigel, what a snag!'

'I wouldn't have, only the swine was hanging round the studio and practically asked me straight out. That's gratitude for you, after all the custom I've brought him.'

'Oh, never mind, he makes wonderfully, and it's my favourite suit. Now, quite sure you've got rid of all your brown money?'

Nigel went through each pocket carefully and made two little piles of pennies and halfpennies on the table. 'That's the last,' he said, 'you haven't any in your purse, I hope.'

'Not a bean. Think I'd risk our lucky star for a brownie?'

'Well, that's everything then, so let's be on our way. Ring for a car, will you, sweet.'

Claire dialled for several minutes. 'No one answering.'

'Give them another tinkle.'

Claire tried again. 'Nothing doing, I'm afraid.'

'Oh, darn it all. We'll have to go down and try for a taxi. Private hire service has gone to pot these days like everything else. Will I be glad to see the end of the Yanks!'

They came out from the flats and went up to the corner of Macleay Street, where Nigel hailed a cruising taxi. It drew up.

'This is a miracle,' Claire cried.

'It ain't yours,' the taxi-driver snarled at them. 'These coves called me before you.'

Two American privates sauntered to the edge of the pavement. He opened the door and they stepped in.

'This,' said Nigel bitterly, 'is what you have to put up with when you have an Army of Occupation. Once they're gone the taxis'll be glad enough to come crawling round.'

An empty cab circled beside them ignoring their signal, drew up in front of the American Naval Hostel on the opposite side of the street and took on a quartette of sailors who had just come out of the canteen.

Claire sighed resignedly. 'We'll stand here waving all night at this rate. Better get a trolleybus; there ought to be one leaving Wylde Street about now. Oh, here it is—our luck is certainly in!'

BOB HERBERT

from *No Names . . . No Pack Drill*

SETTING:

A flat on the second floor of an apartment building in Kings Cross, Sydney. The time is December 1942.

Stage right is a round dining table, upstage right an archway leading to the kitchenette. A window in the right wall overlooks the street. Upstage centre is a short passage leading to the bathroom; off this passage to stage left is the only bedroom. The door giving entrance to the flat is in the left wall, well downstage. Set against the upstage wall is a divan.

The flat is neither luxurious nor squalid but favours, like the play itself, the red end of the experiential spectrum.

[KATHY *goes into the bathroom.* REBEL *picks up his shoes and, after inner debate, puts them down again.* KATHY *comes back.*]

REBEL: Know where Ah come from?

KATHY: Georgia . . . and LA.

REBEL: Ah mean, what part of the war Ah come from?

KATHY: No, and I don't want to. You shouldn't be telling people.

REBEL: Guadalcanal.

KATHY: [*Pause*] Why didn't your buddies take you back to camp?

REBEL: Those two last night? They wasn't mah buddies. They wasn't even

Marines. And most important of all, nobody's gonna take me back to camp.

KATHY: The provosts will.

REBEL: Who?

KATHY: Your MPs.

REBEL: First they gotta find me.

KATHY: But you've got to go back some time.

REBEL: [*negatively*] Uh uh.

KATHY: Oh, Rebel, you're a sergeant, and a Marine, and you can't just . . . leave . . .

REBEL: Yeah, Ah'm a Marine . . . but Ah'm not a Marine the Marine Corps gonna be proud to own . . .

KATHY: Why not?

REBEL: Because Ah'm also a member of the Coward Corps. [*An uncomfortable silence.*]

KATHY: Who isn't?

REBEL: Yup. The first time Ah heard a little ole hornet go buzzin' past mah ear, Ah said to myself: 'Harry, ole pal, you're a coward.'

KATHY: Everybody must get scared.

REBEL: [*quietly*] Not everybody . . . bolts . . . like a . . . like a rabbit. Not everybody . . . messes up their pants.

[KATHY *avoids his gaze.*]

Know what a woodpecker is?

KATHY: The bird?

REBEL: It's a Jap machine gun. Fires real slow . . . tutta tutta tutta tutta . . . Like a woodpecker. Well, Ah was behind this little thin tree an' a Jap was sprayin' all round me with his woodpecker. One bullet went right through the edge of that tree. It missed me, but a chip of the tree hit me and scared the bejeezus outa me. 'Smatter of fact, scared a lot more'n that outa me. Ah just bolted, lookin' for a bigger tree, Ah guess. He got me . . . right here, right in the offal. One of the guys grabbed mah foot and dragged me behind a log. Ah love that guy. Just chewed his gum an' said: 'Take it easy, Sarge.' Dressed the hole in mah offal. Looked after me till the medics come. Saved mah life, that's for sure.

[*Pause.*]

KATHY: How . . . how is it now?

REBEL: Fine. Patched me up just fine, they did. Doc says Ah'm fighting fit. Like hell. Ah'm runnin' fit. They ain't gettin' me back in that jungle.

KATHY: Somebody's got to do the fighting.

REBEL: Somebody else.

KATHY: [*matter-of-fact, not reproachful*] My husband's up in New Guinea with the Sixth Division.

REBEL: Ah appreciate the point you're makin'.

KATHY: My brother Jimmy's up North too.

REBEL: [*nodding*] Doin'—what has to be done . . .

KATHY: And what about your buddies? What about the other Marines on Guadalcanal?

REBEL: [*with a sigh*] Yeah. They're doin' 'what has to be done', hunh?

KATHY: And don't you think they're scared?

REBEL: Sure they're scared. Even the li'l yellow Nip men are scared when mah hornets go whizzin' past them. But they don't have to be scared o' me no more. Ah ain't goin' back.

KATHY: [*after a moment*] Where'd you say you got shot?

REBEL: [*taking her hand*] Point your finger.

[*KATHY points. REBEL places her finger over his liver. He prods her finger a couple of times into his abdomen.*]

Right there.

KATHY: [*aping his accent*] In the offal.

[*They chuckle and smile at each other. There is a knock at the door.*]

Go in the kitchen. Might be my landlady.

REBEL: What would she want?

KATHY: A good old whinge—about last night.

REBEL: Oh.

[*KATHY closes the door. REBEL comes out of the kitchen and moves to the living-room window. He looks down at the street below.*]

KATHY: [*eyeing him speculatively for a moment*] That Bernie.

REBEL: Uh huh.

KATHY: Ought to be ashamed of himself.

REBEL: He's a guy.

KATHY: That makes it all right? Look, would you mind staying away from that window? People know I live up here. On my own.

[REBEL *leaves the window.*]

'He's a guy.'

REBEL: Ah didn't notice him puttin' no headlock on her.

KATHY: She's only nineteen.

REBEL: That's old enough to know what she's doin'. How come *you're so* worried about her?

KATHY: [*shrugging*] We work in the same section. She was a lonely little thing. Attached herself to me . . . we started going around together. She's so unhappy at home. I don't know why, Rebel, but I feel *responsible* for her.

REBEL: She's not gonna listen to you while Bernie's showin' her a time.

KATHY: Uniforms, money, taxis, waiters, flowers—

REBEL: The old routine.

KATHY: It's pretty new here. It's all gone to her head. [*Sighing*] Mine too, I suppose. Don't know what I'd do if my husband found out. He'd be so— understanding. I couldn't bear it. Hey, that was quick of you to say I asked you to stay for breakfast. [*Chuckling*] Suppose I'd better get you some now.

REBEL: Thanks, but Ah really ain't hungry.

KATHY: Come on. Have something. [*A beat*] Please.

[*Pause.*]

REBEL: Got any corn flakes?

KATHY: You really want corn flakes?

REBEL: Yeah. They're kinda neutral.

KATHY: I'll join you. I'm going to be so late, but I don't care.

[KATHY *goes into the kitchen.*]

[*Off*] We've got a real pig of a supervisor. The girls call him 'Bubbles'. God knows why. Where's the teapot?

[*She pokes her head around the corner.*]

How'd you get to be a sergeant?

REBEL: [*grinning*] Ah know just what you're thinkin'. Well, Ah've been in the Marines over three years now, and when the war started—

KATHY: For you lot.

REBEL: Ah'll ignore that. When *our* war started anybody who'd been in for a while and 'd behaved himself couldn't help gettin' promoted. If Ah'd only been able to stop sayin' 'ain't' Ah reckon Ah'd've been an officer.

KATHY: Couldn't've gone AWOL then. ......

REBEL: Mightn't've had to. Might've wangled me a nice little job here in Sydney.

KATHY: How long do you think it'll be before they start looking for you?

REBEL: They'll be lookin' for me already. Hospitals and the morgue first, then the saloons . . . Guess Ah occupy a lot o' men's thoughts these days. You don't put the sugar on first, do you?

KATHY: Sugar and milk'll be on the table.

REBEL: Thanks. Corn flakes is tricky things, and kinda personal. [*Sitting at the table*] First thing Ah gotta do is get some civilian clothes.

KATHY: [*sitting also*] You'll need coupons.

[*They help themselves to cereal.*]

REBEL: Must be a black market somewhere. Got to get back to the States.

KATHY: How?

REBEL: Ship, Ah guess.

KATHY: Stowaway?

REBEL: That's kid stuff. Gotta get some papers, then sign up as a crewman. Jump ship as soon as she gets Stateside.

KATHY: You're serious.

REBEL: Unless you got a better idea.

KATHY: These papers—where'll you get them?

REBEL: Any city this big, everything's for sale. Just gotta find the guy. Don't forget, Ah got five hundred dollars.

KATHY: [*with simple curiosity*] You married, Rebel?

REBEL: Nope. Never met anyone Ah was fond of.

[*Pause.*]

KATHY: How old are you?

REBEL: Twenty-three. Ah'll be twenty-four on Christmas day.

KATHY: Go on.

REBEL: Somebody has to get born on Christmas day.

[*Pause.*]

KATHY: Twenty-three, nearly twenty-four. You must've liked quite a few girls.

REBEL: Ah liked plenty of 'em, but that ain't the same as bein' fond of 'em. Like, Ah guess, you're fond of your husband.

KATHY: [*quietly*] I don't know.

[*Pause.*]

We got married on his final leave. Had a three-day honeymoon, then he was gone. We shouldn't've got married, but he wanted to . . .

REBEL: You didn't?

KATHY: I did . . . and I didn't. I'm twenty-six. My mother's been nagging me for years—reckoned I'd missed the boat. Steve, my husband, he was so keen. I didn't like to disappoint him.

[*Pause.*]

Steve McLeod. I'm [*wry grin*] Mrs McLeod.

REBEL: [*codding*] Ah'm mighty pleased to meet you, Mrs McLeod. Pleased to meet your corn flakes, too.

KATHY: They're Weeties.

REBEL: With you servin' 'em up, they're gonna be the best chow Ah ever had.

KATHY: No smoodging.

REBEL: Hell, you talk funny.

KATHY: I'm scared.

TIGER: Don't you start.

KATHY: [*to* REBEL] Pictures of you. They're going to a lot of trouble. [*To* TIGER] You're calling for us at eleven?

TIGER: Make it a quarter to. Be ready.

REBEL: Ah'm ready now.

[KATHY *looks at* REBEL *sharply. He looks away.* TIGER *opens the door to leave, then closes it again.*]

TIGER: One little thing.

KATHY: And what's that?

TIGER: Supposin' we did get lumbered. Just supposin'. You're on your own. I'm on me own. An' no dobbin'.

KATHY: [*formally agreeing*] No names . . . no pack drill.

[TIGER *looks enquiringly at* REBEL.]

REBEL: [*responding*] No names . . . no . . . pack drill.

[TIGER *gives a satisfied nod.*]

TIGER: Hooroo.

[*He leaves.* KATHY *stares at* REBEL.]

KATHY: So you're off.

REBEL: [*subdued*] Yuh.

KATHY: I'd better start cooking. The butcher's been beaut about the meat. I told him my brother was home on leave and he'd lost his coupons. You should see the steak he gave me.

REBEL: Ah'm . . . Ah'm gonna miss you, Kathy.

KATHY: [*nodding slightly*] Funny. People come into your life—by accident. Strangers. Next thing, you know them better than your own family. Then—they're gone.

REBEL: Ah gotta go, Kathy.

KATHY: I know.

REBEL: Ah've felt awfully guilty this last week.

KATHY: What about?

REBEL: You, honey. Guilty as hell.

KATHY: Don't. I was happy to have somebody here, hearing about Steve that way.

REBEL: Just . . . somebody?

KATHY: You.

[*There is a short silence. They look at each other.* REBEL *moves towards her. She turns away towards the kitchen.*]

I'd better start cooking.

REBEL: Kathy, Ah'm sorry to disappoint you, but Ah ain't hungry.

KATHY: Yes, it's been stinking hot all day. Take away anybody's appetite. Would you like a drink?

REBEL: Ah was hopin' you'd suggest it.

KATHY: You didn't have to wait to be asked. It never occurred to me we were strangers.

REBEL: We ain't strangers.

KATHY: Aren't we?

[*Again* REBEL *moves tentatively towards her. Again she evades him.*]

REBEL: There's a drop of bourbon in the kitchen. Mind if Ah tickle that?

KATHY: Let's both tickle the bourbon.

[REBEL *goes into the kitchen.*]

Got a family, Rebel? You never talk about them.

REBEL: Nah. Ah try to forget 'em.

KATHY: You didn't get on?

REBEL: Well, my Ma an' Pa was almost all the time in a state of war an' us kids was out there in no man's land coppin' it from both sides.

KATHY: Happens a lot.

REBEL: Yeah. Didn't help matters much, my ol' man bein' a nut case.

[*Pause.*]

KATHY: Not—really mad?

REBEL: Well, they never locked him up, if that's what you mean. But he was nuts, all right. Not all the time . . . just . . . [*looking at the bottle*] especially when he was on this stuff. On the whisky . . .

[REBEL *brings the bottle, two glasses and some water out to the table. They sit down while he pours the drinks.*]

Hey, you never did make that cup of tea.

KATHY: I can drink cups of tea when I'm on my own.

[*Pause.*]

What did your parents fight about?

REBEL: Mostly, Ah guess, about the old man drinkin'. What they was really fightin' about, Ah think, was bein' locked in the same cage together. Usually weekends they'd do their fightin', 'cause that's when he'd do his drinkin'. Ma'd start naggin' him with an awful mean tongue, an' he'd start sayin' her family was nothin' but a gang o' rustlers an' moonshiners, an' she'd come back with some pretty tellin' comments about his family, an' if he was losin' the argument, which he mostly did, he'd start bouncin' her off the walls of the kitchen an' us kids'd get whumped just for bein' there. Then he'd get quiet an' mean an' get his shotgun an' say he was gonna finish us all off then shoot hisself. All Ah wanted him to do was reverse the order. He'd herd us into the bedroom, make us kneel down at the beds an' say our prayers. 'Now, kiss each other goodbye,' he'd say. Then he'd say: 'close your eyes.' Ah can still hear the clicks as he cocked both barrels. Ah'd look out the corner of an eye an' those barrels'd be pointin' right at me. Ah'd think, this time he's gonna do it . . . But he never did. [*Chuckling*] Obviously, eh? Then he'd say he'd changed his mind—and he'd go down into his tool shed where he'd have a bottle hid from Ma. Then Ma'd put us to bed an' we wouldn't see him till morning, except once, Ah remember, the shotgun went off down in the shed, an' Ma kept sayin': 'Thank God! Thank God! He's killed hisself.' But—no such luck. He only shot a hole in the wall of the shed. [*Changing tone*] Ah should practise waitin' on table. Which side do Ah serve the drinks?

KATHY: Right side. Food on the left. Take away the same sides.

REBEL: That's simple enough. [*Holding up his glass*] Cheerio! Is that what you say?

KATHY: No . . . but I suppose it's what we're saying.

REBEL: Cheerio, then.

KATHY: Cheerio.

[*They drink.*]

REBEL: Ah guess Ah deserved my share of spankin', like any kid . . . but he couldn't do it like other fathers, you know, just his hand or his belt. No, he'd have to use his boots, or a goddam great lump of wood, or what he really liked was to bail me up in the barn an' lay into me with a rawhide whip. God, how Ah hated that son of a bitch. How Ah still hate him.

[*Pause.*]

An' Ah'm still scared of him. Stupid, ain't it? Ah could lick him now, but Ah'm still scared of him.

[*Pause.*]

KATHY: Does . . . [*touching his hand*] does your Mum write to you?

REBEL: [*shaking his head*] They don't know where Ah am. One day—Ah was fifteen, just turned fifteen—he came at me with that rawhide whip. Instead of standing there like a mouse waitin' for a snake, Ah ran. An' Ah kept on runnin' until Ah got to LA.

KATHY: How'd you live?

REBEL: Pinchin' stuff. Doin' odd jobs here an' there. In LA Ah met an ol' fairy man who took me to stay at his place. You've never seen an apartment like he had. Of course he wanted to fiddle at bit, but Ah got even. Ah pinched about two hundred dollars an' found mahself a boardin' house. Then Ah worked on a gasoline pump for a while. Then soda jerk. Then . . . Ah dunno, kinda got mixed up with a bunch of bums like mahself. We used to take turns walkin' round Pershing Square at night, catch the eye of a fairy boy, take him in the park. The rest o' the gang'd be waitin' behind the trees, an' we'd roll him.

KATHY: Oh no.

REBEL: [*mildly*] Hell, Ah had to live.

[*A slight pause.*]

KATHY: You wouldn't go back to that sort of life, would you?

REBEL: Rollin' fairy boys?

KATHY: Well, not necessarily that. I mean crime in general.

REBEL: Nah. Most of the guys Ah used to bum around with are in and out of the pen like it was a revolvin' door. What kinda life's that? How's your drink?

KATHY: [*who hasn't touched it*] It smells fine.

REBEL: Tastes even better.

KATHY: [*wrinkling her nose*] Tastes dreadful. But I'm going to drink it.

REBEL: Why? We've got—

KATHY: Advokaat?

REBEL: Guess that'll be here a long time, eh?

KATHY: It'll go down the sink as soon as you leave. [*Raising her glass*] To . . . old acquaintances?

REBEL: [*raising his glass*] To us.

KATHY: *What* us? To you and me.

[*Neither of them drink.*]

Rebel?

REBEL: Yuh?

KATHY: Why is it . . . ? [*Making a fresh start*] I want to ask you something.

REBEL: Sure.

KATHY: I don't know how to.

REBEL: Just pretend Ah ain't here.

KATHY: That's not very hard.

[*Silence.*]

Why haven't you ever made a pass at me?

REBEL: That's what you wanted to ask me?

KATHY: Yes.

[*Pause.*]

REBEL: First night here, night of—

KATHY: Yes, I know. But we were strangers then. It's a bit different making a pass at a stranger, isn't it?

REBEL: Hadn't thought of that, but Ah guess you're right. With a stranger it doesn't matter if the whole thing blows up. Just go an' find yourself another stranger. [*Drinking*] Did . . . did you want me to make a pass at you?

KATHY: I didn't say that. But—staying here—together in the same flat— most blokes would've.

REBEL: You did have that bad news about your husband.

KATHY: Is that what stopped you?

REBEL: Partly that.

KATHY: But something else too?

REBEL: Yeah.

KATHY: What?

    [*Pause.*]

REBEL: Guess . . . guess Ah was scared . . .

KATHY: Scared? Of me?

REBEL: Not exactly . . . *of* you . . .

KATHY: You're not—scared of women?

REBEL: [*laughing*] Hell, no. Well, only a bit. Not enough to . . . you know . . .

KATHY: Then what were you scared of?

REBEL: Scared that if it back-fired you'd—kick me out. Where would Ah have gone?

    [*Pause.*]

KATHY: You sure figure things out.

REBEL: Ah'm sorry.

KATHY: It's all right. I understand.

REBEL: But Ah had another reason too.

KATHY: And what was that?

REBEL: Ah like you, Kathy. Ah didn't want to do nothin' to hurt you, or upset you.

KATHY: You . . . you really like me?

REBEL: More'n any girl Ah ever met—or ever expect to.

KATHY: Thank you, Rebel.

REBEL: Kathy, Ah'm holdin' back. Ah don't just like you. Ah'm . . . Ah'm fond of you. Ah'm fond of you like Ah could burst with it.

KATHY: Why didn't you tell me?

REBEL: Ah guess saying goodbye's gonna be tough enough anyhow. Ah didn't want to make it too tough.

KATHY: Too late, Rebel.

REBEL: You . . . you're fond of me?

    [KATHY *nods.* REBEL *reaches out and touches her cheek. She takes his hand and presses it to her face. They stand up and kiss.* REBEL *picks her up and carries her towards the bedroom. There is a knock at the door.*]

  Goddam! Who's that?

KATHY: I'll have to see. Go inside.

KENNETH 'SEAFORTH' MACKENZIE

from *The Refuge*

We reached the Cross. Light seemed to swallow us; the coloured glare of the neon signs made the face of humanity into a livid mask. By contrast with the empty city streets we had just left, the place was still restless with life, sleepless and hectic, a gleaming nightmare of faces and eyes seen as it were through greenish-red water, drowning. We had turned cautiously left into Darlinghurst Road, the street of greatest activity at any hour. At this time of night people were walking in the roadway without care, and the clearest sound, rising above the throb of engines and the scraps of music like torn flags in a wind, was the intermittent blare of taxi-cab horns. When we were forced to halt for some seconds at the Springfield Avenue corner, the voices reached us; and I thought again, as always, how there must be less English spoken in this quarter than in any other equivalent area in the whole country. As the world's most thickly-populated district of comparable size, it had long ago become a refuge within a refuge. Every foreigner who landed from Sydney harbour or stepped to earth at Mascot aerodrome knew of the Cross already, and went there as though drawn by an irresistible passion, there to fade—if he chose—into a consoling anonymity until, like the beetle or the butterfly from its chrysalis, he was ready to emerge, full of plans for conquest.

Irma had come here from her ship, she told me; and I knew she had never lived anywhere else in Sydney, never sought or thought of another refuge until she was driven to it; for here she felt at first she had reached her Ultima Thule, the end and the beginning of the world. Like thousands of others in the years just before the second world-war and during it, she felt the safety of the place, its air of plenty, the security of many tongues, most of which she herself knew, and the more animal security of the herd actuated by one itching idea, which was, as I had learned with dismay and a sort of shame, to outwit the Australian hosts in every way, at every turn in every affair, however small. It was when I myself had become a dupe, a voluntary victim of this almost unconscious intention striking at my most real life, my integrity and my very self—it was then that I had been driven, by a force beyond analysis and so beyond proper control, to act.

'Thank God for the Cross,' Hubble was murmuring; and he seemed to have forgotten the matter to which he had been giving such cold, intense thought two minutes earlier. 'Where would we poor policemen be without it? Crime—I dote on it. Don't you?'

'Like you,' I said, 'I live by it. If it interests me, it is for reasons you would not understand.'

'Ho-ho-ho.'

At the end of Darlinghurst Road we turned right, and the car's head-lights swept through sudden comparative gloom and silence. Through the cleared half-moon of glass before me, on which the windscreen-wiper was working with awkward urgency, I could see the wet street above which the night brooded, heavy with rain. We were going downhill now, to the maze of dead-end streets at water-level on the city side of Rushcutters Bay; we were nearly home. Again the despair, the fruitless sense of completion, the loneliness, came upon me, as for days past they had done hereabouts when in the small hours I made my way back, usually on foot from the Cross, to my own flat night after night, knowing that only a wall divided from each other the only two people I had ever fully loved, disinterestedly with my mind as well as with my heart and, indeed, all my flesh, all my spirit, my whole self. Now the two flats would be empty.

'Right at the end still, isn't it?' Hubble said doubtfully.

'Right at the end, on the right.'

'On the very edge of the water.'

'Almost in the water. The harbour-side foundation is carried straight ahead to make a tidal breakwater for the swimming pool belonging to the building.'

We ran gently down the last incline, almost as steep as a ramp, and stopped before the dimly-lighted front entrance. When he cut off the engine, a profound silence enveloped us emphasized by the faint contracting clicks of hot metal cooling under the bonnet. This was one of the quietest parts of the whole city, for the streets were all *culs-de-sac*, and there was no passage for through traffic within half a mile. Cars could not even approach at speed without risk, and the noise of accelerated departures up the steep street was always a diminishing noise; nor did we whose flats faced north-east, looking out across the vast beauty and peace of the outer harbour, hear any sounds of street traffic at all—nothing but the hush and splash of the ocean, landlocked and serene, against the break-water and the boat-house piles, the grating screams of the grey gulls shearing for ever across the sky's huge disclosure, and the mild and distant sounds of the ceaseless traffic of the sea as the ships came and went, by night and by day . . . Yes, it was a place of peace, where the spirit could, if it would, be still.

This time I led the way, and Maybee stayed in the darkness of the rear seat, smoking in silence. The caretaker's small flat was on the floor below street level, and while Hubble waited I went down the single unlit flight of stairs, and rang the bell. It was a bad hour in which to wake a man out of his first sleep. For some time there was no answer. I tossed up my keys to Hubble and told him to go up to the third landing and let himself into the flat next to mine. A deep silence filled the building, for it was almost one o'clock, and though we who were tenants lived near the Cross we had, for the most part, suburban habits. Irma was the only one, besides myself, who had kept late hours; and now, of course, time would never again mean any more to her than she meant to time, or to me. She was gone, and sometimes during this long night my own desire to live had wavered, as though willing to be gone with her; and only the thought of Alan, so young and proud and bright with happiness and intelligence, had steadied and fed the flame of that desire when it seemed to weaken within me.

I realized now, as I listened to Hubble's ascending steps soften into silence on the carpeted stair, that never again would I return home in the hours after midnight to find her lying on the blue rug, open-eyed and quite motionless before her low-tuned wireless receiver, listening to foreign broadcasts; never again would she pull me down on to the floor beside her, roughly and without a word, and invariably begin to rub my hair with almost ruthless fingers until, although refreshed by this and by her bodily nearness, I could bear neither without moving for a moment longer.

Standing down there in the dark, I felt very tired. No sound of movement could be heard from Alec's little flat, and I pressed the bell-button a second time, holding it down a little longer. The abrupt opening of the door inwards, away from my face, startled me, but in spite of the sensation of profound weariness, I had command of myself; and in any case, I am not a nervous man. Alec's daughter, prepared I think to be indignant, stood against the light of the small entrance hall, wearing like a cloak a woollen dressing-gown that partly concealed her winter pyjamas. She was still half-asleep.

'It's Lloyd Fitzherbert, Emmy,' I said quietly. 'I'd like to see your father for a minute.'

''S asleep, Mr. Fitz,' she struggled to say. 'Won't I do?'

Alec had no wife alive, but had got his job of caretaker on the under-standing that his daughter shared the work and the living quarters with him. He once told me she was better than any wife, as she would not bother to quarrel with him and took his mild orders obediently; and it is certain that this was one of the best-cared-for buildings in the whole rabbit-warren of a residential district in which it unobtrusively stood. It is no less certain that I never knew a young woman, as generally presentable as Emmy, who gave such an immediate impression of having no private life of her own whatever.

'I think you had better get him up for me,' I said; and though we spoke only in casual murmurs, our voices seemed to echo up the stair-well with a ghastly hollowness, like the voices of conspirators in a cellar.

She went away from the door, and I heard her call her father in a hushed and regretful tone, and heard his sudden answer in the brisk voice of a man who wishes to be thought wide awake and expectant. A minute later he came himself, owl-eyed in the light, hitching his dressing-gown about his shoulders.

'What's trouble, Mr. Fitz?' he said in a surprised voice.

I told him, and explained that I wanted his master-key. I did not tell him Hubble had used my own duplicate and was already in the flat next to mine.

'Don't go to bed for a few minutes,' I said. 'There is a police detective with me who may want to ask you a few purely formal questions, as you are in charge here. It is for him I want the key.'

Speechless, he took a ring of keys from somewhere behind the door, looked at them and pushed them about until he could isolate a particular one. I saw he was well awake by now; when he spoke at last, it was with his own peculiar intonation and emphasis which always put me in mind of some radio comedian I had once heard on a B.B.C. programme.

'*That* one is *her* key,' he said in his queer falsetto voice. 'There *is* no *master* key, Mr. Fitz, but *that* one is *hers*. Or . . . should I *say*—er—*was?* Dear me. This is *indeed* a dreadful *thing*, and *you* and your *boy* and *her* such *friends*. Dear me, what a dreadful *thing*. I do *hope*, Mr. Fitz, it doesn't get in the *papers*, I mean to *say*, the *flats*, you know—it's the *letting* what I'm *thinking* of, Mr. Fitz. People don't *like* it, goodness knows *why*, but they *don't*.'

'We'll keep the address out of it, Alec,' I said. 'Just wait for a minute or two, and I'll call down to you if Sergeant Hubble wants you.'

'As you *say*, Mr. Fitz,' he said rather doubtfully; and I left him there in the doorway with his pinched, precise face turned up as he watched me go with some anxiety, and began the climb up that so-familiar stairway to the third landing and—as I hoped—the beginning of the last act in this drama of my own devising, which would be almost at an end when I brought Alan home. It was a heavy and an interminable ascent, for while my will led me up and on with desperate determination, my whole body was in open rebellion now, and I had actually to resist a strong urge to sit down on the top step of the first flight and lean my forehead against the coldness of the pale-green wall. Only the knowledge that Hubble was in her flat, alone, drove me on without a pause. When I reached the landing I saw the lighted doorway, and saw his bulky shadow move slowly across the slab of light on the corridor carpet outside it. Without hesitation I went in to join him. One look about, as I entered the big room from the entrance lobby, assured me that all was as it should be. Hubble, very solid and serious in his heavy overcoat, stood still now in the middle of the deep-blue carpet.

His regard met mine without suspicion, with—I thought —an expression of simple compassion at last.

'There's a note for you on the radio,' he said. 'I want you to tell me, for the sake of formality, if it's her handwriting. If you have any letters of hers you've saved, you'd better show me one. Just formality, you know. The note about settles it, I think.'

I took up the note with both hands. In these matters you cannot be too careful, particularly under the very eye of the police; and that folded sheet of paper, did he but know it, already had my finger-prints on it, as well as Irma's. I did not enjoy this active deceiving of a man who had long been my good friend, but I had determined that it should be he, and no one else from his branch if possible, who would be with me at this moment, for now much depended upon his casual goodwill towards me. It must be understood that I was thinking throughout not of myself and my own safety, but of Alan. Once determined upon, once begun, the business must not be botched through any over-confidence of mine, for the boy's whole well-being depended upon me now.

Our friends, as well as those who love us much, are of course our easiest dupes. I had recently tasted this duplicity myself, and was as yet no judge upon it; but it was then that, by the action of that terrible and subtle poison, part of my inner self had withered and died, in a space of minutes, like green leaves in a quick fire. Not for the world would I have had Hubble experience, through my own action, anything like this.

I read the note. Though I knew it by heart, I read it again with an irresistible fascination now, for now, after so many months, it had true and fatal meaning. That meaning I myself had infused into the half-hysterical words so clearly and neatly written:

LLOYD *darling, I have no world of my own and can't can't live in yours any more. I look at the water of the beautiful harbour and it calls me all night and day even when I sleep. So I am going. This time it is true. I thank you for loving me so kindly and I kiss you*

*Goodbye Fitzi darling—*IRMA

After handling the paper a little more, turning it over as though seeking some added word, some more definite explanation of that least natural of all human actions, suicide, I held it out to Hubble.

'You'll want this, I suppose,' I said. 'It's certainly her handwriting.'

Without speaking he took it, folded it, and put it neatly into his large wallet. Then he walked to the window, and from the light folding table that always stood there, at which we had taken so many good and happy meals, he lifted up the empty glass tube by sliding a pencil into it. Turning back to the room, he waved it briefly at me.

'Morphine hydrochloride,' he said conversationally. 'Quarter grains. I wonder how much there was in this? Did you know she had the stuff?'

'I knew she used to have it. She used it with a needle, she told me, years ago when she had some painful trouble—I think she brought it into the country with her. A great many of them—the refugees—did that. They carted the stuff about with them wherever they went in Europe, after nineteen thirty-three, I believe—only it was usually one of the cyanides. In small glass capsules that could be hidden, or even swallowed unbroken and recovered. You will know all about it, I expect. She had one of those too, but I threw it into the harbour. About the morphine, she told me she had lost that years ago. She must have come across it again since. I could not disbelieve her, anyhow. Possibly she got more. They used to get those things easily enough from Jewish chemists in Europe. You know what the casual traffic in it was like here after nineteen thirty-nine. They were the people responsible, the refugees. And it all began because they were frightened even of Australia. They made sure they had a way out. Apparently she did too. If I had known she had that . . .'

I left it to him to finish the sentence, for although not a nervous man, I am a bad hand at telling lies.

'If you'd known, she might be still alive, you mean?' Hubble said softly. 'Well, Fitz—maybe. But in view of that note I doubt it. She meant business, Fitz. But why in God's name do they do it?'

I sighed. He was not, in his manly kindness of heart, to know that it was a sigh of relief, as well as of utter weariness and that sick despair which I could neither understand nor fight down. All was now ended—all but the task of getting Alan home and telling him, somehow without lying, of Irma's fate; and such was my unforeseen relief at Hubble's last remarks that this task did not now seem so hard in prospect. Often before tonight I had consoled the boy's grief and hidden my own caused by the sight of his; I could do it again, I could do it as long as I lived, for this love knows no exhaustion, asks no return; it is like the spring of water near Hill Farm, in the mountains: no man has ever known it to falter or dry and cease from flowing.

'I've looked round,' Hubble said. 'There's that coffee cup on the radio—can you find me a bottle of some sort, I'll take the dregs for Maybee. It's likely she took the stuff in that.'

In the kitchen, off the small passage that opened upon the service-staircase outside, I looked about for a small container. The complete tidiness of the place, scrubbed and immaculate as though never used, gave me again that subtle feeling of pleasure I had always had when looking at the indications of her manner of living; for she was tidy and clean to a truly exquisite degree, yet in so casual a manner that one never seemed to catch her at it. This was especially true of her person, though her natural physical perfection was nothing at all like the aseptic and repellent American magazine-advertisement sort, but arose and emanated rather from an abundance of good health and her use of leisure for being idle than from the pursuit either of health or of leisure so miserably character-istic of the age. I never knew a woman with her capacity for immobility and ease. Like her strange, animal ability to sleep at will, from which I think it sprang, it was at first disconcerting, though in time I learned its virtue and lost my earlier desire to make her move and speak; to ask—like any love-sick boy—'What are you thinking about?' Her reply, which in another woman might have sounded foolishly affected, was the simple truth: 'I think of nothing at all. My mind is a blank, so do not talk to me, darling.'

I could hear that voice with its light, strong, un-English inflections and accent as I opened the doors of the cupboard under the shining sink. It was so clear in my hearing, memory was so faithful and vivid, that an inadver-tent thrill of intense, unreasonable happiness passed through my nerves and seemed to lodge like an obstruction in my throat, bringing a sting of tears, while I bent down to search for one of the small brandy flasks she kept for replenishments, to lace her morning and evening coffee with the spirits. I had forgotten she was dead.

'Fine,' Hubble said, when I took the little flat bottle in to him. 'Did she drink much of this, by the way?'

'Two tablespoons a day,' I said. 'One in the morning, one in the evening, always in coffee. She considered it a sort of tonic medicine. Otherwise, she drank wine sometimes with meals. Not always. She was as abstemious as—as I am myself.'

Hubble laughed softly as he drained the porcelain coffee cup with delicate precision into the flask.

'What a nice sober couple you must have been, then,' he said. 'Personally, I could do with a drink right now.'

'When you are ready,' I said, 'we can go next door and you can have some whisky, if that will do. I have the caretaker waiting, if you want to see him.'

'Fine,' he said again without much interest. 'Better see him, I suppose. He may be able to give us some idea of the time.'

While he took the empty cup and its saucer to the kitchen to rinse them—for, like some fat men and not all police officers, he was a neat and tidy fellow in all things—I looked in at the bedroom. It was, of course, just as I had seen it last, like the rest of the flat, not many hours before. On the white dressing-table lay her hairbrush which I had picked up from where it fell out of her hands; and I thought I could see still on the bedcover the faint imprint of her half-conscious form, though I had smoothed the ruffled material after I got her off the bed and into a chair in the big room. Neither of us would ever wake again in that firm and comfortable bed, as until recently we had so often done when the light of dawn warned me that it was time to go softly back to my own flat. I supposed that to the rest of the world it would have seemed a fantastic marriage, had the facts of it been known; but as it was it suited us both very well, for there was something innocently clandestine about it besides the freedom of movement made possible by those two separate and adjacent establishments, each of which one of us commanded without question.

Standing there just inside the doorway, breathing her most intimate atmosphere for the last time, while she lay cold and lifeless in an airtight refrigeration chamber, a body among other unwanted bodies each in its narrow deathly little cell, I decided that Alec should arrange with the owners, if possible, to purchase the entire furnishings of the flat for what they cared to pay, so that like certain others in the building it could be rented furnished. I would probably never enter or see into it again, and I was not inclined to have anything more to do with what had belonged to her, even though many of the material things I myself had given her cried out softly to be remembered and taken away. Miss Werther could look after it—that would be better still, better than Alec. For the rest, all was ended tonight, all, and there must be no loose threads. On this I was absolutely determined, just as I was determined that Alan too should never come in here again. There must be no loose threads for him either, for youth can become entangled in such things more easily even than maturity, to its own confusion.

I became aware that Hubble had returned to the room behind me and was waiting, so I switched off the bedside lamp at the door switch and closed the door. As I turned to him I saw again that look of simple compassion in his blue friendly eyes.

'Shall we go?' he said. 'There's nothing more, I think.'

The place suddenly felt dead and empty, as though no one had ever lived there. I looked at none of it as we let ourselves out; I would have welcomed the suggestion of a haunting ghost, but there was no ghost, nothing but a still emptiness containing nothing, expecting no one.

There was still much to be done, and I clung to that thought. When Hubble was settled in my flat, I went down and called Alec from the first landing, apologizing for having kept him out of bed for so long. He followed me up in silence. No doubt the thought of meeting a policeman professionally in some way outraged his law-abiding soul. But Hubble was all kindliness and brevity now, when he questioned him.

'I heard *her* wireless,' Alec said in a more confident tone. 'That would *be* at seven p.m., *sir*, because I had just gone *up* to *look* at one of the *off-peak* hot-water *tanks*, and it was coming *down* I heard *it*, quite a while after Mr. Fitz, I should say Mr. Fitz*herbert*, had gone off to the office, which is why I remember, for as you know Mr. Fitz and Alan was very friendly with Miss Martin, poor thing, and they was always in and out of one another's flats when at home. Oh—I hope I do not divulge unwanted information, Mr. Fitz?'

'Go ahead, Alec,' I said. 'Did you hear the wireless stop?'

'No, sir, but one of her *friends* came, and when he *knocked* he could not *get* an answer, so *he* came downstairs to *me* and says was Miss Martin *out?* and I says not that I am aware of, because mostly I hear the tenants *come* and *go*, and he says "*Well*," he says, "she does not *answer* her door so I presume," he says, "she has gone *out*, though *she* was *expecting* me." So I said to him, "*Well . . .*"'

'What time was this?' Hubble asked gently. Alec, interrupted, looked confused for a moment; his fixed stare over Hubble's head wavered and came back to the present.

'About eight o'clock I think it was,' he said.

'And what was the visitor like?' Hubble asked.

'Like, sir? *He* was one of these *foreigners*, very foreign in his way of *speaking*, with a big dark mo and glasses.'

'Kalmikoff,' I said. 'He's a musician, an irritating fellow she seemed to have known for years. One of those fugitives from Communist Russia who become rabidly communist the moment they reach a country of refuge. Like most of them, he is quite futile and harmless—irritating to talk with, but an excellent musician. You may have heard of him, even if you have not heard him play. He is a violinist.'

'I may have heard of him,' Hubble said. 'As for music, I know nothing about it. Did he stay or go?' he asked Alec.

'Him? Oh—*he* went away, sir, and rather *angry* I should say *he* was, muttering to himself in some foreign lingo. *I* went upstairs again, but Miss *Martin* had turned her wireless *off*, and if she has gone *out*, I thought, why, *she* has been pretty quiet about it. Most likely she didn't want to see *this* chap, I thought, but too kind to say so. She was always very kind in that way, sir. And that is all I know.'

His information could not have satisfied me more if I had dictated it to him myself. Fortunate fellow, he would return to sleep not knowing that when he had heard her wireless tuned to Radio Luxembourg—the only foreign station I knew how to find—Irma was already dead in the early darkness of the placid harbour beyond the breakwater; while I, not she, had heard his quick steps softly pass that door and continue the descent towards dinner and a peaceful evening with the papers and the commercial broadcasting programmes. Before Kalmikoff banged at the door, before Alec returned to listen, I had gone by the way I came after my earlier and more ostentatious departure.

'Thank you,' Hubble said. 'This is quite helpful. And now you had better be off to bed—catch up on your beauty-sleep, lucky man.'

Alec made a sudden clucking noise, his queer way of laughing, and went towards the door, saying, '*Beauty*-sleep. That's a good one. Wait till Emmy *hears* that one. Good night, sir, good night Mr. Fitz*herbert* . . . *Beauty*-sleep!'

He let himself out and clucked softly downstairs. Hubble smiled at the closed door while I set out whisky and a soda-water siphon on the book-table beside my reading chair where he sat, and poured us a stiff peg each. As he took the tumbler, he motioned with his head at the telephone on my work-table in the corner near the windows.

'Hadn't you better ring your office?' he said. 'Then we'll go and get that boy of yours out of the clutches of the law. He must have cooled off enough by now.'

'What about Maybee?' I said. 'Would he join us?'

'Don't bother him. He's most probably asleep, if I know the doc. A hard-working, hard-tongued chap, but one of the best. Now.'

I went to the table and unlocked the only drawer in the whole place that had a key to it. It contained my small revolver, which I had bought and had licensed in my early, youthful days on police rounds, and had never used; and weighted down by this were some half-dozen letters from Irma which for reasons of somewhat weakly sentiment I had kept, meaning always to destroy them yet somehow never being quite willing to part with them or anything else that had been hers. I had never looked at them again. The most recent one, more than three years old, I took out and carried to Hubble where he sat holding his glass near his mouth, enjoying the whisky and at the same time smoking his pipe for all the world as though he were seated by his own fireside. I was pleased to observe the finality of his relaxation; it made my own mind easier, and I filled and lighted a pipe for myself. Then I went back to the table and sat down, and took up the telephone receiver to speak to Blake. As I did so, it occurred to me that I had never had and now never would have that telephone call on which my whole future had seemed to hang; and this I took as a warning not to count on the preconceived mechanics of a carefully devised situation when such a situation depends however lightly upon tides and men and other factors not mechanical.

'Thanks,' Hubble said, coming over when I had given Blake the brief story. ('Can't you do better than a bloody suicide, Fitz? Give us blood, man,' Blake said when I had finished.) 'That puts it beyond doubt.'

He was holding out the letter, looking down at me, his fat, strong face serenely quizzical and apologetic. We met each other's gaze for some seconds; then he smiled.

'Don't forget what I said earlier. One day you can tell me the whole story. You can answer all the questions you know I haven't asked you . . . And now let's go and get that precious boy of yours.'

It was then that I decided to write this down, as time allowed, partly to ease my soul of a burden I had not even then foreseen, partly to help memory shrug off the weight of what is now past and irrevocable. Until I die, it can remain in that locked drawer with the useless revolver and the now meaningless letters from the woman I loved, for whose death may God forgive me in the end.

BETTY ROLAND

'Kings Cross' from *The Devious Being*

Kings Cross with its noise, uneasy crowds, its cheap cafes, beggars, touts and tattered women lurking in the doorways, has always held a strong attraction for me from the first day I had seen it. The Cross was where Guido and I had stayed when we first came to Sydney; it was where Gilda had been conceived, and where I would now begin a new life and forget the old. But the Americans had inundated Sydney and the Cross was their favourite haunt, so there wasn't a flat or a room or a hotel bed that was unoccupied in the whole square mile and my chance of finding a place in which to start my life again seemed remote.

But whatever misfortunes may have befallen me, I have always managed to find a pleasant place to live, even in such an unlikely place as Moscow, where I had been saved from a vermin-infested room on the fringes of the city by the fortunate chance that a friend was due to go on leave to England and offered me her flat. By the time she had returned I was due to go to Leningrad, where the shortage was not so acute, and I had been given a room in a brand new building so recently completed that the ubiquitous bedbugs had not had time to move in.

My luck held good in Sydney. I saw an advertisement in the morning paper, hurried to the address and, to my amazement, there was no queue outside the door and the rent was within my means. I could scarcely believe my luck and it shows the wisdom of never failing to read the daily paper, even the advertisements. I had already found a tenant for the house, but before handing over the keys and moving out, a final distressing event took place.

Early in the year Alan Marshall and his wife had spent a few days with me as they passed through Sydney on their way to Queensland. Alan was going in search of material for his book *These Are My Tribesmen*, and Olive, despite the fact that she was three months pregnant, was going with him for as long as her condition allowed it. It was not very long, and she soon returned to Melbourne, leaving Alan to pursue his search alone. I was in the throes of packing up when he unexpectedly appeared. I was delighted to see him and listened eagerly to his account of the weeks spent with the people of Arnhem Land, how they had accepted him into their tribe and even allowed him to witness their most secret ceremonies.

Still troubled by the memory of Nick and the fair-haired boy, I told him what had happened, knowing he would understand and not condemn. He listened with growing concern on his face, and said it was not love that I had felt for Nick, but a thing of the flesh and not of the spirit, and that my present troubled mood would pass. I was not convinced but lay awake that night while he put up his camp-bed in what had been Guido's study and, presumably, went to sleep.

I must have dozed off because I was disturbed by the sound of his crutches padding across the floor of the big room, the circular room, between us. I listened and a sudden suspicion that he was coming to my room shot through me. It couldn't be, I told myself, it was impossible! But the sound continued, and he came through the door. Neither of us spoke. He drew back the bedclothes and eased himself beside me, while I lay in frozen silence, stunned by the knowledge that the impossible had happened.

I have a deep-seated aversion to physical deformity of any kind. I know it to be reprehensible on my part and reproach myself for being that way, but I cannot bear to look at the twisted limbs and distorted bodies of the handicapped. I have to avert my eyes, and feel ashamed at doing so. And here was this man of whom I was so fond, whom I respected for his gifts as a writer and his undefeated courage, but whose body was a mockery of all that the human body should be. If I rejected him it would tell him that I found him repulsive, if I acquiesced it would be with shrinking flesh, and how could I inflict another wound on this courageous being who had had to endure so much?

As I ran my hands along that poor distorted back and felt the twisted spine, I wept inwardly, not solely for Alan but for myself as well.

He left quite soon after breakfast the following morning. Neither of us alluded in any way to what had happened in the night, but it had cost me a friend. He was always elusive after that and seemed to avoid my eyes, which made me very sad.

Opinions are sharply divided about Kings Cross. It is looked upon as either a modern Gomorrah or a source of endless interest and variety. I belong to the latter category. The place had cast its spell over me when, newly come from Melbourne, I had walked with Guido down that unique half-mile that lies between the top of William Street and the Fountain of El Alamein. Neither the litter on the street, the pornographic shops, the touts and pimps, or the scrofulous old deadbeats with their bottles of cheap wine in any way offended me. On the contrary, I found them all immensely interesting—and still do—so it was inevitable that I should choose the Cross as the place in which to exercise my right as a fully liberated woman. The fact that Guido and Ula were living in Darlinghurst Road may have had something to do with it, and I was glad of their proximity as, contrary to my expectations, I was just as lonely in the Cross as I had been at Castlecrag.

As Norman Haire had said, the place was swarming with men, but the majority were Americans and they, I soon discovered, were only interested in the youngest and least intellectual members of the female sex. I marvelled to see them sitting in the most expensive restaurants, orchids cascading down their bosoms, not knowing which fork or spoon to pick up first, totally overwhelmed by the visitation of these god-like creatures from another world. Of course, I envied them; most women of my age shared my feelings. We wanted the attention, nylon stockings, good manners, good looks and tailored uniforms of Uncle Sam's brave boys who had swept into Sydney like an army of conquerors and claimed the spoils of war.

I find it difficult to reconcile the woman that I am now with the woman of those tumultuous years. I ask myself what it was that drove me to such excesses, what it was that I was searching for, and what did I achieve?

There is no simple answer. Primarily I think that I was searching for a permanent relationship that would replace the one that I had been deprived of, though Kings Cross was not a good place in which to look for it. There was also the strong biological urge, which was fully gratified but brought me no peace or happiness, rather the reverse. All it did was help restore my damaged self-esteem by knowing that I had not lost my power to attract the men. But what kind of men? None of them in any way measured up to the standard Guido had set for me, and with him constantly in front of me, the image could not fade. I should not have come to the Cross, yet being as I am, where else was I to go?

There was another element in the reckless way I went from man to man: a deep inner resentment at having been forced out of the comfortable cocoon of domesticity and into the role of being the sole support of my child. I was now the breadwinner and had to traffic in the marketplace and return with the spoils. In other words, the pay envelope. Having been forced to accept the disadvantages of being a man, was I not then entitled to the advantages? So, when the urge was on me, I was free to gratify it, coldly and dispassionately as a man would do when going to a brothel. In which case, Kings Cross was the place for me to be.

It was confused thinking, self-defeating and extremely hazardous. Even Norman Haire was a little perturbed when I gave him an account of some of my adventures. He warned me of the dangers of VD, of which I was fully aware and which on a number of occasions prompted me to make the biological urge give way to caution. For example, there was the Norwegian sailor Olaf Pedersen.

He was standing on the corner of Market Street waiting for a tram—there were still trams in Sydney then—and was obviously very drunk. He leaned against a light pole and had a wilted carnation in his hand. I had been at a Christmas party; George Edwards and Nell Stirling made it a standard practice. Everyone had been there, everyone who was in any way associated with their production team, and everyone with the exception of myself had appeared to be having a marvellous time. I had gone alone, which always made me feel depressed.

As a mark of their esteem I had been given a place at the top table, presided over by Nell and George, who distributed smiles and goodwill to everyone. Two by two, the couples got up to dance until there was only George and myself and a row of empty chairs. He looked decidedly uneasy, glanced at me and seemed to be on the point of asking me to dance, but I ended his dilemma by getting up and going to the powder room. I didn't shed any tears of self-pity, though I felt like doing so. Instead, I made my way through the crowd and left. And there on the corner of the street was Olaf Pedersen, all six feet of him, propped against the pole, the wilted carnation in his hand.

'Six thousand miles away from Norvay, and I vish that I vos dere,' he proclaimed in a loud voice.

Something touched my heart. He was so lonely, so unhappy, and so was I.

'What's the matter, sailor?' I asked. He was about to reply when a taxi came along. By a miracle, it was empty. 'Would you like to come with me?'

His face lit up with astonishment but he lost no time in joining me and we were on our way to the Cross.

It happened a long time ago and the details are now blurred, but I can remember helping him up the stairs and making him drink black coffee. Of course, he was intent on going to bed with me, but I had no similar wish. He found it difficult to understand my motive in refusing him but gradually he sobered up a little and grew less aggressive. He asked about myself and prowled about the room, picking up a book and pausing at Gilda's picture hanging on the wall, and said 'That's your bulwark'. I agreed.

He was a member of the crew of an oil tanker, just about the least desirable and most dangerous occupation any seaman can engage in when a war such as the present one was raging. He was due to sail the following day and I watched him stumble down the stairs and felt sorry I had let him go uncomforted. Months afterwards, I had a letter from him. He was then on the Atlantic run and wrote rather wistfully about the time we met in Sydney and wished 'dat he vas dere.' I never heard from him again and the chance that a torpedo from a German submarine had silenced him is good.

Norman Haire commended me for my discretion. 'Norwegian sailors are notorious for having syphilis,' he said.

Then there was the American Sergeant of Marines. Troop ships and naval vessels were frequently anchored off Rushcutters Bay and the men would be ferried ashore on cutters that ran a shuttle service to the jetty at the foot of Ithaca Road, which meant that they had to pass the door of The Raymond on their way up to the Cross and again as they returned. One night, as I was walking down Elizabeth Bay Road, I became aware of heavy footsteps coming after me. Those were civilised days, despite the war, and the sound of pursuing footsteps did not chill a woman's blood, nor did the voice that said, 'Hi miss, what's the hurry? Got to catch a train or sumpin?'

All I did was walk a little faster. 'Gee, you must be training for a race,' continued the impudent voice. By now he was walking level with me. He was a hulking figure with a roguish look on his quite attractive face, a cap on the side of his head and massive combat boots ringing on the pavement.

We were now at the point where the road swings to the right and continues its downward course towards Ithaca Road. The Raymond was only a few feet away. There was nothing to prevent me from answering that roguish smile and taking him inside, but something in me said: 'Don't!' It was as though a warning bell had rung, so I crossed the road until I reached the door. 'What's the matter? You got a husband or sumthin' in there?' he asked. 'Something,' I replied. 'And I'll bet it's pretty good at that,' were his final words as I put the key in the lock. He would probably have passed any Wasserman test with honours, not that I will ever know.

It was a different story with Heinrich von Hamburgh. That wasn't his name, but he insisted that it was. It was VE Day, the war in Europe was finally at an end and I was sitting rather dejectedly in a tram after spending the evening among the frenzied crowd that was celebrating victory. I was dejected because, once again, I had been made aware of my solitary state— it is difficult to celebrate anything by oneself. The paper hats, the flags, the coloured streamers had made me feel depressed, so I failed to notice the man at the far end of the tram who stared at me and followed me as I got out. He said: 'Goodnight', and I looked at him for the first time.

He was dressed in a dark blue sweater and dark pants; the sweater had a crew neck which made me think he was a seaman of some sort, but I was mistaken. He had been released that day from the concentration camp in which he had spent the past four years as an enemy alien.

'Four years without a woman,' so he told me as we sat on the top of a low stone wall on the corner of Macleay Street. He had noticed me in the tram and thought 'wonderful woman type' and decided he would try his luck with me.

The thought of being the woman who would experience the pent-up force of a man who had been deprived for so long excited me, but I was wary and evaded him. He pleaded with me to change my mind. How he pleaded, and with what eloquence! There was something of the poet in him, which further helped his cause, so my resistance grew steadily less and eventually gave way. The warning signal may have sounded, but I did not listen to it. Not that I got venereal disease in any of its forms, but I did get a man who refused to be dismissed when I had had enough of him.

He would wait for me as I came home, would be lurking at the corner of the street as I went out, would come knocking at the door when I wanted to work, and I grew afraid to look out the window in case I saw him staring at me from the fire-escape. I went to the police, but got little sympathy.

'What's he done? Assaulted you? Do you want to lay a charge?'

'No. He follows me about.'

The answer was a shrug and a withering glance.

Once we were walking in Victoria Street and he pointed to the basement of one of the dilapidated buildings there. Evidently that was where he had a room. He tried every way he knew to persuade me to go down the steps with him, but a sudden panic made me refuse to do so. I don't know why I felt that sense of menace; he had never been violent, just persistent, a nuisance more than anything else. But something evil seemed to emanate from that darkened room. I could picture nameless horrors, and tried to break away, but he held me firmly by the arm. Then a taxi came along and I hailed it. The grip on my arm slackened enough for me to break away and open the taxi door. He leaped in after me and I had the wit to tell the driver to take me to the nearest police station. That had the desired effect. Heinrich von Hamburgh leapt out as smartly as he had leapt in and the last I saw of him was standing on the kerb staring after the taxi as it drove away.

I never saw him again. I sometimes wondered why the threat of the police was enough to scare him away. It might have had something to do with his recent release from the concentration camp, that he was under surveillance and might be sent back to Germany if he proved troublesome. What if he had got drunk that night and been arrested with the same result. What did it matter to me? I was free of him and had been taught a sharp lesson.

It was not a pretty incident and I only record it because it illustrates the kind of folly a 'fully liberated' woman can be guilty of. Not every woman, however liberated, would behave with the reckless disregard of consequences that I displayed during those frenzied war years, nor would I advise her to—she might lack 'kind beneficent Jupiter' to watch over her! How I managed to emerge unscathed I do not know, but I did, and I can't help feeling that I became a better person because of the things I learned about my fellow creatures in the process. Be that as it may, it explains why Kings Cross does not surprise or repel me; it is an integral part of myself.

I did not tell Norman Haire about Heinrich von Hamburgh. He was busily engaged in packing up prior to his return to Harley Street.

SUMNER LOCKE ELLIOTT

'What'll I do with my rubber?' from *Fairyland*

Nobody was really prepared for the peace that came with such suddenness following the fire over Hiroshima; no one was adjusted after nearly six years to being without the war and to be expected to join in the celebration of the bomb, which to some was a horrendous jollification. After two false alarms when misguided folks rushed into the street blowing whistles, when the sirens finally announced the real McCoy, in the late morning, at first there was a curious stillness before the thunderstorm of joy.

Mrs. Dolly Hollingshead went immediately down Macleay Street to The Gin Cask and purchased six bottles of Gilbey's gin and two of Penfold's sherry, one sweet and one dry before they ran out. In the street people were already slightly tipsy and smiling foolishly at strangers. Strung around her neck on a mock gold chain was her air-raid precaution gear: a tin whistle, a toy flashlight, a wee penknife, and a large flat pink India rubber eraser to be slipped into her mouth to prevent her biting off her tongue even though, goodness knows, she often had need of it being bitten off, with the unfortunate and funny things she said. In the last few years she had entertained (less charitable people might have said enticed) numerous American servicemen to her second-floor apartment. Among them Captain Orville G. Bentley from Oshkosh, Lieutenant Ward Q. Applegate from Racine, Staff Sergeant Willis J. Nutley from New Canaan, and Major John Phillip Sousa MacElroy from Kalamazoo. She had also entertained with less enthusiasm Lieutenants Betty Jean Kirkwood and Delphine Weinstein of the U.S. Navy. Currently there was Lootenant (as he said it) Lloyd C. Manville of Grosse Point, Michigan, for whom she had secreted a preciously saved bottle of Johnnie Walker whiskey given to her by Captain Mick Leatherbee of North Hollywood, said to be a close friend of the character actress Cora Witherspoon, who, oddly enough, greatly resembled Dolly.

Dolly naturally had been on the stage, her height and nose contributing to her comicality, and she had specialized in the kind of run-on, run-off socialite ladies wearing floral chiffon who contributed to the piffling plots in musical comedies. None of the comedy dialogue forced on her was one-tenth as witty or original as the things she said herself, the little barbs and acerbities that came from her. Her comedic self was said to have had many catastrophic effects on her love life; many partners were said to have fallen out of bed laughing at her and not gotten back in. Something about her nose perched beakishly over her small mouth and the glasses quivering on the bridge of it set people to laughing even before she delivered her punch line. When she was seriously and deeply in love, which was continually, she would want desperately to communicate in as simple and truthful a way as she could muster, the emotion she felt to the man, but oftentimes before she reached halfway into the simple declaration of love, her wretched nose would appear to grow even larger and her small mouth to curl up in exquisite disdain at herself and lo and behold instead of being in each other's arms, she and the paramour would be rolling on the floor and holding their sides because she had transformed the situation into a moment of comicality so rich and true that it could not support any modicum of emotion, let alone sensuality. Gentlemen, on the point of eloquent lust, would be unsexed by something she said, usually in a low aside, about their deportment or underwear and, unable to maintain their lustful stance, wilting, would take her in their arms, chortling that never in their lives had they encountered her equal. God almighty, they said, you are the berries, they told her. They told her that she took the cake.

Which had made for a lonely life on the whole. Being followed by gusts of laughter instead of guitars, reviving the bored, succoring the melancholy. Some of the gentlemen were not always gentlemen. During the New Zealand train tour of *Roberta* in which she ran-on, ran-off with the skimpy plot, her current adoration, a tall good-looking chorus boy, had tried it on with one of the night porters who made up the sleeper berths, tried to get the porter into the upper and was assaulted for it, loosening two front teeth and getting a black eye, when Dolly burst into the compartment and began beating the night porter. How dare he make approaches to her *husband*, she demanded to know and, hand on the emergency cord, threatened to stop the train and hand him over to the authorities for making lewd and obscene advances. Nothing more was heard of or from the night porter.

Who Mr. Hollingshead, her real husband, was and where he was remained a mystery, and Mr. Hollingshead remained silent in an enamel frame on her dressing table. Alongside him was the small oval framed picture of a little boy in a sailor suit and occasionally when her eyes lighted on it, her nose swelled and her glance moistened. Someone knew and passed on the information that her little boy had died at age seven from acute mononucleosis; more likely, a less-kind person opined, he had died laughing at something Dolly said.

Well, if this was the end of the war, it was going to go out with a whizbang as far as Dolly was concerned. By the time Seaton got out of the lift, the small flat was already spilling out into the hall with people and Dolly's store of drinking glasses had run out; several people were drinking out of Horlick's Malted Milk tins and jam jars; the noise of talk and laughter was uproarious. Saying excuse me, pardon me, Seaton pushed his way into the crowded living room and embraced Dolly, who was weeping with laughter. 'Too awful to tell,' she said and introduced her American love.

Lootenant Lloyd C. Manville (all Americans, it seemed, were born with a middle initial) was so young and boyish that he could have been a twelve-year-old dressed up in an army uniform for some school play. He blinked behind gold-rimmed glasses, his baby-smooth skin might never have felt a razor. 'Hi, Season,' Lloyd said and gave a warm child hand. He was amiable to the point of caricature. Yes, sir, yes, ma'am, he said, smiling, and offered to get drinks, give up his chair, move the lamp so it

wasn't in your eyes, get you a napkin, ask after your folks. When congratulated on his country's bomb, he smiled modestly but stood to attention
and murmured that people would now have to recognize that America was
the greatest country on earth and such was his innocence and genuine
pride that to discountenance any such statement would have amounted to
treason. 'If you don't mind my saying,' Lloyd C. Manville, said, blinking.

One person who emphatically did not agree with him and who was
becoming drunker and louder by the second was Julia Montrose, British to
the core, or as she was now, on her umpteenth gin, obliged to pronounce,
'Brish-ish.' Thank God, she said for the Brishish. 'I'm proud to remind you
tonight it was the simple Brishish folk in their bloody little fishing boats
at Dunkirk that got us through, not the bloody Yanks and their detestable
bomb.'

'Oh, Julie,' Dolly said, 'when you get smashed you get more and more to
look like Disraeli.'

The party swayed back and forth from the hallway to the kitchen as
more people arrived and some left. Some, Dolly said, she had never seen
before. 'Darling,' Dolly said, pulling a face, 'this sherry's as thin as tin, get
me something robust to drink.' Lloyd C. Manville ran to get it. Dolly
drank and laughed, laughed and drank, but it wasn't until after midnight,
when most of the crowd had gone, that Seaton found her alone in the
kitchen, crying.

'Damn their bomb,' Dolly said, mopping her eyes. 'Light me a Philip
Morris.'

She had been metamorphosed by the war; all the years of feeding off
Hollywood films had translated her, unbeknownst, into a vicarious Yankee
Doodle and then suddenly the avalanche of GIs and officers had transcended the cinema; the huge mysterious country known only on
black-and-white film where lustrous people moved and lived in unreality
became suddenly as real as the corner grocery, and there in their beautiful
pink-and-beige uniforms were the prototypes of John Hodiak and Dana
Andrews; the American girls, the WACS and WAVES spoke and behaved
like Gene Tierney or Jeanne Crain. America came to Kings Cross, Sydney,
and just around Dolly's corner was New York or New Orleans, the pure
childlike GI faces, pleased to present you with a carton of Lucky Strike or
a pair of precious nylons if you'd give kindness in return and not syphilis.

Dolly was a born mother and she mothered the army orphans, gave them drinks, and made them laugh and in return they admitted her to the United States or the nearest approximation of it.

Now in one fell swoop of atomic fission, the Mardi Gras was over, the boys and girls would be going home to Omaha and Bakersfield, many boys with brides from Oatley and Strathfield, none would be taking Dolly back with them to the old folks at home; she would be left stranded on the beach with only the poignancy of them and a see-through plastic cigarette case left her by Private First Class Clarence B. Rosenquat.

Now, as Seaton put his arms around her and squeezed her, she fingered her air-raid precautions kit and said, 'Now what'll I do with my *rubber?*'

That set them off giggling like nincompoops. The way she said 'my rubber,' sounded so suggestive and they knew about the 'pro' stations and what was handed out to the boys on furlough (they now never said 'leave,' always furlough; vacation, not holiday; ketchup, not tomato sauce; and Dolly would say wait a sec till she looked at her 'skedule'—without being conscious of it Seaton and Dolly had become imitation GIs) and being, both of them, exclusive, Dolly because of middle age, Seaton by nature, they looked askance at the eagerness with which the Australian girls took in the bewildered aliens in more ways than one. There was, of course, xeno-phobia, the natural hostility aroused by the invasion of these substantially funded foreigners with their marvelous teeth and crew cuts (the wellworn joke was 'oversexed, overpaid, and over here'), and there had been at least one terrifying incident in a Brisbane bar in which a harmless American GI had been savagely beaten to death by a mob of drunken Australian bullies incensed over some triviality, and there were complaints from the unbear-ably prudish North Shore Liners that Wynyard Station underground was becoming a honeycomb of prostitution at night. Still, everyone sang along with Bing, and Dolly took to eating American-style, cutting her meat and then laying down the knife and transferring the fork to her right hand. 'I'll be hornswoggled,' she was heard to say.

'Go and see if Lloyd's all right,' she said. 'I'll be there in a minute. I want to put on some eyebrows so I'll look bold enough to face the future.'

Lloyd C. Manville had been taken over by Madge Trimble, who, Dolly said, was known to bend over backward to be raped. Sure enough, Madge Trimble was leaning over backward in an attitude of presenting her private commodity to Lloyd C. Manville. She was wearing a black openwork lace dress over a fleshcolored slip that suggested she had nothing on but cobwebs and she was by now lavishly 'shickered' and unable to stop talking. Back and back she leaned, one hand on the fake fireplace mantel, until literally she was all but pushing what Dolly called her 'credenza' into Lloyd's crotch. While Lloyd, glass in hand, stood in his immaculate uniform as motionless as a sentry and stupefied with boredom as, makeup-smeared, hair awry, she drove relentlessly on with some pointless anecdote. When he caught sight of Seaton, relief flooded his prep school face and he reached out and put an arm around Seaton, drawing him into the conversation. 'Oh, hey there, Season,' Lloyd said and smiled a message that read 'For God's sake, don't leave me alone with this dame.'

And so on, my dear, and so on, Madge went on, seemingly unaware of Seaton, all about how she had shaken off the unwanted advances of some 'Lootnant Colonel.' She laughed at her artifices and poked Lloyd Manville in and around his confidential parts. 'Not that I'm any f-f-finicky little virgin, as anyone will tell you,' she said, catching hold of his lapel and spilling her drink on him, wiping him off and pushing up her ravaged face into his with a gargoyle smile, revealing expensively re-created teeth. 'You betcha bottom dollar, sweetheart.' She was one of those drunks who reach a plateau, never passing out or actually falling down, but beyond accountability. 'Bet your arse, sweetart,' Madge said, swaying toward Lloyd who, to avoid her, swayed back and in doing so hugged Seaton. In a very low voice Lloyd said into Seaton's ear, 'Are you going to come home with me?'

'If you want,' Seaton said, surprised.

'Oh, please, I want you to, will you, will you, please?'

When Seaton nodded, Lloyd laughed pleasantly and poor Madge mistakenly thought she had spoken some witticism; her unfocused glare changed to one of pleased acquiescence. 'Tol' you so, I'm *fun*, you wanna know something, I'm fun, more ways 'n one, darling.' Now she dropped her glass on the carpet and, coiling herself around Lloyd, she attempted to put her teeth around his earlobe while he smiled, sweating slightly, holding her at arm's length while she mooed incomprehensibly into his left ear some garbled nonsense about not being a common whore because she cared about those she loved, like Lloyd. 'I car 'bout you, you darling boy, see? How big's your *ontraynoo*, swee'heart? I'll bet you're no midget.'

Lloyd was scarlet now, holding her away from him as if he had been lewdly groped in church. Come to think of it, he was rather like a pleasant young Sunday school teacher out on a picnic treat with his pupils. 'I think, ma'am, you ought to sit down,' he said and firmly put Madge in a chair where she dropped into a glum silence, the beginning of what would become the outraged virulence of the often-scorned. But Dolly would have to cope with that, and could.

As they went down in the lift, Lloyd's fingers brushed Seaton's.

'Thanks an awful lot,' Lloyd said.

'For what?'

'Rescuing me. That poor unhappy dame.'

He was putting up at the Oriental Hotel. Putting up 'with' would have been more likely. It had had a loose reputation even before the war and since the American invasion it had deteriorated to a new low only a notch above a bordello; its tawdry lobby was a hive of tarty girls trying to pick up the army and navy officers who couldn't get in anywhere else and now two of the tartiest approached Seaton and Lloyd as they came in. 'Yew boys look a bit *laoenly*,' one of them said. They were inches deep in rouge and both wore chandelier paste earrings and tight, livid green imitation silk dresses. 'Excuse us ladies, good night,' Lloyd said and pushed Seaton past them toward the lift. 'Oh, they want to be excused,' the other girl said scathingly. 'They want to be alone, the dear things. Whoo-oo, whoo-OO,' the tarts chorused and they swished into an imitation sissy walk, hand on hip and loose-wristed. 'Oh, you sweet things,' they sang derisively and some sailors laughed with them.

In the narrow talcum-smelling little room lit with only blatant ceiling light and with only one three-quarter bed covered in raspberry terrycloth, Seaton asked to use the phone and awoke Essie to tell her the crowds in the streets had gotten out of hand and that he was safer being put up on Dolly's sofa, what with the carryings-on. Essie, more than usually woolly-headed because of being awakened, asked seriously was this because of the war being over. 'When will they let you out, pet?' she asked as if it might be Tuesday.

Lloyd had a bottle of warming champagne sitting in melted ice.

'I didn't want to welcome the peace in all on my own and so I went downstairs in search of a friendly face but all there was was what we've just seen and the thought of having a drink with any of them was too depressing. Now let *us* drink to the peace, Season.'

'To the peace.'

'Long may it last.'

'Long may it last.'

'God bless America.'

'America.'

'And us.'

'And us.'

They sat side by side on the bed and sipped the tepid champagne, an Adelaide brew more like lemonade. It was somehow appropriate to the harmlessness of the situation, more like being sequestered with the vicar, and when Lloyd leaned toward him and said without a trace of irony, 'May I?' before kissing him quickly and dryly on the lips he almost expected that the next thing Lloyd would say might be that the scriptural text for today's Bible lesson was from Thessalonians. Everything was so unlustful and highly proper that their proximity to each other seemed accidental and even had Lloyd's mother come into the room, entirely moral. But then Lloyd put an arm around him and kissed him emphatically and said, exactly like a boyish scoutmaster, 'Shall we proceed?'

They undressed in silence and Lloyd, naked, wound his watch and placed it on the bedside table and then took off his gold-rimmed glasses, which left a pink mark on the bridge of his nose and made him seem nuder than the taking off of his clothes, and younger. The smooth hairless adolescent body suggested that one could be contributing to the delinquency of a minor.

Off went the ceiling light, leaving them in the neutrality of the glow from Darlinghurst Road streetlights as though Lloyd reasoned that there was less sinfulness in the opaque. Sinfulness was hardly the word for the boyishness of his behavior, waggish was more the word for the flip-flopping gymnastics that went on as if it were taking place in a rubber boat shooting the rapids, their heads bumping on the headboard (Gosh, did you hurt yourself?); it reminded Seaton of his schoolday afternoons with sex mates (Quick, in case Mum should come) in toolsheds and cellars, seeing who would be first.

Yet there was an overall sense of simplicity and innocence in Lloyd that made it, in a sense, endearing. Completed, they lay side by side in silence like stone effigies and Lloyd took hold of Seaton's hand and said, 'I just couldn't have borne to be alone tonight on this wonderful night for the world. Thank you, Season, I deeply appreciate it, I do indeed, guy. Thanks a heap, Season.'

'The name is Sea*ton*,' he said. But in the silence that followed he heard only deep breathing.

Over greasy eggs in the Kings Cross Hot Cross Bun, Lloyd said, 'How long do you have off?'

'All today.'

'And I have till seven this evening when they *say* they've got a transport for me to Manila. Let's spend the day together. Would you like that, or am I taking up too much of your time?'

'No, Lloyd.'

Even after all that fumbling and touching last night, Seaton couldn't quite be obvious in the daylight; Lloyd was too polite to make approaches to, too manly to be told that he was sweet. He merely smiled a lot.

They went to the Botanic Gardens; there might never have been a war, they might have been actors dressed in uniform for a film. Right off, doing the right thing, Lloyd rushed after a speeding child headed pell-mell for a pond and scooped her up in his arms, presenting her to her grateful mother with a salute. He half-bowed, half-lifted his hand to his cap to people who passed by. He was dead serious about the telling of himself and it was not all wildly encouraging. He was with a small law firm in Detroit, he liked a good basketball game, he had seen *Bambi* nineteen times (said without a glimmer of embarrassment). Hold on, he would say at the sight of a banyan tree, I want to remember that. Stand there a minute so's I can remember you there, too. And once, in a secluded bamboo garden, he stopped still and said, 'Do you mind, while no one's around?' And kissed Seaton. Remember me, he said out of the blue, dewy with the warm day and with good-natured affection. He was so absolutely decent, taking off and polishing his glasses and smiling up at Seaton, the young American lieutenant doing his bit to save a world for the very same decency of himself that Seaton wanted to take him in his arms. In the quietest way possible and in dead seriousness, as if he were now taking an oath on his mother's Bible, he said, 'If you ever want to come to America, I'd be honored to be your sponsor, Season.'

As they parted in front of the Grace Building U.S. headquarters, he gave Seaton a wilted personal card left over from his prewar days. It read 'Lloyd C. Manville, Attorney. Lord and Tomkins Attorneys at Law, 200 Edsel Square, Detroit, Michigan.' On the back he had written in high-school handwriting 'Don't lose me.'

'So long, pal,' he said as the cab whirled him away forever.

GEORGE JOHNSTON

'Sydney, 1946' from *Clean Straw for Nothing*

When Cressida came back she said, 'Have you been along to the bathroom yet?' and I said no, I'd been waiting for her to clean up, and asked her why. 'Oh, it's interesting,' she said.

The bathroom—there was only one to each floor of the Princeton Apartments—was at the far end of a corridor angled around a euphemistic light-well from which came weird clankings and groanings and the catarrhal cleansings of other residents. The corridor was all gloomy tones of brown, and the excremental colour and smell of this dingy byway went with the bathroom, which had stains on the walls like old maps and blotches more repellent in the toilet-bowl where something seemed to have happened with Condy's Crystals. The cracked wash-basin was a mess of squeezed-out toothpaste tubes and rusted bobby-pins, and the final sordid touch was a framed printed sign screwed above the ringmarked bathtub which said; GUESTS ARE POLITELY REQUESTED PLEASE NOT TO SHIT IN THE BATH. 'Politely' was the bit I liked. It was hard to believe that this had been set up in type, in Bodoni Bold, and printed.

When I went back to the musty bedroom I said hopelessly, 'We should have looked around more. We should have tried for something better than this dreadful bloody dump.'

'It's cheap,' she said, not pointing out that the Princeton had been my choice. 'It will do for a few days while we sort out. When you get a job we can look around for something else.'

'Someone said it was used as a kind of leave place for the troops, GI's mostly, a brothel, I suppose, more than a residential,' I said as if this was a mitigation. 'Put toilet-paper down on the seat first,' I warned.

Cressida went to a window so opaque with city grime that it seemed as if a wartime black-out screen was still pasted over the glass. 'Well, at least it's in the Cross,' she said, as if she could see out. 'It's a pretty street. There's a flower-stall over there. And we don't have to sit up here. We can always go out.'

She turned away and sat on the edge of the bed and wiggled her toes. 'I think I'd better tell you now,' she said evenly. 'I'm going to have a baby.' The expression on my face made her laugh. 'It's hardly surprising, darling,' she said. 'I suspected it a while back. Now I'm sure.'

'But are you sure?' I said stupidly, hardly hearing what she said.

She laughed again. 'I'm a very regular girl. Yes, darling, I am quite sure.' She came across and put her arms around me. 'It's all right,' she said. 'It's not anything to worry about.'

'It is something to worry about.' I tried to fight down a flurry of panic. 'I'm not divorced. We can't get married.'

'Who said anything about getting married? I haven't said anything about it. We love each other, don't we?'

'Yes, but . . . You see . . . Well, listen, this is serious. I mean, do you want to . . .'

'Get rid of it? Oh no, I don't want to get rid of it. It'll be our baby. I want to have it.' She didn't seem frightened or worried or excited, just serene and calm.

'Well, that fixes it,' I said. 'We're going to get out of this bloody terrible dump! You're not going to have it here.'

'Crikey, I hope not,' she said, and flung herself back on the bed, hugging her laughter into herself. 'Nor am I going to have it for quite a long time, darling,' she added after a while, her mouth twitching. 'So while we're waiting why don't we get dressed and go down and have some coffee at the Arabian?'

Coffee in cramped dim cellar lounges and the soft play of branch- and leaf-shadow in the autumn streets, as much as the emotional and physical raptures of a love still sublime even in the sleazy room of the Princeton, have been the palliatives of this uneasy arrival time of the last few weeks. There really are flower-stalls in Kings Cross and the one run by old fat Maggie has become *our* flower-stall, and we now have *our* tobacco kiosk where Cressida has charmed an old dragon of a woman into letting her have under-the-counter cigarettes, so we no longer have to save the tobacco from our used butts to be rolled up in airmail paper or smoke those terrible South African things that smell as if they are made from wilde-beeste dung. And we have our own coffee-lounge where we can hear *our* songs on the juke-box, 'Laura' and 'It Might As Well Be Spring' and 'The Breeze and I' and 'Deep Purple' and 'Night and Day'. And in the evenings we can walk through light-dazzle and cacophony under the bronzing leaves, and nobody takes any notice of us or cares who we are, although heads turn wherever Cressida walks.

Kings Cross is a little spurious and more than a little self-conscious, and its air of cosmopolitanism is an awkward masquerade, but there are misfit-ting foreigners about and odd eccentrics, and a raffishness has persisted, and it is better than Melbourne, and better than the rest of Sydney, which is even more war-scarred from its self-inflicted injuries. A coarser, tougher city, poised on an edge of violence. A cocky, callous place. Amid the merciless tensions of the town these past weeks have been a time of abeyance, of putting things off.

But that all came to an end this morning.

I think in spite of everything we have both become very depressed by the Princeton and the furtive faces we see in odorous corridors and the sounds we hear from behind closed doors and the sneaky hoverings around the institutional entrance hall, but I have been moody about making a change, and hardly able to afford one anyway.

This morning over coffee, Cressida said, 'It's time you thought about a job, darling. Or I did. We keep putting it off.'

'They know I'm here,' I said.

'But do they? You haven't even tried to contact Mr Tomlinson.'

'He knows,' I said impatiently. 'It's nearly five months since I quit the *Post*. Christ, he knows. Why should I go cap in hand, pleading for favours?'

'A job, darling, isn't necessarily a favour. The phone's there in the corner. Why don't you ring him?'

'All right, I will,' I said. And when I got through to Tomlinson he said, 'Where the devil have you been, Meredith? Been waiting weeks for you to contact me. Where are you speaking from? Yes, well grab a cab and come straight in. And make it snappy. I've an editorial conference at eleven.'

In the event it was he who made it snappy. He seemed petulant about something and was brusque and caustic with his secretary, but he greeted me warmly enough and made a point of recalling a wartime meeting we had had in Washington and indulged himself with a brief tonic scatter of dropped names, then came to the point crisply:

'Right. We could use a good feature writer. We do have Brian Jefferson but he's getting very unreliable. Turned into a parlour pink. Can't be trusted any longer. So, yes, there's a place on the *Globe* for you, Meredith, if you want it. You can have a senior grading, a flat thousand a year, and no bargaining.'

His secretary, still sulking, took me through the clamorous big reporters' room, which was in the frenzy of edition time, and down newspaper-smelling labyrinths to the small cluttered cubby the feature writers used. Jefferson was there, looking uncertain, a thin gaunt man with a pale, twitching face. He was polite and helpful but not effusive. We went across to the Long Bar of the Australia for a drink. Although quite early in the day, the huge bar was crowded: with most of the city's bottled beer running to the black market, all the bars were doing boom business and the swill began early. Jefferson drank Australian whisky, doubles, with beer chasers. His drinking hand had the shakes and he kept the other hand in his trouser-pocket jingling keys and coins. He told me he had been a colonel in Intelligence during the war, right through from the Middle East (he was one of the few in the bar, though, not wearing a returned serviceman's badge), and when he mentioned that we had a mutual friend in Archie Calverton, the penny dropped and I remembered some very passable war poems Jefferson had written. Calverton, he said, had come back to Sydney and was acting with a new Little Theatre group—'a bit leftish' he said—doing Ben Jonson's *The Alchemist*. Calverton, he said, was a bloody promising actor. I ought to go along.

'What does Tomlinson want you to do exactly?' he asked, trying to sound casual but with his uneasiness showing through.

'I don't know,' I said evasively. 'He's going to work something out.'

'They might give you a column,' Jefferson suggested hopefully. 'The gen around the office is they're planning to run a daily column.' He thought about this, jingling his pocket frantically, then said rather timidly, 'You'll like the *Globe*. It's not a bad paper to work for. Tomlinson's a pretty good bloke really.'

I was anxious to tell Cressida the news, and I suggested walking back to the office with him, but he said no, he'd stick on there for a bit, so we shook hands and he went over and joined a big bunch of other early drinkers around Freda, the popular one among the Long Bar barmaids. His left hand kept fumbling away in his pocket.

Walking up to Elizabeth Street for a tram, I kept on hearing that jiggling rhythm from Jefferson's pocket, and this brought back a few suddenly recaptured lines from one of his poems about the retreat to Crete. A good poem, as I remembered. As the words went through my mind they moved to the jingling sound of the coins and keys in his pocket.

There was a big crowd on the safety-zone and the trams, as usual, were banked up halfway along the street. Near me stood a nervous little European refugee—the odd round shape of the hat and the long coat and briefcase and thick-soled shoes testified his origins—and as the line of trams began to move again he turned to the man next to him, a tall rawboned type with a trap mouth and jutting chin, and asked in a heavy, thick accent. 'Iss zhis, z' next one, for z' Bellyview 'Ill?' The rawboned man looked at him with sidelong contempt and snarled, 'Why don't you reffo bastards learn t' talk English!'

I still don't know what made me react the way I did, but I had him by the shoulder almost before I realized what I was doing, and I threw a wild punch at him and began snarling myself, 'You wait till *you're* in Prague, you rotten uncouth bastard, and you're asking directions in *your* impeccable bloody Czech!' And then we had bumped through the crowd and were lurching across to the gutter, flailing at one another and brawling and swearing, knocking over the newspaper billboards, and the like refugee scuttled aboard the first tram that came along, whether it was for Bellevue Hill or not, but by this time a red-faced policeman had us both by our jackets and he was snarling too, 'You break it up, you two bastards, or you'll both be in *real* trouble!'

Coming back to the Cross, I smarted with humiliation and anger— anger with myself, mostly, that I had allowed myself to become trapped in the snarling violence and vulgarity of the place.

But tonight Cressida dug into almost the last of her army deferred pay so we could settle the account at the Princeton and have a celebration dinner in candlelight at Gleneagles. I drank too much of the wine, but it helped to make it gay. I said nothing about Jefferson or the incident at the safety-zone. Although Jefferson was much in my mind, with the words of his damned poem going round and round: it would have been easier to tell her, I have just realized, if I really knew what is going to happen here.

M. BARNARD ELDERSHAW

'Morning' from *Tomorrow and Tomorrow and Tomorrow*

It was almost dark, the premature darkness of a stormy sky, when Harry Munster brought the truck, piled with his furniture, to the kerb outside his new home. It had been a long day on the road, coming from Old Toongabbie by the Great Western Highway and the Parramatta Road, those great culverts draining into the city, to the steep little gut of a street in Darlinghurst. He had had some trouble on the way with the engine, delaying him beyond his expectations. Ally had come in by train in the morning with Ruthie and Jackie. She shouldn't be carrying Jackie now, he was far too heavy for her, but there had been no other way to manage. He'd put her into the train and her sister-in-law, Arnie's wife, had promised to meet her at Central. Ruthie at four was a sensible little thing, already more a help than a responsibility, with the eldest child's premature grasp of reality. Wanda, Harry had brought with him in the truck. She had been wildly excited and full of chatter. He had humoured her all day, bought her penny icecream cones and chocolate bars at their numerous stops and let her take fizzy drinks, triumphantly and noisily, through a straw into her unaccustomed stomach. He let her stand on the seat beside him, holding her securely with his left arm to look at the new world. Her little cheeks grew scarlet. She knew that she felt like a little queen and

lorded it very happily. She was three years old. He was ready to spoil her
out of a dim sense of guilt. He was taking her away from a world he
believed to be safe, however hard, into one he didn't trust. The bright
prizes of the city awoke his countryman's distrust. Poor little kid, let her be
happy when she got the chance. He owed her something. His heart
dragged with an obscure pity and a heavy tenderness. More obscurely still,
he was sorry for himself, and the day alone with the child, so dependent
and, in her little demanding way, so loving, had comforted him. But it
ended badly. Emotion and strange foods had had their way with her. She
had grown tired and sick, had cried and vomited, and at last, tired, dirty,
sticky, miserable, had fallen asleep against his side and so, tired himself, he
had held her and still found a weary joy in having her there.

As they turned into what was to be their street the storm broke. First,
in the heavy calm, slow drops made large dark circles on the asphalt. Then
came a gust, the rush of rain and wind sounded like a procession in the
narrow street, a procession that became a rabble. The light changed
sharply from grey to steel, a cold wet breath, and then rain and wind,
turning the corner, poured down the street in a torrent of air and water,
every surface darkened with wet, white flapping of a newspaper before the
rain bore it down, a white curtain flapping from a window, a white curl of
water in the gutters, pedestrians like leaves, the solitary tree straining at
its roots, leaves cast up, fixed buildings seeming to stir and flicker in the
downrush of the rain.

Harry could only disentangle Wanda and run with her into the house.
The child began to cry with fear of the storm. Ally met them, heavy and
querulous. She'd been waiting for hours, whatever had he been doing, and
look at the state Wanda was in; there wasn't any electric light because the
Council wouldn't connect them until they paid a deposit, the place was
filthy, and she couldn't do a thing about it even if she was fit to, because
the brooms and buckets were on the truck, she was dead tired, Jacky had
been playing up, she didn't know what had got into him, he was asleep
now, and for God's sake, don't wake him up. Chris was still there and it
was a good thing she was, what with Jackie nearly screaming himself into
fits and not so much as a chair to sit down on and Harry taking his time
on the road till she began to think there'd been an accident. Chris, Arnie's
wife, came forward in the midst of this interior downpour, shook hands

with Harry, vaguely muttering 'What oh' and retired again. She was a phlegmatic girl, wholesome looking and willing enough to do anything she was asked. She was of passive rather than active assistance.

The Munsters had the upper floor of a terrace house, two rooms, one behind the other, a latticed-in balcony in front where the two little girls would sleep and a latticed-in balcony at the back which served as a kitchen. The rooms would always be dark because they depended for natural light on the two balconies which were now both screened. They were now as dark as night. Ally had bought a couple of candles from the corner shop and they burned in their guttering wax with a wan yellow light. There was a box lent by the lady downstairs, so that Ally could sit down; the remains or beginnings of a meal, a cut loaf, butter in its paper, a large tin of sardines, lay on the kitchen sink, and Jackie slept on a coat spread in a corner, a handkerchief under his head. There was a girl in the attic above, an oven-like room with a surprised gabled window poking out of the slates, a family downstairs, and an old age pensioner tucked away at the back.

Harry levered up one of the candles and went to look at Jackie. The child was a bad colour, and breathing rather hoarsely with his mouth open. The relief of the city doctor's reassurances had quite worn off and Harry was again oppressed by a foreboding that the little boy was really ill. These screaming fits, were they temper, as his mother said, or were they pain? He was a year old now but backward. He had not begun to walk and wasn't lively or happy as a baby should be. Ally said it was his teeth. She didn't worry. Lots of babies had difficult babyhoods and grew up none the worse. It was just another trial for their mothers. All Harry's fears rose up in him now. He told himself it was the light, veering and flickering in the empty room. Ally stood watching him, her grotesque shadow thrown on the wall. He looked up at her from where he knelt on the floor. Their eyes met as they rarely met now. She said nothing, but he was laid open to her jeering silence. Her burdened body was a reproach to him, the sickly child was a reproach to him. There was no need for words. The strain and weariness of the day, the savourless weight of the change they had made, had for the moment stripped them in one another's eyes. This was the communication they had with one another. Her eyes were alive in her sick, sullen face. They asked a question he could not answer. 'A bob both ways,' he thought.

Whichever way things went for them, well or badly, she'd have her cut. She meant to have all there was to be got, and if there was nothing, then she could still feed her resentment. Nothing dismayed her, she was invulnerable, and that was the measure of her power and their estrangement. They had this grudge against one another but they could never express it. When it broke out in the pustules of a quarrel it could only be in terms they both understood—a quarrel in the accents of other people's quarrels, the debased small change of hostility that passed as meaningless as pennies through hands greedy for all that money cannot buy. There was no quarrel tonight. Harry got awkwardly to his feet and put down the candle. He wanted to get into the open air. This room was like a bad taste in his mouth.

He went downstairs and stood on the oblong of iron-railed verandah beside the gas box, looking at the rain. It was still falling heavily but with less conviction. The storm was passing. The stormy twilight was like a bruise. This wasn't like the open air. Houses and streets crowded in, acres of them, square miles of them, as far as the mind could reach. The sky itself was cut into a narrow thoroughfare between buildings. People were standing on verandahs and balconies staring at the rain. Unseen they were looking out from opaque curtained windows in the dark caves of houses. No one greeted him nor did he greet anyone. Maybe they were curious about him or maybe there were too many coming and going for them to notice. He had the feeling that the rules were different here and that at any moment he would blunder into someone else's world. It made him feel inferior and angry. Probably this strip of verandah belonged behind that window—mean-looking, tight-shut window. The rain didn't mean anything here. It never reached the ground at all, it ran down gutters and into concrete pipes and away, something to be got rid of as soon as possible. It was waste. Under the asphalt the earth was dry and barren. He didn't like it. It made him feel bad. It wasn't anything to do with him, of course, and he'd get over it. He couldn't unload the furniture until it stopped raining. It'd be dark. He could manage by himself, there were only a few sticks. The thought that one of those lounging men might offer to help filled him with embarrassment.

Behind him in the house Wanda was crying. Her mother was washing the grime and stickiness of the day off her, ungently, at the sink. The child cried because everything was strange. Ally slapped her and she stopped. Ruthie came and stood by her father, holding to his trouser leg. He twisted a finger in her hair. They hadn't anything to say to one another. They just looked at the rain. It beat him where the children would play. Not in the slip of backyard at the back among the garbage tins. Out in the road. They'd have to learn they couldn't go where they liked. There wasn't any place for them and they'd have to learn it. He hadn't liked this place, looked like a slum to him. Agent was quite shocked when he said so. Not a slum rent anyhow. It wasn't easy to get a place. This would have to do until they could look round them. Wait till Ally could look for herself. They'd shake down. Bit hard to get used to after the country. Funny, didn't know he'd liked the country. Always said it was a lousy life, poultry farming. Everyone did. Still . . .

The rain was stopping. Chris came downstairs. She'd have to be getting along as soon as it stopped, she said. It was late. Arnie went to market if his tea wasn't ready. She tittered as she did when sex was referred to, however remotely. She'd be along tomorrow to see how they were settling in. She gave Harry a nerveless hand, and he noticed that she had a strong cottony smell. 'Goodbye, love.' She kissed Ruthie, who was shy, stepped into the dwindling rain. Harry went down and began to unknot the rope which held the tarpaulin. Tomorrow would be Sunday. He'd have to drive the truck back to Toongabbie and hand her over to the man he'd sold her to, and come back by train. After he'd finished paying for her there'd just be enough for his fare. Maybe he'd take Ruthie. Get her out in the open for the day. Ally would say he wasn't to be trusted after the way he'd brought Wanda home. Monday, he'd see about the job. Arnie said it would be all right. Arnie always said that. Plenty of jobs going just now. Don't go pulling the returned soldier, though.

He carried up a kerosene case packed with crockery.

'Bring up a bed, can't you?' said Ally, 'I got ter put the children somewhere.' Wanda had fallen asleep in a corner and Jackie was whimpering.

The dismembered beds were underneath. He got Jackie's cot out first and was carrying it upstairs when he heard the screams. They broke out suddenly and they weren't like a baby's cries at all. He rushed up stairs. Ally had just picked Jackie up. He was bent backwards in her arms, screaming, his face bluish and distorted, in a fit or a convulsion. She could barely hold him. Harry took him. He had the poor man's instinct to run with him to the nearest doctor or hospital, but it was still raining, and he did not know where to find either. His fear of the strange world was stronger. The woman from downstairs was already at the door.

'Is she took bad?'

'No, it's the baby.'

She would help. Better to leave Jackie with them to do what they could while he got a doctor. He knew it was urgent, they all did. The air itself changed. He plunged downstairs. The hoarse screams followed him. He ran towards William Street. All these people—there must be a doctor near. He caught a passer-by by the shoulder and gasped out his enquiry. The man gaped at him oafishly and he let him go, ran on, turned up the hill. A river of traffic flowed in the great thoroughfare, a blaze of light and noise. He cannoned into an old man, repeated his enquiry. The old man took his time. 'Dr Jones will be the nearest, over the road and straight along Darlinghurst Road, not the first one, that's Victoria Street, the second one. On the left, straight on, you'll see the red lamp . . .'

He jumped into the river, cars hooted, brakes screamed, a tram clanged very near him, he thought in an unheeded flash, 'What would they do if I was run over?' but he was on the other bank, crossing another road, battling against a leisurely stream of people, lights, noise. There were many red lights. There was a chemist's. A chemist would know. Then he saw the square red lamp with Dr Jones in white letters. It looked calm and steady, rebuking. It was a big building, trees in front, a car at the kerb. He ran up the steps. The doctor's name was printed on a door, a bell marked Night Bell. He rang it. A stocky, middle-aged man opened it.

'The doctor in?'

'I'm the doctor. This isn't my consulting hours.'

'The baby's taken bad, please come.'

The doctor sized him up, unperturbed. 'You should have gone to the hospital,' he said.

'I don't know where it is. We only moved in tonight.'

'You could telephone the ambulance. That's what they are for.'

Harry shook off the entangling argument. 'Please come. I think he's dying.' An idea crossed his mind. He thrust his hand into his pocket and brought out two crumpled pound notes. 'I can pay.'

The doctor seemed offended. 'Wait here,' he said, and went back into his rooms. Harry didn't know if he were coming or not, whether to wait or look for some one else. He heard an altercation going on, a woman's voice, the doctor's answering brusquely as he had spoken to him. At least the door wasn't shut. After what seemed an interminable time the doctor came out with a bag.

'Look sharp,' he said, 'Where do we go? I've an engagement.'

They got into the car outside. Harry gave the address. The doctor grunted. It was nearly eight o'clock and the theatre traffic was at its peak, shining cars in a long fluent stream under the lights. Harry saw now that the doctor was in evening dress.

The upstairs room seemed full of women. The fat woman from downstairs was in charge. She was putting Jackie into a hot bath rigged on the kerosene box. His little body was rigid between her hands. He wasn't screaming now but breathing in choking gasps. There was no mistaking the look on his face, it was one common to all in extremis.

'Are you the mother?' the doctor asked.

'It's her, poor soul.'

The doctor drove them all out except Ally and the fat woman. Ally was collapsed in a chair someone had brought in, a swollen frightened look on her face. The fat woman held a candle in each hand to give the doctor light as he laid Jackie in the cot and began his examination. Harry stood by the door. The doctor took his time.

He wasn't doing anything. It was quiet. Harry even heard the whining of the trams in William Street. The doctor's shirt front was splashed with water, his face expressionless, only intent.

The fat woman screamed, 'He's going, doctor.' He told her harshly to be quiet. There was a pause. He could not see what the doctor was doing. The wavering light danced on the wall. Harry clenched his fists.

The doctor touched him on the arm. There wasn't anywhere for them to talk but down on the street. The other room was dark and Wanda asleep on the floor. Ruthie had woken up and come in, her eyes big with fright, but silent. Ally was crying hysterically and the fat woman was soothing her. It was about half-past eight.

They were down in the street standing by the doctor's car. The rain was over and the pavements were dry. There was the partly unloaded truck.

The doctor was explaining something. He could not give a certificate because he could not state with any certainty the cause of death. There would have to be a post-mortem, an inquest. He'd get in touch with the authorities. Jackie would have to be taken away, it emerged. Harry rebelled. The doctor was dry and matter of fact. It had to be. He didn't like the business. He'd had an engagement. Well. He hoped he'd made it clear.

'This is bad for your wife in her present condition. She shouldn't be left. Can you get her mother or some one responsible? Keep her quiet.'

Ally would be all right. The doctor started his car. It took itself off neatly and suavely, turned the corner and disappeared. Harry stood on the kerb.

A policeman with an open notebook had to speak to him twice.

'That your truck?'

'Yes.'

'Can't leave it here like that, you know. Been standing a couple of hours, obstructing the traffic. I'll have to book you if you don't get busy.'

Harry balled his fists. 'You get to hell,' he shouted. 'Me bloody kid's dead, ain't that enough?'

'Now Dig, now, none of that,' said the policeman, kind but admonitory.

The Fifties

'First, man chases dragon.
Later, dragon chases man'
—*Peter Doyle*

During the war years, sophisticated nightclubs had defined Kings Cross. In the Fifties, however, with the absence of American G.I.s, many nightclubs were driven to bankruptcy. Entertainment tastes were changing, and most Australian veterans preferred to fraternise in the R.S.L. clubs that were being built in many of Sydney's suburbs. Australian society was becoming more permissive, and in the Cross, nightclubs were replaced with more strip clubs. At the same time, the underworld brothel racket, controlled by madams such as Tilly Devine, was losing its hold. As prostitution became more accepted, women began to work on the street independently.

By 1950, the Cross housed over 60,000 residents. The area had always been densely populated, but now it was overcrowded. The increase was partly due to the government's immigration policy, which was at its peak soon after the war. During this decade, Sydney received hundreds of Greeks, Italians, Dutch, Germans, Jews, Turks, and Maltese, many of whom made a beeline to the Cross and established businesses and restaurants.

Kings Cross soon became the place to dine out. Due to the influx of immigrant restauranteurs, traditional Australian cuisine like steak and mashed potato was replaced by more exotic dishes like spaghetti, risotto, and beef stroganoff. Tea was substituted by coffee as the preferred hot refreshment, and the Cross was the only place in Sydney where you could have an espresso after eleven o'clock at night.

Not only did the strip clubs flourish during the 1950s, but the café culture which had been interrupted during the war was gradually revived. At the Arabian Cafe on Darlinghurst Road, you could hear poetry readings in the evenings, and be waited on by Norman Lindsay's favourite nude model. As described in John Clare's *Bodgie Dada & The Cult of Cool*, the El Rocco was the centre of Sydney's modern jazz scene and was named by *Down Beat* magazine as one of the greatest jazz clubs in the world. The

Kashmir was another café that welcomed creative eccentrics, and soon became a venue for many local musicians. Uncorked wine bottles were hidden beneath the tables, and many people surreptitiously poured whisky into their coffee. Most of the waiters were drag queens, and criminals frequented the upholstered booths to divide up stolen goods. The Kashmir was the second coffee shop in Australia to install an espresso machine, though a special licence had to be obtained from the city council to operate it, because it was regarded as a steam engine.

The Kashmir was also at the centre of one of the decade's most memorable scandals. Owner Pop Goodman contracted Kings Cross artist and witch Rosaleen Norton to paint a number of murals on the café's walls. The erotic, Gothic images of naked Pans, which blended religiosity with sexuality, led to both Pop and Rosaleen being charged with creating and exhibiting obscene pictures. Norton's notoriety escalated over the years, and she was later accused of performing satanic rituals in her home on Brougham Street, along with perverse erotic acts. It is difficult to separate fact from fiction, but in the following extract of the Inez Baranay novel, *Pagan*, loosely based on the Kings Cross witch and her lover Gavin Greenlees, it is obvious that much of Norton's mythology has seeped into the public imagination.

Just as Kings Cross, and the El Rocco in particular, became the centre of modern and experimental jazz, abstract painting was growing more popular, too. Nowhere was this in more evidence than at the Terry Clune Gallery on Macleay Street. Clune encouraged new and risky work, and introduced Sydneysiders to such innovators as Robert Hughes, Robert Klippel, and Stan Rapotec. The gallery soon became a bohemian haunt.

In the 1950s, Robin Eakin's ancestral home, the sprawling Victorian mansion, Maramanah, became a casualty of the development boom and was demolished. In its place was built what would become a defining icon of Kings Cross—the El Alamein Fountain, surrounded by the Fitzroy Gardens. With its dandelion, puff-ball orbs of water, from the 1950s onwards the fountain would be a natural backdrop for tourist photographs and a place where locals would score drugs. It would also become an obvious receptacle for dyes and detergents, occasionally transforming itself into a frothing, scarlet effluvia.

In the meantime, the Sydney Stadium, which was just at the foot of

Kings Cross Road, was converted to a rock 'n' roll venue, managed by American promoter Lee Gordon. From 1956, most touring overseas artists performed there, including Frank Sinatra, Nat King Cole, and Ray Charles. With the new international face of Kings Cross came more serious drug abuse, particularly in the form of heroin. Peter Doyle's chapter from *Get Rich Quick* provides a witty and unsentimental portrait of the drug and crime problems of the time. Part of the development craze and the stride towards modernity was realised in the construction of the Rex Hotel, which opened in the mid-1950s. The hotel became the definition of American sophistication, boasting several bars with live entertainment and a sidewalk espresso bar. The hotel was *the* place to stay for visiting international celebrities, and its Bottoms Up Bar became a favourite hang-out for the district's growing gay population.

In the meantime, the eccentric Bea Miles moved into a storm-water drain in Rushcutters Bay, as fictionalised in the following excerpt from Kate Grenville's novel, *Lilian's Story*.

KATE GRENVILLE

from *Lilian's Story*

Glory Boxes

Frank had stopped driving his taxi some time before. I think there was an accident, police, a great deal of meaningless noise. Now his room had arreared so far that he had been dislodged from it, and lived in the storm-water channel in the park. We found that the storm-water channel was as good a place for two as for one. *This is the life, Lil,* Frank said, and leaned back against the curve of the concrete. *I could live here real well.*

Frank was a tidy man, house-proud in our storm-water channel. *Everything in its place and a place for everything,* he said, and propped the bottle upright between two bricks. *Things go missing, Lil, if you are not neat,* he said, and kept a hand on the neck of that bottle, even though propped between its bricks it could not go missing anywhere.

My room at the Cross was becoming smaller, meaner, stuffier, each time I went back to it, and Aunt Kitty's money was shrinking week by week. In any case, there is no wallpaper like stars, and no bed as soft as the sound of a sea breeze in leaves. *Come on, Lil,* Frank urged, *I will even have a go at carrying you over the threshold.* And at last, with my book bag full of the few things I treasured, I joined Frank in the great room of the park. *There is plenty of wood for fires, come the winter,* Frank said. *The abos did okay, and so will we.*

I loved my life with Frank. I had never set up house with anyone before, and loved the feeling of coming home at the end of the day to the place Frank and I shared. Frank had tried to carry me over the threshold, and we had clawed and grasped at each other, panting noisily and gasping, until we fell together on the grass. Frank had wheezed noisily for a few minutes and then said, You *cannot say I did not try, Lil, but you are a bride and a half, and I am only half a husband.*

I enjoyed the way Frank rolled us into our newspapers for the night, and loved to wake up when the birds were being insistent in the trees overhead and the sun was sending yellow fingers along the wet grass. Frank snored on beside me and I heard the city wake slowly, and the birds take second place as hurrying men in suits and women in high heels began to clatter along the paths to the city, and everyone got ready to die another day away. When Frank woke up, gradually, nodding off again before he got up and tidied his newspapers into a pile under a stone, we had the pleasure of sharing our dreams. I had not often woken up in the company of others, and shared dreams while they were fresh, except in the loony-bin, and no one wants to share their dreams in a loony-bin. Most there do not know that there is a difference between a dream and a life.

The sleep of the chaste is full of dreams. Mine were of burning towers and seas sweeping in over strange lands, lapping at trees and castle walls. *I do not admire chastity,* I told Frank, nodding off again over his bottle. *I do not admire chastity, although I am a virgin.* He woke from his stupor at that word and suddenly thrust his jacket sleeve up and flexed his skinny arm at me. *We will soon put that right,* he cried, and strained to make muscle appear, so that veins engorged along his arm and he began to cough. *I like my dreams,* I told him, and helped him pull his sleeve back down. *Deflowered, I might miss out on dreams.*

Our bliss was not conjugal, but chaste, but I did not envy anyone, and told the people on the buses, *I am a contented woman, and wish for nothing,* and they stared at me, and none could say the same for themselves.

A Life in a Bag

Jewel joined Frank and me in our storm-water channel when she came across us there. *Jeeze but you have got yourselves a good spot*, she admired, but would not drink out of the bottle that Frank waved at her. *I am expecting*, she said primly. *I do not drink while expecting*. Jewel had been expecting God's baby for as long as I had known her, but now she was certainly expecting something from the bulge under her dress. *Jeeze, I like it here*, Jewel said with satisfaction, and became part of our household, bringing with her a dowry of her belly and a plastic bag full of stolen baby bootees.

This is my life, Frank told her with pride, and held up his gunny-sack, which held all that he owned. Jewel stared with her mouth open, breathing audibly in the way she did when she concentrated, then crowed suddenly. *And this is mine!* patting her gigantic stomach. *Ah, but Jewel, can you wear your life?* Frank asked, winking at me and pulling his boots out of his bag. *Or shave with it?* He held up his razor, for Frank was still fastidious about his face, and shaved after a fashion from time to time up at the hostel. Jewel frowned in silence, but finally thought of her answer. *Your life will not be able to talk back to you*, she cried, *but mine will, and will be famous!* Frank winked at me again but had no answer for Jewel, because it was true that his life would never grow up to be anything very much now.

All Happy Families

It is a funny kind of family, Frank said, but seemed to enjoy it. In the nights we built fires from wood frayed by the tides, and invented a few hard names for the stars. Like the others of long ago, we who sat on this dark beach had been slowly transported, by the nature of our lives and the choices we had made, to the stern lip of another land. The privilege of the first ones has always been to impose names of their own invention on the new world. *Hebdomedary*, Frank would say after a long silence. *How about that, Lil? Or concupiscence*. When the flames reached in and singed the wood it spat salt embers that pulsed on the sand before dying.

Those autumn nights were the times when we told the stories of our lives, either the ones we had or the ones we would rather have had. Jewel and I watched by cool starlight and hot flames as the tears slimed down Frank's cheeks. *The wife*, he'd say and look for the bottle leaning against his leg. *Me little girl*, he'd say, and the cork would make a hollow mocking sound. Those who spent their days smiling and worrying at each other, and their nights behind walls and windows, would claim that Frank had never had a wife or a daughter and had never wanted anything but the loving boy he had never quite had. But we listened and threw another stick onto the flames, and later I held him as he shuddered and hiccupped under the dew.

Across the water, as black as the inside of an ear, the yellow lights of those in the old country winked feebly at us. When our memories or inventions failed us we watched the yellow semaphore. *Snug as a bug in a rug*, Jewel said. She could just as easily have meant the three of us by the fire, or those secure in their houses and beds around the bay.

Mother and Young

Jewel was close to her time now, she thought, and had stopped being sick every morning, and moved slowly, like a cart. *No hospital*, she always said. *I will not have no hospital where they lock you up*. On those occasions when I tried to reason with her—*But, Jewel, if there are complications;* whatever *complications* were, I knew them only from *Gone With the Wind*—her eyes began to roll and her breath came faster. If I persisted—*Jewel, we must be realistic*, I would say, wondering at myself for the words—she would run down to the beach and sit among the rubbish, threatening to drown herself, baby and all. *Won't catch me locked up again*, she said, and hissed, *Incineration, that's what it is*. Her face as she sat among the rotting oranges was anxious but determined, her chin very pointed. *It is mine*, she said, shielding the lump under her dress. *Mine*. When I tried to come closer, saying something that was meant to soothe, she stood up, stumbling on rubbish, and waded out heavily into the water until she was standing up to her thighs in it, and I turned back. *It is mine*, she tried to explain more calmly later, *and they are all jealous because it is me that will have God's baby*. She stared down at her belly and made round gestures with her hands. *It is mine, see?* was finally all she was able to say.

No Humbug in a Baby's Bottom

Some women have babies and others have stories. I would have liked to have both. Nothing in my experience equipped me to be a midwife, but as a student of life I knew it was never too late to learn, and I wanted to add all experiences to my store. It was necessary to prepare for Jewel to become God's mum, because her bulge was getting bigger by the day. She still insisted that God would not be born in any hospital, but would emerge into the world on our beach, among the orange peels and lost sandals, where the storm-water channel deposited its gifts. I could not imagine this, but life had astonished me before now, so I did what I could to prepare myself.

I read books, spending days in the library, and the librarians looked twice when they saw what kinds of book Lil Singer was asking for. *I am a student of life*, I told them with dignity, Jewel's secret safe with me, and they were silenced, these young librarians who knew nothing except how to whisper. The books had not been quite as specific as an earnest student of life could have wished, but I learned what I could from them, and then went out into the streets, where I had always learned so much, and looked for some practical experience.

When a baby dribbled at me invitingly, up at the Cross, I decided it was time to begin to learn. *I would like to hold it*, I told the man, barring his path. The passage of years had not made me any less monumental, and this was a small man. *I am on my way home*, he said, but I only moved closer. I saw his fear in his eyes. He was afraid that I would rip the baby from his arms and gallop down the street with it, or squeeze its round head like an orange. *She needs changing, you see*, he tried once more, a male animal defending its young, but I was already reaching for the thick padded bottom and the swaddling chest. This father was graceful in defeat. *Here, get a hold of her like this*, he said, and in a moment I had a baby in my arms for the first time. *She is Dianne*, the father said, and blushed with pride in spite of everything. *She is our first.*

The baby pouted up at me like a tease, grinned gummily, frowned. Her hand waved up and down at my face, a finger brushed into my laughing mouth, and she laughed a small wicked laugh. *Aaaah*, she crowed, and I crowed back, *Aaaaah!* A man in woman's clothes stopped and looked with a hand up to his mouth; two ladies of the night waved across the street at me and called, *Pretty as a picture, Lil!* I asked, *Were you at the birth?* and this man, who would never parade his baby down the street again, blushed fiercely as he said, *Yes.* I held Dianne high in the air, my thumbs hooked in her tiny armpits, and said, *I need to know.* This father, whose pride in his daughter was more powerful than any fear, said suddenly, *She popped out just like a pea out of a pod,* and nodded around at the small crowd that had gathered. *Lil Singer,* I heard voices whisper at each other. *With a baby.*

This was a father not used to crowds, it was easy to see, but he nodded at the man in frills, and at the lady of the night on his left, whose black eye was at the yellow stage. *Just popped out like she'd been doing it all her life,* he said, and everyone laughed, even the policeman who had decided to stand on the edge of the crowd and *keep an eye on things.* I knew that little Dianne would grow up listening to the telling and retelling of the story of the day she was dandled by Lil Singer, and might tell it herself at last.

What Is Needed

I was anxious, but Jewel was serene, knowing she was prepared to become the mother of God. *I got all the necessary,* she said haughtily when Frank had had a bottle or two, or began to screech that she was loony, thinking she could have a baby on our beach. *Look,* Jewel said, and held up her plastic bag of bootees. *I am ready, see?* But Frank sprayed spittle in his derision. *It's nappies you need, Jewel,* he cried. *Use your loaf, Jewel, think of all that shit!* His laugh made Jewel cup her belly with her hands, *Nappies for its bum, nappies for its bummy bum bum,* Frank sang lustily. Only his cough stopped his song going on until dawn.

Frank was scandalised, too, that Jewel was not preparing a name for her baby. *Got to think of a few names,* Frank said. *It's just a thing till it's got a name.* Jewel looked frightened, as she always did when called upon to act. *What will I do, Lil?* she appealed, and although I did not feel strongly about names, I disagreed with Frank. *For years you were only F.J. Stroud to me,* I reminded him, and he smiled so that I could see how grooved and stained his teeth were from the years of smoke and drink. *Yes, Lil,* he said, and Jewel watched as if to surprise a secret. *Those were the days, eh?* Jewel continued to stare, but what lay between Frank, or F.J. Stroud, and me, was opaque to anyone but us. But something in the way we smiled at our memories made silent Jewel speak: *Was youse two sweethearts, then, was that it?* and our Jewel was preparing to become sentimental over sweethearts of long ago.

Leaving the Nest

No one came for Jewel, but she left in any case. She had become much more silent as the nights in the storm-water channel became colder, and her belly became an unmanageable size, and things began to fall apart. *We are gunna go north, Lil,* she said at last one morning, her eyes crazed now with the idea of the north and how it would be warm there, and mangoes falling off the trees. *They will not find us up there, to lock me up.* She could not stop herself glancing over her shoulder, and jumping at small sounds. *I will change my name,* Jewel said cunningly. *Then we will be right.* She winked at me and nodded. *I have got it all worked out, see.* Frank woke up with a snort and a fart and waved the bottle at her. *What do you mean,* he shouted, *change your name?* Jewel looked sly and pursed her lips, but could not resist telling us, *I will call myself Ruby,* she said. *Get it?* She began to wink at me as if she intended never to stop. *We will be right as rain,* she said, and picked up her plastic bag of bootees and left for the north. *Bye-bye, Lil,* she called from the fence where Frank and I stood watching and waving as she laboured away up the street. When she had disappeared Frank burped and put his arm around me so suddenly that he knocked the wind out of me, and said, *Well, Lil, it is just me and you now, like a pair of old farts,* and we both laughed so loudly the birds flew up in fear out of the trees.

The Last Loss

Frank took good care of me in our home by the water, tucking my feet into the newspapers at night, combing my thin old hair for me by the hour as we sat like a pair of baboons in the grass, grooming each other in peaceful silence. He took good care of me, but he was a sick man. He was yellow in the morning, yellow and trembling until he had sucked long enough at the bottle in the brown paper bag.

We are gunna die, Lil, Frank told me one dank night when the tankers mooed to each other like full udders in the fog. *And you will be the lucky one, Frank, and go first,* I said, and we both let slide some cool tears, thinking of how lonely I was going to be without Frank. *You will go first, and quickly, Frank, but I feel my death will come at me slowly,* I told him, but I did not try to resist, because if my death wanted to come at me slowly, that would be what happened.

Frank was planning his death, one step ahead of its arrival, and lay shivering and coughing by our fire with a few last tales to keep him warm. He was once a wealthy man, he said, and had written a will, he said, and left his estate in its entirety to me, he said. Another bottle, and he would claim to be the lost scion of the podgy House of Windsor.

I thought of my own death while Frank fended off his. Every third thought, on such cold nights, was my grave. There were noises in my head, too, rushing and roaring noises from time to time, and a feeling of birds massing behind my eyes, getting ready to fly somewhere. I would have liked to go like that, on the sand, with Frank making noises in his sleep beside me. Stars had never frightened me, even the black spaces between them had never frightened me. But Frank went first, as we had guessed. It was not in my arms, as we would both have wished, but on some street somewhere, staggering into the gutter with a last cough, or in some cold hospital bed with the screen drawn around him, because they had picked him off the street only to give him a bed to die in, or on some stretcher with the wailing of the ambulance filling his last moments. I had held his sick old hand, and embraced his thin old body, and watched him walk up into the city, and when at last it had been clear that he would never return, I wept long tears, but regretted nothing, because Frank and I had given all there was to give, and no love had ever been more true than ours had been.

INEZ BARANAY

'The Great Rite: Sex Magick' from *Pagan*

She is waiting for him. The flickering lights of candles create shadows in the darkness, create dancing phantoms on the green glass globe that was her scrying-glass, illuminate the face of the Horned God who leers and grins in delight, cause the skulls and bones that remind of endless rebirth and endless rebirth to shine then disappear then shine to the same candle-flame rhythms.

All has been agreed upon. The script has been written and learned; not a word out of place; all is set for a perfect play, a shadow-play, a transcendent reality.

Inside her dusky, musty room, the rickety sofa has been pushed into the centre, east-west. It now stands before the altar, facing south, from which the Elemental gave his blessing. On it she has thrown all her precious, tattered odd cloths—velvet and brocade and animal prints—that in this mysterious half light seem rich and exotic and make a bed fit for gods to sport on, as indeed they will. On this bed lies the scourge, the smooth stick with the many cords. Not a word! Not yet! As arranged. It is the witching hour and he enters, enters the room, to enter, oh but not yet. In the corner he removes his clothes and pulls on the simple robe left there for him. She is clad in a similar robe. These are soon to be removed, for sky-clad the ceremony must proceed. But first, to cross the border between this mundane reality and the greater reality that lies beyond . . .

In his robe he approaches the altar, where she is lighting many thick sticks of incense; the air in that closed room is soon laden with overpoweringly sweet, oriental scents: musk and ambergris and aphrodisia. An old gramophone has been wound up and its needle placed on a record of Tibetan chanting. On the altar, alongside the athame and the white-handled knife, the pentacle, the salt and the candles in their holders, some marijuana cigarettes have been placed beside a large goblet of wine: substances to facilitate the initiate's entry into the illusion, substances to enhance the movement to the realms of the Other.

The wine is handed to him. He swallows and shudders as it burns its way down: some spirit has been mixed into it, and there is a bitter chemical taste as well. Bravely he swallows again. She swallows deeply too. The candle she holds up to her face as she lights the first cigarette shows her slanted eyes glistening bright; she is already high on her speed pills. She draws in and hands it to him; they hold acrid smoke deep in their lungs and swallow the burning potion until their heads rise, up off their bodies, revolving and orbiting in endless dizzy motion.

Each has a task: each has developed a supreme ability to concentrate and, as they swallow and as they smoke, each concentrates on the Other—not as the human beings they know, no, no longer those poor imperfect mortals, but as the embodiment of the Deity, the Divine Lover.

Four candles are burning at the points of the four elements. The circle has already been cast: the consecrated sphere within which they finally shed their human identity through the ritual scourging that purifies the body completely so that the Deity might enter.

The record turns round on its round turntable and the chanting it plays, scratchy, hollow, other-earthly sounds whose notes arch and dip like satellites, is circular too, and the smoke drifts in rings, and his breathing goes in then out but round, round, inbreath becomes outbreath in an endless circle of breath that breathes him, and he sees the magic spirals painted on the walls and feels his whole being go into the same twirling spiral. He kneels, and the lashes of the lustrating scourge caress and sting his flesh in arcs of tender pain.

Heat rises as they remove the robes, and, sky-clad now, begin the invocations. In the measured, poetic language that is pleasing to the gods (and is easier for humans to learn by heart) they invoke their Deities, call them, and with respect and knowledge of them command them to manifest in the body of the man and the woman. He begins his invocation with eyes closed, oh the whirlpool he's in, while she looks right at him; as they repeat and repeat the magic phrases, he opens his eyes, the words turning circles in the air, their bodies, the smoke, the sounds of breathing in the now still room, all a complex of intertwining, dancing circles . . .

Then the sound (from where?) of a mighty rushing wind, a gale that arises in that very room, storms around it in a whirlwind of immense force, a force that is answered by a rising force in the body. The brave little candleflames rise huge but do not go out, and oh yes, look at her, the woman, the woman before you, indeed she is, oh Hecate, Artemis, Isis, Luna! Before you is the Divine Female manifest, the Goddess incarnate, oh and his body is grown straight and strong, broad-shouldered and silken-skinned like a youth in his powers, strong and hard and huge, with a desire a lust a need a power a fierce triumphant raging randy lust, and like Pan himself he seizes the woman, the princess, the goddess, the Divine Lover, his own Daemon, his own Other, seizes and enters and ravages and he takes her and oh the swirls and eddies of their frenzied, perfect motions; she becomes a pulsation, a tender vice, a point of light, taking unto herself again again her dear god her lusty Elemental her vigorous half-man half-goat; he seizes her by the hair and throws her face down, he hammers her delicate centre, he splits her in twain, he grinds himself deeper and deeper within, he is lord of Nature he is Supreme Intelligence, he enters the heart of all mystery. Gods are fucking the universe spins they are planets in the firmament and they cause explosions great enough to create new worlds, he roars like an erupting volcano and the scorching river of larva drowns the earth.

Which heaves great sighs and becomes still. And now it begins.

Now for the greater purpose of this rite: the first matter transmuted to Elixir. They take the 'matter which is neither alive nor dead', the transmuted substance, the spirit made flesh, the Magickal Child, the White Eagle and the Red Lion, the transubstantiation, and they will feed upon the flesh of God. The bodies have parted. Her fingers reach for the still throbbing, gently softening male organ, the Athanor, the furnace; his fingers reach for her sticky lower lips, Cucurbita, the gourd; they take the sweet sticky Nectar, and take it into their mouths: they consume the most holy sacrament, the rejuvenating Quintessence, the Elixir.

And she takes her awaiting bowl. And in the last seconds of divine incarnation she takes from his cock and from her vulva and the drops that streak their thighs she takes into her bowl, the most magickal essence, for using this she possesses the universal key of all Magick, she can make Nature change to her will.

This is only a start, she thinks. You will want more of this, there is more we can do. You will scourge me till my pain becomes ecstasy and you will need to come back to me again and again; you, my Chokmah, my Baphomet, my own Great Beast 666, and from this thunderous union of deities the power will rise in you, power to create to control to make music beyond your dreams, together oh the power to create!

A cold, naked man is lying, robbed and drained, in a dingy little Kings Cross room. He stirs and it is cold now, these coldest, darkest hours. He will leave. He will put on his clothes, and leave. There will be no words. He will leave.

JOHN CLARE

'El Rocco' from *Bodgie Dada & The Cult of Cool*

On the ledge of a red phone box in Darlinghurst in the late 1950s someone had written 'AUSTRALIA, LAND OF MEN WITHOUT WOMEN!' in thick black paint. If you walked back along Darlinghurst Road toward Sydney's Kings Cross, you would pass a number of coffee-shops that were usually filled with European men. Some of these expatriates were bearded. Many smoked pipes and there was usually a chess game in progress. Most women found the feeling of frustrated masculinity oppressive and soon asked to leave. One had the feeling that there were probably a number of formidable intellects there, with no-one to impress but each other. They were too alien to interest Australian women. Some of them ventured from these enclaves and visited El Rocco, a block away in Kings Cross itself, where their male singleness was somehow diluted.

'The most daring thing you could do in the late 1950s,' Clive James once said, 'was to listen to Errol Buddle at the El Rocco'. Daring had nothing to do with it for many listeners and musicians. By 1959, El Rocco had become the best and most famous modern jazz venue in the country and almost certainly one of the better clubs in the world. Certain factions would turn up for certain bands, but a sense that they were on to something beyond the mainstream was all that united the audiences on many nights. But there were hipsters there. Graeme Lyall said, 'They always knew what were the best new records to hear. When I came up from Melbourne I remember saying that I liked Benny Golson on tenor, and immediately this guy said that I should listen to Billy Mitchell with the Dizzy Gillespie band. He knew exactly what I was looking for, and he knew where I could hear it. He was always on the ball. There were a number of these guys. For the new-comer it was very difficult to tell who they were. Unlike the hippies of the next decade, or the beatniks of their own era, the hipsters betrayed no obvi-ous need to proselytise. Perhaps that would have seemed like the best way to wreck a good thing. If you asked their opinion, however, they would deliver it with a confidentiality that bordered on the secretive.

As long as you didn't try to talk over the music, you were left entirely to your own devices at El Rocco. There was no sense that anyone was judging, or even taking any notice of you. Daring? It was a sanctuary from the Cold War ethos, from an aggressively conformist suburbia in which bronzed Anzacs invited you outside to digest a knuckle sandwich if you accidentally said 'the magic word' in front of a sheila.

The mother of a young Sydney musician told me that she used to go to El Rocco with some other girls from a drama class. 'We thought of ourselves as beatniks,' she said. 'We smoked cigarettes and dressed in black and tried to look pale and interesting. I found the music incredibly exciting, and I'm still interested in it.' Yet people who thought of them-selves as beatniks were usually in the minority at El Rocco. Australian beatniks were more often interested in folk music (this is the scene from which Joan Baez and Bob Dylan emerged). Traditional jazz could conceiv-ably be seen in these terms, but certainly not modern jazz. The notion that beatniks were the main audience for modern jazz stems from the belated publication of Jack Kerouac's On the Road. Kerouac's novel was written in the 1940s. He called his protagonists 'beats'. This meant, more or less, that they were beatific deadbeats who eschewed material concerns and pursued the pleasures of the moment. These pleasures included rhythm and blues and bop, the two sides of 1940s black music. Some fans of Dizzy Gillespie aped his little ziff or goatee, his beret and his glasses (if they themselves did not need glasses, as Dizzy did, they wore dark ones). Perhaps they looked a bit like the beatniks of the late 1950s, who had been named by a

Los Angeles columnist, following the habit of putting 'nik' after every-thing (sputnik began orbiting in 1957). As Kerouac's novel was not published until the late 1950s, many readers have since assumed that he was writing about that era, instead of the 1940s. Many of the hipsters who went to El Rocco did resemble Kerouac's beats, in that they wore jeans and T-shirts or casual long-sleeved shirts. Few of them went in for the duffle coats and Jesus Christ mien of the beatniks.

Some of the younger musicians who began appearing at El Rocco devel-oped a taste for Ivy League clothes and for the clothes worn by black musi-cians on the covers of Blue Note, Prestige, Candid and other East Coast independent record labels. In fact, the two styles were hard to distinguish. The blacks for their part liked the idea of looking like English gentlemen. Ivy League—the reference is of course to the elite American college circuit—did have some vague echoes of English country life. The button-down collars, for instance, were said to have been invented by fox hunters to stop the peaks of their collars blowing up into their faces as they cleared fence and hedge.

The big suits of the bodgies had shrunk down to these tight three-button jobs which, with small modifications, were worn by advertising executives, rock and roll singers on 'Bandstand' and 'Six O'Clock Rock' (where the trousers were a little tighter, the shoes longer and pointier), plus black jazz and rhythm and blues musicians. The three-button suit was probably the most versatile cultural signifier of all time. Young musicians at El Rocco rarely wore suits, however.

El Rocco proprietor Arthur James was a great fan of Ivy League clothes. He had friends in advertising and the clothing trade who often hung around with him at his desk near the bottom of the stairs, impeccable at all times. To the more anonymous hipsters, these guardians of the gate were a bit of a joke, even though one of them owned the place. They certainly did not set the tone for other regulars, although there were certain musicians among the immaculates—most notably the drummer Lennie Young, whose playing was also greatly admired.

In fact, there was no dress code. 'The crowd,' according to Bruce Johnson, 'was as heterogeneous as white middle-class Sydney could produce. There would be Cross people but also outlanders from straight society: professionals and academics, TV and film people with an interest in music as an element of visual theatre.' Nor was the audience, in fact, limited to the middle class. It is interesting that jazz is called elitist to this day, even by people who submit themselves to the style police on the doors of their favourite dance clubs. Indeed, the hipsters may have been practising a form of elitism, but not of the ostentatious kind we are familiar with in the 90s. As we shall see, there was a particular kind of elitism among some musicians, but the jazz club at its best is a temple of egalitarianism, and El Rocco was one of the very best anywhere.

Melbourne's Jazz Centre 44 was up in a sort of tower beside a fun fair by a wide bay. Its main performances took place in the daytime. The room was actually quite big. El Rocco was downstairs in a tiny room below an apartment block on the corner of Brougham and William Streets, Kings Cross, and it was very much a night place. Both became modern jazz clubs in 1957. El Rocco opened in 1955 as a coffee-shop. The original space was a boiler room. This could only be expanded by quarrying out several tons of sandstone. Those who assisted in this back-breaking task dubbed the place the Rock. This was soon changed to El Rocco, which struck exactly the right tone for a Kings Cross coffee-shop. The Cross was in those days a very liveable environment in which an underworld (who didn't bother you so long as you didn't bother them, as the cliché goes) rubbed shoulders with an artistic and intellectual bohemia—to identify but two strands of the populace. Bassist and composer Bruce Cale, who later spent many years in America, said 'Kings Cross was very akin to Greenwich Village then. There was gangster element, but there was a lovely feeling of going to the Cross, to coffee-lounges, and talking about music until four or five in the morning.' One of those coffee-lounges was the Piccolo, which actually had a jazz jukebox. Knowing that musicians and chess-playing Europeans congregated here, Bumper Farrell's Vice Squad would sometimes rush in and sniff patrons' coffee to see whether they had put whisky in it. Rocco was a French saint. The artist Rocco Fazzari informs me that it also means a castle or fortification, but that it should be Il Rocco. 'El' is Spanish. In 1957, Arthur James—the manager of the coffee-lounge and son of the owner of the premises—installed a television. At a time when many people would stand in the street watching a TV set in a store window, this swelled custom. It might be imagined that TV was a despised symbol of materialism, but the fact is that musicians found certain shows to be very hip and came in to meet and to watch them.

The problem was that transmission finished at about 10 pm, leaving a certain vacuum. Drummer Ralph Stock suggested to Arthur James that a jazz group might be suitable on Sunday nights after the TV closed down. Stock then moved his existing combo from the Arabian Coffee Lounge to El Rocco. The Arabian was itself a most exotic place run by a flamboyant Russian woman who had come to Australia in the 1930s. It was upstairs near the El Alamein fountain. Bodgie David Perry remembers hearing two blonde women—sisters perhaps—scat-singing wildly at the Arabian in the early 1950s.

Needless to say, the jazz soon took over from the TV at El Rocco and more and more nights were thrown open to bands until the club was presenting contemporary music five nights a week. Some of the musicians who played there in the first couple of years were Don Burrows, Ron Falson, Col Nolan, David Levy, Judy Bailey, Ken Morrow, Joe Lane and Warren Leroy. Later, two distinct factions formed: the older musicians who were still largely involved with the cooler styles, and a younger group who wanted to sound hard and black. Bob Bertles said, 'We heard what Don [Burrows] was playing as gentleman's jazz. My idols were Sonny Stitt and Jackie McLean—a cracking New York alto player. I liked the sound of that Jazz Messengers front line of trumpet and alto—Bill Hardman and Jackie McLean—that brittle sound, like a whip cracking, you know. It was happening. Of course we were very young. Now I draw from all areas, including Lee Konitz and Paul Desmond and try to make something of my own from it.

Drummer Barry Woods arrived from New Zealand at the height of the hard/cool split. He began working on 'Bandstand' with Don Burrows. 'Don was really helpful, until one night I said I'd been to the El Rocco and heard these guys Bertles and Keith Stirling, playing some fantastic music. Don hardly spoke to me after that.' Some older musicians—Errol Buddle and Frank Smith most notably—transcended these divisions, as did Burrows himself often enough on a purely musical level. Nor was the hot and cool split always along age lines. Dave Levy was a very young advocate of the Dave Brubeck school. 'I thought the hard bop stuff was disgusting,' he said, 'until I got stoned one day and listened to Art Blakey and the Jazz Messengers. I wish I'd left it there as far as the pot was concerned. I remember seeing Bob Bertles leaning right forward over his saxophone, playing very hard, and I thought that was terrible. Later I began to think that East/West, Black/White division must have been created by writers.'

Above the narrow doorway a thin, condensed but rounded species of art deco lettering spelled JAZZ CELLAR in caps. This was not a neon, but raised lettering within a shallow lightbox, which was extended down a certain way on either side of the door, where current attractions were advertised in dynamic hand-lettering or elegant modern typefaces (you simply unlocked the light box and stuck the printed material in there). As a result, most likely, of the expansion of the advertising industry, this was an era that seemed very conscious of typefaces. Reid Miles and other designers made great use of typography—which became the major design element on the covers of Blue Note albums. There was a sense that one should do as much as possible with existing fonts before breaking into the free forms of hand-lettering. Contrary to rumour, modern design and modern jazz thrived on rigorous discipline. It is difficult to know to what degree Blue Note covers influenced or drew on advertising.

Down in the cellar, the band played on the same level as the audience. In fact, a stage in such a tiny space would have been ludicrous. A false ceiling of hessian seemed to improve the acoustics and also to give the place a kind of sawdust-coloured ambience that aided concentration. The wooden tables were glass-topped and the chairs skeletal, with woven cloth backs. The walls were bare, except for a couple of sets of parallel wooden strips, or brackets, between which some photos of jazz musicians were fixed, giving a rudimentary Mondrian effect in black and white. The double bass could be played unamplified and, when the tiny place was packed with sound-absorbing bodies, horns could be played hard and loud—and also very softly—without distortion. The sound was direct, and the performances were often very intense. I remember going down there and hearing Lyn Christie singing in unison harmony with his bass and thinking that this was the most eerie and evocative sound I had heard (of course it was a modern adaptation of a technique used by Slam Stewart in the 1930s), or reaching the bottom of the stairs with tenor saxophonist Keith Barr in full cry and thinking that it couldn't be much better than this in New York.

Arthur James made several unsuccessful applications for a liquor licence, but decided in the end that the place was probably better off without one. 'You couldn't get this to happen anywhere else,' he said. 'Once people start to drink, the main drawcard will be the drink. When you have that, they'll start to get more rowdy, and they'll listen to the music in a different way altogether. People go down there to have a drink. That'll be first, and then the music . . . This is what made the whole place . . . You sat in a room, all squashed up together—and they were in there like sardines—and you could hear a pin drop.'

John Sangster, who moved into a funny little penthouse on the roof (which had been vacated by drummer John Pochée) and stayed there through the life of El Rocco, puts it more bluntly: 'The coffee was undrinkable and the sandwiches were made of cardboard. There was nothing else to go there for. Just the music. It might have started to get a bit fashionable towards the end, but most of the time, people were there for one thing: the music.'

When pianist and composer Judy Bailey arrived from New Zealand, she found '. . . an atmosphere that I had not experienced before—or since. The coffee was awful, but the tea wasn't too bad. The diversity of people who went there was incredible. Over the years I've had many people come up to me and say they first heard me at this tiny little place. A lot of them can't remember the name, but as soon as I say it, recognition dawns. The thing that strikes me is that these people come from all walks of life. I don't think there was any particular image, because jazz was—this is something that [Melbourne pianist] Tony Gould said—jazz was almost beyond culture. Many of us were drawn to the music before we ever got to see a photo of our heroes. I know I was. If an image came, it was later. The music came first.

✳

By 1959, the TV was long gone and El Rocco was purely a jazz club. In that year Mike Nock caused a sensation with his 3-Out Trio. With Dutch expatriate Freddy Logan on bass and Greek-born Chris Karan on drums, this trio played a steaming, non-stop, bluesy, ecstatic power jazz that was influenced by such Americans as Bobby Timmons and Oscar Peterson. At times these performances also included some 'free' improvisation without predetermined chord changes. Grimacing, his eyes screwed shut and his feet stamping, the small, wiry Nock was like a little monkey of passion. People queued around the block to get in when the trio was playing.

'That was a cathartic experience,' said Nock. 'There was a woman called Babs who used to sort of moan and keen through the music, and there were these characters who'd get up in that tiny space and dance by themselves. Dancing by yourself was very unusual in those days. Something happened there. We'd be sweating heaps and there'd be all these people going apeshit over it. The club was like a church then. It was like a black gospel church. Everything was new. We felt like an élite. You'd be stoned, walking the streets, and nobody around you knew. It was almost like the hashish clubs of France. Actually I was against all authority, and from an early age it was only the fear of missing out on the music that kept me straight, or I'd be in jail now. There was a whole scene around jazz. Jazz comics, like Lenny Bruce, Mort Sahl, Ken Nordine. John Olsen used to come to the El Rocco. People like that. You know, everyone had the cool pads with the blue lights or the red lights. Cats who wouldn't come out until after dark. People who dressed immaculately. The music had a lot of the blues in it. A lot of energy. It was the centre of most esoteric activity. Am I right in thinking that Rosaleen Norton the witch used to come down to the El Rocco?'

I told Nock that I thought not. Most people who were around in that era have a Rosaleen Norton story. A friend and I used to sit in the Kashmir coffee lounge opposite the Rex Hotel in McLeay Street while Norton painted a mural around the top of the walls from a ladder. We talked a great deal about art and music, possibly in the most excruciatingly earnest and naive terms and Norton seemed to grow older and more world-weary by the minute as this drivel floated up to her. To us she looked very old to begin with. I never saw her at El Rocco.

Certain of Arthur James' friends would put whisky in their coffee, whether he was aware of it or not; joints were sometimes smoked on the roof or around the corner and the pub opposite was handy during the breaks, but El Rocco itself was not generally a place of such indulgence. The one drug raid there was a fruitless follow-up to a bust that had taken place elsewhere. Dave Levy was caught smoking a joint in his flat. Then, as a matter of form, the Vice Squad swooped again in ridiculous numbers while he was playing in the club. 'I'd just finished a tune, but there was no applause, so I thought I'd better just play the next one and hope that went over better. At that point I heard Sergeant Abbott's voice behind me, saying, "I think you'd better announce a break, David." I looked up and there were cops at intervals all around the walls. Of course, I didn't have anything on me. The whole thing was very distressing, though. They'd thrown me up against the wall at my place. In fact, one had a sledge-hammer and another one had an axe and they smashed the door off its hinges. I was held in remand, sent to Goulbourn jail in a train with these two characters who seemed to be planning to shoot a warden and there was a headline in the *Sydney Morning Herald* along the lines of "Jazz Musician on Sex Drug Charge!" That's right, they still thought it was a sex drug. They wanted me to dob people in. All of that. I was amazed at how much information they had on people I knew. It was quite disturbing. As a result, I had a bit of a nervous breakdown.'

Heroin use was rare. Keith Barr, a truly great tenor saxophonist, arrived here from England with a heroin habit (and diabetes). He came in the band of Basil Kirchen, which was brought out by Lee Gordon to play in one of his clubs. Kirchen was one of the first people busted for marijuana in Australia. Like Lester Young, with whom he had played on passenger liners in bands led by Tadd Dameron, Barr was of diverse and exotic descent— Armenian and Chinese—but spoke with a cockney accent. He took his place with Frank Smith, Errol Buddle and Bob Gillett as one of the absolute kings of the saxophone to whom all the young players looked for inspiration and guidance. Bob Gebert remembers Coleman Hawkins putting his arm around him and saying, 'This is my man!'

In the last years of El Rocco, John Sangster led a band which usually included saxophonist Graeme Lyall, pianist Judy Bailey, bassist George

Thompson and drummer Alan Turnbull. Sometimes trombonist Bob McIvor was added. It should be noted that these experiments were far from rarefied or unpopular. As with the 3-Out Trio, queues often formed outside the club. 'Not all our experiments were greeted with wild enthusiasm by our mentor Arthur James,' said Sangster. 'Sometimes we went "too far out", but the audiences loved it. I'd been to two World Expos with Don Burrows, and had brought back all kinds of fresh and new ideas and approaches to the music, which dear long-suffering Arthur sometimes went along with. Which tolerance, during those early years of their musical development, gave encouragement and impetus to such important figures as Bob Gebert, Bernie McGann—who has become an internationally known and respected composer and player, both through his recordings and his cultural tours abroad—and John Pochée.

'Arthur, far from being your average get-rich-quick entrepreneur, had more than his share of setbacks and financial difficulties. He also managed to handle our crowd of young incipient prima donnas, pour oil on troubled waters when necessary, and generally keep the music coming out and the audiences coming in.'

Sangster has elsewhere attributed the explosion of creativity that has occurred in Australian jazz in the nineties to a climate of experimentation, first established at El Rocco, in which players dared to find '. . . a sound and style that was distinctly theirs, not carbon copies of Americans'.

Such was the international reputation of El Rocco—*Down Beat* magazine cited it as one of the great jazz clubs of the world. Most jazz musicians who came to town, whether as concert artists in their own right or as accompanists to popular artists, sought the place out and usually played there. Graeme Lyall remembers hiding in the tiny kitchen because American drummer Larry Bunker was sitting in and he did not want to make a fool of himself in such exalted company.

Only three women played at El Rocco: pianists Judy Bailey and Marie Francis, and an excellent drummer, the late Molly Parkinson. Then, there was only one other female modern jazz instrumentalist playing at a high level at the time: guitarist Valda Hammock. Bailey said, 'I was not aware of any barrier, but in retrospect I think there may have been a few. Just a few particular incidents lead me to believe that I was living in blissful ignorance. Everyone was very encouraging. I was often complimented. In a way, I wish people had been a little more honest, which would have helped me with some of the problems I had.' Coming from a religious background in New Zealand, Bailey was also quite shocked by the dope smoking. As a result, she was not invited when the men went off to have a smoke, and this made her feel excluded.

El Rocco finally became part of mainstream Sydney culture. Fashion parades were held there. Clive James' statement, with its implication that this was a convenient place to sight some bohemia, was true enough in the end. It was rumoured that a high society debutante had taken a job as a waitress there in order to make herself more pale and interesting, so to speak, and no doubt more newsworthy. It is to Arthur James' considerable credit that this made no difference whatsoever to the music policy. In fact, some of the most adventurous music of all was played at that time. That he did not try to 'commercialise' the place or present some Hollywood version of jazz to the tourists was some kind of a miracle, given the instincts of most club owners. What he did do in the end was close it. James had actually planned to make further extensions, possibly linking the cellar with space that was available on the first floor, but a trip overseas convinced him that big changes were coming in entertainment, so he closed down in 1969. This was the height of the hippie era and the club was as popular as ever. I can't help but think that if El Rocco had continued, the place of jazz in the great effusion of 1950s, and 1960s, creativity would now be more readily acknowledged locally.

PETER DOYLE

from *Get Rich Quick*

Two years before, Lee Gordon had been worth half a million pounds, now he was stony broke. His last few Big Shows, with Abbott and Costello, Betty Hutton and Bob Hope, had all stiffed. He'd made back some good dough with Bill Haley, but that had gone on debts. He was doing the Little Richard show on the cheap, meaning we'd be paid after he collected. Lee was used to the high fall. Back in the States he'd made a million dollars and blown it again before he was more than twenty-one years old.

Turned out he was doing the whole promotion on the nod—he'd persuaded Pan Am to fly the show out here on a promise, the promise being that if they covered him now, he could pay back the thousands of quid he already owed them from the last few shows. Likewise the hotels, stadiums and internal flight costs were all on tick. As well, he'd managed to scab some brand new Chevs from a hire-car company in William St. I said Jesus, Lee, I'd love to know how you manage to run up so much credit. He said sure, he'd tell me the secrets of his success one day, if he ever managed to climb out of this present hole.

'I'll tell you one thing though, Billy. Your creditors are your greatest business allies—they're the ones with the biggest stake in your future success.'

'Yeah, I can personally vouch for that, Lee, me being one of them.'

'And you know you'll triple your investment if this show goes well.'

I rang Max, who I knew to be presently financially embarrassed, seeing how he'd invested all his and his mum's money in Teddy Rallis's caper. He was happy to do the driving job. He was a fan of Little Richard records, looked forward to meeting the band.

I asked Teddy to drive one of the cars. He said beaut, he'd like to meet Little Timmy. I said, Teddy, it's Richard, Little Richard. He said yeah, he knew. I arranged for his goon baby-sitters to drive another three of the cars. Vic Camellieri, who used to work in his father's milk bar at Bondi, took the remaining car. He thought it was great, wanted to meet Gene Vincent, told me he was certain Vincent was actually Maltese—just look at him, he said, Maltese, just like Presley.

Busy week. That same Thursday night Laurie O'Brien knocked on my door. I hadn't spoken to him since Max and I screwed him for six thousand pounds in 1952. I'd seen him once or twice at the races, but I'd been careful to keep clear of him.

He stood at my door with an old suitcase in his hand.

'How are you, Billy?'

'The fuck do you want?'

'You could invite me in and give me a drink. I haven't had anything but homebrew for the past two years.'

'Laurie, you tried to get me killed. I brassed you for six grand. To tell you truth, I'm not too clear on what the correct etiquette is in this situation.'

'Let's have a drink and try to figure it out.'

'What do you want, Laurie?'

'I just got out of the Bay this very day. I've got nowhere else to go, Billy. Let me in, son.'

Son. Jesus, he could lay it on thick.

'You better come in then.'

A couple of years before, Laurie had fallen out with Ray Waters, who was a Chief Superintendent by then. Waters had formed an alliance with Little Jim Swain, Laurie's rival. Waters pinched him for conspiracy to rig a race—substitute a good horse for a nag—which was like getting done for lying on a tax return—a bit illegal but it went on all the time.

While Laurie was on remand, Waters repeatedly raided his SP premises until he went right out of business. He sold his house at Maroubra to pay his legal costs and to keep himself afloat. They set fire to his block of flats at Maroubra Junction. No one was hurt, but it was so obviously arson that the insurance company refused to pay up. Then Laurie copped two years for the conspiracy.

Swain and Waters had set themselves the project of taking over Laurie's business. Pretty easy with Laurie out of action, but six months later Swain keeled over dead from a heart attack in the dining room at Big Tatts.

Laurie did his time. They sent him out to Oberon for a while. Laurie spent the rest of his money trying to keep himself comfortable in the nick. When that ran out he started a book, which only kept him in gaol currency, cigs and homebrew.

'So that's it, son. I'm up the creek.'

We were sitting around the coffee table in my flat, well into a bottle of Cutty.

'What are you going to do?'

'I've got my plans, don't you worry about that.'

'So what do you want from me, Laurie?'

'Can I stay here for a few days while I sort myself out?'

'I don't think so, Laurie.'

'I know I owe you, Bill, but please give me a chance. Come on, Bill, I know you're not the type to keep a grudge.'

'I've got things on this week, Laurie.'

'I'll keep out of your way, son, I promise.'

'Well, a few days then, Laurie, but that's it, I don't want you thinking this is the People's Palace.'

That night he drank himself unconscious, fell asleep muttering about something I couldn't quite catch. I put a blanket over him and left the fire on.

He woke before me the next morning. When I got up at eight, he'd already showered and folded up his bedding. He'd made a pot of tea.

It was a cold morning and I took my cup of tea over to the front window, which copped a bit of sun at this time of year.

Thirty yards down Barcom Avenue, behind my car, a Hillman was parked with two men in the front seat. They didn't seem to be doing anything much.

Laurie was pretty spry. He took my cup away and washed it after I'd finished it. I asked him what his plans were. He said he'd say hello to a few people, maybe go see his brother across town in Lakemba.

'Do you want to take my car?'

'Really?'

'Yeah, take the car if you want.'

'Are you sure?'

I looked out again. The two were looking at the flats, talking.

'Yeah, go for it.'

Fifteen minutes later when he left, the two blokes were still outside. When Laurie took off in my Customline, they started up and pulled out behind him.

I waited half an hour then got the port full of hot jewellery from my room and tied it up with cord and an old belt, and walked down to Bayswater Rd.

The morning was still cold. The south-westerly wind had blown in some scrappy, low cloud off the sea, turning it into a half-grey day.

I flagged a cab which had just turned out of the Red De-Luxe base, told him to take me to Central Station, steam platform.

There were thirty cabs on the rank there, so I didn't get him to wait.

I put the case into a locker. The sign said the lockers were cleared out every Monday morning, so I had till Sunday night to find a better hiding place for the loot.

I rang Teddy from the public phone at the station. He told me nothing much had happened, good or bad. I told him about the car outside my flat. He said that was bad news, did I get their number plate. I said no, I didn't think of that. He asked where the gear was now, I told him, he said good.

'But Teddy, how could anyone possibly know that I'm involved? For that matter, how could anyone know that *you're* in it?'

'The hoisters might have dobbed us in.'

'But why?'

'They've got their money once. If they get the stuff back again, they're laughing. We're not going to the jacks to complain, are we?'

'But isn't it the Darling Harbour mob that put the wind up you in the first place? How do these mugs fit in?'

'Maybe they're connected. Maybe they heard something around the traps. Maybe they're cops. I just don't know, Billy.'

I rang Max, filled him in.

'Oh yeah, one more thing. Guess who arrived at my place last night, wanting a roof over his head?'

'Who?'

'Laurie O'Brien.'

'The fuck does he want?'

'He got out of the slot yesterday. He says he wants to forgive and forget.'

'Kind of strange, him arriving out of the blue, you with forty grand's worth of hot jewellery in your sock drawer.'

'Might be coincidence.'

'Don't forget, pilgrim, this is the same geezer who arranged to have you bumped off.'

'We took his money.'

'So what's that mean—you're even? Bullshit. Billy, keep an eye on the old cunt. I speak partly out of self-interest here, so you know I'm dinkum.'

'Thanks a heap for the concern. Why don't you come around later on, say hello to him.'

'Yeah, maybe.'

I walked east through the steam train terminal, down the stairs to the electric train platforms, straight through to Elizabeth Street. I bought a *Telegraph* and went across the road to the Oceanic Cafe. I was cashed up enough to eat at a classier place, but I had a sentimental attachment to the Oceanic. I ordered a mixed grill and read the paper.

There was a cartoon on page three, of a giant Chesty Bond lookalike, labelled 'Australian Worker', rolling up his sleeves and making a fist at a lowbrowed, thuggish-looking character, labelled 'standover rackets'. There was nothing new on the J. Farren Price robbery. On the page with the movie and stage show reviews there was an ad for the next Big Show. It said, 'Lee Gordon presents ROCK 'N' ROLL.' Little

Richard had top billing. There was a photo of him with his arms spread, his head thrown back like a wild man.

I finished my breakfast and walked home.

That night I stayed in and so did Laurie. If the Hillman really had followed him, and if he'd noticed it, he didn't mention it. In fact he didn't say much at all. Television had come in while he'd been at the Bay, and I had a 21-inch Kriesler in the lounge room. Laurie sat staring at it all night, and he had it on again already when I got up on Saturday morning. 'That Crusader Rabbit's a clever little chap, isn't he?' he said.

The day's race meeting was at Randwick. I thought Laurie might go out there, show the world he was back in the action, but he said he'd stay in, if it was all the same to me. I said suit yourself.

I made a few selections from the *Telegraph* form guide that morning and went up to the Mansions to place some bets and grab a counter lunch. I could have rung the bets through, but I wanted to get away from Laurie for a while, have a couple with the lads in the pub.

The Hillman was parked up near the corner. I walked past it around the corner and up Craigend Street, stopping to light a cig after a hundred yards or so. Two blokes came walking up the road behind me. One of them had a crew cut. He had on a leather jacket, the other one was wearing a blue cardigan, fair-haired bloke. Tough-looking lairs. The fair-haired one had a broken nose, maybe did a bit of boxing. I walked briskly up to the Mansions and saw them walk past the door. They didn't come in. I spent the afternoon in the bar but I didn't see them again all that day.

I rolled out of the hotel at five o'clock, half-stung, seventy quid ahead on the day's punting. I swallowed a couple of dexedrine pills, which straightened me up well enough and then I went on to the Astoria for some dinner. The dexes pretty well killed my appetite, but I always liked to finish up an afternoon's punting with a visit to the Astoria. I managed half a vienna schnitzel and some strong coffee, then ambled back to Barcom Ave.

Max was back at the flat when I got there. He'd done his last forty pounds that afternoon, and needed some petrol and drinking money to get to a gig he had at the Manly Hotel. Since late closing had come in, some of the bigger pubs had taken to putting on floor shows. The publicans were playing it safe, though, avoiding boogie-woogie or rock 'n' roll combinations, figuring that they'd attract the riffraff.

Not that Max was too put out about that. When Del up and left town and the music business, he sort of gave up on rock 'n' roll. His style of boogie-woogie piano in the key of C was looking and sounding a little old-fashioned for the young crowd and though his guitar playing was pretty good, he didn't really twang it the way they did now. So he started up a hawaiian act which he took around to the pubs and RSL clubs. The feature of the act was a couple of hula dancers who did a semi-blue dance routine—more like a striptease cum belly dance than a hula. They billed it as 'The Forbidden Dance of the Islands'. Max gave the publicans and club secretary-managers a spiel he'd written himself but attributed to a supposed anthropologist called 'Dr Kutisarki', from Cutty Sark, and another one attributed to Prof. Benjamin Zadrine, as in benzedrine, which authenticated the performance as being Polynesian native rituals with profound spiritual significance.

Max and Laurie were kind of sizing one another up when I lobbed, doing the small talk thing. Max had found my piss but Laurie seemed to be staying dry again.

'Back any winners?' I asked Max.

'I backed Narcolepsy. It ran so wide it knocked a pie out of a bloke's hand in the leger.'

'Yeah. Bad luck.'

'I'll say. I was fucking robbed. By rights it should have won.'

'A good thing beaten, eh?'

Laurie spoke to Max. 'So you still like a punt, Max?'

'Oh, yeah, Laurie, I suppose so, a flutter now and then, you know.'

'Why do you bet, Max?'

'Why? What kind of question's that? I don't know, for fun, for profit, to keep bookies like you in fancy houses.'

Laurie looked at him, a bit of a smirk on his face.

The next morning, Monday, was cold and windy. The bushfires around town were burning fiercely, and you could smell eucalyptus smoke in the air, along with the dust and coal smoke. The air was so dry I was getting electric shocks off anything I touched. The wind gave me a headache, or maybe it was just a dexedrine hangover.

I walked up to the Cross and bought the papers, read them over a cup of tea. The Russians had just launched the Sputnik. They reckoned it would be going right over Sydney in a couple of nights' time. In America they'd sent the army into Little Rock, Arkansas where the governor was being a shit in regard to Negro schoolkids. The Russians said the Sputnik would be flying over Little Rock, as a symbol of hope to enslaved people everywhere.

There was nothing about the J. Farren Price robbery. Last I'd seen was a week ago, a story saying that the police investigation was proceeding, a number of leads were being looked into, the sort of stuff which usually means the cops didn't have a clue and were waiting for some give-up to come forward and tell them who did it.

I left my kero heater going all morning, it was that cold.

So that afternoon I was driving the crew back into the Hampton Court Hotel, with my old girlfriend nagging me to buy her some heroin, and the jewellery in the boot of the borrowed Chev. We were driving along South Dowling Street.

'Molly, I wouldn't even know where to get heroin. I don't know anyone who uses it, and even if I did, I still don't think I'd get it. Jesus, didn't you see *The Man with the Golden Arm?*'

'Come on, Billy, don't turn square on us. This is really serious.'

'Is that what's wrong with your pal Marty?'

'Yeah.'

'Then he should lay off it.'

'It's lack of heroin that's making him sick.'

'What about you, Molly, do you take it too?'

'A little.'

'How come you're not sick?'

'I am.'

'Shit!'

Eddie Cochran and Alis Lesley hadn't said anything through all of this. Marty was in the back seat groaning.

We got to the hotel and got them all settled in their rooms.

Lee arrived a little later, looking like a big shot, welcoming the artistes, pouring champagne, introducing radio announcers to the stars, arranging interviews. Lee knew Marty from years ago in the States. After a while Lee signalled me to meet him across the room, away from the journos.

'We gotta do something for Marty. He's dope sick.'

'Yeah, I know. But shit, Lee, he'll get better, won't he?'

'Not in time for the show tomorrow.'

'Sack him then.'

'It's not that simple, Billy. His girl's an old sweetheart of yours?'

'Yeah. Small world, eh?'

'Would you cop for him if it wasn't for the chick?'

'Listen, Lee, it's like I told her, I wouldn't even know where to get any. And if you mean that I'm dirty on him and that's why I won't go hunting for dope, that's not it. Me and Molly were years ago, like back in the Dark Ages.'

'Whatever, Billy, it's not my business, but you know, maybe you don't really know your own mind on it, if you'll pardon me for being Mr Know-Everything.'

'That's alright. Back in '52 when I last saw her it was "she loves me, she loves me not", and it finished up on the "not", for her anyway. I got there later, I guess. I was off tap about it for a while, but not now, not for a long time.' I didn't add that Molly and I went back to the war years, when we were both teenagers and learning fast, together and separately, and I could never really be neutral towards her either.

'Yeah, alright. I can dig it. The chick has gone to their room. She asked for you to drop in on her.'

The Little Richard entourage had the top two floors of the hotel. I took the lift up there.

Molly answered the door to their room when I knocked. She was wearing satin slacks, looked like a burnt out Mamie Van Doren, except she had a blanket around her shoulders. The electric radiator was on full.

'Grab yourself a drink, Billy.'

'Where's the clown?'

'Marty? He's in the bedroom. He's taken some pills to knock himself out.'

'How'd you get mixed up in this shit, Molly?'

'In stages, I guess.'

As I was looking at her, a sweat broke out on her face. Then she sneezed, once, twice and again. She had a hanky to her face. Her eyes were watering and her nose was running. Then she started sneezing in earnest, maybe twenty times. She finished with a fit of coughing that turned into retching.

She flopped down on the armchair, drew her knees up to her face and started crying.

She sat there shivering and sweating. I went over to her and put my hand on her shoulder. She recoiled like she'd been given an electric shock.

'Is this from the dope?' I said.

She nodded, her head on her knees.

'Christ, Molly. This is terrible. I'll see what I can scrounge.'

'Really?'

'I can't promise anything. I'll try but.'

She stood up immediately, started brushing her hair. 'I'll come with you. You got anything at all?'

'Some dexedrine.'

'Give me some. Anything's better than this.'

'Have you got any money?'

'Not really.'

'How about Marty?'

'As if. But Lee's an old friend of his. He'll give you some.'

'As if. He's broke. Don't worry, if we do actually find any, I've got a few bob.'

'This is very good of you, Billy.'

'Listen, Molly, I'll try to get some for you, but before I do that, tell me, why don't you just kick it now while you've got the opportunity?'

'It's not like that.'

'No?'

'In a few days I won't be sick any more, but there's more to it than the sickness. It's like you've got nothing left to live for. Nothing else counts.'

'But in time, doesn't that pass?'

'It never passes, not really.'

Marty tagged along. If we were going to find any dope, he wanted to be there when we did. In the lift we bumped into Eddie Cochran. He motioned me aside.

'Listen, man, I know you kinda got your hands full, but, ah, hell, I'd really like to have a look at the town before it gets dark.'

'Jeez, Eddie, I'm headed for the dives and dens, we're not really doing the tourist route.'

Eddie beamed. 'That's OK, brother, that's my kind of guided tour. I'll ride shotgun. Hell, man, you might be grateful to have me along as back-shooter.'

I walked down and picked up the Customline from outside my flat and drove back to the Hampton Court. I didn't want to drive around town looking for drugs in a hire car. Back at the hotel I took the Globite out of the Chev and put it in the boot of my car.

It was four in the afternoon when we started at the Macquarie Hotel at the 'Loo. Marty and Molly waited in the car. Eddie had a couple of beers with some bodgies who had recognised him, while I made some enquiries with a couple of the crims there. No result.

We went to the Ship Inn, the Orient, and then Monty's, all with no result. Eddie was recognised by the bodgies everywhere we went, had a beer with them all while I spoke to the fences and lurk men.

In the end it was Eddie who got the tip on where to get some dope. He was having a drink with a Scottish teddy boy, a seaman, down at the First and Last Hotel. Eddie called me over and introduced me. The Scot, Andy, had asked Eddie if he'd like some reefer. He'd got hold of some marijuana in Sumatra last time he'd passed through, said it was the strongest dope in the world. I told him we were looking for heroin.

'No, I'd never touch that stuff. But some of the fellers on the boat do, and they got some here in Sydney.'

'Who from?'

'Ask the old grey bloke. He put them on to it.' He pointed to a fellow drinking alone at a table.

'Thanks, Andrew. While I'm at it, I'll have some of that reefer if you can spare it.'

'It's not rolled up into ciggies yet. You'll have to do that yourself. Can you roll a cigarette?'

'Yeah, that'll be alright.' When I'd bought dope before from Chet, it was already made up into reefers.

'Just mix this stuff half and half with tobacco.' He passed me a matchbox, I gave him five quid.

I bought two scotches and went over to the old bloke Andy had pointed out. He was a dead-eyed, unsmiling old codger. He still had his hat on, drawn low over his face. He must have been nearly sixty, but I wouldn't have wanted to scrap with him. He looked like he'd glass you in a second.

He took the drink from me, gave a slight nod which might have meant thanks.

We talked racing for a while, then yarned about the old days. He opened up a little. Turned out he'd been a heavy before the war, a crony of some of the notorious old gangsters, people like Phil the Jew and Frank Green. I came clean about what I wanted, why I wanted it. He said, 'It'll cost you.'

'Yeah, I know the stuff's expensive.'

'I don't mean that. *I'll* want something.'

I gave him a five-quid note.

'Try the Chows.'

'But who?'

'There's a bloke who runs the pak-a-pu in Dixon Street. Louis something.'

'Louis Hoon?'

'Yeah, that's him. If he can't get you some, there isn't any to be had.'

'Thanks, dad.' I bought him another drink and left.

I knew Louis Hoon. He was a Malayan Chinese, about my age, supposed to be out here on the Colombo Plan or something. He was a big gambler and a racegoer, which was how I knew him. I'd heard he was an occasional opium user as well, but they said that about every Chinese. I'd never heard of him selling drugs.

When we left the First and Last, Eddie was half-drunk, so I gave him some dexes. Marty and Molly were in despair, sniffing and sneezing all the while, complaining of the cold.

I drove to Dixon Street and parked outside the Come Luck restaurant.

I went in a side door and up two flights of stairs and knocked on a door. It was opened by an old bloke who didn't say anything but grunted an enquiry.

I said, 'Where's Louis?'

'No Louis.'

I knew there *was* Louis. He ran his pak-a-pu from here.

'Tell Louis to come downstairs. I'm Billy.'

The door slammed closed and I turned around to go downstairs. It opened before I'd got out of earshot, and a voice called out to me. I walked back upstairs and Louis Hoon gestured me in.

There were twenty or thirty Chinese men inside in a large room. Louis took me into a side room bare except for a couple of chairs.

'How are you, Billy?'

'Good, very good. You?'

'So-so. I am not win daily double for very long time. What you want?'

'Louis, my friends from America are here. They are sick. They need something to make them OK. Heroin.'

'Like Golden Arm man?'

'Yeah, that's right.'

'This is very bad, Billy. You should leave them.'

'No, I can't Louis.'

'Who is friend, boy or girl?'

'My old girlfriend and her new boyfriend.'

'Ah! Americans are rich?'

'Not rich, Louis, but they can pay.'

'OK, come with me, maybe we can find. Do you take?'

'No, it's not for me, just for them.'

He nodded. 'That's good.'

He sent me back to the car and ten minutes later he came down himself, got in the front seat and told me to drive to Surry Hills. I introduced him to everyone, first names only.

Louis turned to Eddie and said, 'You sick man?'

'Not me, brother. Them.' He pointed to Molly and Marty beside him. Marty had brightened up at the prospect of a score. He smiled sweetly at Louis, gave him a friendly nod. Louis looked closely at him.

'You do this?' He made a miming gesture, pointing at the crook of his arm, jabbing his finger like it was a needle.

Marty nodded.

I drove up Campbell Street, across Elizabeth. It was dark now. People were walking up the hill from Central Station, going home. Others were going down to the station, leaving the small rag-trade factories and machine shops around the Surry Hills gully.

Louis directed me into Commonwealth Street and told me to stop. Some little Chinese kids were playing in the street. Nearly all the faces in the street were Chinese.

Louis went into a tiny terrace house. Ten minutes later he walked out of a different house, three doors down.

He came back to the car, said, 'Come.'

Marty and Molly were out in a flash. I followed. Eddie said he'd wait in the car, he wasn't of a mind to go kicking old Buddha's gong.

Louis took us inside a different terrace yet again, led us out the back, through a smoky, greasy kitchen where an old guy was frying noodles. We went through a door to the left and into an almost completely dark room and through a door at the other side. I figured we must be a couple of doors away from the house we started out in. Louis took us upstairs and through another doorway, into a dim room with a tattered couch, a mattress by the wall and a low table in the centre. Magazine pictures of women—mainly Hollywood movie stars—had been pasted up on the walls. The photos were of faces only.

Louis said, 'Wait here. Give me money.'

'How much?'

'Ten quid.'

I gave him the money and he was gone. I could hear noises from all around us, a mother calling out to a child, somewhere else men's voices, talking rapidly and laughing loudly. Elsewhere a regular dull thumping noise, like someone beating a carpet, except it went on and on.

Marty said, 'I think that guy's taken your bread, man. What'll we do if he doesn't come back? Have you got any more?' There was panic in his voice.

I didn't answer him.

An older Chinese man came into the room, lit a candle in a stick on the table and gestured us over. He drew a particle from a paper package and put it on a tin ashtray and handed a straw to Marty. He held the candle under the tray and after a few seconds the particle began to smoulder. He indicated to Marty to inhale the smoke through the straw.

Suddenly the particle, which was about the size of a peppercorn, started fizzing and darting around the tray as it liquefied momentarily before it burned. Marty inhaled but missed most of the smoke which tailed off from the little rock. The Chinese guy gestured that he'd have to use the end of the straw to chase the burning particle around the tray.

'This is called "chasing the dragon". You chase the dragon! OK?'

Marty nodded. The guy put another piece of the pink stuff onto the tray and this time Marty got it all. He drew it down deep like it was reefer smoke and passed the straw to Molly. The guy dropped another particle down and she repeated the act. Then he gestured to me. I shook my head.

Marty sighed deeply and said, 'Man, that's good shit.'

He had another couple of turns and so did Molly.

They stopped their sniffing and coughing. Their skin took on a dry, dead look and their mouths sagged in a strange way. They'd stopped complaining but to me they looked worse now than they had before.

We got up to leave and the Chinese guy gave the package to Marty and smiled.

He took us to the door, opened it, and Marty and Molly went out. As I went through the door, he gestured to Marty and said to me, 'First, man chases dragon. Later, dragon chases man.' He thought that was quite a hoot.

Louis met us outside the room and led us back to the street, a different way. We came out in a house around the corner in Ann St. Good trick.

Eddie was leaning on the bonnet of the Customline, talking to some Chinese kids.

We drove Louis back to Dixon Street.

When he got out, he said, 'Good luck.'

On the way back to the Hampton Court Marty spewed out the window of the car again.

'What's wrong with him now?' I said to Molly.

'It's the shit doing it to him.'

'I thought *not* having it made him spew.'

'So does having it. It's a different kind of spew, though.'

'Gee, some people sure know how to have a good time.'

Back at the Hampton Court I went upstairs to see if Max or Teddy was still there. There was a party going on in the main suite. A bunch of women had been rounded up somewhere and a couple were dancing. One of the girls had her blouse off, dancing in her bra. Gordon was there, and so was Little Richard, walking around kissing the women, kissing the men. O'Keefe was there, along with Catfish Purser, his drummer, having a pretty good time.

Gordon saw us all walk in, glanced at Marty, then called him aside. They both left the room. Molly went with them.

I couldn't see Ted, but Max was there whooping it up. He had a guitar out and was jamming along with one of Richard's band, who was bashing on the piano. Cochran picked up a bottle of champagne and joined them.

I interrupted Max, who told me Ted had split a while ago. I had a couple of drinks and circulated for a while, then after half an hour I went down to the Chev and got the Globite from the boot.

I took it upstairs and put it in the hotel room where they'd stored all the gear, the stage suits and instruments.

I went back to the party and said goodbye. I was nearly at the door when Lee re-entered the room with Marty. Lee looked ashen, his eyes were dim. He said was I right for tomorrow? I said yeah.

Before I left he said, 'And thanks for doing that for Marty and Molly.'

'It's no big deal. Are you alright, Lee?'

'Yeah, I'm fine.'

He was scratching his nose, running his hand around his mouth.

'Hey, Lee, watch out for that dragon, they reckon it bites.'

I rang Vic and Ted when I got home. Vic was OK for Wollongong, so was Ted, but the other two guys, his muscle men, wouldn't be available, they had jobs to get back to. I said that was OK, I'd get replacements.

'Actually, Bill, it might be a good thing to be out of town for a day or two with Little whatsisname, keep out of reach of those blokes.'

'Ted, we can't keep this up forever. Sooner or later we've either got to get rid of the stuff or have a showdown with the mugs.'

'I don't want a showdown. Don't worry, it shouldn't be too long now. I'm working on a contact now for the stuff. With a bit of luck I might be able to get rid of it in a few days.'

'Really? Thank Christ for that.'

'Sit tight. Gee, that Little Robert's a funny bloke isn't he?' he said.

'Ted, the name is *Richard*.'

'Yeah, whatever.'

The Sixties

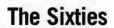

'Thus began my year of living
dangerously . . .'

—*Roberta Sykes*

By the early 1960s, crime had once again become a problem for Kings Cross, though it had nothing to do with sly grog or prostitution. Juvenile delinquency was on the rise, echoing the violence of the razor gangs of the 1920s. In 1963, the old Kings Cross Theatre on the corner of Victoria Street and Darlinghurst Road was remodelled into a rock 'n' roll dance venue called Surf City, though of course the only surf in sight at that time were the waves of screaming teenagers. There were some nights when as many as 2000 youths jammed into the new discotheque. Similarly, the Minerva Theatre changed its name to the Metro and also became a rock venue. American promoter Lee Gordon brought out rock'n' rollers such as Bill Haley to perform at the Stadium in Rushcutters Bay.

In the early 1960s, Reverend Ted Noffs of the Methodist Church responded to these growing problems by setting up the Wayside Chapel. It was established in two rooms of a ground-floor block of flats on Hughes Street. The chapel was open to all faiths, and attempted to meet the specific needs of the community in a direct and non-judgmental way. During the decade, Noffs opened a coffee shop as part of the Chapel, encouraging the flower children, the hippies, and the Beats to exchange artistic and spiritual beliefs. Since the Cross was becoming a haven for runaways from all over the country, and underage alcohol and drug abuse was on the rise, Noffs also opened a Crisis Centre.

However, it wasn't just juveniles who were beginning to rebel. In the 1960s, the famous Clune Gallery was converted into what was known locally as the Yellow House. It was Martin Sharp's urban shrine to surrealism, and soon became the Mecca for Australia's artistic avant-garde, housing many of Sydney's painters, photographers, writers, and musicians.

Meanwhile, a police station was established beneath the newly-built Crest Hotel. Its proximity to the loud and unpredictable Surf City venue, which was just across the road, was intentional. Still, when the then young poet Viv Smith first descended upon the Cross, he was too timid to be a delinquent (see the poem 'Twenty Years of Sydney'). Unlike his poetic forefather Kenneth Slessor, who was inspired by the seedy grandeur of the Cross, Bruce Beaver's poems about the 1960s in the Cross flinch from the brazen glare of neon lights and prefer instead the leafy foliage of Rushcutters Bay Park, with its scalloping seagulls and transcendental light.

It was also in 1967 that the first American servicemen on leave from the Vietnam War strode up the Wylde Street hill, just as their compatriots had done 25 years before. Like the R&R culture of the Second World War, prices skyrocketed, and the Cross became Americanised once again. Instead of the plush nightclubs and muted jazz of the 1940s, bars and taverns boasting American names and themes sprung up to accommodate the carousing G.I.s: the Texas Tavern, the Bourbon and Beefsteak, the R&R Restaurant, and the Arizona Inn. The Chevron Hotel on Macleay Street had already opened (see Ivor Indyk's essay 'The Silver Spade'), becoming Australia's first international hotel and its first bow toward modernity. Various international celebrities performed at the Chevron, including Jerry Lewis and Eartha Kitt. The American G.I.s established their headquarters in the bridal suite of the celebrated hotel. Figures reveal that at any one time during the late 1960s there were almost 1500 servicemen roaming through Kings Cross. Like their mothers before them, many young women flocked to the area in the hope of having a fling with a horny American marine with not much time on his hands but plenty of money.

As detailed in Roberta Sykes' chapter from her autobiography, *Snake Dancing*, go-go dancing was extremely popular in the Cross in the 1960s. At the beginning of in the decade, Sykes performed a sensual dance act with snakes in various local venues. As the years passed, clubs and bars were embellished with gyrating dancers locked inside cages suspended from the ceilings, the women wearing only skimpy G-strings and tasselled pasties glued over their nipples. Bars like the Whiskey a Go-Go on William Street proved hugely successful with the R&R boys, perhaps due to the fact that, unlike the perfunctory and sometimes confronting acts performed in the strip clubs, the go-go bars were more socially acceptable:

they were places where you could take your girl, have a few drinks, and be fairly confident that you wouldn't offend her. Topless waitressing also grew in popularity, with the famous, all-night Hasty Tasty Cafe at the top of William Street initiating the new trend towards the end of the decade.

Meanwhile, the regular strip clubs responded to the new permissiveness of the 1960s by taking it one step further—women dancing in venues like the Pink Pussycat and the Pink Panther now had to take off every stitch of their gear if they wanted to keep their jobs. Local prostitutes at that time adapted to the needs of their many patrons by establishing mobile brothels inside Kombi vans, and coordinating business via walkie-talkies.

ROBERTA SYKES

from *Snake Dancing*

I was soon to discover that the poorest people have a greater sense of caring for strangers than anyone else I have ever met. Despite having so little themselves, they look out for and respond to need.

Finishing up my last shift for the day, I found myself outside the hospital with my suitcase in my hand, a few coins in my pocket and nowhere to go. The Black woman told me that she had friends we'd run into on William Street who were bound to know what I should do. We also ran into the young man who had, with great chivalry, given up his bed for me the night before. With two shillings from here, another from there, and advice about where a clean room costing one pound seven and sixpence a week had recently been vacated, I was soon the proud occupant of a very tiny attic in Victoria Street, Kings Cross. The ceiling sloped sharply so that I could only stand upright on one side of the narrow room, but it had the luxury of the smallest refrigerator I had ever seen and I felt like a queen. The gift of a battered half-pint saucepan enabled me to heat water or cans of baked beans on a gas ring in the kitchenette one floor below, but the most precious present of all that I received at this time was the unquestioning friendship from the people I met.

They were all young, none more than about twenty years old. Most, like me, could fit all their worldly possessions into a suitcase, though some did not even own a suitcase. In the many long talks we shared, I learned that they all had aspirations, all wanted to do something better with their lives, had an eye on the future, and each had a story of family disintegration or alienation which had to a very large extent determined their present circumstances. However, despite their frankness with me, I felt unable to share my own story. Instead I picked out bits and pieces to tell them when it became my turn to speak. The secret pain I carried was still too raw, too ugly, too heavy, for me to lay at another's door. Thus began my year of living dangerously.

My path home from Sydney Hospital took me past a discotheque, then known as Sound Lounge, which my new Black friend had taken me to one night after work. It became the centre of my life. Scarcely a night went by without me slipping in there and dancing myself into a state of exhaustion, before going home to sleep. It was, I found, a very good way of keeping the demons at bay, of preventing myself from going into 'shocks'.

My frenzied rhythmic dancing, with which I had already won applause and competitions in Townsville, transformed me and I spent as much time dancing as I possibly could. Soon the manager of a Kings Cross nightclub asked me if I would be interested in dancing on stage and being paid to do so. I couldn't believe it. And when he said that I'd be paid more than double what I earned carrying plates backwards and forwards at the hospital, I thought I was having a fantasy. Because my life had been so unsettled I had been unable to write to my previous employers for copies of my references. Carrying dishes had begun to look like being my entire life.

It was not until I had given notice at the hospital that I learned there was a catch to the offer to dance. The costume I was to wear was brief. By today's standards it would be considered seriously over-dressed for work on the stage, but at the time any skimpy costume was generally thought to be downright immoral. Police came into the clubs from time to time with tape measures to ensure that the sides of the bottom of women's two piece costumes were no narrower than four inches. In these days of the string bikini, see-through clothes and topless beaches, the norms of the early 1960s seem ludicrous in retrospect. Still, even at the time New South Wales laws were considered progressive when compared to Victoria, where hotels closed at 6 pm and no alcoholic beverage could be served without being consumed with a meal after that hour.

I wasn't particularly happy about dancing around on a stage in a brief costume with everyone in the audience, fully dressed, watching, and my attitude showed. Another entertainer, Kahu, a Maori who used fire and snakes in his acts, took me under his wing. He suggested I include a snake in my own performance and I nearly fell off my chair. Why hadn't I thought of this myself? After all, my totem is the snake and I got along with them very well.

Under Kahu's guidance I bought a large python from a pet store near Central Station, made an appropriate costume which couldn't snag on the snake's skin and had a wooden case made in which to carry the snake from one venue to another, with a fine brass gauze panel installed in the top so it could breathe.

Kabu became a special friend to me, perhaps because he, too, was a long way from home and knew about depression and isolation. Also probably because we were two dark-skinned people trying to survive in the otherwise very white and quite closed world of entertainment. The other Black entertainers we saw were Americans—big-name stars visiting Australia for a few days to perform at expensive venues, such as Chequers, the Chevron Hotel and other classy nightclubs. They were often surprised to see our brown faces in their audience and some came out front after their shows to talk with us. A few even came to watch Kahu's performances or to sit around and chat. I particularly remember Earl Grant because he perched on my snake box when he joined us as there weren't enough chairs. After half an hour or so someone at our table told him that his uncomfortable seat was a snake carry-case. In disbelief he bent down and peered through the shiny panel, then let out a scream and went running up the stairs and into the street. We didn't see him back there that night.

Kahu was the first man I had met who could cook and sew. He kept his tiny flat immaculate and I was always a welcome guest. On what could have been the loneliest day of my life, Christmas Day 1961, in the late morning Kahu sent two of his friends to rouse me from my bed and bring me to his place for lunch and a small festive celebration. I was so overwhelmingly grateful for his concern for me that my tears threatened to ruin the day until he took me aside and said, 'We're all in the same boat here, all alone, and we all look out for each other. I cooked. Your job is to smile.' He had the capacity to make the complexity of life seem quite simple.

Over time I had several rock pythons, carpet and diamond snakes come to live with me. I named them, depending upon their gender, Lucifer, Satan, Diablo, Delilah and Jezebel, reflecting the way society reacts to these beautiful but largely unknown and unloved creatures.

Snakes provided me with personal security. As well as carrying them around with me in their box, I put up mesh on the windows and gave them free rein in my apartment. I often wore them under my coat, draped around me, and I would bring them to parks for sunshine and air, and the chance to climb in the trees. The snakes, like me, were from the north and unused to being in an urban environment. I took them mainly to Rush-cutters Bay Park to start their training and get them accustomed to being handled. Snakes are used to having their ten and twelve-foot long bodies almost completely supported along their length. Each one, therefore, required a great deal of love and patience to develop sufficient trust to allow it to be held aloft with only my hand beneath it for support.

To gain the snake's trust I would let it slide across my hand on the ground and lay there, then successively raise my hand a little higher, until at last the snake would have only its head and tail on the ground, the bulk of its body supported by my hand. It often took weeks to get this far. When at last I felt we were both ready, I'd raise the snake that last little bit further, and if my intuition was correct, the snake would allow itself to stay suspended for a few minutes. If not, the creature would whip its head and tail frantically and lash itself around me, struggling for purchase, some-times almost strangling me in the process!

The snake was happier to be worn when I was out walking than to be carried in its box. It would cling to me with the minimum strength required to hold itself in place, wound two or three times around my waist. If I stopped along the way to have a coffee or chat, however, it would squirm around to see why we'd come to a halt. Snakes love warmth but are unable to generate their own heat, so it's easy to see why they are so happy to nestle against a warm body.

Snakes do not hear but they pick up vibrations—and there aren't too many vibrations in their natural habitat. So exposure to loud music was another source of anxiety for them until they became used to it.

Because of my experience, and although I struggled against it, being out on the street, especially at night, made me very fearful. With my snakes, however, I felt much more in control since most people are afraid of snakes and know very little about them. On my occasional dates with men, for instance, it was not difficult to manoeuvre the outing to finish up at my place, where, of course, my snake would be just where I wanted it, waiting for me inside the door. In winter I'd leave the radiator on and thus be assured that it would be curled up in front of it. In summer, a baby's bath weighted down with a few inches of water in the bottom of it had the same effect—snakes love to lay in cool water on a very hot day. Otherwise the snake could be found in warm places, such as on top of my refrigerator or water heater. Men invited in for a coffee after an outing were usually on edge and anxious to leave at the earliest opportunity as soon as they realised we had company, that is if they didn't go screaming up the hall and out of the building as soon as I opened the door. I was asked to leave quite a few apartment buildings because of men screaming on their way out.

By accident, therefore, I had found the perfect way to keep men at arm's length. Rapists or potential suitors, they were all the same to me. Emotionally I was badly damaged and needed time to heal. I was not ready to get involved in relationships of a sexual nature. My lack of interest in men in this way was a source of curiosity and sometimes mirth to my small circle of friends, who nicknamed me 'Capon'—a desexed chicken. A couple of women who referred to themselves as 'camp' picked up on my disinterest in men, but I had no interest in sex with them either, though one in particular made a tremendous effort to befriend me. She always seemed to arrive at one of my favourite haunts just before me and arrange for the staff to have the strains of 'I want to be Bobby's girl' playing as I walked in.

I had moved from Victoria Street, Kings Cross into a variety of bed-sitters and flats, including a period living in the Tor, a large old castle that housed entertainers, writers and eccentrics. It had seen grander days and been subdivided into huge rooms-to-let.

Leila knew the area where I was living and started hanging around Kings Cross and trying to get into my group of friends by telling them she was my sister. I was extremely unamused. She managed to pick up people who I knew only slightly, and I was forever being given messages from her. I met two Canadians, Buddy and Jimmy, who Leila latched on to, initially as a channel to pass on titbits of irrelevant information to me. However, when she broke into their boarding house and stole some of their musical equipment and cameras, she became more than just a nuisance.

One morning I was walking along Darlinghurst Road and the proprietor of a small cafe was standing in his doorway. He greeted me and cheerily told me that he had given my 'sister, Leila' a loan to enable her to fly to Townsville and bring back her son. My blood ran cold. Leila had shown him a photo. When he described the child, I knew it was my son, Russel, who she was talking about and that the photo was one of those she had stolen from my suitcase.

I ran to the nearest post office and hastily wrote a note to Mum. Although I had told Mum what I was doing and how I was making a living, and sent her money for Russel, I had not written to her about the drama that had occurred between Leila and myself. My message to her was brief. *I am concerned for Russel's life and safety. Please do not leave him alone with Leila for any reason. Do not let her take him out anywhere. I'll write a longer letter later to explain.* I sent it off airmail express and special delivery.

My concern that Leila intended to abduct Russel was well founded, but Mum was alerted and no opportunity arose. I had begun to suspect that Leila was taking some sort of drugs, a guess based on the company I had heard she was being seen with. She returned to Sydney but did not pay back the cafe proprietor's 'loan', a fact he apprised me of from time to time. Instead of moving back to the Coogee flat she briefly took a room in Kings Cross.

I next heard that Leila had gone to work at a hospital somewhere around Surfers Paradise. I felt relieved as she was a threat to me in so many ways—embarrassing me by telling people she was my sister in order to get close to them, then stealing from them, telling lies, not to mention the physical threat that she posed. When I learned that she had gone, I arranged for Russel to spend a few weeks with me.

What a lovely time we had together! He was about eighteen months old and full of mischief, and his stunning looks turned heads. However, he wasn't very interested in learning to talk as he could get anything he wanted by pointing and raising his expressive face towards any adult within cooee. What money I had I squandered on him, buying him a wardrobe of little Italian shoes and dapper clothes. When he returned to Townsville, Mum wrote to me: 'He went to Sydney a baby and came back a little man.'

A few weeks after Russel had gone home, I answered a knock at the door to find a man from the government welfare department standing in the hall. He had come, he said, to inspect my flat and ask me some questions, having learned that I had a child with me. He looked around my small but spotless flat, even though I told him that my son had returned to North Queensland. When I offered him a cup of tea he accepted and, more relaxed now, became quite chatty. He explained that it was his job to remove children from unsuitable premises and family situations, and that a large number of these removals were 'dark' children. They were sent to homes, he said, and some were adopted out.

Towards the end of his visit he assured me that, since Russel was no longer with me, I would not be bothered again. As I was seeing him out, I asked him who had drawn the attention of the department to me. 'Your mother,' he said. I was shocked. How could she have done this, I wondered, after all the trouble she had had from the welfare when I was a child? Much later, when I was again living in Townsville, I told her about this caller and asked why she had done it. 'I wrote to ask them to look at your place,' she said, 'because I couldn't get down there to see for myself,' as if this response was completely self-explanatory.

Not long after Russel went home Mum wrote to me of Leila's death. Like her mother before her, Leila had committed suicide. Following her many attempts over the years, she had finally succeeded. But, Mum said, at the last minute, as the emergency staff were pumping the pills out of her stomach yet again, she had changed her mind and begged them to save her. Her father, Laaka, was broken-hearted as Leila was his only child. 'She has gone to a peace,' Mum wrote, 'that she was never able to find on this earth.'

Despite Russel's recent visit and the veneer of exuberance that permeates the entertainment industry, I envied Leila in the peace of complete oblivion.

Mum's regular correspondence kept me informed about some of the events happening in Townsville and with the movements of my sisters. In my early teenage years, two brothers had, for a time, hung around in our area and visited us at our house. The elder, Bobby, was tall, dark-haired, good-looking, articulate and bright; the younger, Barry, was much fairer and a little slower, physically and mentally. He was always lagging behind, and we called him DK, which meant 'Dumb Kid', even though he was a little older than Dellie and me. The brothers had been around for a short while and then disappeared, as youthful friends seemed to do. We had never been very close and I had all but forgotten them.

Out of the blue I received an extremely angry letter from Mum telling me that '*your friend*, Barry Hadlow, has committed a heinous crime'. He had raped and murdered a five-year-old girl and hidden her body in the boot of a car. This was in November 1962. When her parents had reported her missing and a search had been mounted, Barry had joined the search parties, but eventually he was charged with the crime. Perhaps Mum used her letters to vent the repugnance which all Townsville residents, indeed people everywhere, feel towards this type of crime, but it seemed terribly unjust to slant it somehow towards me—claiming that he had been *my* friend, instead of someone who was just about the place when I was thirteen.

Following her letter I endured a period when I had very short, troubled sleep and suffered recurring nightmares in which this poor raped and murdered child and I were constantly changing places. I would wake screaming and sweating profusely, from a dream in which I was trapped in the boot of a car. 'Let me out, let me out, I'm not dead,' I yelled in my sleep, yet, awake, I often wished that I was the one who was dead.

A few years later, Barry's brother, Bobby Hadlow, stopped me in the street. I told him how surprised I was that he would dare to speak to me in view of what his brother had done, but I joined him for a cup of coffee. His brother, he said, had enlisted in the Army and had been shot in the head during training on the rifle range. A metal plate had been inserted in his head, and he'd been discharged a completely different person from the one I had known. He was so odd even his family didn't know him. The court had disallowed evidence regarding this accident to be admitted during the trial and the Army had refused to release information about it. Bobby and his family were devastated by everything that had happened, but the streets were a safer place with Barry, so severely mentally damaged, not walking along them, Bobby said. Although, he would have preferred Barry to be in a hospital rather than a prison.

I was learning more about the awful things that can go wrong in this life, and that such a series of tragedies had touched people I knew made me feel both afraid and reckless. What meaning did life have, if things can go wrong at any time, regardless of our own best efforts?

Some time later I was again walking down Darlinghurst Road when I experienced an overwhelming urge to go into a newsagency and buy a newspaper. I regularly bought the *Australasian Post* for its giant crosswords, but apart from that my reading consisted of fiction and non-fiction books. The feeling that I must buy a paper was surrounded by other sensations I had experienced when I was receiving paranormal messages: light-headedness, no thoughts other than the direction I was somehow being given, and an urgency and anxiety about the mission that caused me to do it immediately in order to alleviate my distress about it.

Running home with the paper in my hand, I was very hot and bothered, though there had been nothing in the headlines to alarm me. I couldn't imagine what would have any significance for me in the paper. But as I flicked through its pages, moving towards the centre where news items grew smaller and smaller, the paper itself became warmer and warmer. When I arrived at that page which it was obviously my destiny to read, the paper felt positively hot. There, a tiny paragraph, a bare few lines, informed me that a child had been killed in a bicycle accident in Newcastle. I read it over two or three times, trying to work out its meaning, before it hit me. The child's surname, Appleby, was the name Mum had told me was the surname of my brother, the child Mum had given birth to and reared almost twenty years before I was born. From somewhere deep in my memory, I recalled that my brother Jimmy lived in Newcastle, though I had never known his address. Certainly it hadn't occurred to me when I was staying with Skip's relatives in Newcastle. I was filled with the certainty that in my hand was a notice of the death of my nephew, a child I hadn't known existed.

I immediately mailed the clipping to Mum. I knew such a small item of New South Wales news would never make it into the *Townsville Daily Bulletin*, and she would be unlikely to find out otherwise. She had lost all contact with her son, James. Strangely, while Mum responded to the little note I included, she didn't mention that she'd received the clipping. What grief she felt, she bore in silence.

I continued to meet with my two Canadian friends. Buddy was excited at the prospect that his wife, Brunie, would soon join him, although I noticed that his friend, Jimmy, did not seem as pleased. Perhaps he regarded her arrival as a dampener to their mateship and running around together. We three had met for breakfast at a tiny cafe in a sidestreet in the Cross and, after ordering, Jimmy walked around the corner to buy a newspaper. When he returned he was deeply distressed and told us, and everyone else within earshot, that President Kennedy had been shot.

Although not a close follower of politics at the time, either here or overseas, I knew who President Kennedy was. Buddy, Jimmy and I had talked about the wind of change that we felt his youthful presence in the White House signalled. We were all thunder-struck, and spent the next few days huddled together, supporting each other through the shock, because the safety of everyone in the entire world now seemed to be under threat. This experience gave us a common bond, and we remained friends for several years.

I had met a wide variety of people by living and working in Kings Cross: business people, crooks, sharks, gamblers, hoons, standover merchants, as well as poets, painters and artists. Rosslyn Norton, or Rowie as she was called, was a Kings Cross identity who was commonly considered to be a witch. I didn't meet her—she once sent me a gift of a dead toad in a shoebox and had stood outside the window of my first-floor flat in the night, yelling out that she loved me. After that I made sure I never met her.

Despite my work in the entertainment industry where the demands are for laughs and smiles, I remained a very serious person. Between shows I sat in the dressing rooms, reading books and doing my Aus-tralasian Post crossword puzzles, to which I was virtually addicted, while the other performers circulated amongst the patrons, encouraging them to buy expensive drinks and sometimes arranging to meet them after the show. From time to time unknown fans sent champagne and imported boxes of chocolates backstage to me via the waiters. At first I sent them back, but the other women became cross, telling me that women with any class at all *do not* refuse expensive gifts. My ways, I must confess, did not endear me to some of the other performers, who often jibed me, saying I was dull, even though I gave them my gifts of champagne because I didn't drink.

After work, while others dressed glamorously and went off to night-clubs, I put on my tights, long jerkin and flat dancing shoes and went down to the Sound Lounge. There, from about midnight, I held impromptu dance classes for prostitutes who had just finished work. It was not unusual for me to put in three or four hours of near solid dancing, pausing to sip orange juice or to run to the women's toilet when it was reported to me that one of my 'charges' had passed out there from taking amphetamines. Once Adrian Keefe, the sound operator, passed out from drugs and I employed my nursing skills to help him too.

My time at the Sound Lounge was spent helping the girls of the night feel better about their own bodies, after they had been abusing them all evening. I would encourage everyone to get up and move rhythmically to reach a state of exhaustion, after which, I thought, we could all go home and have a peaceful sleep without the need for any form of sedation.

Eventually the petty jealousies amongst some of the other performers at one of the clubs I worked in festered. I found some of my costumes shredded with a razor in the dressing room on the night before I was to audition for a new job. I found cigarettes dropped into cold drinks which I had left in my cubicle, and once the word 'Nigger' was written in lipstick on my makeup mirror. No one would own up to writing it or to seeing anyone else do it.

I left the clubs and went to an agent to find work. This meant carrying my costumes, snake box and music with me to a new venue each night, and not everywhere provided the luxury of a dressing room. At some venues I found that performers had to prepare for their act in the ladies' rooms shared by the patrons, and it was often difficult to secure my purse or valuables in those places. The work was not steady, and I was staggered to learn that some agents dole out jobs on the basis of which of their clients gives them the most expensive gifts. The irregularity of shows and the very moderate fees we were paid often barely covered rent, food and the few pounds' remittance I tried to send my mother, without the whole operation being contingent upon my showering agents with presents.

The regular exercise of dancing had contributed to my physical growth and general look and feeling of good health. Since Russel's birth I had grown three inches taller and, for the first time in my life, weighed in at more than seven stone. The switch from being a club employee to working through an agent, however, had a negative effect on me as I began to worry and skip meals in an effort to meet my commitments. Mum wrote that I wasn't to panic if I sometimes couldn't send any money—she said there was always enough in her house to feed one small child—but the feeling of responsibility rested heavily upon me.

Then I fell ill. I had been moving around, seeking always cheaper but still clean accommodation in an effort to make do, and at the time of falling ill I lived in a private hotel in Potts Point. As well as security, these quarters had the added advantage of having a switchboard to take messages for me from my agent, relieving me of the need to pay for a phone. But I had to bundle my snakes into the wardrobe twice a week when the housemaid came to clean the room and change the linen.

When the illness didn't pass, I went to see a doctor. After he examined me and found nothing physically wrong to cause such distress and lethargy, he began to ask questions about my life and state of mind. Instead of answering him, much to his astonishment I burst into tears.

'I want you to see a specialist,' he told me when my grief had subsided, and he wrote out a referral. A few days later I took a bus into the city to find the Macquarie Street address he had carefully written on the envelope. I was dismayed when I reached the building to find the specialist's name on a brass plaque with 'Psychiatrist' stamped under it. I was sure I had some physical complaint, some parasite perhaps which had invaded my intestines, so to find that the doctor had sent me off to a shrink greatly disturbed me.

Still, as I had found it an effort to reach the surgery I decided I shouldn't waste the trip. After I had registered my attendance with the receptionist, I asked to use the ladies' room. In the privacy of the cubicle I carefully opened the referral letter and prepared to leave if its contents alarmed me. Instead, the few lines contained a request for the doctor to talk with me as the referring doctor suspected I had deep concerns, the nature of which he personally had been unable to determine.

The psychiatrist was a man of middle age, or so it appeared to me at the time. His dark hair showed wisps of grey although his face seemed youthful. After making a few preliminary notes on his pad, he turned his full attention to me and began to ask some very general questions. What did I do for a living? Was I in touch with my parents? Then he asked if I was happy. His question seemed so terrible that I was completely unable to answer. After a few moments of silence I felt tears welling up in my eyes and to my great embarrassment I began to weep quietly. I could not stop the tears flowing down my face. He got up and snibbed the lock on his door, came back and put what he may have hoped was a reassuring hand on my shoulder. I flinched.

He took his cue from my reaction and went back behind his desk; the distance and barrier made me feel a bit safer. In a sort of shorthand I told him I had been the victim of a crime in which a large number of men had raped and tried to kill me, and that there had been many court cases. His eyes opened wide, though not in disbelief, and he was obviously aghast by what I was saying.

Eventually he said that he didn't think he could help me, that I didn't need and possibly couldn't afford psychiatric help, and that I would find that time would prove to be the greatest healer. I went home feeling quite stunned, suspecting that perhaps I was *so* crazy that even a psychiatrist couldn't help me. I lived through the next few days in a haze, so filled with self-doubt I could barely function.

I was more than a little surprised when, about a week later, the psychiatrist sent me a message asking me to phone him. When I did so his receptionist put me through to him immediately. He asked if I would like to meet him for a coffee. I was wary and agreed to meet him, but not for coffee. I was so suspicious of any sort of personal attention from a male that, away from the surgery, I would only speak with the psychiatrist in broad daylight and in a public place outdoors. We set up a meeting for an early afternoon at a bench in Rushcutters Bay Park. He brought bottles of cool drink. I brought one of my snakes.

Altogether we met about five or six times. It was evident that what I had told him about myself at his surgery had deeply disturbed him and he was concerned that I may have felt fobbed off by him. In his role as 'friend', he thought we could just meet occasionally to chat about my life and what progress I might be making. He kept encouraging me to 'get back into life' and made suggestions about how I could do this. He was concerned about the huge gulf and contradiction between my career as an entertainer—apparently social, outgoing, gregarious—and the enormously isolated and pained soul I became off-stage.

Coincidentally, several other things of importance happened around this time. I was walking up the hill along Bayswater Road one day when I noticed a dress store, but it only had two frocks in it. One was stunning, and I peeped around the door to look at it more closely. A quite young and extremely handsome blond man sat behind the counter, sewing sequins onto some shiny fabric, and we started to talk. He told me he was Dutch and that his partner, also European, had gone overseas to visit his parents. This was his shop and in it he tailored very special and expensive outfits for wealthy women and prostitutes in the area. He was taken with my exotic looks, he said after a while, and wished to make me a dress, for free, to complement my style. I had been given a lot of guff from some of the entertainers with whom I had worked. They had tried to erode my self-confidence by telling me that I was 'unladylike', didn't do my hair properly, didn't wear enough makeup, and so on. So I was absolutely thrilled to hear this man who had such obvious dress sense and charm tell me otherwise.

We became friends and began to spend a lot of time together, laying about on the beach and meeting up with his friends for cocktails at the Quarterdeck Bar. He made me several items of beautiful clothing—fancy dresses and day frocks—always inspired by particular locations we visited. When I had a work engagement some of his friends, many of whom were employed in theatrical and other flamboyant professions, spent time making up my face and generally turning me out to look eye-catching.

We would often go to his tastefully decorated apartment, which was in a luxury block of units, and several times I stayed overnight. He missed his partner, he told me, and welcomed my company. We made up exotic recipes, he was an excellent cook, and listened to music and laughed a lot. He delighted in trying out new ideas and clothing on me. In his large and modern bathroom we took bubble baths together, and later we would both put on some of the glamorous nightwear he owned, and he'd hold me gently when we went to sleep.

This sexually non-threatening and emotionally rewarding relationship with a man went a long way, I feel, towards allowing me to reconsider the position of men in society and in my life. My psychiatrist friend encouraged me in this friendship, telling me that, although it didn't really fall into a 'normal' relationship between a man and a woman, the security and joy that it brought me was definitely very healthy and a step in the right direction.

Otherwise, my relationships with men remained dismal. I sought care, encouragement and emotional support, while the men I met were in a seemingly constant search for sex. Through my work I came into contact with a wide variety of men from all walks of life, and those exceptions who were not on the hunt were few and far between.

Kings Cross was a hub, a place where people who lived in the suburbs came to have a good time, even if they only made such an excursion once or twice a year to celebrate birthdays, anniversaries or promotions. The streets teemed with people all night, and the dregs and stayers—women in bedraggled evening dresses and camp guys in women's clothes and five o'clock shadows, as well as straight men in a variety of guises—could always be seen limping home at dawn while street-sweepers and milkmen made their early morning rounds.

Cross-titutes, as people who lived in, rather than visited, the Cross used to call themselves, were also a very mixed bag. The area seemed to beckon to all manner of eccentrics, the rich and the poor, and Kings Cross garrets attracted artists, writers and others who wished to live close to the city and in the company of hopefully like-minded people.

I was walking into an expensive and popular nightclub in Darlinghurst Road one night to meet friends when I saw a short, swarthy and well-dressed man standing alone against a wall. He seemed to glower at me as I passed. When I joined my friends they remarked that they had watched him staring at me, and that I had better be on alert. His name was Abe Saffron. I had heard of his almost legendary reputation as a crime boss and owner of illegal gambling houses, as well as tales told by some of the entertainers about his brutal treatment of women. One woman had told me that she was his short-term 'girlfriend', 'the girlfriend you have when your real girlfriend is pregnant' she'd said. When Saffron discovered that she had been seen with some other man he had stood by while his thugs smacked her around so seriously that she had to be hospitalised. I strained in my chair to take a look at him. It was wise, I thought, to know what people look like if you want to avoid them.

Not too long after that I was hired to perform in a small club in the southern suburbs on a Friday night. After completing the work, I packed up and went to collect my pay. The manager told me to go to a table in the back where 'a man will pay you'. This area of the club was poorly lit, in fact it was downright gloomy, and only by peering could I see a figure sitting alone at one of the tables. I was right up at the table before I realised the man was Abe Saffron. A crisp white envelope lay on the table between us, my pay. Mr Saffron nudged the envelope towards me, but as I reached for it, he lay his hand over it. I wished I was still wearing my snake, but I'd returned it to its box after the show and, with my costume bag, it was on the floor near the dressing-room door. Mr Saffron, however, couldn't have been more charming.

'I'd like to invite you to a party,' he said. His mouth was smiling but the geniality didn't reach his eyes.

'I'm sorry, but I'm expected somewhere else as soon as I finish here,' I replied.

'The party's *tomorrow* night.' The smile didn't leave his face. I could feel panic rise in my heart, and I was glad the room was dark enough for him not to see my alarm. I was lost for a rejoinder.

From his pocket he took a square of paper on which was written an address. He put the piece of paper on top of my pay envelope. I reached across and picked them both up, watching him watching me, feeling the tension like predator and prey. I had heard talk of his 'parties' and they didn't sound like somewhere I'd want to go, but I didn't feel I could say anything. His tone was more like an order than an invitation.

'Where are you going now? I'll give you a lift,' he said, and this time I was quick.

'My boyfriend is waiting for me in a car outside.'

'Well, I'll see you tomorrow night then. Goodnight.'

There was no boyfriend waiting for me, and I picked up my things and left by the back entrance. I ran down the stairs and into a dark suburban street, then around the block and back onto the main street. I thought it was too much of a risk to try to flag a cab there, still too close to the club, so I sat on my snake box in the dark around the corner from the highway and waited for an hour or so to pass, sweating about what I should do. As I didn't know the area I had no option but to stay where I was until I felt sufficient time had elapsed to make it safe for me to hail a taxi. I took Jezebel, my snake, out of her box and let her wind herself around me—just in case.

The following Tuesday I rang my agent to inquire about bookings, however, I was met with a strained silence at her end. 'Anything the matter?' I asked.

'Can you come in?' she replied.

Work for individual entertainers was often difficult to obtain. Clubs rang, wanting 'an act', 'a singer', 'a comedian'. Only rarely did they specify any particular act, so if agents asked you to stand on your head, most entertainers would try to oblige. And so it was that I found myself in her office, watching her flutter through sheafs of paper as she prepared herself to offload her problem.

'I don't know who you've offended or what you've done,' she at last said, 'but it's unlikely you'll get much work in this town now.'

'What?' I spluttered. 'What do you mean?'

'Well, let me put it this way. I can't give you any work.'

I reeled out onto the street and was dazzled by the brightness of the sunshine. Such a perfect looking day for something this bizarre to happen, I thought. I crossed Oxford Street and wandered into Hyde Park, needing a few minutes to comprehend this sudden news. So this was my 'punishment' for not turning up at Abe Saffron's party, I realised, and was angry. For Mr Saffron or whichever of his henchmen had called the agent, the action meant nothing at all. Like swatting a mosquito, they would probably never think about it again. But for me, it was monumental, a demonstration of the power of money and influence over the destiny of a tiny nobody just minding her own business, trying to stay alive and earn enough to keep herself and her son.

I had heard of other girls who had been starved of work, shut out of the industry. Some had gone back to live with their parents in the suburbs, others latched on to their boyfriends and convinced them they were ready to settle down, but a few had hung around until they reached the point of starvation, leaving themselves with few options but to debase themselves in front of whoever they'd upset, hoping for mercy, or move into prostitution. I would not allow any of these things to happen to me. It was time for me to go, but go where?

IVOR INDYK

'The Silver Spade'

He has a vivid memory, not shared by his parents, nor by his brother, of being borrowed by his great-uncle for the afternoon, and taken to visit an elderly couple living in a terrace house in Kings Cross. The couple appeared not to trust his uncle, since they talked through their fly-screen door, from deep inside the corridor of their house, the woman standing even further back, behind the man. Their suspicion must have heightened his own feeling of awkwardness, and of being out of place, for it is this feeling which he remembers most.

For many years afterwards he believed that what he had witnessed was his Uncle Stan completing the groundwork for one of his great visionary projects, buying the last properties in the block fronting Macleay Street, between Manning Street and Rockwall Crescent, so that the area could be cleared for the building of the Chevron Hilton, Australia's first international hotel. This was in 1959, when he was nearly ten years old, his brother eight. The elderly couple didn't want to move, or were holding out for a higher price. His Uncle Stan might have thought that if he approached them as a family man, with two nephews in tow—two great-nephews—their resistance would weaken.

He has only a few memories of his Uncle Stan, and his parents' testi-

236

mony is also fragmentary, since they lived in Sydney and his uncle lived in Melbourne. What happened to Uncle Stan later also influences their recollections. So he researches the matter in the State Library, something that comes easily to him as an academic, reading old newspapers on microfilm, and reports prepared by the special investigator appointed by the Government to enquire into his uncle's complicated and sometimes illegal business dealings. The last time he was in the State Library, he was working on Kenneth Slessor. Now, like many others around him, he's reading family history.

He discovers another possible explanation for their afternoon visit to the Cross. Plans for the Chevron Hotel were submitted to the City Council late in August 1959. There they were opposed by Labor aldermen concerned about the number of demolitions required—thirteen terraces in Manning Street, two private hotels and four shops in Macleay Street, and a private hotel in Rockwall Crescent—one hundred and twenty two 'dwelling units' in all. There was an acute shortage of housing. The local ALP branches were about to vote in pre-selection ballots which could determine the fate of the aldermen themselves. The plans were held up through September 1959, while the delay, and the reasons for it, received considerable attention in the press. At the very same time, the company his Uncle Stan had floated to build the hotel, Chevron Sydney Ltd, was engaged in raising two and a half million pounds from the public through the issue of shares and debentures. The *Sun-Herald*, already warming to the grand perspectives inherent in the idea of an 'international' hotel, described it as 'the biggest-ever approach to the public for a new enterprise'.

Stanley Korman was always careful to present his best face to the public, since he depended on its money to fund his visionary projects. The Lord Mayor, Harry Jensen, clearly wanted the hotel for the city. When he suggested that things might go more easily for the Chevron if the company agreed to build new housing to replace what it wanted to demolish, the company responded immediately, with a magnanimous gesture that made front-page news: it would provide three hundred new dwellings in the vicinity, more than twice the number required, and a public assurance that all the affected tenants would be treated in a 'fair and decent manner'. Lord Mayor Jensen described the offer as 'more generous than any proposal ever submitted to the Council in recent times'.

Meanwhile, the *Sydney Morning Herald* had found anxious tenants in Manning Street with testimonies unlikely to encourage investors or aldermen—a totally and permanently incapacitated soldier living on a pension, a single woman with a heart condition who could only work part-time, and a swimming-teacher who lived with her mother and grand-mother. There was also a shoemaker with a shop in Macleay Street, who said he had lost one business when Hitler annexed Austria, and was now afraid of losing another.

Poring over the newspaper accounts of the controversy in the library, he wondered if, in being taken to Kings Cross that afternoon forty years ago, he hadn't been his uncle's guarantee that the tenants would be treated in 'a fair and decent manner'. It wasn't the incapacitated soldier he had seen in the corridor of the terrace, nor the single woman with a heart condi-tion, nor was it the shoemaker, though that was a meeting he could easily imagine. Perhaps the couple had been the organisers of the petition signed by fifty-seven tenants, which was presented to the City Council at its meeting early in September, when it voted to defer a decision on the hotel. Time was passing. Qantas and L.J. Hooker also had plans for inter-national hotels. It was essential to Stanley Korman's vision that the Chevron be the first. He was about to depart for the US, for discussions with the Hilton Hotel Corporation on plans to build Chevron hotels in all the major cities of Australia. The hotels would be part of the world-wide Hilton network. There was an empire being built, and there he was, the great-nephew, in at the ground floor, in short pants and white socks, lending his innocent demeanour to the business of persuasion.

Six or seven years later, when the empire was in ruins, and Stanley Korman stood accused of fraudulently putting the best possible face on his dealings, through the manipulation of balance sheets, and the misrepre-sentation of his companies' prospects, he told the special investigator that he was prepared to play the role of a scapegoat, if that is what the public wanted, but he objected to being portrayed as a confidence man. The investigator noted, wryly, that if the essential thing about a scapegoat was that it had been charged with sins which it had not committed, then Stanley Korman was clearly unqualified for the role. The question remains as to whether he was a confidence man.

It was no ordinary task, in the early 1960s, first to acquire, and then to lose, twenty five million pounds of public money. Although it would be difficult to doubt the unscrupulous nature of Stanley Korman's financial dealings, once they had been disclosed, there were many who testified to the visionary quality of his ideas, and his persuasive power as a negotiator. He was a small, dapper man, with an appealing honest face, and a pencil-thin moustache. He had a soft voice, which exuded sincerity and intimacy. It was the perfect vehicle for his visions of the future. He seemed like the modest agent of larger, inevitable forces. He was going to build a chain of department stores, to rival Coles and Woolworths, selling everything from underwear to speedboats. He bought Queensland Mines, well before it became a household name, in order to mine uranium. His companies planned subdivisions, dredged swamps and created islands. They were growing forests for timber and paper, and in New Zealand where his brother Hillel directed textile mills and an ammunition factory, they were planning a twenty million-pound iron- and steel-making plant. And then there were the hotels, the motor inns, the tourist resorts . . .

Clearly this was the modern way of doing things, in 1960, with the past forgotten, and the world in glittering freshness all before you. In every aspect of Uncle Stan's plans for the future, not only the grand scale, but the method of implementation, even the 'factoring' by which he made the public's money seem to grow and grow in his hands, there was the example of America, the idea of 'America'. He travelled there frequently when his plans were forming, and stayed for long periods. After being released from prison he went into exile there, arranging big property deals from Phoenix and Las Vegas, or so it was rumoured, not that anything seemed to come of them. Of all his great schemes, the Chevron Hilton would have been the clearest expression of the modern ideal, an American-style skyscraper rooted in Sydney sandstone, an icon of the jet-age. Towering above the harbour, from what was then the most cosmopolitan part of Sydney, it gave the assurance of Australia's standing in the contemporary world order. As the xenophobia of the Cold War waned, the idea of the 'international' hotel, built on a grand scale, took on a magical quality. Stanley Korman had tapped into the public imagination. The money flowed.

Within two months of the City Council overcoming its qualms about the demolition of fourteen two-story terraces, approval was given to increase the height of the hotel's second-stage building from two hundred and fifty to four hundred and ten feet. Thirty five stories high, soaring out of the closely settled precinct at its base, the slim-line curtain-wall skyscraper would stand seventy feet above the Harbour Bridge, making it Australia's tallest building, and the Chevron one of the biggest hotels in the British Commonwealth. True to its role as a jet-age icon, the hotel was to have a heliport on top of its thirty-fifth floor, and its own overseas air passenger terminal down below, so that, according to the somewhat exaggerated publicity, the rest of the world would never be more than a few hours away for its guests.

In other respects the hotel would be its own world, with nine hundred bedrooms, banks, a hospital, shops, four international restaurants, cocktail bars, gymnasiums, Turkish baths, a nuclear fallout shelter for eighteen hundred people, closed-circuit television, and simultaneous translation into six different languages direct to individual rooms, so that conference delegates could hear proceedings in their own language while lying in bed. Outside, there were to be Parisian street cafés, a Polynesian-style village with dining facilities, and an Olympic standard swimming pool in which Australia's leading swimmers would train, while at night, lit from below, it provided the setting for performances of water ballet.

The second-stage tower was never built: instead, the excavations for its foundations created an enormous hole in the ground, sixty feet deep, between Manning Street and Rockwall Crescent, which remained unfilled for a quarter of a century. Yet the appeal of the tower was such, that it lived on as an image, an integral part of the iconography of the Chevron Hilton. Representations of the hotel always showed it complete, as if the tower already existed, side-on to Macleay Street, anchored at right angles to the thirteen-storey wing which was all that would be built, the pure geometry of its elegant rectangular profile a monument to the modernity of Sydney.

And since it was built with the tower in mind, and with facilities large enough to service the whole hotel, there was enough in the thirteen-storey wing that did exist, by the end of 1960, along Macleay Street, to give the public a taste of what modernity offered Australia, its dream of cosmopolitanism, its abolition of distance, the sense of simultaneity, across time as well as space. Down in the Quarter Deck Bar, murals depicted scenes from Sydney's early history, starting with Cook's landing;

upstairs, the Oasis Lounge emphasised Australia's outback, while the Namatjira Room made a show of presenting the country's Aboriginal heritage on its walls. In 1962 *Talk of the Town*, the Chevron's in-house magazine, described its hosting of the first-ever exhibition of Aboriginal bark-paintings for direct sale to the public, presided over by Mawalan, chief of the Yirrkala tribe. 'He came to sit in the lounge of a modern hotel—a stone age man painting as his tribal forebears have done for untold thousands of years'. The hotel bought a bark-painting, for its Namatjira Room.

When the *Sydney Morning Herald* devoted seven full pages to the Chevron after its opening in September 1960, one of its reporters noted that the hotel's simultaneous translation equipment was like that used by the United Nations, and testified to Australia's growing role in world affairs. But then, didn't the hotel, complete with its imagined thirty-five story tower, look uncannily like the United Nations building in New York? When the deal between the Hilton Hotel Corporation and the Chevron hotel chain was finally struck, in Honolulu on 5 April 1960, it made front-page news. The 'Big Two', as Stanley Korman and Conrad Hilton were called, as if they were Khrushchev and JFK discussing the future of the world, had agreed in principle. Negotiations were continuing 'throughout the night'. It was, using the hyperbole typical of news about the Chevron, 'the biggest hotel deal in the world'.

On the day of the opening, 16 September 1960, motorists cruised up and down Macleay Street, marvelling at the illuminated glass facade of the new thirteen-storey building, and creating traffic jams back to Darlinghurst Road. Scores of police struggled to control the traffic and the crowds gathered outside the hotel. Ten thousand people were said to have inspected the Chevron's public spaces on that first afternoon and evening. Of particular interest was the staircase from the lobby to the Silver Spade Room, slabs of pure white polished Sicilian marble suspended on stainless-steel rods, the whole surrounded by mirrored glass: the height of elegance, it was made to seem timeless, weightless, multiple to infinity. That night, in the Silver Spade Room, the Black and White committee held its 'Very First Night Dinner Dance', hosted by Mrs Marcel Dekyvere, wearing a sheath dress of cream and gold brocade, with the Governor, Lt. General Sir Eric Woodward, and Lady Woodward, as guests of honour.

The bouffant hair-style was in fashion. 'Many guests favoured the high beehive, either plain or with brilliants arranged among the swirls of hair.'

It was here, in the Silver Spade Room, that the American-inspired internationalist dream of his uncle finally found its most lasting expression, though perhaps not in the exact form that he had intended. The Silver Spade was only a small part of what the Chevron Hilton might have been. But as it was designed to serve the whole hotel, the unbuilt part as well as the built, it was a huge room, seventy feet wide by ninety feet deep, free of supporting columns, and with an extendable stage one thousand square feet in area. Its sophisticated control room housed state-of-the-art sound and lighting equipment and, remarkably for the time, a television production unit. Its over-sized kitchen could serve six-hundred guests with ease. Soon international stars, mainly from America, began appearing, and more followed.

He remembers, as a child, seeing a line of Can-Can girls performing, legs kicked high in the air, and glimpses of their underwear, then a disturbance at the back of the stage, and the body of one of them passed over the heads of the others, to receive medical attention from his father.

He saw Johnny Ray weeping on stage, and Eartha Kitt purring. He heard Wayne Newton sing with a young boy's voice. He was taken to meet Ray Charles, who spoke to him kindly, with his face averted.

He had his *bar mitzvah* reception in the Silver Spade Room.

It was impossible to be part of a family that was building an empire, and not be affected by it, even if it was the doing of his grandfather's and his great uncle's generation, even if the empire was over before it had been fully built. He can't remember if he felt proprietorial about the Silver Spade Room in the way he had a year or so before his *bar mitzvah*, when at the head of a group of children, he had followed Ricky Nelson around the Chevron Hotel in Surfers Paradise. This is our place he had thought, and our pop star too. This Chevron Hotel had also been the creation of his Uncle Stan, who was credited with being one of the founders of Surfers Paradise. It had an elevated barrel-shaped swimming-pool with glass sides, through which you really could watch performances of water ballet. All around there were coloured telephones in plastic mushrooms, to be used by the guests to call for drinks while they lay in the sun. The American star Sabrina, who had the biggest breasts ever seen in Australia, performed at the Skyline Cabaret, though not for him. That night, he ate Chicken Maryland, and danced with his six-year-old sister, in the air-conditioned Fontainebleu Room.

The Chevron in Sydney was different, a playground for adults, not children. Yet his *bar mitzvah* marked his entry into adulthood—and coming only two years after the Chevron's opening, and three years after his visit to the Cross with his great uncle, it must have occurred near the high point of the Korman family's fortunes. His father was a director of the Chevron, his mother Uncle Stan's favourite niece, his grandfather Stan's brother and business partner. It would have been difficult to separate the celebration of his own coming of age, in the Silver Spade Room, from all that the place stood for as an expression of his family's social standing.

He recognises this, not from his memory of the *bar mitzvah* itself, but from an incident that occurred a few years later, when his family were taking their summer holidays with his grandfather at Lake Rotorua in New Zealand. By this time the glory days of the Chevron were well in the past. The Hilton Hotel Corporation had been gone from the scene for many years. Suddenly, and without apparent cause, a rumour swept the beach that Mr Conrad Hilton was about to arrive in a flying boat. No-one had ever landed on their stretch of the lake in a flying boat. He ran to fetch his grandfather. 'Mr Hilton is coming. Mr Hilton is coming.' His grandfather, who was creosoting the letterbox, mumbled dismissively around the stub of his cigar, and went on painting. 'But he's coming to see *you*!' When the plane splashed down and taxied noisily towards the shore, his father advanced down the beach, right hand extended in greeting. It was Mr Hilton, though not Conrad Hilton—a tourist from Sydney, sightseeing the modern way, by air, he was in the dress business. The idea was an impossible one, but the will to believe was clearly there, among the children especially, that Mr Hilton might one day descend from the skies, promise to fill the big hole in the ground, restore the Chevron to its original grandeur, and remove the financial and legal difficulties that now cast a long shadow over the adults' conversation.

As he sits reading the official investigator's reports in the library, he is conscious of the fact that virtually nothing of what his Uncle Stan imagined, and gave concrete form to, remains. The Chevron has itself

been demolished, the hole filled in, another less interesting but economi-
cally viable hotel put in its place. The Chevron in Surfers Paradise, after
a long decline, has gone too. Of what his great uncle might have built for
the future, only the Bertil Romberg-designed Stanhill Apartments, in
Melbourne, remains as a legacy. And this raises another prospect in his
mind: how aware would they have been, at the time of his *bar mitzvah*,
that Stan's great modern vision, so intense in the imagining, and so faulty
in the management, was in the process of coming to nothing?

The preparations for the party, which took place in the Silver Spade
Room on 23 September 1962, were long and elaborate. He remembers
languishing for hours in a coffee shop in Bayswater Road while his mother
went through every detail with the kosher caterer, a large woman called
Mrs Goodkind. The final menu ran to twenty four dishes, and was mostly
in French—only Gefillte Fish and Lemon Meringue Chiffon Pie, his
mother's favourite, defied translation. He was taken with his brother to be
fitted for suits by a tailor in a dark old building near Central Station. He
was puzzled and offended when, at the beginning of the second sitting, the
tailor had wrongly called his mother Mrs Barboutis. There was serious
panic with the invitations, when it was discovered that a Hebrew letter
had got out of its natural order. Of the night itself, he most remembers
sitting at the centre of the long head table, which was elevated, looking
out over the two hundred guests. From time to time the guests would come
up and offer their congratulations. The layout was imperial, but he felt
uncomfortable, facing the whole room.

In fact his uncle, who had an honoured place among the guests, was in
serious trouble. Only three months after the Chevron had opened, in
November 1960, Harold Holt had announced the credit squeeze. Uncle
Stan had sought to traverse the land with hotels and motor inns, department stores and whole new suburbs, but the money to finance his plans
had been borrowed and lent in magical circular transactions which
showed profits where none existed. The fact that there was no money left,
because there was no possibility of borrowing more, now became apparent.
In March 1961 Conrad Hilton scrapped his deal with Stanley Korman,
leaving his name on the hotel, but taking his money with him. At the
same time, work stopped on the thirty-five storey tower, leaving the hole
built for its foundations yawning under the Silver Spade. The company

announced that it would be unable to build the three hundred dwelling units generously promised two years before as a replacement for the terrace houses it had demolished. By the time of the *bar mitzvah* the shares of Chevron Sydney Ltd, and its parent company Stanhill Consolidated Ltd, were close to worthless. Three months later, the Chevron Hilton was placed in the hands of receivers.

It was some years yet before his parents' names, and his grandfather's, would follow his great uncle's into the newspapers, and anonymous callers would ring in the middle of the night, and tell them they should all go back to where they came from. Five years later his great uncle would be sent to Pentridge gaol for six months for issuing a false prospectus. There Stanley Korman was attended and protected by two murderers, or so the newspapers reported, a final inglorious testament to his powers of persuasion.

KENNETH SLESSOR

from *Life At the Cross*

At the apex of the park, the Alamein Fountain, floating in the
... wind like a giant, crystal puffball, is a constant and unwearying
magnet for tourists, photographers, and bare-legged children. Resident
citizens have grown accustomed to an occasional, gentle showerbath from
the spray, some even have a kind of affection for this baptism of King's
Cross. The Fountain also seems to fascinate the oafs, the vandals, and the
village idiots, who never tire of adding dye to the water, so that the
Fountain, with monotonous frequency, turns purple or green. The people
who delight in this form of elemental humour are not the people of the
Cross or the park. The true possessors of Fitzroy Gardens are the pigeons,
the sparrows, the butterflies, the boys and girls, the book-borrowers
coming from the Municipal Library, the lunch-time crowds listening to
open-air music, the sailors and travellers taking photographs, and the old
gentlemen dozing on benches under the plane trees. Sydney amuses itself
in its traditional playgrounds at King's Cross in much the same way as
other big cities—nightclubs and floorshows, eating and drinking, flirting,
joking, gossiping, coffee-sipping, dancing to romantic music or rock and
stomp and twist, sitting at bars, giving parties, going to banquets and festi-
vals and baccarat. For two million people the Cross is the centre of the

city's indoor entertainment. It has clusters of nightspots, from the glittering Silver Spade of the Chevron-Hilton Hotel, to the tiny pink and pea-green Rio of Penny's Lane. It has splendid restaurants with some of the best French, Italian, and Chinese cooking in Australia. It has nickel-plated snack-bars and hamburger counters, and chicken 'barbecue' windows. It has costly and plushy hotels with even costlier floorshows. It has folk-singing cellars and sound-lounges and strip-shows and 'all male revues'. It can, in short, help you to spend 5/- or £50 on anything from a 'brandy crusta' to an orgy in a private room . . .

To find the Pink Pussy Cat you climb up a steep and narrow staircase from Darlinghurst Road. It is not the kind of marble and gilt facade traditional in nightclub-land. It is rather more like visiting someone on the third floor back in a doubtful apartment house. Even in the faint glare of a 60-watt globe, the walls at the side of the steps are frowsy and grease-marked. Halfway to the top, on a small landing, there is a knot of unidentified, slick-haired, blue-chinned men, gossiping, laughing, smoking, picking their teeth. From one of them (who turns out to be 'Last Card Louis', the manager) you get an admission ticket for £1. You also get a 'souvenir card', a pink-printed bit of pasteboard certifying that you have been 'duly admitted to the inner sanctum of the Pink Pussy Cat and appointed an Honorary Tom Cat of King's Cross'. Visitors from the country or more sedate suburbs may treasure it as visible proof of their sophistication . . .

Girl follows girl, each performing the same ritual of exfoliation with minor variations of pretended shyness or belligerency, each coming to the same culmination of naked flesh. Contrary to the belief that this is an occupation for chromium-plated professionals, they seem mostly young and untutored, even unsophisticated. Their figures, too, are mostly slim, sun-darkened, and youthful—the figures, in fact, of any half-dozen Australian girls on any surf beach on any summer afternoon. The strippers circulate. There are at least three other shows like the Pink Pussy Cat in King's Cross, and the regular girls go round 'the circuit', so that you are likely to see Princess Aloha or Genevieve or Anito-Vivo again at one of the other places if you make the circuit of them too.

At the Staccato, only a few hundred yards away, you will find much the same scene, except that the room is bigger, the platform longer, and the audience a little less decorous. There is the same smoky, pink light, the same faintly choking smell of pepper and perfume, and there are the same deadpan faces with fixed smiles and intent eyes. There are 80 or 90 men and about a dozen women, some drinking coffee, some staring without interest at plates of biscuits and gherkins. While they wait for the performance to begin, colour slides of nudes and semi-nudes are projected on a screen fixed to a side wall. The room is lined with mirrors so that every inch of body exhibited on the platform is reflected at a score of angles.

Again there is a lull in the recorded music and again the disembodied voice flows like golden syrup, while the lights concentrate on the dancers' runway. The girls begin the midnight show. Angeline drops her skirt. Natalie, yielding to persuasion, sheds her breastplates. A 'little French girl from Noumea' is succeeded by 'the tall, blonde bombshell from Perth, W.A.' One girl divests herself of a filmy, lilac-tinted nightgown. Another appears as a St. Trinian schoolgirl, artlessly taking off her sailor hat, long, black stockings, big, black spectacles, skirt, blouse, pants, and brassiere, and stowing them carefully in her school case. The ritual dance repeats itself. Gold and silver nozzles and streamers of brilliant ribbon sparkle as the breasts rotate. The girls go through their postures and gestures with automatic smiles. It is nudity with the benefit of lights and music—but you would see more bare flesh at Manly. This is King's Cross striptease, some of it saucy and gay, some of it sad, some of it even dreary, but none of it really depraved or obscene, as the moralists thunder . . .

In another corner of King's Cross there is another kind of church.

This is the 'Wayside Chapel of the Cross' in Hughes Street, a narrow and crowded tributary of Macleay Street, noisy with little shops, continuously moving cars, and the traffic of the hundreds of penthouses, apartments, 'flatettes', and bed-sitters which line it on both sides . . . the Wayside Chapel gives fierce battle to the chromium and plateglass, neon lights, sky signs, restaurants, and espresso bars. It fights them with their own weapons—publicity, 'glamour', and incandescence. It is really (as befits King's Cross) a church combined with a coffee shop.

The crowds include grey-haired spinsters, pensioners, office workers, factory and shop workers, artists, writers, musicians, beardies, weirdies, beatniks, boys and girls, and all the junior flotsam who would otherwise be roaming Darlinghurst Road. The chapel and its coffee-shop offer them an antidote for the worst and most terrible disease of King's Cross—loneliness.

BRUCE BEAVER

'Angel's Weather'

Watching Rushcutters' bright bayful of masts and coloured keels,
Half-sensing Dufy's muse walking on that gull, sail
And cobalt sky reflecting surface,
I open my senses to the gift of it and hear
The yacht club telecommunication paging
A Mr Fairweather over the water;
Watch gulls wheeling one after the other
After another with sustenance in its beak.
Frantic as white sharks they thresh the blue waters of the air.
Perched on a dory a shag replete
Flaps dry and stretches out its black umbrella wings.
On the mud-flat's rank solarium
A few grounded parent birds are teaching their young
To walk tip-web-toe,
Heads pointed up at the sun-mote
Swarms of gnat-fry,
Fishing the citron-scented shallows of noon.

Passing are pattern stockinged girls
With old dogs and strollers full of family.
Prim seated or grass floored the sun imbibers,
Some still hung from last night's
Vinegary round of dark: the White Lady presiding
Somewhere near the toiling two o'clock till,
Honing her crescent. Now only
The grass poking its tongues out at our fears;
The coral trees' crimson beaks of bloom pecking the blue.
Above the doughy park's arena of tiger-striped
And cougar-charcoaled athletes
A murmuration of applause for no-one in particular
From the immense and yellow foliaged
Fig leafing through the wind;
Spectator of the sportive weather.
Olympiads of effort are stored, restored
Within that echo-memory of clapping leaf.

Now we are all sun lovers, steaming in tweeds and combinations.
Be it upon our own heads
This blessed incontinent surrendering
To the open handed noon broadcasting silence
And the bright winged seeds of peace which find their nest
In an evening of visionary trees.

VIVIAN SMITH

'Twenty Years of Sydney' and 'A Few Words for Maxi'

Twenty Years of Sydney

It's twenty years of Sydney to the month
I came here first out of my fog-bound south
to frangipani trees in old backyards,
and late at night the moon distorting palms.

Even then the Cross was crumby, out of touch.
I was too timid for Bohemia as a style
or living long in rooms in dark Rose Bay hotels.
All one night a storm flogged herds of Moreton Bays,
for days the esplanade was stuck with purple figs.
The flying boat circled for hours and couldn't land.

That was the week I met Slessor alone
walking down Phillip Street smoking his cigar,
his pink scrubbed skin never touched by the sun.
Fastidious, bow tie, he smiled like the Cheshire cat:
'If you change your city you are sure to change your style.'
A kind man, he always praised the young.

251

A Few Words for Maxi

Dear Maxi, it's already seven years
you left us in your bandages and plaster,
smiling your sudden smile, refusing tears,
declaring I'm not getting younger faster—
and thirty years or more since you came here.
Your family park became the bonsai trees
you watered with a dropper for the moss,
and you became a Sydney Viennese.

There was so much we never spoke about.
The past you knew. We tried to stick to Strauss,
reciting bits from Hofmannsthal
and nodding at mots from Kraus.

Last summer I had twice hallucinations:
in one I thought I saw you at the Cross
standing with some shadows in the shade.
It was your presence and my sense of loss.

And when I pass your B'nai B'rith flat
I see you still alone with your last creeper
coiling its weekly way along the wall,
growing away, your illness growing deeper.

This is the season that you always loved
seeing the semi-tropics fade and bloom:
the surface of the sea stained shrill with light,
reflections waving through your darkened room
as all the windows of a tower of flats
catch the sun's last rays and start to glow.
I see you watching from your balcony,
yachts and gardens streaming away below.

GINA LENNOX AND
FRANCES RUSH

'Living the Piccolo Mondo: Vittorio Bianchi, maestro of the cappuccino machine' from People of the Cross—True Stories from People Who Live and Work in Kings Cross

I have worked at the Piccolo for over twenty-five years. It has opened different doors for me—doors into madness. It's a small place, very small. I've filled up the walls with photos and posters of my favourite people. I like James Dean—just a little. There's twenty-nine of him. Sometimes somebody takes a fancy to one of my collection and I come to work and find a hole in the wall. There are benches along the walls, a few chairs, six tables, a jukebox squeezed into the corner, a kitchen at the back. Everything is in earshot and arms reach. There is no room for people to remain strangers. We have a poster, 'Smoking and free thinking strongly encouraged here'. People get together in the Piccolo. They talk. I make sure of it. I'm like a matchmaker, even though my matchmaking in my own life is a disaster. I think it's very rude if you sit down at a table with three other people and you don't introduce yourself. I always try to make people comfortable—I hand them something to read, feed them plums, or get them talking across tables. Then it's up to them. Some people have even married a person they've met here. Some come back to thank me, some to curse me.

My childhood is such a long, long time ago I don't remember much about it at all. I was born in Italy in 1934, and grew up with two sisters and one brother. I remember the war. When I was eight I was raped by an American soldier, but I was too young to know what he was doing. Afterwards I took him home and introduced him to my family and he gave us all chocolate. I was his prize and the chocolate was my prize. It did not leave a scar on me. The poverty left more of a scar. During the war no-one in our village had enough to eat. Me and my sister used to steal cabbages out of trucks and we'd survive on cabbage, no salt, nothing. I remember watching Napoli being bombed from our verandah, and my mother crying. Now I hate fireworks.

My mother used to send me to church to pray for her. She knew she was dying and she was desperate for her children. One day I was visiting my aunt. All of a sudden I went quiet, and when I got home my mother was dead. So much for prayers.

My father was blind—he was a First World War soldier. Anyway he lost his eyes. I didn't know him. I suppose he was a kind person but he used to beat the shit out of me. That's all I remember. When I was fourteen he sent us to Australia by ship—me, my elder sister, Maria, and my younger sister, Rosa. I was sad about leaving. I knew nothing about Australia. We arrived in this wonderful new country and it was a shock—everything was different. All the people spoke English and I didn't know a word, not a bloody word. It was foreign territory, with foreign people, but my family were nice—my uncle, my aunt and all that rubbish, except they made me give up smoking!

Two weeks after arriving I started working in my uncle's box factory in Homebush to pay back our fares out here. My brother, who'd been in Australia for a while, also worked there. He was driving this huge truck, I mean huge—a semi-trailer. I was getting on top of it when I fell down under the tyres and broke my leg. I was in plaster for six months and too shy to go out.

It was very hard. I had my own problems of growing up, personal problems, but for a long time I didn't know what they were exactly. I wasn't allowed out by myself. As a family we'd go to the movies on Saturday night, a big night in Enfield. I had to pick the English up bit by bit. I was very, very shy. I used to be friendly with the children next door who I'd see when I was doing my uncle's garden on weekends, but my uncle and aunt didn't want us to have anything to do with Australian children. They didn't want us to become contaminated by Australian customs. My family was very old-fashioned, very strict.

My uncle and aunt eventually had a child of their own and, after both my grandparents died, the families disintegrated a bit. Rosa and I went and lived with Maria who was married by that time, and life became much better. I was free to come and go. Until then I didn't make any friends, not like now. Now it's easy, just a snap of the fingers for me to make friends.

I was working with my uncle in a big grocery store which served coffee and sandwiches at the markets near Chinatown when I met Ossie. Ossie owned the Piccolo Bar and worked as an accountant in the markets. He used to come in every day to have lunch. Ossie is short for Osvaldo. Australians are lazy—people call me Vittor, Victa, Vitti, Vitt, everything except Vittorio, so, that's how Ossie got his name. I always called him Osvaldone because he was so huge, he loved eating and drinking. He was sort of Italian—half Italian, half Egyptian, born in Alexandria, but he spoke Italian very well. We became friends, and he asked me to work at the Piccolo three nights a week.

When the markets moved to Flemington, I refused to go and got the sack. Ossie heard about it and straight away offered me full-time work. He was an absolutely amazing man in many, many ways. We used to fight a lot, but I loved him. Everybody loved Ossie. I never liked jazz but Osvaldo was crazy about it. The old jukebox was full of it. The jazz people would come down and we'd play their records—people like Wendy Saddington and Rene Geyer. Ossie loved horses too. I think he had one but I used to dread it when he came from the races because he was always cranky—he always lost his money. At least, I never knew if he won, but when he lost he used to go on like a house on fire. I'd never say anything back, never. What can you say? He'd get into the most terrible rages, oh, horrendous, but then it was all over. Finish. And he was very kind. He was perhaps the kindest man I have ever known. He used to give away money and offer coffee or food to friends and people who couldn't pay. He did lots of things without making a big thing of it. He was a gentleman. It's largess of heart, and he had it. It's something you're born with. And then he died.

Twenty-five years ago the Cross was a beautiful, wonderful place. It was like a village, where everybody knew everybody, everybody was kind, with lots of ideas, and always doing things—artists, writers, actors, musicians, people who didn't have much money.

The poor ones and the celebrities came to the Piccolo—Peter Allen, Adrian Rowlings, and so on. Sometimes I didn't have a clue who they were and I would find out later, after I saw their show. That's how I became friends with Jeannie Lewis. One day I just walked off the street into the Regent, not knowing who the hell she was, and heard her sing—she was absolutely mesmerising.

My sister and I saw Lindsay Kemp in his show *Flowers*—it was a fantastic experience, like taking a trip. I've never taken a trip, but we were walking on air when we came out of the theatre, and then one day there's this man with a white face and shaven head outside the Piccolo. I said, 'Lindsay! What are you doing here?' and he said, 'I'm lost.' I said, 'What do you mean you're lost? You're in Roslyn Street.' He was staying at the Sebel Town House and he was doing a season of plays at the Valhalla in Glebe—*Flowers*, *Salome* and *Clowns*. He would come and have dinner, him and lots of people in his show. I was in awe of him. Absolutely. It was embarrassing to take money from him because he was a genius. But what else could I do? He ate so much—all this spaghetti and lasagne, yet he had such a beautiful body—I know because in his shows you saw all these naked people.

I didn't go to the shows around the Cross. I'd go to Les Girls occasionally but I never went to the strip shows. I don't really like them, it's a personal thing. Strippers should be paid a lot of money to show their secret parts. The only show I've seen was at the Pink Pussycat with Elizabeth Burton. She is fabulous— like poetry in motion. That first time I watched her it was so beautiful tears came to my eyes. I'd met Elizabeth through Lloyd. I was in love with him. Out of the blue they came to the Piccolo and she was so stunning with flowers all through her hair. Since then, every time she comes in, the place lights up—she talks to everybody.

Another person who came to the Piccolo—I nearly died—was this magnificent woman, nothing like in the movies, but I recognised her straight away: Liv Ullman. She was with Jeremy Irons but I didn't recognise him. They were doing a film together. She wanted a key to the toilet next door, and I didn't want to give it to her knowing the state the toilet was in! She insisted: 'Don't worry. I've been to India.'

I love the people in the theatre, I love the theatre, I love acting. Before I worked at the Piccolo I was involved with the Independent Theatre and then the Ensemble with Hayes Gordon. When Hayes Gordon moved theatres we all moved with him. At that time I lived at Silverwater in the box factory which my sister and brother and I had just opened, and I was choofing off to the theatre every night after work. In the acting classes we'd do improvisation and method acting and I did little bit parts in some of the plays. I played a gigolo in *Camino Real* and a Negro servant, with nothing to say, in *Cat on a Hot Tin Roof.* Tennessee Williams was very good for my acting career! Otherwise it was mainly backstage work and running the coffee lounge at the Ensemble for seven years. It was all a work of love—money was not important. It was the people—they were fantastic. I still have some of the friends I made then, people like Reg Livermore and Helen Morse.

In the early 1980s Elizabeth Burton and I became part of the Sideshow Company and we put on cabaret shows at the Garibaldi in Riley Street every Sunday. I was a white-faced master of ceremonies and sometimes I'd sing songs. It was fantastic. There was Martin Raphael, Fi Fi L'amour, Boom Boom La Berne, and Michael Metou (he's dead now). I know lots of dead people. Later I put on play readings and musical evenings at a coffee lounge in Victoria Street called the Sad Clown. We used to charge two dollars and the place was packed.

Later Gail Austin from Triple J rang me up and asked if I would do a half-hour weekly show on radio. It was called the 'Voice of the Piccolo' and I just rattled on about all the shows in town, all my friends' shows, the books I read, and the music I love. The first time we did the show everybody in the Piccolo was listening—it was very embarrassing—but I got used to it. Another labour of love.

Actors would come into the Piccolo and I would start chatting to them. I've made lots of friends that way—Kate Fitzpatrick, Jennifer Claire, a divine actress. She's also written plays and a film script called *Luigi Ladies*, which I don't think a dog saw. Who else? Margaret Roadnight, Jeannie Lewis of course—all friends of mine. And also Brett Whiteley and Frank Hardy—but they were not friends of mine. The list goes on and on. Roslyn Norton used to pass and wave and call out my name. I don't know about all that witch rubbish—maybe she was a witch, she knew how to work spells, she had the powers, and the notoriety, but I don't believe in all that myself. She was an artist, a big talent, very intelligent and amazingly strange looking.

The Piccolo would get so packed people would wait outside to get in. They'd take their coffee to the park across the road. I don't know what it was that brought them here. Maybe the jukebox. And then they used to love the rubbish I put on the walls. Maybe it's because the Piccolo and I have been here so long and everything else has changed. The Piccolo feels like home. A lot of people think it's their home . . .

We still get all the painters, poets, writers, and film makers, lots of fiery talk about politics and movies and stuff. It all sounds so important—like life and death. A full moon brings out the crazies and they all want to argue and somebody has a fit. I don't find anything extraordinary anymore. I'm lucky that I can hide behind the cappuccino machine and escape the madness.

I'm not a traveller. Never have been. In 1972 I went back to my little village of Seiano near Napoli after twenty-one years. They knew I was a foreigner because I didn't speak Italian like they did, and I looked at things in a different way. They were religious, and I'm not a religious person whatsoever. I lost my belief a long time ago. If there is God, where is he if he is not inside us? I certainly don't go to church to find God. They're always shut when you need them anyway. My family were always asking, 'Why didn't you get married?' and of course they couldn't see, and I couldn't tell them. I left it too long to go back, too long. My father was still alive then, but he was a sick, blind old man. We spent a lot of time together. I took him for long walks, and we talked and then he died and I haven't been back. That's it.

I'm one of those people who don't change around. I have been living in the same place for twenty years and my friends go back over thirty years. Friends are sacred, like family, like marriage, and I work very hard to keep them. But I get too attached to people, which is not a very good thing for me. I've always had very good strong relations with women, perhaps because my mother died when I was very young. At fifty-eight years I'm still looking for a mother! I have lots of men friends, but my relationships with men are completely different—not as good. I can talk to women. I don't want anything from them—just to give my friendship, my love, whatever I can offer. From men I want something. I want love from them and they don't give love easily. It's completely, completely fucked up, really.

I like people who are strong but if somebody says, 'Can I have five dollars?' and I have only five dollars, I give to them. I've been taken many times. I was so naive when I started working for Ossie. There used to be this guy who came in, and he would fall asleep in his lentil soup. Years later I discovered he was on mandrax. Lots of times I didn't know what was the matter with people but now I see the signs. I see through all the tricks. Sadly. Some people don't want their problems to go away—their problems become their crutch.

Drunks are the worst of the lot—they want to fight. When they start a fight I just tell them, 'Get out! You can't fight in here. Get out!' They've always obeyed me, I don't know why. I don't have as much trouble with people who are on drugs. They just live in a fantasy land or fall asleep.

They sell all this rubbish around the area—heroin and grass. I think it's garden grass they sell sometimes. But that doesn't worry me as much as the hard drugs—I'm horrified. I say, 'When you take drugs, don't come around me.' Those heroin addicts are crazy. They'd rip off their own sister. They are sick, and sick people are very cunning—they need hospital. They know it kills you. I wish they'd do it sooner. At least you'd feel sorry for them once—not this long drawn-out process. I don't drink alcohol, take drugs or pills. The only vice I have is smoking.

I work five nights from six to six. Night people are different from day people. As the hours go from night to morning, people get more desperate, or lost, more full of booze, or pills, or whatever they're into. They're looking for friendship, love, a fuck in the night, especially between the hours of one and four. Even when it's daylight some people don't give up looking. There's a lot of lonely people around and they congregate in places like the Piccolo. Often they are lonely by choice—they don't want to extend themselves. You can be lonely and unhappy in a room full of people. It's something you bring inside you and people smell it and keep away.

Sometimes I think I'm more mad than the people who come here. We're all a bit mad. My madness is I'm still working at the Piccolo, but I will work until the day I drop dead. My life is my work. I find holidays a kind of death. I respect people who work. I believe in a socialist way of thinking—we all have to produce something even if it's a garden full of flowers or cutting pictures from newspapers and pasting them in a collage.

If you keep yourself busy you don't dwell on things, you have no time for nonsense.

I used to be mad when I thought I could help people. Look at Annie Crowe. Is she still around doing whatever she does? What a waste of time. There are so many street people. One lady I've known for twenty-five years. I knew her when she could sing in a big voice next to the jukebox when she was young and beautiful and very intelligent. She used to write and read poetry, but then she went strange. She'd go to Rosa's coffee lounge in Oxford Street and my sister was very kind to her. But look at her now, she's still around. She has lost everything through her drinking problem, but I can't do anything for her.

For a person who wants to live alone there's always people living with me. People come to stay for a few days and end up staying three or four years. But if there is room, you should give your space. This friend of mine had a young son and she threw him out. I said, 'What are you doing living on the street? Come and stay with me.' He turned out to be a real bastard. He'd lost his own soul and didn't give a stuff about other people. These days I think twice before I take anyone home but I still have someone living on my couch. I don't think he'll ever leave. I just try to do some good without trying to be Mother Teresa of Roslyn Street. I'm not cut out for that sort of rubbish.

On my days off I read, I love books, I go to the cinema and the theatre, that's it—those are my great loves, my great passions. I like autobiography—to find out about people. The trouble is, the more I read about people, the more I don't like them.

As far as love is concerned I am a disaster area. I love the idea of being in love—it's wonderful, it's amazing, it's a miracle, but I choose the wrong people. All my boyfriends are dead—Lloyd, Billy, Roger. I was in love with one man for fifteen years, I was crazy about him. Then one day I realised, what's the point? We never went to bed together. Another man used to come to the Piccolo, then, years later, he came in and my heart went gasp and I said, 'My God, I'm in love with him.' It just happened like that. But of course nothing came of it.

People say that you become homosexual, but I think I was born with it. I was maybe ten years old when I fell in love with this man. I kept it to myself—my family would have been horrified. I knew it wasn't right. I felt guilt and I still have guilt feelings, so nothing ever changes, but I have never felt sexual towards a woman and I'm glad. Those men who want both—what a mess.

Two years is the longest relationship I've ever had. I would have to find some very special person that could put up with the terrible hours I work. I come home, I'm buggered, and all I do is go to sleep. Then I go to work again. I have lived with people but I don't like to. People need their own space. And also there's things I don't like about me. I see it in other people and I'm the same—I make too many demands on people. I find that the few men I've loved have never loved me as much as I loved them. I'm jealous, I'm suspicious, I feel mean, and I find all that very demeaning. I want to trust people, but I can't. All my relationships have been disastrous, very stormy, and at the end—it's diabolical. I hate to see them with other men because I think they still belong to me. Love and hate—it's the same thing, don't you think?

When I was young I was silly and I did lots of silly things. I was looking for happiness—lasting love, money, all that rubbish. As you get older you're supposed to learn, but you still fall in love and you still make the same mistakes. My idea of true love is to love somebody without having any sex—real unselfish love. Sex changes everything. It's like an outside force which is catastrophic on a relationship. It's supposed to bring people together, but it doesn't—it destroys this very fragile thing. Not that I have had too much good sex in my life. When I have, I've wanted to die, I haven't wanted this orgasm of happiness to ever end—but of course it does, and I go on living.

Dying terrifies me. When I found out that Lloyd was dying of AIDS in hospital I went and saw him every day and gave him foot massages. He lost so much weight and he was all eyes. He went through a personality change but I had this strong belief that he was going to get well, simply because I believed in it. I don't pray for myself, I pray for others—so I'm a hypocrite, I must believe in God. I prayed for Lloyd's life, for a miracle, and then he died. He was thirty-four years old. I thought I was going to die from a broken heart. It can happen you know. But it's a choice you make—to live or to die. I just talked and cried, and talked and cried it out, and then my body took over and I went back to work.

When Ossie died, I cried for a week, and then a week later my sister Rosa died of a heart attack. I had no tears left for her, I had given everything to Ossie. Rosa—she was so young and beautiful. She was only fifty-two. I loved her very much. We were like twins—so much alike—I'll never get over it. Sometimes, as much as I want to keep it together, I feel I'm going mad—I lose it completely. I like to control my feelings, but I don't accept death, I don't understand it. Where does all that energy go? It's a mystery. Maybe it goes into plants and animals, and into other children who are born—I don't know so I don't fool myself. I like to see facts in front of my eyes, and even then I have my doubts.

The trouble is dead people are more alive when they're dead than when they're alive. They're always with me. I talk to them and they visit me. Sometimes I wake up with an incredible start and I'm in this sweat because I've been dreaming about Rosa or Lloyd, or someone. I know I'm dreaming, but they're so much alive. And it is not only in dreams that you see people. You see them everywhere. I don't know—when people are dead you should let them go, let them rest in peace, but I can't. I want them with me all the time.

Perhaps it is because half the family is in Australia and the other half is in Italy. After all these years I still feel more Italian than Australian. It's a different mentality, very family orientated, but when I visited Italy I was a stranger. I became sick for Australia, my friends, my sisters, my animals. I am Italian but this is my home. But then I get so angry when I see what they are doing. I mean who is planning this city? Monsters from out of space? The Cross is losing its heart and soul. The artists and writers will go on doing wonderful things for very little money but they may not come back to the Cross.

I am full of contradictions but somehow I live with myself. It's not easy. I am a creative person—my life is my creation. I don't want to be part of this throwaway society where you sit down and somebody tells you the story of all their life in five minutes and you never see them again. I want to keep what's beautiful, and go on believing that as one door closes a window opens, otherwise you're dead. To me, there's two kind of angels: children and old people—those who haven't seen the cruelty and the hardness of the world, and the others who've seen it all. Love is the strongest force. It keeps us alive. I'm always looking for it in every person—different kinds of love.

JOHN TRANTER

'Leaving The Sixties'
—*i.m.* M.D.

There you are, nineteen,
in the alleys at the back of William Street,
smoke skeining the sky at dusk, a light rain
just beginning to fall,
                                    the smell of coffee
catching in the back of your throat . . .

and when the machines shut down at night
certain people gather on the edge of town—

a huge aircraft, a Zeppelin with wings,
motors like a dozen old tractors starting up,
dust and rubbish blowing, the excitement, that
European gentleman with something under his arm—
a bottle, a book wrapped in waxed paper—
the sky lit with a faint orange glow, and
off to one side, along a catwalk
near a cargo door you hadn't noticed

a gang of angels in hats and overcoats
pushing and fighting with the crew.

The Seventies

'I always thought the whole point of death
was to make life more exciting.'

—*Mandy Sayer*

During the early part of the 1970s, Kings Cross remained a sanctuary for eccentrics and outsiders. The American counter-culture of the 1960s had leapt across the Pacific, due to the ongoing Vietnam War and Australia's growing access to the American media. Nowhere was the counter-culture more evident in Australia than in the Cross. Basement flea markets were opened, brimming with cheesecloth dresses, embroidered Indian shirts, mood rings, and incense. Flower children drifted through the new village square on Springfield Avenue, high on LSD. The Children of God moved into a deteriorating mansion on Victoria Street. Artists, musicians, and writers lived in bed-sitters and single rooms, along with working-class families and pensioners. The Cross still maintained a village atmosphere—one of informality and casual acceptance of anything new or unusual. In the Frank Moorhouse extract, "The American, Paul Jonson" the male narrator, between protests about American imperialism, comes to the Cross to discover the pleasures of gay sexuality with a man who is his political enemy. In an extract from his autobiography, *More Please*, it is to Kings Cross that Barry Humphries flees after being released from a year-long stint in a Melbourne Psychiatric Hospital. (He relates how he goes on a rambunctious bender in the Gazebo Hotel, displaying behaviour that anywhere else in Australia would have been considered shocking: see Patrick White's letter, written from the comfortable distance of Centennial Park.)

By 1973, however, the urban village was already being dismantled in a way that would change its face forever. Multimillionaire Frank Theeman had joined forces with underworld investors and bought up almost all the low-income housing along Victoria Street. Cross-ites who had lived there all their lives were suddenly evicted from their rooms and bedsits inside the crumbling but beautiful Victorian mansions. Of course, throughout the decades, Kings Cross was constantly changing and reinventing itself.

However, one aspect had always remained constant: the way in which the underworld culture had always happily coexisted with the bohemian. The Kings Cross artistic community had often rubbed shoulders—and other parts of their anatomy—with those of drug dealers, gangsters, prostitutes, and nightclub owners. But with the advent of the massive redevelopment by Theeman and his crime bosses, bohemia and the underworld were in direct opposition for the first time in the history of the Cross.

The rest of the decade is known locally as the Age of the Green Bans. Merchant seaman, union activist, and Dixieland drummer Mick Fowler joined forces with his neighbour Juanita Nielsen to oppose the redevelopment, and to protect both the historic buildings and the low-income residents who lived in them. Nielsen was one of the most fascinating characters of the Cross at that time. She was the statuesque heiress to the Mark Foys' fortune, who lived in a small terrace on Victoria Street, writing and publishing her own newspaper, *Now*, which soon became a vehicle for promoting her own radical socialist views. As described in Mandy Sayer's novelisation of the conflict, *The Cross*, Fowler and Nielsen conspired to save the community through any means possible, and in the process unwittingly created one of Australia's most enduring unsolved mysteries.

Nielsen and Fowler joined forces with Jack Mundy and the Builders Labourers Federation (BLF), who eventually enforced a ban on demolition of the homes. The federation managed to hold up the redevelopment for a number of years, but not before Nielsen went missing on 4 July 1975. Over the years, theories have flourished throughout the country as to what really happened to the famous heiress. As the saying goes, 'Every gangster in Australia knows what happened to Juanita Nielsen, and every story is different.' Though there have been several enquiries and trials concerning her disappearance, most observers agree that police investigations were tampered by the underworld investors and the influence they had on a corrupt police force. Nielsen's body was never found, and no one has ever been convicted of her murder.

Nonetheless, Fowler and the B.L.F. were able to reach a compromise with the developers toward the end of the Seventies. The high-rise apartment blocks were built around and at the back of the grand Victorian terraces, blocking out the harbour views and creating an ugly and disturbing visual juxtaposition. The homes might have been saved, but the community was not. Along with Juanita Nielsen, most of the bohemians, the pensioners, and the working-class families disappeared from the Cross, driven by eviction and escalating rents.

With the changing cast of characters came a growing climate of intolerance. The Cross had always embraced difference, particularly in terms of lifestyle and sexual preference. Over the years, Jessica Anderson, Sumner Locke Elliott, Jon Rose, and Frank Moorhouse have described the area as a welcoming environment for homosexuals. By the late 1970s, a more conservative element was rising, along with the modern apartment blocks. In 1978, the first Gay and Lesbian Mardi Gras produced a shocking reaction from Kings Cross police, resulting in brutal bashings of gay activists and fifty-eight arrests.

BARRY HUMPHRIES

'Don't Wake Me For Cocktails',
'A letter from Patrick White' from *More Please*

Don't Wake Me for Cocktails

Christmas was approaching, and I was still writing my weekly column for the *Age*, but the editor was being difficult over petty things: cutting out my best jokes, censoring my more outspoken material. I was in an irritable frame of mind when I caught the flight to Sydney for my historic *rapprochement* with Mr Miller. While I was in Sydney I thought I might even telephone Roslyn, whom I had rather caddishly abandoned in London, and tell her I was 'on the wagon'. She would be so pleased that she would undoubtedly fly out to Australia on the next plane. The stewardess asked me if I would like a drink. 'No thanks,' I smiled smugly, 'I don't use the stuff.'

'That's funny,' she said, pointing to the little plastic tray that unfolds from the seat in front, 'you've just had one.' I looked at the tray. There was an empty glass, and a miniature bottle of brandy. I must have drunk that automatically, unconsciously, I thought with more curiosity than alarm. An AA phrase came back to me: *It's the first drink that does the damage.* Well, it seemed that I had had the first, so a second would do no harm so long as I kept it at that. I thanked God that I had rediscovered my will-power.

269

He checked in to the Gazebo Hotel in Kings Cross, a brand-new cylindrical building, rather like a cocktail-shaker. The room was large, with a view of Sydney Harbour, but he telephoned the desk and asked to be moved to a suite. Then he telephoned a florist and ordered lilies, dozens of them. It was so exciting to be back in Sydney, with all those hospitals and doctors a thing of the past. A relief too, not to have to go to those AA meetings any more—he had helped those people enough.

The doorbell rang and a room-service waiter pushed a jingling trolley of champagne and glasses into the suite, followed by another waiter bearing oysters and lobster.

Harry Miller was not returning his calls. It was disgraceful under the circumstances, and he decided that it was demeaning to be always ringing those patronizing secretaries. Who did that shaygets and schlockmeister—he relished the Yiddish epithets—think he was? Instead, he would call around to Miller's apartment in person.

A housekeeper opened the door, Irish, and, he suspected, very slightly drunk. Mr Miller was not at home, she explained, and he couldn't come in. What nonsense. He pushed past and took a comfortable chair in the sitting-room. The pictures looked to him as though they might have been hired, and he mentioned this to the agitated woman who hovered in the background. He demanded a cocktail, but after several of these it was apparent that his unwitting host was not immediately returning.

Back in his suite at the Gazebo, heavy with the intoxicating efflux of too many lilies, he decided to have a party to celebrate the resuscitation of his career, and his new sobriety. He telephoned Patrick White and left an urgent message for him to come to dinner at his hotel. He telephoned his old girlfriend Margaret, who was now married to a charming property tycoon, and invited them both. He called all his old girlfriends. He telephoned everyone he could think of, he even telephoned the Sydney switchboard of AA. Someone there could surely do with a party, he thought.

But nobody came. He nibbled the oysters, drank some more champagne and obscurely wondered how he would ultimately pay for all this, for he had absolutely no money. No more, in fact, than his return ticket to Melbourne, and a chequebook on a bank account that no longer existed. He was sick a few times, unfortunately into the sunken bath, or as near to it as he could manage. It must have been nerves, he reflected. Nervousness from being in the world again after

so many months 'inside'. The doorbell rang and a stranger called Guy stood
there looking embarrassed. He said he was a member of AA, a pretty new one,
too, but he had been told about a phone call, and did he need help? The man in
the suite with the lilies, and the trolley laden with half-opened wine bottles, and
the debris of several seafood suppers, laughed. 'Do I look as though I need help?'
he said.

All night long, and well into the next day Guy sat there watching the man
make phone calls, sleep, drink, weep and vomit. A secretary phoned to say that
Mr Miller's housekeeper had been insulted yesterday and that Mr Miller never
wished to hear from him again. The man then telephoned the florist and ordered
twelve dozen gladioli to be delivered immediately to Mrs Nora O'Sullivan, care
of Mr Miller's residence.

At some point he went off in a taxi to visit his friend Patrick (see Asides), and
at another time Margaret arrived and fed the man with some potent vitamin B
compound. Late the next afternoon a psychiatrist turned up and persuaded him
to go to hospital, but at the very gates of the institution the man escaped and
thumbed down a car-load of students whom he conned into buying him a bottle
of vodka. With this in his pocket he somehow found the airport, and was reluctantly admitted on to a flight to Melbourne. There, it seems, some plans had
been laid, by persons he did not know, for his admission to a small hospital called
Delmont, run by a Dr John Moon. It was a hospital for 'thirsty people'.

After the doctor had been to see him, he was given, at his own importunate
request, a large glass of brandy. It was his last drink.

As he sank deeper and deeper into sleep, he felt like a character in a remembered story by Kafka, who, as he dropped into the river Moldau, cried softly:
'Dear parents, I have always loved you, all the same.'

A letter from Patrick White

Patrick White to Geoffrey and Ninette Dutton, 27.7.70

... A few days ago Barry Humphries suddenly came up on the telephone (it turned out he had got my silent number from that strumpet at the British Council!). He was in Sydney, in a state, after blotting his copybook in several places. The *Age* had given him the sack after he had written a column sending up the rich Melbourne Jews who celebrate Christmas. He had then rushed (perhaps even escaped) from his hospital in Melbourne to come to Sydney to ask Harry Miller to take him on. Harry had given him an appointment at the office but before this was due, Barry had burst into Harry's flat in Harry's absence and insulted the housekeeper by saying rude things about the paintings and furniture. According to Barry he was confused by his first day of freedom after a year of hospital. According to the housekeeper, he was drunk. Next day he rang up the secretary and insulted her too, according to Harry; amongst other things he said, 'I'm trying to get in touch with a friend who's become an acquaintance: a Christian writer called Patrick White.' Barry's call to me was to see whether I would try to make the peace with Harry M. We had Barry out here to lunch. He arrived an hour late, after two more telephone calls announcing himself, and a taxi-driver at the door to ask whether I still expected to see Barry Humphries. Barry, in a grazier's hat and monocle, was looking rather strange. He says he has been 'weaned off one or two toxic breasts' but I felt he must have got on to at least one of them again on his way to Martin Road. I'd be most interested to see his medical report. He still has flashes of great brilliance, but moments of despair, one feels. Very difficult to assess. He is such an actor one can't decide when the acting has stopped. I spoke to Harry Miller on the phone, and he agreed to talk to Barry. Whether he did, I don't know, and I didn't feel strong enough to ring Barry and ask. He was staying at the Gazebo, in spite of being on the rocks financially, and was planning a party for the following night to which so far he had invited Sculthorpe, Peter Coleman, and Peter Scrivener. He said: 'I suppose you wouldn't care to come?' I didn't feel I wanted to. Nor do I like to think what must have happened to Barry when faced with the toxicity.

Patrick White to Ronald Waters, 8.1.71

[After an abbreviated account of the visit to the flat and the call to the office:]

How insulting the insults were, I don't know. Both the housekeeper and the secretary told Harry that Barry was drunk. Barry comes here and wants me to make the peace. I, in my Martita Hunt role, try to do so. At least I rang Harry and told him he ought to see Barry: although he's crazy, he's a genius and one can't dismiss him just like that. Harry said he would see him. Since then I haven't had a word from either of them. I expect both are angry with me: Harry because I tried to make him do something. Barry because Harry either made no attempt to get in touch, or did and gave him the brush-off.

FRANK MOORHOUSE

'The American, Paul Jonson' from *The Americans, Baby*

They'd met the American Paul Jonson in the bar of a hotel near the university.

He'd offered to buy them beers and they'd let him, amused by the chance to bait an American.

'I graduated AB from New York City College,' he told them.

And they went at him about the standard of American universities.

And then they went at him about the Negroes.

'I can appreciate your admiration for Brown and Carmichael—but they aggravate—they don't solve,' he stated, doggedly.

And then about Vietnam.

He looked at them with an easy grin, 'Am I to gather,' he said, reaching for money for another round, 'that you fellows don't particularly like America?'

They laughed. He said to Jonson, 'Why should we?' speaking for all of them.

Jonson shrugged, 'Let me buy you another beer—as a gesture of international goodwill.'

They let him.

'Let's get one thing straight,' he said. 'I'm not blind to my country's ills,' handing them the beers.

At closing time they were still on about Vietnam.

Outside the hotel on the footpath, Jonson said, 'Well, it's been—how shall I put it?—stimulating?' He laughed. He wanted to meet them again. 'I'm kind of new here and don't know over many people. Next time, though, I'll bone up on Vietnam and debate you.'

He found himself exchanging telephone numbers with the American, for the sake of form.

He drove home with Kim. 'We sent the American up,' he said.

'He took it OK,' Kim said.

'They all talk like public relations men.'

'Bloody articulate,' Kim said, 'They put things well.'

'Don't say you fell for the charisma.'

The American rang a few days later.

'It's Paul Jonson—that dumb American you fought the Vietnam war with in the pub the other night.'

'Oh yes—hullo,' he was not enthusiastic, he'd been working on an essay, something that involved him.

'Let's meet for drinks,' Paul Jonson said.

He hesitated, it was a nuisance.

'OK—only I'm broke—could we leave it until next week?'

'Forget the expense—the night's on me. American aid.'

This made him uneasy. Not CIA? He didn't have the CIA look, whatever that was. When had he ever met a CIA agent anyway? Why not let him pay?—the rest of the world did.

They met in the same pub. He didn't tell the others. He meant to. He saw Kim and forgot to mention it to him and then it was too late to do anything about it. Perhaps he was guilty about it.

'The others not coming?' Jonson had asked.

'No, they couldn't make it.'

'Probably makes for better discussion—just two.'

They leaned there on the bar and the conversation came easily.

'Protesting lately?' Jonson asked with a smile.

'No,' he was defensive, 'but we have a demonstration next month.'

'Give me the date—I'll do a cover,' Jonson said, 'let the people back home know how much they're hated.'

Jonson talked a little about the news agency he worked with. Then they talked about Cuba and he said how he'd like to have a look at it.

They argued about Berkeley.

The conversation had a fire about it which came from the aggressiveness he showed now and then, and the way Jonson handled it. The aggression was a way of resisting the blandishment of Jonson's accent and his style of arguing. In some ways he was whipping Jonson too and he thought Jonson liked that. And when Jonson lashed back the sting of it wasn't a bad feeling.

Paul Jonson bought the drinks. He felt obliged to mutter to him something about paying him back next week. But Jonson was unembarrassing about money—as though Americans had made a special skill of being generous.

Standing in the lavatory pissing it occurred to him that he should remember to note down the things Paul Jonson told him as a source of 'informed American opinion' or something. Somehow he felt he should make use of Jonson. He wasn't quite sure how or why. Except that Jonson was in one sense the 'enemy'. But it wasn't like that.

Back in the bar the bell was ringing. Inside he felt slightly unsteady but not too drunk. He thought he was still coherent and didn't sound drunk. Above the ringing of the bell Paul Jonson was saying, 'Why don't you come back to my apartment—sorry flat—I've got some cans on ice.'

They caught a cab. 'You didn't mind me coming back at you a few times tonight?' Jonson said.

'No, no—it's good practice for me.'

It was a standardised, expensive, bachelor flat—'ultra modern'. It had no signs of Paul Jonson the American—except for a pile of books which had not yet been stacked into the built-in shelving. *War and Peace, Strait Is the Gate, For Whom the Bell Tolls, An American Dream*, and a *Short History of Australia*.

'I've only been in the place—what would it be now?—three days,' Paul called from the kitchen. He heard the spurt of beer cans. 'My books and records are in some trunk on some wharf between here and the Panama Canal.'

'I notice you've bought some pamphlets about Vietnam.'

'Yes, I was in your Left Bookshop,' Paul called, 'I thought I'd better get some reading done if I was going to drink with you.'

Paul came out with the cans of beer. 'Can't offer you elaborate hospitality—nothing but crackers—the bachelor existence—I'm living one meal to the next.'

'I wouldn't mind something.'

Paul went to the kitchen and brought back a packet of biscuits.

'Cheers.'

'Cheers.'

They sat on the settee and looked across Elizabeth Bay. Drinking beer from cold cans and eating bacon biscuits.

Paul switched off the main light, 'You catch the view better.'

It was a view of harmonising blacks: black textures, of dark water, dark parkland, dark streetscapes—all black, hit by a random scatter of electric yellows from lights and some neon pinks and purples.

'Do you really feel animosity towards us Americans—in particular me?' Paul asked, 'I know,' he held up his free hand, 'I know, you have any number of criticisms of American life, but me, do you specifically resent me?'

'I guess I hold every American responsible,' he said, not believing it, but feeling that he had to be tough.

'Now wait on—what if I held you responsible for everything your government did?'

'I protest against what I don't like.'

'Right. To some degree I am culpable on those grounds.'

'Silence means consent.'

'Oh come on now, stop talking like a banner. Some of us would not have the damn time for anything else if we protested everything we didn't like.'

'You should protest on major issues,' he responded. He remembered how the conversation had begun and knew it was going wrongly. He didn't want to attack Paul now. He didn't particularly want to talk politics. He sort of liked Paul and he had wanted to let him know this. He turned to him grinning, and said as casually as possible, 'No, you're OK,' smiled and added, 'for an American.'

'Gee, thanks,' Paul said amiably.

He couldn't understand how it happened. The conversation suddenly hung in midair and, without looking at each other, he reached out and they took each other's hand. His next thought was, 'Paul is camp,' and before he could even see the implications of this he was moving, of his own free volition, into Paul's arms. His heart was gasping. He had an erection, Paul and he were hugging.

Paul said something about his boyish body. Their hands were under each other's shirt. All he allowed himself to see was the rough-cast texture of the cement on the ceiling. Paul was taking down his trousers. The bay lapped without sound, way down amid the blackness. He was in a clean modern flat making love to a man.

They had not moved from the settee. He had ejaculated. The breathless slide into the pleasure of it had stopped against revulsion. It was shuddering through him. He felt flung and dazed as though in a road accident. Jonson got up and went to the bathroom.

He salivated his mouth which the beer had left dry and ravaged.

Jonson came back and threw him a towel and said something about having another drink. He didn't reply but went to the bathroom, holding his trousers as he walked, avoiding getting come on his clothes. He washed himself, drying with Jonson's towel. It had Jonson's personal odour and caused another wave of revulsion.

As he came out to the main room Jonson was drinking from a can and staring at him. An uncertain smile on his face.

He ignored Jonson and picked up his brief-case.

'I'm going.'

'No need to rush,' Jonson said in a soft voice.

He didn't reply but went to the door.

'Don't be mad at me,' Jonson said to him.

'If I'd known you were bloody queer I wouldn't have come anywhere near the place,' he said, letting himself out, slamming the door, hearing Jonson say, 'But that's bloody unfair . . .'

He ran down the stairs. The running made him feel less guilty as though he was running away from his guilt.

He had been trapped. He felt not only guilty but humiliated by his own naivety. He had not been able to see that Jonson was camp. He'd fallen for a glib American. Not that Jonson looked like a poofter.

He thought of Sylvia and boiled with guilt and agonised with something else which, he guessed, was shame.

He kept it away from his mind during the next week. But it crept to the
edge while he was writing his anti-Vietnam war speech and in a way it
made it easier by feeding his anti-Americanism. But when it came back to
his mind fully, it buckled him. Bringing with it a feeling of illness. But later
the same evening he had moved over to his bed, feeling slightly weary, and
had masturbated. While masturbating Jonson came to his mind and he
imagined Jonson's hand on him. When he finished some of the shame had
come back too.

His mother took two phone calls from Jonson but he didn't return
them.

He gave his speech to the group at university before they moved
downtown for the August Mobilisation Against the War. In his speech he
talked about the phoney American innocence and their pathological
destructiveness. Their 'humanity' which was contradicted by their history
of violence against the oppressed—the Indians, the Mexicans, the
Negroes, the working class, the immigrants, the Filipinos, the Koreans,
and now the Vietnamese. They had been guilty of racial, industrial and
imperialistic oppression. They had produced a public relations and mass
communications industry without precedent—geared to justifying themselves and selling an image of an innocent, humane nation. 'They are now
a military presence in fifty nations,' he said.

His speech was one of a few but he thought it was received better than
the others. Some of the committee congratulated him later. Sylvia
thought it was great, jumping with adrenalin.

Students were milling around chanting, 'Let's go, let's go, let's go.'

They moved off. He'd hoped for a larger crowd and somehow a more
'solid' crowd. He felt they all looked . . . too weird or something. But
downtown the non-students would be joining them and they would
change the way it all looked. He felt conspicuous although he was with a
thousand others. Workmen at the roads looked up, paused on their
shovels, handkerchiefs knotted around their heads, and he felt they were
looking at him. A Greek in a milk bar, one arm deep in an ice cream
canister, looked up for a second and then served his cone.

When they reached the main demonstration he felt less self-conscious. It was larger. The chanting began, 'Bring the boys back.' It faltered and then like an intermittent wind grew alternatively loud and strong and low. He said it soundlessly and then began to give it volume and repeated it until it lost its meaning and became like walking.

'Anything could happen here today,' he said to Sylvia, feeling a hankering for violent eruption. Although he was against violence.

Then a hand on his arm and Paul Jonson was walking beside him, wearing sun-glasses, a Leica camera around his neck.

He had feared Jonson would come.

'Some crowd you've got,' Jonson said.

'Yes,' he said with an effort, 'better than last time.' His face flushed, internally he shrank. All he wanted to do was bury his face in the chanting and the movement.

'Why aren't you carrying a poster?' he forced himself to say to Jonson.

'I'd infringe my status as an observer.'

He could not stir enough aggressive energy to attack. He was using it all to overcome his trembling tension.

Then as they moved together he realised that Sylvia was looking at them both a little puzzled. She had for a moment been excluded by the hot presence of Jonson.

'Sylvia, I'd like you to meet Paul Jonson.' He introduced them without looking at either. 'He's a journalist. From America.'

Jonson was effusively polite and interested in Sylvia.

'Carl's been breaking down my neutrality with inexorable argument,' he said to her.

'You should have heard his speech,' she laughed.

'I must see a copy,' Jonson said. 'I'll flash it across every wire service in the States.'

Sylvia moved off slightly to a friend who had called her.

'I'll be back,' she said, weaving away.

'You didn't return my calls,' Jonson said quietly to him.

They walked together.

'I've been studying—working on the speech. Other things.'

'Look,' Jonson said with intensity, 'I'm sorry about the other night. Deeply sorry.'

He clenched inside as Jonson mentioned it.

'I promise it will never happen again,' Jonson said.

A bystander scuffled with a demonstrator and the police moved in to separate them. Other demonstrators bulged around the scuffle and were moved on. Jonson lifted his camera but shrugged and lowered it, turning back to him.

'You're sure it's OK between us?' Jonson pressed.

'Yes, let's forget it,' he said, wanting to forget Jonson.

'I'd hate for us not to be able to talk,' Jonson said, quietly. 'I value what we have . . . intellectually.'

He didn't answer, although feeling vaguely flattered, he wanted to be away from Jonson.

'You will meet me again . . . and talk?'

'Yes. I've been busy, that's all,' he lied.

'Meet me after the demonstration for a beer?'

'I don't know what's happening after the demonstration.'

'I'll watch for a while and then go to the Kings Head—try to make it.'

Paul Jonson walked beside him for a few minutes, asking questions about the demonstration, and then left. 'Try to make it,' he said.

'Who was the American?' a fellow near him asked, grinning, 'CIA?'

When the demonstration broke up he found himself uncomfortably debating whether to meet Paul Jonson. He'd been quite certain during the demonstration that he wouldn't. But like it or not, he enjoyed his company. But Kim and Sylvia decided it for him; 'Come and have a beer,' Kim said, and he went with them. They raved about the demonstration. 'But we should have sat down—we need dramatic confrontation,' Kim said.

Others joined the group.

'You're not with us,' Sylvia said quietly to him.

'Oh—just thinking about something,' he said.

His mind was on Paul Jonson. He was tired of the demonstration talk. He was tired of their voices. After two beers he said he had to go.

Sylvia went to the door of the hotel with him, 'Is something wrong?' she asked.

'No,' he said, 'I want to go home to study.'

'Wait a second,' she said, 'I'll go some of the way with you.'

'No,' he said, caught unawares, 'no, I want to do a few things first.'

'Well, I'll come along with you.'

She was searching his face for a sign which would explain his evasiveness.

'I'd rather be alone,' he said, avoiding her eyes, angry at her for putting him in a corner. 'I just feel like being alone.'

'Oh, all right,' she said, shortly.

He gave her a perfunctory squeeze of the arm and left the bar.

He walked quickly to the Kings Head Hotel and was relieved to find Paul still there.

'I'm glad you came,' Paul said.

'I nearly didn't make it,' he said, carelessly. 'Sent your propaganda to the States?'

'No. I'm doing a full length "backgrounder"—the climate of opinion—that sort of crap.'

He wondered if his speech would be printed in the States. That would be one reason to be friendly with Jonson. An opportunity to get stuff across.

They talked and drank. Paul took him to dinner and then they went to another hotel and drank until closing time.

They stood outside the hotel. A burning silence after a garrulous evening.

'Well,' Paul said sheepishly, trying to smile away any implication, 'I've got some cans back at the flat.'

They looked at each other. He looked away.

'I don't know,' he said, 'I should get home, study early in the morning.'

'Just a quick beer. I'll shout you a cab home.'

And then he added, 'Just for a drink.'

Without really waiting for him to answer, Paul hailed a cab. They rode back to the flat making only desultory conversation.

In the flat, Paul's books were now on shelves. There was a record player. A print of the Australian outback by Arthur Boyd. Paul went to the kitchen and again he heard the spurting of cans. He felt his heart thumping. He sat on the settee and picked up a copy of U.S. News and World Report.

'Eats?' Paul called.

'What you got?'

'More than last time.' Paul's voice faltered slightly on the 'last time'. He heard Paul open the refrigerator. 'Crackers, cheese, meat loaf, pizza pies, eggs, ham.'

'Cheese and biscuits.'

Paul carried out the beers and then brought the cheese and butter and biscuits. 'Cut the cheese yourself,' he said.

They talked quietly while they drank and ate. Paul stood up and switched off the main light. 'You can take in the view better.'

'I took it in last time.'

He looked across Elizabeth Bay, conscious of the smell of the flat as Paul's smell which was the smell of Paul's body and the smell that had been on the towel. A smell which had been branded on him that other night.

'You said the same thing last time.'

'I know,' Paul replied.

Without any invitation their eyes met and they let their hands go out to each other.

'Oh baby,' Paul said with relief.

'Oh, yes Paul,' he heard himself say.

This time they went to Paul's bed. Afterwards he lay there bewildered, wanting to run from the flat. The distance between himself in the bed and the clothes, crumpled on the floor beside the bed, was too great. He could not make the move.

'Christ,' he said bitterly, 'you said we wouldn't.'

'We're too attracted,' Paul said hopelessly.

'I didn't want it. I didn't want to do it. I'm not like this.'

'I'm not homosexual either,' Paul said defensively, 'we have affinity—it happens to people sometimes.'

Jonson tried to take him in his arms again. He pulled away and got out of bed. With disgust he washed himself and dressed. He was bewildered and shaken.

'You're ten years older than me,' he said accusingly at Jonson.

'Eight years.'

'You're responsible for what happens.'

Jonson shrugged unhappily, 'You know that's not true.'

They didn't speak again. He let himself out without saying goodbye.

On the streets he remembered that he'd been demonstrating that day—and it seemed that he'd betrayed the demonstration. What he'd done with Jonson was inconsistent with his way of life. Against his way of life. And he'd done the wrong thing by Sylvia. He winced when he remembered pissing her off in the hotel. Sylvia and he weren't 'in love' but they were somehow *on* with each other. They'd drifted together. They had sex now and then, but it was difficult to arrange. Perhaps he didn't have enough. Perhaps he was sexually frustrated. He'd spend more time with Sylvia. He had to be finished with Jonson. Jonson had manoeuvred him into a trap twice. But he was just not like *that*.

He came home from university the next day to find a message in his bedroom from his mother—'Ring Paul.'

He screwed it up and didn't ring, hoping that Jonson would leave him alone.

A few nights later he was working in his bedroom when the telephone rang. He heard his mother say, 'I'll get him—who shall I say is calling?'

He went to the telephone, 'It's Paul Jonson,' she said, handing him the phone. He stood holding it.

'Hullo?' Jonson said. 'Hullo?'

He stood silent for a second or two.

'Hullo? Hullo?' Jonson said again.

'Hullo.'

'Where you been hiding?' Jonson said, an attempt at breeziness.

He was dumb with embarrassment.

'Hullo?' Jonson said, 'you still there?'

'I've been busy.'

'Take a break—let me buy you a beer.'

'I've got term essays and stuff to do.'

'Oh come on now—you can't be that busy you couldn't stop for a beer.'

'I am,' he was firm.

There was a short silence, then Jonson said, 'if it's the other thing that's bugging you—forget it.' The exuberance was gone, Jonson sounded a little desperate, 'Let's forget it ever happened and leave the matter alone.'

Forget it! Jesus.

'I don't think we see eye-to-eye politically or in any other way.'

'Don't say you're running away from an argument. That doesn't sound like you.'

'I think we are basically different.'

'Let's have dinner and maybe I'll change a little.'

He was being backed into a verbal alley. The only way out was to drop the receiver.

He didn't. 'I'm just frightfully busy,' he said.

'Look—we'll meet Thursday after you finish school—we'll have a couple or three beers, a quick meal, and then you can get back to your books.'

He didn't reply.

'Hello?—now Carl, that's a fair bargain.'

He knew he couldn't escape.

'OK, just for a meal.' He was chagrined. He felt like throwing the telephone.

'That's fine, Carl, that's wonderful.'

His mother asked him who Jonson was. He felt himself blush. 'Oh, an American, I met him at university.'

'He's been trying to get you for days. You should bring him home—he's probably lonely.'

He decided not to keep the appointment.

What had ever possessed him to go up to his flat the second time? He felt sick.

He went to the University Thursday morning and did not remember the appointment until after lunch when he was having coffee with Sylvia in the foyer.

'Oh God,' he said aloud to himself as he remembered.

'What's up?' she asked.

'I just remembered something unpleasant.'

She looked at him, waiting for him to go on.

'Oh, it's nothing,' he said to her.

She frowned.

They talked and Sylvia said, 'Will you be putting your draft to the committee tonight?'

'Tonight?'

'Yes,' she said, 'remember—the meeting was brought forward a week—because of end of term.'

'Christ,' he remembered. And he hadn't done the draft. 'I haven't, shit. But I'll go along anyhow.'

'Kim said he was going to raise something about links with the downtown group.'

'Not again.'

He didn't know whether he was going to the meeting. He knew that, despite the fact he had told himself that he wouldn't keep the appointment with Jonson, it was still a possibility.

The meeting wasn't until 7.30. Perhaps he could meet Jonson and then get back for the meeting.

'Are you eating at the Union before the meeting?' Sylvia asked.

'No—I've got something to do in the city.'

'I'll come with you and eat when you do.'

'No,' he said, writhing, 'I'll just grab something to eat on the bus.'

'OK,' she said disappointed.

There was a pause.

Then Sylvia said, 'Are you meeting someone else?'

'No,' he said, 'of course not.'

'If there's someone else—you can tell me.'

'Of course there isn't anyone else,' he said, almost angrily, 'whatever that means.'

'You know what it means.'

'No, there isn't.'

'I didn't mean to pry.'

'That's all right,' he said, touching her hand, 'there isn't anyone else.'

It was resolved. He would meet Jonson and then go to the meeting.

During the next two hours he found himself resolving not to meet Jonson. But as he left the last lecture shortly before six he found himself thinking, 'What the hell, it's a free meal.'

Jonson was reading in the pub.

'I thought you mightn't come,' he said, looking up with a warm grin.

'I thought I wouldn't come,' he said toughly, as Jonson ordered him a beer.

'I'm glad you did.'

'I have a meeting at seven-thirty.'

'Bringing the Government to its knees again?'

He was a little hurt by the remark. He didn't want to be attacked. He felt sensitive.

'At least we do something.'

'Now, now,' Jonson said, 'take it easy. I didn't mean to get at you.'

Jonson bent down to his brief-case. 'I have a present for you.' He handed him a book, *The Voice of the People—Readings in Public Opinion and Propaganda*. 'I apologise,' Jonson said grinning, 'it's an American book.'

He stood, uncertain and confused. He knew that despite himself the friendship with Paul was growing. Like the beanstalk perhaps, entangling him. He didn't see much he could do about it. Or much he wanted to do about it.

He opened the book. It was inscribed, 'To Carl—outspoken friend— Paul', and the date.

'Thank you, Paul', he said haltingly, 'it's the sort of subject I want to read more about.'

'It seems to cover the ground.'

'I'm . . . touched,' he said and looked at Paul.

Embarrassed, they looked into each other's eyes.

'Drink up,' Paul said turning away. 'If you have a meeting we'd better rush.'

'No rush—it doesn't matter if I'm a little late.'

'Let's talk about music,' Paul said. 'We'll give politics a rest.'

He didn't answer. He felt immobilised. He wished suddenly he hadn't come. He wished the gift hadn't been given.

'My record collection has arrived—I'd like you to come up one day and we'll play some.'

'I bet.' He blushed at the audacity of his remark.

'Don't be like that, Carl,' Paul said, slightly upset. ' I didn't mean it that way.'

'Let's have another beer, then,' Paul said.

'I should study,' he giggled.

Paul stopped. 'If you feel you should . . .'

'Let's drink', he said, 'if you have the money.'

'The evening's on me.'

They drank until closing time.

Outside on the footpath he found himself reckless.

Paul said something about the uncivilised drinking hours.

'Why, back home we'd be able to sit in a bar drinking until the early hours.'

This time he said it, not Jonson. 'Get a cab. Let's go back to your place.'

'I've got cans on ice,' Paul said, in the cab, intimately.

They held hands.

Afterwards in bed with Paul he cried.

'Why are we doing this?' he said, from the same bewilderment as before, though it was less savage. He folded his arms around a pillow knowing that he was going to stay the night.

'Calm now,' Paul said, rubbing his back. 'Be calm. I guess this is the way it is with us.'

MANDY SAYER

'The Heiress' and 'The Receptionist' from *The Cross*

The heiress

There are three kinds of people in the world. One wants to know every-thing about you. One wants to know nothing about you. And one wants you to lie very well. Though we always want to get down to the happen word. Did that really happen? Where was it happening? But rarely, very rarely, Why did it happen?

This is because we have an insatiable appetite for facts. At a young age we cultivate it by learning two plus two equals four, that there are sixty seconds to the minute and sixty minutes to the hour, when what's really happening is our lives.

Why are there three hundred and sixty-five days in a year? Because somebody chose to measure it that way. Time is not a fact. It is a fiction. Yet, in measuring it, we grant it a position of power in our lives and believing it makes it real. That's why changing currency from pounds to dollars, and changing weights and measurements from pounds and miles to kilos and metres was so traumatic for Australians. How could some-thing as elemental as money and space be conceptually transformed? The good, concrete facts we rehearsed as children and upon which we relied as adults suddenly decomposed.

You want me to expose myself. Because by listening to me, you believe that I might expose a kernel of you, something more personal than the mole on the inside of your right thigh or the word for shit you used as a two year old. You want to be the protagonist of your own life. You're listening to me because you want to know everything about yourself.

My adult years as a widow far outnumbered my years as a married woman. I was twenty-three. We were married in my father's garden in Kirribilli. My father was widowed himself at thirty-five, and I was only seven when she died. My father just adored my husband. Enriqué was an interpreter for the embassy and used to make love to me in Mandarin. On our honeymoon, we flew to South America and travelled by boat down the Amazon. In the jungle, a thrill always trembled at the edge of each day. The heat, the relentless vegetation, the sweet stench of ripe mangos compelled us into an exotic dream of ourselves. He often held my hand and joked in Spanish to the boys manning the boat, while the muchachas washed their hair in the river.

He adored my name and would suddenly turn and whisper it in my ear. He often called me Latina cariñosa, because of my long dark hair, my features. He bought me lots of peasant dresses and lacy fans and scarves, and one night, in a small township in Ecuador, after copious amounts of sangria, I got up and danced a solo adagio for him in front of a trio of guitarists. I danced because perhaps for the first time I was gracing the outskirts of what it meant to be in love.

Afterwards, the locals applauded noisily, additional pitchers of sangria burst from the kitchen, and the men elbowed my husband in the ribs and laughed. It would be something that we would tell our children at a Christmas gathering; the first anecdote that would spring into their mouths when my children spoke of me. I thought then it would be one of the most prominent things for which I would be remembered. But how could I have known?

So there was my new interpreter husband, the jungle, and my adagio in Ecuador. But I haven't told you about the kidnapping. In that very same town, two days later, I was abducted. I had just been shopping in the market and I hopped into the moored boat that was to transport me to our larger boat a little farther downstream, when three men clambered in, too, started the engine, and began motoring up stream.

I politely leaned forward and asked, *Están seguro vamos en la dirección razón?*

They just smiled and nodded in a patronising way, as if my Spanish was so broken they deemed it unnecessary to reply. The boat puttered on, away from the town. I was sweating more than usual. And the straps of my new *sandalias* were killing me.

Suddenly, the boat stopped and three men stepped forward. *Give us all your money,* they demanded.

No, I said, and crossed my arms. The smell of rotting bananas and the heat was stultifying.

Dinero! they repeated, pretending not to understand.

You want me to take your picture? I lifted my Minolta, focused and snapped a shot of them, and that seemed to scare them off considerably, for they went scuttling to the other end of the boat to confer. I donned the new straw hat I had just bought, and waited. When I grew bored, I snapped off a banana from a nearby bunch and ate it.

Soon the older of the three braved his way back.

If you don't give us your money, we will throw you to the crocodiles.

Good, I remarked. *I'm from Australia. I'll be right at home.*

I lifted my camera and began fiddling with the light meter, and that was enough to send him backtracking to the others.

Take me back to the boat, I demanded, *immediately.* The heat and stench was dizzying and I was afraid I might faint.

They started the engine again and I dropped one hand in the water, relieved. But moments later I realised we were not going downstream at all, but edging off to the bank.

Soon they were conferring with another man at the river's edge, while I scooped up water and splashed my face. Finally, the new man marched up and said, *Give us one American dollar.*

No, I replied, emphatically. *Take me back to the boat.*

Just enough to pay for the gas, he persisted. *The cost of bringing you here.*

Absolutely and unequivocally NO. I didn't ask to be brought here.

I scooped another handful of water to my face. He called me an unreasonable woman. I replied that that was like a frog accusing a tadpole of being ugly.

Finally, after much grumbling and conferring, they took me back to the boat, and even helped me on with my shopping bags.

When Enriqué, my husband, asked where I had been all afternoon, I replied, *Being kidnapped, actually*.

The problem is never the problem itself, but our reaction to it. Fear gets embedded in our unconscious, gaining malignancy as we age. I told my husband that and he laughed and called me *tonto*.

But he was a careful man who was always uneasy about the potential consequences of undotted Is or a crooked part in his hair and he radiated a neurotic kind of polish and perfection and died on the fifteenth day of our honeymoon from an allergic reaction to p'au tea.

I have meditated upon this supreme irony for years. The universe demands a little reverse psychology. Pretending that you don't care, that you're not scared—something in your environment reshuffles and exempts you from danger. Sometimes circumstances necessitate that we accept this as a fact, like when I needed to believe that the real cause of my husband's death was his fear of it, when I was stranded in the jungle with a beautiful corpse in my arms, my menstrual blood mixed with his semen from the night before running down my thigh.

I always thought the whole point of death was to make life more exciting. Limits enable the universe to remain within our grasp, something we can hold in our hands or contain within our imagination, like gravity.

I remember the moment this thought first occurred to me. It occupies its own space in my mind, as does the first time I rode a camel, or saw a wild peacock. It occurred to me when I was standing between a condemned Victorian house and a bulldozer. I'd had plenty of time to get out of the way if I'd wanted to. A crowd had gathered and I was wearing my white vinyl jacket zipped almost to the top (nothing underneath), my black bellbottom pants and platforms. I had my beehive wig on and was all made up—eyelashes, the lot—and my boyfriend, Ben, was darting about, snapping photographs with his Pentax.

But the truth is, I almost enjoyed the way the bulldozer made the earth tremble, enjoyed my balancing act on that fragile border between times—the elegance and charm of the century-old Victorian house and the impending progress of bulldozers and high-rise hotels. But I also had a sense of balancing on the ambiguous line between my own life and non-life, between my own lightness and darkness, and I'm not ashamed to say that perhaps teasing the limits of each made me feel complete.

I had first seen the bulldozer from my lounge room window. It came grumbling down the street with that parasitical ex-cop in the driver's seat. He was wearing this corny railway cap—like something straight out of 'Petticoat Junction'—and was cruising down the street as if he'd just bought it. Now tell me, where does an ex-cop involved with organised crime suddenly learn how to operate heavy earth-moving machinery?

Luckily, I had just finished putting on my face—it usually took about an hour—and I shouted to Ben to grab the camera because I knew we could get some great shots for the paper if we could catch up with the dozer. As we ran down the street I was already composing a headline in my mind for the following week: EX-COP ATTEMPTS TO BREAK GREEN BAN—AND LAW!

It was common knowledge that this ex-cop'd been retired as medically unfit. Actually, he suddenly became medically unfit one month after the prostitute was murdered. Interesting, isn't it? When a common citizen murders someone they usually go to gaol for life, but when Lacey, a member of the New South Wales Police Force, murders a prostitute he gets retired with a pension.

Well, Ben and I are running down the street after the ex-cop. Back then he was working for Sol Levine, that midget businessman who made his fortune in underwear. We were about ten yards behind the dozer when it slowed down and began veering left, heading straight for number 115, the last house in the row that Levine owned. I knew that there were one or two people still living in 115, and so I raced ahead and planted myself firmly between it and the bulldozer and announced, *You're breaking the law if you come any closer!*

The man just chuckled to himself and changed gears and, as my heart did a little soft-shoe shuffle against my chest, the bulldozer edged forward, like a cat about to pounce. I was sure that the very fact that I didn't seem to care would make all the difference, and it did. He put the bulldozer in reverse and puttered back up the street, and number 115 was saved.

I'd already lived in Victoria Street six years when Sol Levine bought up a whole chunk of the historical homes and evicted all the low-income tenants. Not that I was directly affected or anything. No, I owned my own little terrace and my business. No, it was the principle of the matter, and the aesthetics of it, too. The Cross had always been this little bohemian, urban village. Full of artists and writers and hippies and old people and migrants, full of cafés and second-hand shops and bookstores and flea markets and corner milk bars, and, yes, up in Darlinghurst Road the strip clubs and jazz joints.

I began using my newspaper to oppose the redevelopment. I thought I could embarrass them into not pulling down the houses. At first, I disagreed with the whole idea of squatting. I felt as if the squatters were sending out the wrong message. I thought they were simply a horde of layabouts; that their strategy was all wrong, too impulsive, too illegal.

I was never given the opportunity to object to them because the squat seemed to happen overnight, as fast as December's first hot day sweltering over the city. It was just before Christmas. I opened my eyes one morning and, through the sheer purple scarf we used as a curtain, I could see, hanging from a balcony across the street, ANDS OF framed by my bedroom window.

After getting out of bed and taking a closer look, I found HANDS OFF OUR HOMES, and a string of other political clichés painted on thin, shabby sheets, hanging from second-floor windows and verandas like a row of crude flags. Further down, I could see that DEFEATED was misspelled—with four Es—and WON'T contained no apostrophe. As a writer and a fairly recognised organiser, I shuddered at the thought of being associated with such mediocrity. Battered suitcases and cardboard boxes with bits of clothing, cushions, bedspreads, and pots and pans spilling out still sat in front yards as if that's as far as they would get in the pilgrimage toward front doors. A stray blue cattle dog, which I'd never seen around before, sat on the footpath across the street, barking incessantly at absolutely nothing.

I drank a cup of coffee, put on my face, and dressed. Outside, it was hot. Perhaps that dog was barking at the sun. A little girl was swinging on a wrought-iron gate, completely naked. The hair was slowly rising on the back of my neck at the element I suspected had suddenly invaded my street. Further down, I kid you not, Alice Cooper's 'Welcome to My Nightmare' blared from the pristine beauty of a Victorian mansion, whose marble steps were flawed by empty Fanta bottles, a half-inflated beach ball, and one wooden crutch. Beyond the Piccadilly Hotel, it was more of the same. An Aboriginal girl—who couldn't have been more than thirteen—seemed to have had all her belongings tied up in a flannelette sheet, and carried them into a house on her back like one of Santa's helpers.

I began to sweat. Who would ever take my plight against the developers seriously now? Of the few people I saw that morning, I recognised none. It wasn't a matter of former residents reclaiming homes, but professional squatters and anarchists and troublemakers leaping onto the proverbial bandwagon. We few home-owners and ratepayers struggling to hold onto what was ours would be summarily dismissed along with the riff-raff pervading the street. All I was worried about was my business, about the advertisers I had to please and the City Council I had to convince. To me that morning, the barking dog, the loud rock, the squeaky gate swinging back and forth sounded like the death knell of possibility. But that was before the fire, and before I got to know my James.

The receptionist

Money. There was a whole lot of it going around in those days. Not that I saw much of it. Lacey was doing really well off that Victoria Street thing. After he got that twenty-five grand advance, he promised me all kinds of things—a string of pearls, that halter-neck lamé dress in *La Mode,* a car. He was going to buy me a little Mini Minor to run about in. He told the police later on that the cheque was for a nightclub he was supposed to be opening down at Bondi. He said Sol Levine wanted him to start a nightclub for Manny De Silva, an American friend of his. The rumour was that Manny couldn't hold a licence in his own name because he'd been busted for drugs in Chicago. That's what he told them, and they actually believed him. And who do you think was *assigned* to investigate Gina Delgado's disappearance? Sergeant Wallace Rggins. Good ol' Wal, the red-haired wonder, and his two goons, Barton and Crane, who'd been on the take for two years and who couldn't find a toilet in a bathroom.

He could have at least bought me the pearls. He knew how much I pined for them. A grain of sand irritated into a round, milky stone. It all makes sense when you think of pearls. Pearls make your life make sense. I even had to pay for my own operation. *He* said he didn't want me to have it. That's what he *said.* That's the excuse he gave me. But I'll tell you what, he certainly didn't have any complaints when I undressed that night. But that was later—I'm getting ahead of myself here.

It was well after eight o'clock, maybe even close to nine, when the boys started getting really uptight. Riggins, in particular, became abusive, his hands caught in some boozy melodrama, waving them about as he whinged: *Didn't I say? Didn't I say no? No later than seven? Bowling. I'm supposed to be. I'm supposed to be bowling right, right now!*

Barton sat polishing his gun with a serviette, always making sure the barrel was pointed directly at Lacey's chest, while Crane's frame filled the doorway as he sipped a double Jim Beam and continued to jingle the change in his pocket with his free hand. Murphy told a story about how he and his partner, Stanley, dug a hole in the ground just outside Windsor and began burying this man alive for holding out on them. They'd already shovelled six inches over him before he broke down and told them where the smack was. And Bobby Boy, our little gentleman in blue, sat there speechless, swigging on his scotch, morose as a tub of cheese. It's the silent ones you've got to watch, the ones who can do the most damage.

It was right then that Lacey jumped up and started dealing out a round of poker, *strip* poker, that is. And I knew at that moment that it was taken for granted that I would save my man's neck—not to mention Lionel Silke's—from an imminent lynching by picking up my hand and playing. My new body that I paid for all on my own would be their decoy when they were desperate enough, and I didn't even get as much as a string of pearls for my trouble.

Bobby Boy didn't want to play. He was actually *blushing*. But Lionel said everyone had to play—it wasn't fair that only one could sit out and watch without taking any of the risks.

Lacey dealt first, of course, and he made damn sure that I got strapped with a lousy hand: seven of hearts, eight of clubs, nine of spades, ten of hearts, and the Queen of diamonds. I kept the two hearts and the Queen. I got back the ten of spades and the nine of diamonds, and moments later was standing up and peeling off my pink angora jumper. All eyes leapt towards my nylon blouse underneath with the black and white stripes imprisoning my breasts. Those boys.

The dealing went around counter-clockwise. From Lacey to Barton to Crane to Riggins. I lost another hand and took off my high heels. *Lowest hand, take off what you can*, murmured Lacey as he cut the deck. Stanley and Murphy lost a hand each, both discarding their shirts. Riggins lost next and condescended to taking off his hat.

To tell you the truth, I thought Dart and Jif had taken the money and shot through. They were a couple of real silly buggers and stupid enough to do something like that. And there was a lot of tension around the Purse at that time between those two and Manny. Silke had flown Manny over from Chicago to work with Lacey on troubleshooting. Apparently, by that time—May of '75—Levine was losing three thousand dollars in interest for every day that the redevelopment was halted on Victoria Street. That's thirty grand a month. And so all that month and the next, right up until the time of the disappearance, Manny was strutting around the Purse all the time as if he owned the place or something. Dart and Jif *hated* him. Manny was always trying to lord it over them, even though he was only nineteen. Even Lacey didn't like him much—Lacey only likes to star in a one-man show. Anyway, I figured maybe they'd had a blue with Manny and shot through with the money to spite him.

I was left trembling inside what few clothes I was left wearing, not only because of the cold, but because I was anticipating what these maniac policemen might do when they finally realised their money wasn't forth-coming.

It was getting late. Riggins was swaying back and forth under the influence of Silke's double shots of overproof Bundy. Murphy, who'd had the misfortune of losing two hands in a row, sat bare-cheated at the table and kept dropping his cards on the floor. Barton went down to look for them, and while he was down there, tried to handcuff my ankles together. Crane, fully dressed, knocked over his drink, and mopped it up with Stanley's discarded shirt, while Stanley himself sat like a parasite in his singlet and undies in exactly the same position as when he's fully dressed—back rounded, hands slipped beneath his thighs as if to warm them.

Lionel Silke sat fully clothed in his white T-shirt, leather jacket, and jeans, and continued to pour the drinks. He hardly ever dressed like a busi-nessman, let alone an entrepreneur. He paid other people to look busi-nesslike on his behalf. Remember when I said he used to rave on about the pleasure principle? Well, he started crapping on about it that night, too. All tied in with the libido, he said. You know, life instincts and death instincts. Something he read in a book. Mastering the trauma of life through death. What was it? You can't understand the beginning and middle without having experienced the end. I never really figured it out. And Riggins and Barton just looked stupid at him, like maybe he was trying to have them on.

Lacey padded across the floor in his socks to call the Purse again. I was down to my nylon blouse and panties, and everyone was just waiting for me to lose again. In this momentary pause in the game, Bobby Boy and I happened to glance at each other at exactly the same time and at that moment I just knew he'd be trouble. Those flaring blue bloodshot eyes. He said hardly anything. Just that look that could burn two holes into you. I'd heard he had money tied up in Victoria Street, too. Shares in Silson, Incorporated. And he was in too far to extricate himself now. Reluctantly and slowly he would take off his jacket and hang it neatly over the back of his chair, next his tie, next his Italian shoes, resting them by his feet.

Lacey padded back in with a look that could've scared Cassius Clay. He dealt the next round and made me lose and so I had to sit there and peel off my nylon blouse while everyone ogled my 38 D-cups, the kind Sol Levine used to manufacture. They all knew then about the operation, though I think some couldn't quite conceive it, and whenever they had the chance, their eyes would travel down to my black lace panties and stare as a man might gaze at a spot of bare earth where the house he was born in once stood.

Most of them had forgotten about how late the money was—all except Bobby Boy—and were trapped somewhere between arousal and nostalgia. As each felt their penis filling with blood, they each contemplated the thought of life without it, and it was most likely this peculiar limbo that caused them to stare at me with such expressions of disbelief.

The tension increased when Riggins lost the next round instead of me. He unbuckled his holster and laid his .45 on the table and though this technically was not an article of clothing, no-one was game to voice an objection.

Bobby Boy dealt next. He placed each card on the table slowly and deliberately, looking everyone in the eye as he went round the table. I could tell he was drunk as a skunk—his face was flushed and his head was swaying back and forth. When he finally finished, we picked up our cards and were taking the first glance at our hands when he suddenly slammed down both fists on the table and yelled, *Where-in-the-fuck is my money?*

His eyes bulged and a string of spittle hung precariously from his bottom lip. He glared at us all, even at the police, as if they were withholding his money, too.

Lionel Silke nodded to Lacey, and Lacey cleared his throat and said, *Don't get upset over a little tardiness, Bob. We're only human.* Silke rose to fix him another drink. And I saw this much with my own eyes: he poured part scotch, part vodka, part Jim Beam, and one part overproof Bundy, and topped it up with a splash of Coke and ice. Bob kept rambling on as Silke mixed it. *No dough, no go.* I remember that, and something about a Council study. I think it had something to do with that environmental impact study the City Council was doing. Only Silke was able to soothe him with a few soft words about trust and long-standing friendships, and coaxed Bobby Boy into tasting the cocktail that was mixed especially for him. Bobby wheezed and wiped his forehead with Silke's powder-blue handkerchief and took a sip.

We played the next hand. I got a rotten one: seven of hearts, eight of clubs, nine of spades, ten of hearts, and the queen of diamonds. I kept the two hearts and the queen and threw out the rest. I got back the ten of spades and the nine of diamonds.

This is what it came to: the panties or the bra.

They'd been waiting to see it all night. You've been waiting to see it all along. Your own genitals feel tender at the thought of it. You think of it often, whenever you hear my name. It's a long process, of books, questions, tests, hormones, implants, stitches. But you want to advance, to go all the way. You convince your doctor you're ready. You sign a document in triplicate stating that he can't be held responsible. They take photographs of your body beforehand for the medical journals, the new breasts, the knot of flesh hanging limply between your legs. They can't believe that anyone would actually want to do it. They'll take photographs afterwards, too, and compare them. Their success will be measured by how beautiful they'll leave you. Perhaps for a second you want to stop it, after the first wave of anaesthesia ripples across your skin. But it's too late. All the documents are signed, and down there in the operating room, scalpels are being sharpened and handsome young surgeons are washing their hands.

And the trepidation only lasts a second. You're just a phantom now, bumping up against white-washed sterility, the scent of disinfectant. A wide-eyed nurse leans over you and mouths secrets you can't hear. They're lifting you up, up onto the stretcher and wheeling you toward a kingdom of primary colours. Only later will they tell you with a conspiratorial grin that you were singing 'Ave Maria' all the way down in the lift.

You've blacked out by now, but it's been explained to you so often you could describe it in your sleep.

In the operating room, you're slipped onto the flat bed and your legs are placed into stirrups, similar to the childbearing ones but wider and your feet are strapped in so they don't fall.

One of the nurses lifts a sterilised razor and begins to shave you, and the coarse, wiry black hair comes off easily against her gloved hand. She shaves you down to a hairless child, a baby, down to a kernel of undivided cells, before mistakes and definition. She wipes you clean with a warm cloth and disinfectant soap. The head surgeon is an attractive man in his mid-forties, brown eyes peering over a white mask. He's only done this once before, in England, eighteen months ago.

The doctors and nurses are like nervous white ghosts hovering about your shallow grave. All the metal instruments glitter under the glare of overhead lights. The head surgeon is dogged by the thought of his own testicles as the nurse fastens the clamp over yours and lifts. His assistant passes him a scalpel. He tries to steady his hand. He's only used to penetrating, to delving delicately about in an unfamiliar body and repairing tissue, organs, veins. He always thought, theoretically, that simple amputation would be easier. Perhaps the nurse holding the clamp nods at him prophetically and he lowers the scalpel and finds the place, the exact invisible dotted line on your body over which you've run your finger a thousand times, the one that, when perforated, would close the separation between you and who you really are. All the scores of children you might have fathered come away in the grasp of the nurse's clamp. He cuts slowly, deliberately. He tries not to think of his own. He instead conjures this object into a cancer, cyst, something his scalpel has grown accustomed to removing.

When it at last falls away completely, his assistants rush a bandage to the wound. The nurse drops the bounty into a tray. Another three doctors descend upon it and whisk it away to another part of the room.

Next, a clamp goes over the other organ, just as soft and lifeless as the first. You've already taken your last piss with it. Your last erection was months ago. The clamp holds it tight and still. The surgeon takes a moment to admire it—a dusky pink, rather large for someone as slight as yourself, the bald, shiny head resting half-submerged in a swaddling of foreskin.

He thinks it's a pity. He's already nostalgic for you. He doesn't aim for that other invisible line you've always imagined around the base, but an eighth of an inch higher. He wants to leave you with something, a cluster of nerves, a fleshy stump that you hope to one day come to know as your little pearl, the one that the fingers of some handsome man will slide down your body to find as you're making love.

It's harder to think of this elegant thing as a cyst or a cancer. The doctor's hands begin to tremble. But you won't think of it as being elegant until much later, not until it's too late. Then you will lie awake at night, missing it.

But right now it's just dead weight you've been trying to shed for years, and the doctor has done this once before—in England, a year and a half ago—and he can do it again, by God, and the nurse holding the clamp pulls the organ taut. The surgeon makes a clean incision. The scalpel slices through vein and tissue as easily as a knife through a ripe tomato. It hurts him to hurt you, to torture you this way. He reaches the first *corpora caver-nosa*—one of your three cylinders; it's a little tougher and so he applies a fraction more pressure. Halfway, at the urethra, he pauses for a breath and his assistant dabs the sweat from his forehead.

It is too late now. It will never be the same. You've already relinquished yourself to what will one day be a feeble stab at reconstruction. The surgeon would like to lay down his scalpel right now and walk away. But he knows already that you've made him your accomplice, that he can't rise above incrimination halfway through the act.

His grip tightens and the blade continues on its journey through you, through blood vessels and the last vestiges of semen your body will produce. Your blood is on his gloved hands. It's hard to hope for the best as the nurse lifts it away from your groin and drops it into a silver tray.

It is over for now.

But in a week or so they will dissect the fascial plane between your legs, sculpting crevices and holes, folds of pink labia—all with the skin grafted from that discarded scrotum that you'll almost have forgotten. Yes, they'll tunnel into you, moulding a cavern lined with your penile skin so that it may close around the fullness of someone else's erection.

The hardest part will be rerouting your urethra. It presently burrows right through your stumpy little pearl and will have to be coaxed down further between your legs. But you don't know yet, do you, that it will never quite work out, that you'll be hooked to a catheter on and off for the next six years and that it will hurt to urinate for the rest of your life. Your problems will begin to bore your lover, and he'll give you some lame excuse and sack you. You'll have to move out of your Elizabeth Bay flat and into a room in Darlinghurst. You'll have medical bills, lots of them. The money your lover man was going to give you never comes through.

The silicone from the implants will one day leak into your system and make your skin rise up in crescent-shaped welts. You'll try to make some quick cash as a temp, but nobody will take on someone like you. And so you'll start hanging out on the corner of William and Bourke Street, and young men will lean out of windows and howl as they drive by. And you'll find yourself talking, talking to anyone who'll listen, anyone who can stand to stay the entire night.

How could you have known? If they'd tried to tell you, you wouldn't have heard, you wouldn't have heard a thing above the titillation of Laura's voice in your throat, seductive and complete.

The card game. Yes. The game . . . The bra or the panties . . . Barton, Crane, and the whole silly lot of them sat there staring at me through blankets of cigar and cigarette smoke, waiting for me to pull down my undies or take off my bra. Except Bobby Boy, of course. He was carked out by then, face-down on the table, his hands still clutching his last few cards.

Go on, then, said Crane. I glanced at Lacey, who wore an expression of feigned indifference, or maybe it was resignation. I couldn't believe it. I bet he wouldn't have treated his wife like that. I pushed my chair back and stood up. My pubic hair had barely begun to grow back. They would see the scars, the dry and reddened skin grafts, the crooked labia. Even Lacey would look away. They don't tell you about that, and all the while you think it's still there. You're aware of the space it took up between your legs. I stood there, my fingers touching the elastic of my black undies, ready to yank them down, when someone—thank God—someone began banging on the locked front door of the Liquor Store.

When Lacey got up to answer it in his trousers and singlet, I fell onto my clothes and pulled them on, and so did all the boys. It was like a mad scene change between acts of a play, all the cops were squabbling over whose belt was whose, pulling each other's shirts on, yanking handcuffs out of one another's grasp.

Only Lionel Silke remained seated, puffing on his cigar, since he hadn't even lost one hand.

When we all looked up, we saw Lacey ushering in this old white-haired woman in a fake leopard skin coat and pink fluffy slippers, and carrying all these plastic bags. Lacey had two briefcases in his hands.

The old woman was Dart McKenzie's *mother*. She told us that Dart and Jif had dropped the bags off at her place and had asked her to drive them over to the store. She said she didn't know where they were. *Apparently,* she said, *they've misplaced one of them and have gone back to get it.*

You should've seen the look on Lacey's face. I thought he was going to punch the old lady in the nose!

That's when Silke stood up and offered her a drink. You could tell she was scared by the way her hands were trembling and how she kept on saying she didn't know where they were.

I'll have to give it to Silke, though. While the police were uttering threats under their breath about what they were going to do to a certain person if they didn't get paid, and while Lacey paced across the room, kicking chairs out of the way, Silke just calmly opened the bags and pulled out the packages with the names printed on them in red ink.

Maybe that's how he got the nickname Smooth as Silke.

It became obvious right away that the missing money belonged to our little Bobby Boy who was carked out. And after Riggins, Crane, Barton, Murphy, and Stanley had donned the remainder of their gear, and had bolted with the cash, it was Lacey and I who carried the dead weight of Bobby out to his silver Alfa Romeo parked two blocks down the street. We laid him down in the back seat. Lacey closed one of Bobby's hands around the keys and locked him in.

I suppose Lacey thought he was lucky because the package that went missing belonged to Bobby Boy, and Bobby was too pissed to know the difference.

But misplacing that package was the beginning of the end. Dart and Jif and the package didn't turn up for a week. And in that time a thousand things went wrong, and the writing was on the wall for one precocious journalist.

The Eighties

'. . . carefully avoiding references to women, love, despair and the pale carnage of the street.'

—*John Tranter*

The 1980s were years of slim literary output in the Cross, as evidenced by the comparatively short section of extracts representing the decade. Unlike earlier decades, during which the literature set in and about Kings Cross was so prodigious that the editors were hard-pressed to choose between them, the work produced in the materialist eighties was sadly lacking, both in quantity and quality. The booming commercialisation of the Cross, and the continuing redevelopment, caused the district's writers and artists to move to more accommodating suburbs like Newtown and Surry Hills. In literary terms, the editors felt the decade was redeemed by two poems by John Tranter and three poems by American writer Yusef Komunyakaa. (It is no coincidence that both poets were inspired by the Piccolo Bar, which was one of the few surviving bohemian haunts in the 1980s.)

At the same time, the growing tourist industry was squeezing out the bohemian community. In the 1940s, the Cross was Americanised; in the Fifties, it was Europeanised. In the Eighties, however, Kings Cross was Asianised. Souvenir shops proliferated (even though the toy kangaroos and boomerangs were manufactured in Japan, shipped to Australia, and resold by Japanese shop owners to visiting Japanese tourists). The Hotel Nikko replaced the Chevron Hotel and became the central venue for Asian tourist dollars. Thai restaurants and Korean takeaways replaced milk bars and coffee shops.

The district was also altered by the dramatic escalation of drug use. Runaways from all over the country continued to flock to the Cross, many of whom acquired expensive heroin habits. As John Ibrahim notes in his oral history of Kings Cross, documented by Gina Lennox and Frances Rush, it was in the 1980s that prostitutes grew younger, strippers were often underage, and teenagers from the suburbs brawled and overdosed for a bit of fun on the weekends.

What had traditionally been a district that welcomed people from all walks of life soon became an area that was sharply divided; those with money belts bulging with foreign currency, and those on the street who hoped to divest them of it.

YUSEF KOMUNYAKAA

'John Says', 'The Piccolo' and 'Messages'

John says

I'm more medicine
        than man. His hair
a white roar on the corner
        of Roslyn & Darlinghurst.
I'm thinking yellow
        skirts grow shorter
when streets are sad.
        On tonight's furlough
from the psychiatric ward,
        he throws his baseball cap
to the sidewalk & recites
        'Kubla Khan'. Working
the crowd closer, he segues
        into 'Snowy River' &
'Marriage' in Lear's voice.
        After years of Thorazine,
Hamlet & Caliban still
        share his tongue. Coins
rain into his upturned cap,

& the crowd drifts toward
The Love Machine
    & McDonald's, before
he scoops up the money
    & dashes to a milkbar
across the street. Sometimes
    among blossoms, we imprison
each other with what we know
    & don't say beneath the moon's
striptease. John's back
    sitting near the footpath.
Between sips of Coke,
    he talks about Strasberg
& his birth on Australia Day,
    as his pink artificial leg
glows like a nude doll.
    A week later at Rozelle,
we're on a red arched bridge
    Japanese POWs erected
in a garden of flame trees.
    He tells almost the same story
Harry told about the LSD
    one Friday night in April,
what God kept telling him.
    Harry said an axe was used,
but John says he cut off a leg
    with a power saw. The trees
ignite the brook. A smile
    flashes among the goldfish,
& he says, *This is what love made me do.*

The Piccolo

'There's Ayisha,'
you say, pointing to a wall
yellowing with snapshots
& theatre posters. Her face
wakes Piaf & Lady Day
on the jukebox, swelling this
12 x 12 room. A voice
behind the espresso machine
says Ayisha's in town,
& another says No,
she's back in New York.
Everyone's like Ehrich
Weiss in a tiger cage,
a season to break
things & make ourselves
whole. Someone puffs a J
rolled in perfumed paper,
& in my head I'm scribbling
you a love note, each word
sealed in amber. A cry
seethes from a semi-dark
corner, hidden like potato
eyes in a root cellar. My lips
brush your right cheek.
It's St. Valentine's Day,
but there's no tommy gun
in a violin case from Chicago
because it is your birthday.
You buy another sweet
for me, & when I take a bite
I taste desire. Another
dollar's dropped into the box:
Bud Powell's 'Jor-Du'
fills The Piccolo,

& we move from one truth
to the next. Fingers
on the keys, on the spine.
Passion & tempo. We kiss
& form the apex that knows
what flesh is, the only
knot made stronger
by time & pressure.

Messages

They brand themselves with hearts
 & dragons, *omni vincit amor*
wreathing the handles of daggers,
skulls with flowers between teeth,
& dotted lines across throats
saying *c-u-t-a-l-o-n-g-h-e-r-e-*.
Epigraphs chiseled into marble
glisten with sweat.
Madonna quivers on a bicep
as fingers dance over a pinball machine.
Women pose with x's drawn through names
to harden features & bring knifethrowers
into their lives. A stripper in the neon
doorway of The Pink Pussycat
shows how the tattoo artist's hands
shook, as if the rose
were traced on her skin
with carbon paper & colored-in by bad luck . . .
red as a lost cartographer's ink.
A signature under her left nipple.

GINA LENNOX AND FRANCES RUSH

*'The Tunnel: John Ibrahim, nightclub owner at nineteen'
from People of the Cross—True Stories from People Who Live
and Work in Kings Cross*

I've never lost a fight. In fact, I've only ever copped one punch in all the years. I've never used weapons. I've fought guys far bigger than me but they lack a game plan or they underestimate me. I'm twenty-two and a lot of people think I'm a lot younger. It's one of my biggest problems. It also has its advantages.

I plan things and follow them through. If you just sit back and wait for things to happen, nothing will. You're just a dreamer. You've got to make things happen. I'm ambitious. I'm also wary. I don't count on people, then I don't get disappointed. If a person turns out to be a good person, with no bad intentions, then it is a nice surprise. I have faith in people that have proven themselves to me, but mainly I count on myself.

Just before the war started in Lebanon my parents travelled to Sydney to visit family. They decided to stay but my father didn't like it here. He hated it. He didn't speak the language, and he didn't think he could learn. In Lebanon he was a well-known businessman. Here he thought he was a nothing. My older brother and myself were born here, and then my father went back to Lebanon, came back for a year, had two more children, went back to Lebanon for four years, came back, had two more children, then went back. We haven't seen him again. Something happened in Lebanon

313

and he's what you call 'missing'. I don't think his absence has influenced me really, but it would have been good to know him. He's a bit of a character himself apparently.

My mother didn't want to take us back to Lebanon because of the conflict over there. She still thinks they're married, they just haven't seen each other for ten years or so. My two younger brothers and two sisters are what I'd call normal. It's my older brother Sam, and myself, that have grown up a different way. Mum knew I was a wild child but she is very naive about the world. She comes from one of those families that thinks the woman's place is in the home and what the man does is his business. I know that doesn't sound good in this day and age, but that's my mother. In Australia she didn't speak the language, so what we told her was what she went by.

Sam started it all off by working as a bouncer at a strip-joint called Studio 44 when he was sixteen. He thought it was magic. I just followed in his footsteps, learning martial arts from the age of nine until I was fifteen. My brother and I aren't exactly bouncer material—we're not tall—so learning how to defend myself was definitely a plus. I represented New South Wales and won a couple of titles and then I gave it away. I still train now, but not with a passion, just to keep fit.

When I was fourteen, I used to have my own little group I moved with and we'd always end up in the Cross, even though we lived out west near Parramatta. We'd come up here at least five nights a week for the bright lights and night life. We liked to think that we were Sam's backup. He used to think of us as little pains in the arse. He'd give us money for food and send us home, but we'd always end up going somewhere else.

We'd go anywhere looking for trouble. It's not like we planned it, but we knew in the back of our minds that we were going to run into people, and get hassled by police and security guards. It was part of the thrill. On a Thursday night we'd pick fights with all the punk rockers. We'd just walk through them, and if we didn't get a reaction we'd walk back through them again until it was annoying for everybody. Something would always happen. But it was nothing like today. Today there's weapons and too much anger. Back then a punch-up was a punch-up. Half the time you'd get up, they'd be laughing at you, you'd be laughing at them. We'd practically wave each other goodbye and say, 'See you next week.'

Six or seven of us can trace each other back to when we were twelve years old. Three of those guys are still with me now. Back then if you'd told us we'd be doing what we're doing now, we'd have laughed and told you to run along. We could've easily gone bad but I like to think we just stayed on the border.

Seven years ago Kings Cross was Kings Cross. You could count on at least ten fights a night, blood everywhere, people going crazy. There were big muscle men that would lift me up with one hand just to pat me on the head. I thought they were magic. People would wind up their windows and lock their doors just to drive through. Others would pull up in their Ferraris, dressed in suits. They were the ones that owned the strip-joints. I used to respect them and their power, and how much control they had over people.

I was dazzled by everything—I had no idea that a world like this existed. Then I started to see the other side of the dazzle, and that wasn't so thrilling. You'd see people overdosing, and young girls on the street. I couldn't understand why people were willing to do it to themselves—I didn't know about the power of money back then. The prostitutes I used to speak to are still around. It's a career for them. I was a little boy they used to pinch on the cheeks. Now they see me and they still try to pinch me on the cheek.

It was fun, but it was also unnerving to see how the world really works. I'd go to school the next day and tell people. Most days I'd go to school. I used to avoid it as much as possible—roll up late all the time. School wasn't for me. It's just buying time 'til you're mature enough to get out and work. All I needed was to learn how to read and write and multiply. I couldn't see the point of learning anything else. I'd come to the Cross and they'd teach me something completely different. I had a few teachers that hated me with a passion. They'd constantly throw me out of the classroom because I couldn't agree with anything they said. The principal made the best sort of prediction. He said I had three options—I'd be a very wealthy man, or I'd be in gaol, or dead.

One day this teacher who I thought of as my worst enemy threw a duster at me to get my attention, and I stood up and threw it back at him. He'd also done martial arts so he called me around the back and urged me on. He didn't think I'd take a shot at him but I did. I was only up to his waist, so he was shocked, and then he sort of caved in, and we sat down and had a talk.

I listened to him. He got me into cadets and playing football. He used to make me feel good about the things that I was good at, instead of highlighting the things that I was bad at. I always had people follow me and that used to get me into trouble, but he showed me how it could benefit me. He was definitely the best influence in my life. Today I'm godfather to his only son.

I got my fourth year certificate when I'd just turned fourteen and I knew I had to leave—the principal was hunting for me, the deputy was hunting for me . . . I worked for a bricklayer, but it wasn't for me. I packed it in after six months and spent most of the days with my friends training and going to the beach. As long as one of us had money we all had money. If we didn't have money, we'd go to the Cross. My brother's boss would slip me a fifty or a hundred, give me a pat on the head and tell me to go and do whatever I wanted. He wasn't so stupid—a year or so later I ended up copping a knife for him.

I'd always go home, it caused my mother too much anguish otherwise. As long as we came home to eat and sleep she was happy. Sometimes I'd just come home and have a shower, get changed, and be off again, but that was good enough. My mother is magic. I could talk her into anything from the time I could speak. I still go home even though I could afford to live wherever I want. I think it's very important to have a base. You can only wander for so long.

Others aren't so lucky. One of my friends, David, has been with me since we were seven years old. When we were about thirteen we went to his place after school and his stepfather was drunk and wanted us to mow the lawn. We didn't want to, so he came out and belted into David the way you'd belt a man. David and I thought we were pretty tough, so I came up from behind and king-hit him, and then David and I belted him with extreme prejudice. David got thrown out of home so he came and lived with my family for seven years. I talk to a lot of street kids in the Cross. The main trick is to get them before they arrive on the streets. A kid comes out of home knowing nothing. The experienced street kids take them under their wing, and in one week they've learnt everything. They think they're a genius.

When I was young, I didn't have the knowledge to be scared. I didn't know the circumstances, or the consequences, of my actions. I didn't know the chain of events that I unleashed, or the chain of events that could unleash on me. When I think about some of the things me and my friends did back then, all I can say is someone must have been watching over us. For instance, over six years ago there was a big punch-up. One nightclub owner was unhappy with another nightclub owner and all his boys were going over to close the other one's place down. I'd spotted this flow of people and went along to check it out. All these doormen were punching it out, the club was a mess. A few guns went off and it was just great for me, like you see in the movies.

A month before my sixteenth birthday I saw my brother's boss in trouble. Two men were harassing him and I sort of came to his rescue. I hit one man so he couldn't do any more damage, then broke up the other two who were still fighting. The guy that I was helping ran off. I had this other guy pinned up against the wall. I didn't want to hit him because it would have been too easy, and I think he just acted out of reflex. He had a kitchen knife wrapped up in newspaper behind his back, and suddenly he just stuck me with the knife. I ended up with something like 5000 stitches, internally and externally, and a punctured lung. He cut my liver in half and my intestines had to be reconstructed. I spent six months in St Vincent's Hospital, and for three weeks I was unconscious. Mum didn't leave the hospital for two weeks. The policeman in charge of the case explained that I was helping a friend so she thought I was being a good boy. What I thought was a simple punch-up turned out to be one tyrant against another tyrant, and I was just a little sheep in the middle. I had no idea that behind them was another hundred people that I'd have to punch out. It was a very big lesson.

I took a year to recover. I thought, 'I'll never go back to the Cross, I've used up all my chances. I'm not going to put my mother through this again.' But as soon as I recovered, I trained so hard, and healed so well, I was back.

Getting stabbed certainly changed things, not necessarily all for the better. I'd proven myself and my status had been lifted. The person I'd helped gave me opportunities. People liked having me around, they knew I'd always be there for them. They figured I had brains and I was young—

whatever they said to me was gold. I moved into different circles with people who had more money and more knowledge. The money didn't so much impress me. People give you money and you spend it, but knowledge is everything and I started to learn how the Cross really works—not only the Cross but how society works, whether it's Kings Cross or Double Bay Shopping Centre. There's always a chain of command with someone pulling the strings. There's politics behind every action. Someone always having something to gain.

I learnt how to read people, how to talk to people and make them do things, how to be one step up on everyone else. People need to think that you know something they don't know, that you know where you're going, then, even if you have no idea, they seem to follow you.

I also learnt it isn't about what you know, it's about who you know. We didn't have to do much, that was the big trick, we just had to be at the right place at the right time with the right people. We were kept men, but it was all right, because that was the thing to do back then. Wherever we went—in the coffee shops, the clubs, the discos—we'd get everything we wanted because of our association with certain people. At sixteen that was a big thrill.

One good influence in my life is that I've been in love with the same girl since I was fourteen. Meagan went to the school next door to my school. Her school was the good school—our school was for all the rejects. It all began at a Blue Light Disco in Parramatta when I belted a guy she knew. She told me I was a bully, and I told her to run along. I had a thing going with the police who ran the discos—I did my martial arts training at the club and because my crowd used to get into so many fights one sergeant said, 'Look, we might as well have you on our side.' Me and all my friends ended up working there. Two weeks later Meagan couldn't get into the disco, so I got her in with me, and we started talking, and it just went on from there.

In the beginning Meagan's parents thought I was the end of the earth, that I was Satan in the disguise of a fourteen-year-old boy. Her older brother would tell their parents, 'This John Ibrahim, he's belted everyone at our school, he's barred from playing sport because he's always getting into fights, he's been thrown out of school because he was accused of punching the principal . . .' When I was stabbed it was big drama. If my daughter came home and said, 'This is my boyfriend,' and I knew all these things about him, I'd take him outside and reverse my car over him a few times, maybe her with him.

The first couple of years of going out with Meagan were my discovery years. I was moving 100 miles an hour around the Cross and she was the only good, pure thing. I'd tell her all these things, and she'd bring me back down to earth with her innocence and faith in human nature. Sometimes knowing too much can make your life miserable.

We'd go out together, and do the little things that fourteen-year-olds do. Mum would catch this little golden-haired girl sitting on the couch with this curly-headed woglett. I'd take her home about 8.30, and the minute I'd drop her off you'd see my guys come and pick me up in a car that we'd borrowed, and I'd be off to start my other adventures for the night—up the Cross, getting into fights, running down a laneway being chased by ten police, hanging around all these people that I thought were magic. A few years later I'd end up in places with some really scary people—people you'd see on television as ones to avoid, and I'd think, 'What am I doing here?' I'd just take it all in and try and keep everything in context. It was all like a game. I'd step into one world and play that role to the max. Then I'd step into another. I never let the worlds cross paths and I'd adapt to every one of them.

There's been times when Meagan and I were going to break up, but there's too much history. Everything I can remember about my life, she's been a part of—the tragic things, the good things. My first car I ever bought, when I got stabbed, when I got shot. She's been my sanctuary where I can leave everything I've done behind me.

There was a lot of things I didn't get caught up in. Gambling or drugs never interested me. I don't drink alcohol or smoke. I was more into fitness. Lots of people around me used drugs and I've tried just about everything, but drugs did nothing for me. It's harder to be off drugs and be your own person, because using drugs goes with the flow. I've seen a lot of good friends go to waste that way. I once helped a guy out with some money. I thought I was doing the right thing by him, but then I sat in the coffee shop and watched him go up to a drug dealer. He overdosed a week later and I saw the grief his family went through. If I ever got to the state I see some junkies in I'd honestly rather be dead. I say all this even though now

I make my living out of selling alcohol. It can be just as bad as any other drug but no-one's forcing it down your throat.

People get as hooked on selling drugs as they do on taking drugs. They get used to making so much money they can't live any other lifestyle—they're an addict like the rest of them. Gambling is an even bigger drug than narcotics. People do crime to get money to gamble, just like people do crime to get money for drugs. They may have closed down Kellett Street, but they've relocated. When a place gets too hot they move. If people want to destroy their lives they find a way, casino or no casino, legal or illegal.

I've seen violence beyond belief. I've seen plots against people, I've seen the end result. People have died in front of me, but one of the things that affected me the most was what I saw when I first bought my club. I was visiting one of the strip clubs nearby, having a friendly talk with the owner and a girl came up and asked me if I wanted a lady for the night. I sort of looked at her and she looked at me, and then she turned around and walked away. Later it was her turn to do a show. She was stripping and I sat there watching her and then it clicked who she was. I'd known this girl all through primary school. All I could think of was this little girl I used to know. To see her like this—taking her clothes off for, say, two hundred men—was earth-shattering. She actually couldn't finish—she got half-undressed, put her clothes back on and left. I also walked out. I think it was one of the saddest nights of my life. I just couldn't get her out of my mind.

A few days later I went and saw her. She told me how she had to move out of home because of her mother's boyfriend. I asked her if she needed anything and she said, 'No.' I ran into her boyfriend a couple of nights later and I pulled him aside to have a talk. It did more damage than good. He left her and she met up with another guy who was probably worse.

You learn to block things out, but things like seeing her affect me so much. People from my childhood mean a lot to me. I remember having an argument with the owner of the strip club over her. To me it was unacceptable, but he said, 'Look, John, I'd sack her but she'll only go to one of the other clubs and what good would that do?'

You become hardened. I see prostitutes standing on the street about to collapse, and they're doing the limbo dance, swaying this way and that, and you're swaying with them waiting for them to fall, but they just keep swaying. After a while instead of trying to help them, you start making bets on whether they're going to tip or not. It's a cold attitude but I've learnt that you can't help people until they want to help themselves.

In Kings Cross there is no such thing as Women's Lib. Women are a way for men to make money, and a way for men to get off. A woman might run a brothel but she's usually only a front person for a man. Not every stripper and prostitute has a hard luck story, some do it because they like it, but no matter how much they make, the man is making double. I could never sell drugs and I could never make money off women. What they do is sad to me. I don't think their childhood dream was to grow up and be a prostitute and have men slobber all over them. Okay, I might have made money in some pretty strange ways but I never exploited anyone. It was all between equals.

The wildest period was when I was sixteen, seventeen, eighteen. If someone said, 'Look, we'll be there for you—you can count on us,' that was good enough for me. But I came to know that it was all make-believe; that if the time and politics didn't suit them, they wouldn't be there, no matter what favours you'd done for them. I was getting burnt by all the conniving and lies and it started chipping away at me, a little bit at a time. I began to think, 'This is ridiculous. These people aren't so magic. They're thugs and they are using us as their bat, that's all.'

What scared me most was it wasn't just my life, I had other people counting on me. That was the biggest pressure and it got me thinking in a more business-minded fashion. I had money saved up—I was the sort of person that knew that the good times weren't going to last forever. I got my security licence, and set up a company. I'd met a businessman who owned a nightclub in Surfer's Paradise. I liked him because he was his own man, a person I could learn from. On a holiday up at Surfers we looked him up and, after sorting out a blue outside his club, we got to talking. I suggested opening a nightclub in the Cross. He'd always wanted to but he was cautious because he didn't know the right people. I did, so we decided to go into partnership.

He came to Sydney and set everything up. I went straight in with a twenty per cent shareholding. The money that I put into the business wasn't as important to my partners as me being able to look after the place.

It was on the verge of getting taken away from them. It's all a game. There's certain people that like to harass and stand-over businesses and supply them with things they don't need—things like protection from the police which doesn't exist.

Four years ago about six or seven people used to organise everything that happened in the Cross. They were always against each other but they were making so much money that they controlled what opened, what closed, who worked, who sold the drugs. If you didn't go along with it, these people had the muscle, and the know-how, to make your business life hell. Unless you were one of them, there'd be nothing you could do about it.

In the last three years things have changed. The organisation element has gone. You can now actually ring up a policeman, tell him what the problem is and count on him to help you. Before, that policeman would probably know the person you've got the problem with and it would cause you even more trouble.

I was nineteen when I bought into the nightclub. I wanted to learn and I learnt quickly. The more people I met in this line of business, the more I liked it. In the beginning everyone told me, 'Don't do it. You know nothing about it. You'll lose money,' but I knew I could do it. The people I had been with didn't like me straying from the flock, becoming my own person. Just like everyone else who tries to hold you back, they told me all the negatives, but it's been the best move I've ever made. After a year I bought my partners out and got a new partner. That was two and a half years ago.

The first year was the most nervous year of my life. Fortunately, when our club first opened, we had a honeymoon period. There was only one other dance club in the area and we were packed. There were people bribing my doorman to get in. But there's been times I haven't been able to sleep at night worrying about whether the weekend was going to cover the bills. I never spent money I didn't have. I'd always think of the worst scenario and work from there. I couldn't believe that I'd ever have so much responsibility. It's in the back of my mind that I've got at least ten guys working with me that I care about, and their lives sort of depend on how well I run this club.

A club's image is important for business. There has to be a weeding out aspect. It's got to be seen as a good and safe place to go where people can relax and not get hassled. If you let everyone in, you end up losing the customers you want and having a club full of yobbos. And then the yobbos won't come because they say, 'There's no-one there but yobbos.' I like to be at the front door anyway to say hello to people, to personalise things, but also I like to think I can see trouble coming. Trouble is five drunk guys walking up the laneway all dressed the same and not one girl among them. Something happens to people when they're in a group. If you get any one of those five guys on their own, or with a girl, they're a totally different person. Ninety-eight per cent of the fights that we've had have been at the front door. We try our best to talk things through, but you've only got two cheeks to turn, and then there's nothing left. It's then I feel my hand start to twitch. If the guy continues to push me, I lose it. When I realise what's happening a minute or so later the guy is on the ground. I might feel sorry for him and see if he's all right. I don't enjoy fighting but sometimes it is necessary.

One problem in owning a nightclub is the licensing laws—they haven't changed in eighty years. I mean, overcrowding and under-age drinking I can understand, but other laws are ridiculous. You've got restrictions on how many people you can have in a certain area, but people move around so what am I supposed to do? Come with a whistle and direct people to different areas?

It's a different crowd each night. On Sunday nights we often have live jazz, but otherwise it's dance music. I enjoy studying people, just sitting back in a dark corner and predicting their next move. When there's alcohol and dancing and dark lights it all just unfolds in front of you.

I meet a lot of beautiful girls and they might think they sort of like me, but I could never meet someone like Meagan at a nightclub. Cheating on Meagan a few times and getting busted definitely wasn't worth the grief. As a nightclub owner you suddenly become someone people want to meet. People pretend to be your friend. It's important not to let it get to your head or become someone you're not. That's the biggest challenge.

I'm there every night until we close. The thing that keeps me going is I'm my own boss. I like the freedom and I like the money. I'd like to think I would be the same person with or without money, but I have always liked being able to do what I want, when I want. I'm thinking of opening up another place, and if I wasn't busy with that I'd be planning something else. In five years' time, I want to be set up so that I never have to worry about money again. Then I can enjoy having a family. In the long run, all you've got is family. For me success is taking care of my family, keeping all my friends, staying with Meagan and at the same time going in a way that I want to go, sticking to my own principles.

I hope never to go backwards. I'm too scared to fail. I know that failing is just a learning experience, but I'll skip that lesson. Losing money and starting all over again doesn't scare me so much as letting myself and others down. That's my biggest fear. My family think I come up with answers from the top of my head, but they don't know how I sit and think about things, that I could be wrong, that I have doubts, that I don't know what I'm talking about sometimes. Even so, I'd rather make the mistakes myself than have someone else make them for me. Meagan thinks I know what I'm doing. Her idea is, 'Look John, you think about things long enough, so if you can't make it, it wasn't meant to be.'

Relationships are very tricky. The more you put into them the more you get out of them, but you gotta be going in the same direction. I have least control in my relationship with Meagan. I don't intimidate her one bit and I really wouldn't want to. You've got to have something that's different. We argue more now, because she's taking a stand. That's all right, I knew it was coming. I like to think I listen and compromise, bargain, give and take, but I hate to bend—it's too hard to straighten back up again.

My older brother's the wild card in the family now. All he thinks about is having a good time. I take care of my two younger brothers. I like playing Dad. My eighteen-year-old brother is doing his second year in a chef's course and works for me part-time. I try and keep him sheltered. He hasn't seen anything Sam and myself have seen and there's no need. He's a different person. I couldn't sit and cut lettuce for three hours—I'd go bananas. But he couldn't argue with people for three hours at the front door of the nightclub like I do. Sure he tries to buck the system— non-stop—but I like to think he loves me enough that me being upset with him does more damage than any I could do to him. Whatever he wants I'll give him, as long as he doesn't turn out to be a no-hoper-bum who does nothing with his life.

My other brother is fourteen, still at school and playing football. A big thrill to him is buying a pushbike. I wouldn't let him leave school—no chance. He has no idea of the things I knew at his age and there's nothing out there for him. In the long run he'll be grateful.

Mum is happy. She doesn't have to worry about money. I'm sort of steering the dinghy. She keeps busy visiting relatives and looking after my sister's baby. One sister went overseas and met one of our distant cousins, and did the Lebanese thing and got married. My youngest sister is seventeen. She has left school and is about to get a job. I don't think she has boyfriends. It's not the Lebanese way.

I like to think nothing much moves me. I've seen things happen that would make policemen go to therapy, and I accept it. It's just that I don't think dying is such a big deal. It's a part of life. You see, I was clinically dead for a few minutes after I got stabbed, and it's the most blissful feeling. It was also the freakiest time of my life. I saw everything that happened to me. I watched them take my clothes off and operate on me. I could tell what they were saying, even though I was unconscious. Then I wasn't even there—I was wandering 'round the hospital. I started hallucinating. I relived everything that I'd done that I'd felt guilty about, as though it was being read back to me from a book.

When I came to I was on a respirator. I was conscious but I couldn't talk to anyone—I was like a zombie. I'd seen and heard things that I couldn't explain and I felt my mind had been playing tricks on me. The doctor knew that I was flipping out. He came and said, 'This might be a good time for us to talk.' He'd obviously experienced it a million times before. I said, 'You're the doctor who operated on me and there was another doctor with glasses.' He said, 'Yes, that's true.' Like, I'm not one of these people that believes in anything unless you show it to me in black and white, but the experience is a part of my character now. It makes you a stronger person, it makes you cope. You put things on a different level. There's some sort of intelligent life after death, some sort of master plan, I just can't see it.

My parents are Muslim but I think I'm the worst Muslim ever made. I don't like family get-togethers at all. Being a Lebanese family, you have to kiss about fifty people before you sit down to eat. It's just not worth the food, no matter how good the food is. I'm the only one in the family that has never been to a mosque. I don't think my mother would take me. It'd be like a sacrilege. I can speak Arabic but I can't read it. When I read the

English version of the Koran I read about three paragraphs, but gave it away because I found it so disheartening. I thought I was a pretty good bloke until I read that. Maybe when I get older, and I'm less hyperactive . . . So many things could be changed, but it's not as simple as it looks. I've tried to be the Good Samaritan, tried a bit of everything—you can't live in Kings Cross without trying a bit of everything. I think when I'm due in heaven God's going to look up his calendar and say, 'I've gotta leave that day free, Johnny's coming up. We got a lot of things to sort out.'

I do some sort of exercise every day. I do a bit of kick-boxing and I've got a punching bag and weights at home. It relaxes me. I come home from work at five in the morning and I've got too much energy. I get changed and have a work-out. I'm pretty active. I love horseriding and bush-walking. The in-thing for me at the moment is scuba diving. We go hunting every now and then on a friend's property. We help the farmer with his sheep and at night we sit around and talk over a fire. We hunt kangaroos and those vicious rabbits that roam the country side. We don't touch the wild life. When we go shooting or fishing none of the women come. If I took Meagan every time I shot something, she'd run out and put a band-aid on it and give it mouth-to-mouth. She'd end up shooting me. There's no point.

Society conditions you from the minute you go to school to be a good citizen, work and keep quiet. You live out your life, pay all your debts to the government, and you really haven't enjoyed any of it. It's the people who don't listen to that, the ones that break away, who let their minds grow, who end up getting somewhere. I still live in about four different worlds, but I think my time is still coming. All I hope is I know when it's there, but I like to think I'm on the right track.

JOHN TRANTER

'At the Piccolo' and 'Storm Over Sydney'

At the Piccolo

Sitting in the jazz café at four a.m.
plotting a future in another country and a change of heart
I see a friend walk past with a striking woman
I happen to know has syphilis. His last girl was a lesbian
the one before that slit her wrist
four times in a week. Sitting at my table
with a Spanish coffee and a diary of despair
scribbling its lunatic message in my eyes
I think of two foreign girls with brutal inclinations
grappling on the gymnasium floor with their legs
awkwardly apart, smelling of stale perfume, honest toil
and a frank desire to please.

The girl thinks she might make the coffee
'on the house'. I'd back out of such a contract
on principle, remembering the advice of a friend
now married to a bitchy hag who used to be 'affectionate'.
Don't shit on your own doorstep, he said. Outside
the street takes on a pale radiance and a hint of mist.
My friend walks in, alone, and we talk
carefully avoiding references to women, love, despair
and the pale carnage of the street.

Storm Over Sydney

Blustering over the Harbour, brilliant rain
slaps and blathers at the rusty Bridge.
I dodge for cover as the sky turns green.
Cars wobble and skid on William Street,
 hot with mechanical rage.

Lightning strikes twice: a blinding white
crack! and the echo whacks the concrete.
I fossick and dawdle in the supermarket aisles
safely underground, among the paper plates
 and the jars of honey.

The thunder has trundled a thousand miles
and boiled the Pacific black to bother us all,
and it's dull and sick from its long journey.
Now I'm trying to wheel a crook trolley
 from the shopping mall:

the chrome's rusty, and a bent wheel clanks.
It's the season of ruby cellophane and holly;
the gutters are chock-full of summer hail
fresh-frozen and smashed into chunks.
 At the café I doze

in a corner, read the messages and the mail,
and unwrap the book I've bought. It's old, old:
the writer's fervour whispering down the years,
epigrams elaborating a narrative—as though
 such fragments could!

On schedule, the weather grumbles and raves
westward over the suburbs. I'm happy. I know
a little park where I can park the car,
sit on a wet bench and watch the waves
 fume in the amethyst air.

The Nineties

'It was like he was part of an opera, only this time he didn't have to pay a small fortune for a walk-on.'

—*Louis Nowra*

In the 1990s, the reputation of Kings Cross was further tarnished by the NSW Royal Commission into police corruption. The following chapter from *Whipping Boy*, by Gabrielle Lord, is a chilling fictionalisation of the ways in which the police force cooperated with criminals in the protection of paedophiles. Under the indifferent gaze of the same police force, heroin use greatly increased, and in the 1990s various pockets evolved in the Cross that catered to the diverse needs of users. There was a 'Kiddies Corner' on Darlinghurst Road, near the railway station, where children aged between twelve and sixteen slouched about on heroin and cocaine. They made their money from kerb crawlers, some of whom would pay them a nominal fee to perform all manners of sexual acts. The Dead Eye Zone, populated by ex-criminals, was across the street, while the Transient Zone was around the El Alamein Fountain, where tourists and first-time users scored, just metres from the Kings Cross Police Station. Most regular addicts repaired to illegal shooting galleries, which were mostly filthy rooms above strip clubs and bars.

Much of the literature produced during this decade reflects the inexorable slide of recreational users into addiction and prostitution. Luke Davies' chapter, from his novel *Candy*, illustrates just how easy it was to procure heroin in the Cross, and the consequences of casual drug use. In the 1990s, deaths in the Cross increased, due to accidental overdoses and the AIDS virus. The chapter extracted from Lorenzo Montesini's autobiography, set in the Sacred Heart Hospice in Darlinghurst, is one man's poignant interpretation of the current of love and loss that was sweeping through the gay community. Local religious organisations, however, responded to the plague. In 1999, the Sisters of Charity tried to set up safe injecting rooms in the Cross, but were duly blocked by the Vatican. The underworld of Kings Cross sided with the Vatican, but for very different reasons—if the church provided shooting galleries, then the crime bosses wouldn't be able to rent out rooms to desperate junkies. In the same year, after several attempts, the Wayside Chapel caused a national controversy by establishing an injecting room on its premises, providing clean needles and any necessary medical attention to local heroin addicts.

In the 1990s, the Cross lost many of its youths to drugs, and it also lost many of its individual businesses, mainly to multinational companies. The German restaurant on the corner of Springfield Avenue became Hungry Jacks. The Cosmopolitan Cafe became the Sunglass Hut. The Rex Hotel and the nearby Kings Cross library were demolished. On the site of the Rex was built a new hotel, albeit an expensive one for visiting tourists, with a bar that only serves drinks to its guests; the library was reestablished in the back of the building. Sweetheart's Restaurant, Pandora's Cake Shop, the Lebanese takeaways, the various clothing stores were replaced by sushi bars, McDonald's, foreign exchange centres, and Asian fast food outlets. Residential high-rise buildings like the Elan and the Horizon—both on William Street—began to disfigure the skyline of the Cross, much to the chagrin of the local community. However, Merlinda Bobis' story 'Fruit Stall' is a short hymn to a surviving small business in Kings Cross, and to the quiet dignity of the individual people who still inhabited the rapidly changing landscape.

The 1990s also ushered in other changes on William Street, mostly in the form of transsexual prostitutes. Infinitely more glamorous than the heterosexual working girls along Darlinghurst Road, each night 'the trannies' and 'crossies', with their sequined mini-skirts and platform shoes, became colourful ornaments to the rows of illuminated car dealerships. Graeme Aitken, in his chapter from *Vanity Fierce*, dramatises the transsexual culture with great detail and humour, and in some ways his prose style and concerns hark back to an earlier, more frivolous time, to Jon Rose's account of a 1940s Drag Ball.

Despite the growing commercialisation of the area, Kings Cross remained a favourite haunt for night life in the 1990s. In Louis Nowra's chapter, excerpted from his novel, *Red Nights*, the Mansions Hotel is a source of endless entertainment—smoky and blaring with music—with its regular drag queens, drug addicts, and standover men.

Finally, after vacating the Cross in the late 1970s and throughout the 1980s, artists slowly began to move back to the area, though most prominently in the form of filmmakers. The annual short film festival, Tropfest, soon became a feature of Sydney, attracting hundreds of would-be directors and writers to the area, and thousands of eager people to screenings in Victoria Street. The offices of Minton House, on the corner of Bayswater and Darlinghurst Roads, evolved into a kind of unofficial headquarters in the 1990s for various industry professionals. The Kennedy Miller Film Production Company was just down the road in the art-deco building formerly known as The Metro.

Individual writers also drifted back to the area, perhaps inspired by both the tawdriness and elegance of the urban village. A café culture soon reemerged along Victoria Street, and at the lower end of Macleay Street. The Tropicana, the Coluzzi, and La Buvette are just a few of the cafés that were popular with authors, artists, and filmmakers. The Darlo Bar and the Green Park Hotel evolved into the main watering hole for the local bohemians.

In the 1990s the Cross housed authors Helen Garner, Justine Ettler, and Susan Geason, amongst others. Recent figures from the NSW Writers' Guild prove that there are now more authors living in the 2011 postcode than in any other postal district in Australia, and this phenomenon is reflected in the abundance of published material the editors of this book had to choose from when making selections to represent the 1990s. Writers who still live in the Cross today include Linda Jaivin, Peter Robb, Murray Bail, Gaby Naher, Matt Condon, Anne Summers, Lorenzo Montesini, and Stephen J Spears, most of whom have fictionalised the Cross with particular affection, as have their literary ancestors since the early 1920s.

GABRIELLE LORD

from *Whipping Boy*

Two of the group of kids near the station entrance were unconscious from drugs or alcohol, lying on the hard and filthy street while their companions argued or sang, faces as mindless as the men with schooners staring out through the glass of a fishbowl lounge nearby.

The spruikers ignored Cass now. They knew she wasn't worth a hussle. She felt self-conscious and was aware that she was walking straighter and taller because the man was following her. The lights were bright around the doorways that led either upstairs or downstairs to dives and bars and strip joints. The winter evening was setting in, and hellish stripes of neon greens, reds and yellow lights seemed to burn on the rain-wet surface of the road. But the weather had cleared, and several young prostitutes were already leaning against walls and doorways. Their eyes were bleak with heroin and their pale skin seemed to be drying out under the harsh lights. One was little more than a child, sadly droll in the trappings of harlotry. A black eye and broken lip were still visible under the glaze of the young woman's make-up.

Cass turned away, not wanting to feel the shame of them within herself. She wanted to look behind her, to see if she could see him. She forced herself instead to stare into a florist's window, pretending interest in an arrangement of Madonna lilies. She jumped when someone spoke her name.

'Miss Meredith?'

Cass turned. She made sure her eyes stayed on the short middle-aged woman in a navy dress who was addressing her, and didn't stray behind to see where Warner or his man might be.

'I'm Margaret Maloney. Loveday's friend.' For a second, Cass was bewildered. There was something so brisk and wise about her, Cass immediately thought she could be a very successful dyke, a woman who smoked Senior Service and gave orders to a thousand people. But then she noticed the tiny silver cross on the lapel.

'I thought you might like this.' The woman handed Cass a pamphlet; a novena card. 'It's not all Popish superstition,' she smiled. 'There's something you need on the other side. God bless.' And she turned and walked towards the fountain.

Cass looked at the card in her hand. It was a novena to St Jude, the patron of hopeless causes. She smiled and turned it over. There, very lightly pencilled in, was an address in Potts Point. Cass pocketed the little card and started walking there, almost forgetting her bodyguard now.

As she neared the place, Cass glanced at the address again. Yes, there it was—a terrace house set in a sodden garden. A huge old palm took up most of the space but there was no strangler fig clenched around it. Masonry from renovations cluttered the verandah and when she knocked, the barking of an invisible dog caused her to jump. The dog barked in sequences of five, sounding like a giant starter motor. Inside, she heard a woman's voice restraining it.

'Who is it?' came the voice in the hall.

'Cass Meredith.'

Cass heard the chain being engaged and the door unlocking. The eye and cheek of a beautiful face peered out the crack. Then the door was closed again briefly so that Loveday could let Cass in.

'Come in. Quick. I hate opening this door. Every time I hear the key go in, I nearly jump out of my skin. Don't mind Sheba. She won't hurt.' The Dobermann stood with her tongue lolling near Cass's hip as her mistress stood back and allowed the visitor in. Down the hallway, on the right, Cass caught a brief glimpse of a room filled with cushions and a tiny flickering light. She imagined it to be a seductive boudoir until she noticed the crucifix hanging in the hall.

'Sister Margaret found you okay? Do you want a drink?'

'Coffee would be nice.' Cass followed Loveday into a larger room at the back of the house and then through into a comfortable kitchen. 'The sisters are out at the moment. Are you sure you don't want a real drink? No? How do you like your coffee?'

Cass told her, enjoying looking at her. Close up, Loveday was quite beautiful; Eurasian, finely boned and delicate, with long dark hair, a glossy fringe and winged eyes. She reminded Cass of a very beautiful hawk. Curious gold earrings, like upside-down question marks, swung near her jawline. It was impossible to tell her age. The mouth was very full, almost African, but the body was frail. The addiction was already emptying her, and her shadowed eyes flickered from haunted sockets; she was far too thin under the cheongsam of vivid green.

Sheba followed her mistress dotingly, almost tripping her up with loving attention, wagging up against the too-slender legs. From upstairs, Cass could hear the sound of the television. Loveday noticed her upwards glance.

'Kismet. My daughter. You know—she's supposed to be doing her homework.'

Cass remembered the last time she'd seen Kismet and tried not to think of the blurred pink image in the spa with her mother and the dog. She stared at Loveday but the woman was looking upwards.

'Turn it off and do your homework,' Loveday suddenly screamed up the stairs. There was no change in the sound level of the television. 'Little bugger. She takes no notice of me. You know what they're like. You're a mother, too.'

Loveday generously topped up her own glass from the scotch bottle on the sideboard. 'You sure you don't want a proper drink?' Cass shook her head. Loveday made the coffee and handed it to Cass. They sat at a long table in the large room, which was simply and quietly furnished. Cases of books filled one wall and the other walls were covered with photos and paintings.

'You're younger than I thought,' said Loveday, sitting opposite Cass and studying her face as relentlessly as a beautician. Then leaning on the table with her elbow, she propped a hand around her sculpted jaw and cheek-bones, and flicked a long strand of dark silk behind her shoulder. One of the question marks swung this way, then that, revealing a dark red stone smoothly set in the gold. 'How old do you think *I* am?'

Cass looked into the shadowed face and its beautiful features. She shook her head. 'You could be anything from late twenties, to, say, late thirties?' Loveday looked pleased.

'That's good. That's very good. I had this operation on my mouth. To make it—you know—fuller. All the American movie stars have had it done. Michelle Pfeiffer. I'm forty-three,' she announced, as if producing herself out of a box. 'And this is all I've got.' She indicated her face and body with an offertory gesture of her hand. 'I didn't—you know—have Kismet till I was twenty-nine. It's a bit late, do you think?'

Cass was intrigued to hear a desperate edge to the woman's voice. 'Not at all,' she said. 'It's quite a good age to have a child.' In the normal way of things, Cass was thinking. *I don't know when is a good time for a working prostitute to have a child.*

Loveday looked relieved. 'Your son looks a real cutie,' she said, mother to mother.

'Loveday. I want you to tell me everything you know. I'll organise money for you. But you must help me in every way you can.'

'I can help you. But don't register me. Or I'll tell you nothing. Promise me. I don't want to be a registered informer. If Arikan ever finds out, I'm dead.' Cass remembered the name on the warehouse at Granville. 'He nearly choked me once. He's got friends in the coppers. I just want to do this informally—you know—like a friend.' Cass nodded. 'Except for the money, I mean,' Loveday continued. 'And I'm only asking for that so I can get clean. I'm writing a book. So no registration.'

Cass nodded again. The system of registered informants, and the official bank accounts from which they were paid, were part of that shifting area where the swirling clouds of the underworld met the precepts of the law and condensed into a confused bureaucracy.

'I'm fairly new in Sydney. I haven't settled in yet. This work is a great chance for me,' said Loveday. 'But I've only ever done straight stuff before—you know—straight adult stuff. Never with youngsters. I feel terrible about *All in the Family*. I was really blasted that time. Kismet had been doing coke. I've told her over and over not to touch drugs. She won't listen to me.' Loveday took two small blue pills from a purse and washed them down with mouthfuls of scotch. 'Arikan was directing it and we were all off our faces and he just said to try it this way and try it that way and there was this kid hanging around and before I knew it, we were all in together, me, Kismet, the boy and the Doctor. Well, I call him the Doctor. I don't know who he is or what he does, really. But he's got this real Pommy way of talking. He's a big customer. He likes little boys. He's got a lot of money and he's got a little doctor's bag like in the movie of Jack the Ripper.' She laughed. It was like a sob. 'So it all just kind of happened that first time. He wants to do more movies. He wants me to get kids for him. And I think that's wrong. You know you can buy a little kid for two hundred and fifty dollars? The kids are numbed out. They're past caring. But I'm not,' she said with real emphasis. 'He thinks I'll do anything because of the drugs. But I haven't got a real habit. I can get off this stuff any time I like. I'm only a recreational user. I'm not a junkie.' Cass watched as the woman's lozenge-shaped eyes flickered at the lie. 'I'm not. I just want to write my book. I love my daughter. I don't want to do anything to hurt her. And I don't want to become the woman who procures kids for Arikan's clients.'

'Tell me about Arikan?' Cass asked.

Loveday shrugged. 'He's a businessman. Dealer. He's got some parlours round here. Properties. He's been around here a long time. He's bought and sold coppers. He gathers information. He knows everyone. He works for himself or for anyone who'll pay him, buying and selling. He does special favours for people. For money, of course. I haven't known him for long but a friend of mine has.' She swallowed the drink and went out to the kitchen.

'Do you know Arikan's first name?' Cass asked through the doorway.

'Not sure,' Loveday called back. 'I think it's Klaus or Claude or something foreign like that. The man he's supposed to be working for these days is a very heavy dude.' Cass made a note of it. Loveday kept talking.

'You know—all I've got to sell is me, one way or another. This—' she had come back to the lounge room and gracefully indicated the length of her body with her free hand—'and the information I get hold of through my work. If I sell information to you, and set up the kids so your people can move in, I'll want a lot of money. It's dangerous work this.' She raised the scotch to her full lips again. 'I heard already a kid died.'

'What happened?' Cass asked, but Loveday closed down and shook her head.

'It's just talk. Don't know if it's true even. Anyway, kids die round here all the time.' She fumed. 'Kismet! Turn that fucking-excuse-the-French-television down, will you!' The green silk of the cheongsam gleamed around the woman's beautiful throat as she yelled. Cass waited till Loveday put the glass down again.

'Something's puzzling me. How come Arikan wants you to work for him again, Loveday? After you going to the press with his latest work of art? I don't understand.'

'Look,' said Loveday, opening her hands. 'Men like him. They don't care. They're not worried about the coppers. They know the papers will have something else to fuss about next day. Nobody really cares. People just like to carry on a bit. And I told him I was sorry. That the drugs sent me off my head and I went to the press.' Her voice was suddenly flat, without vibrancy. 'And I'm good. I'm good at what I do. I enjoy my work. That shows up. And I do have a beautiful body.' Cass noted a strange rehearsed detachment in the way the woman said this, as if she were talking about someone or something else, a piece of merchandise, or a length of fabric. 'Actually, he didn't really mind all that much. He just wanted to scream at me for a while. He said there's no such thing as bad publicity. He's been running off copies like mad. He can't keep up with the demand now. There's a warehouse full, he said. He's charging three hundred for that cassette. And people are coming out of the woodwork wanting more stuff like that. But I won't get kids for him. And that's that.' She made her sobbing laugh again. Then she became serious. 'But he nearly choked me—' she raised her hand to the high-necked silk collar—'and said if I ever mentioned his name, he'd kill me for sure. One of his mates is Shaun Loneregan. The one they call The Vet. You've heard of him?'

Cass nodded in the silence that was punctuated by the static sound of canned laughter from upstairs.

'Okay,' said Cass at last. 'What can you give me?'

'You're not wired, are you?' Loveday suddenly said.

Cass shook her head. 'No. I'm not.'

'Empty your bag. Go on. Do it.' Cass opened her flat little leather envelope. Out dropped lipstick, comb, crushed handkerchief, address book, condoms, eyebrow pencil and compact. Then forty dollars folded together. Loveday sat on the chair opposite, leaning forward, the way a child does when excited.

'Take off your jacket. Open your blouse. Go on.'

'No,' said Cass.

'Well, piss off, then,' said Loveday, suddenly sullen. 'I'm not saying a thing until I'm sure you're not wired.'

Reluctantly, Cass removed her jacket. She slowly undid the tiny buttons of her cream blouse and opened it, like curtains, to show the lace of her bra. There was a long silence.

'You're quite small too,' said Loveday. 'I like small breasts. A lot of men like huge ones.'

Once again, Cass noted the flat voice. She started to do her blouse up. She tucked it in and put her jacket back on.

'Loveday,' she said. 'This is the last time I will do this, or anything like this. If I wanted to record our conversations, I would, and I'd do it in such a way you'd never find out. You have to trust me. I don't lie.'

'Ha!' Loveday's laugh was bitter. 'You just haven't had to, that's all,' she said. 'A woman like you.'

I am the daughter of a thief and a betrayer, Cass thought. What can you know about me? But she remained silent. Then she repeated her earlier question.

'What can you give me, Loveday?'

Loveday became animated again. She swallowed more scotch. 'I can tell you where we'll do it, what time. Everything. When the kids will be there. There's a huge market of people who will pay big money for this sort of thing. But they want special things. Certain sorts of kids. Really weird shit. I can find out who the kids are. How he pays them. If they'll talk. Maybe I can find out where they run the copies off, how they distribute them. Who buys them. Who sells them. Everything. Then you'd just need to watch it all happen and when your team's ready and got everything you need, you could just move in and wipe them all up. That would be the end of your investigation. Another successful one, like Melbourne Customs.'

'You know about that?'

'I'm a Melbourne gal, remember.'

'Loveday. What you've just described to me is great. But on the phone, you implied you already had something for me. You led me to believe you had something in your possession. Some physical piece of evidence. Am I right?'

The earrings became very still and Loveday's voice, remote and mechanical; her face as closed and painted as a Manchu princess.

'You're greedy,' she said. 'Isn't it enough that I can set you up with these scummy rock spiders?'

I'd better make a good offer, Cass was thinking, as Loveday's flat voice continued. She had changed tack and was on another course.

'If anything should happen to me, see Saphra at Babes. She knows about where I store my other stuff. My old man's stuff.'

'Okay,' said Cass to her, keeping her eyes still, excited at hearing Saphra's name again. 'I want you to tell Arikan you'll get the kids for him. Tell him you have a friend who specialises in this line of work. Her name is Angel,' said Cass, improvising. 'Give me his number.'

'I haven't got it,' said Loveday. 'He always rings me. But I think you can contact him at Babes.'

'Tell him you have to have a contact number, Loveday. It's essential. For Angel. Tell him Angel will ring him when she's got what he wants.' Cass felt the hairs on her neck and back start to rise. 'What exactly does he want?' she asked.

'A little girl. And a boy. But the boy can't be older than about ten or eleven. This guy can—you know—smell when they're—um—starting to grow up. And he won't touch them if they don't smell right. And the girl has to be skinny. She's got to have dark hair and plaits with red ribbons. Little girls' dress. Little black court shoes. Little red ribbons. No other colour. These kids are for private use. Someone real important. He'll pay them well.'

Cass swallowed. 'Get me that phone number, Loveday. Tell Arikan about Angel. That she can get what he wants. That she can get anything. That she'll ring soon. Promise.' Just then, feet on the staircase made both women look up. Cass opened her purse quickly and put the forty dollars in Loveday's hand. 'Just do this for me. Please? I'll fix up some decent money for you soon.'

'Okay,' Loveday nodded, shoving the money inside the cheongsam and looking up again.

Kismet was coming downstairs. Cass stared. If the mother was beautiful, the daughter was even more so, with a ripeness and the frailty of adolescence together; her long green eyes were angled in a perfect little cat's face. The only flaw was a very thin top lip, but this somehow added to her elfin grace. Black hair fell like a mantilla around her neck and shoulders. But the voice was a shock. So were the nicotine stained fingers of a heavy smoker and the cigarette hanging from her hand.

'I wanna see Leo.'

'You can't,' said her mother, looking up at her. 'Don't you realise the mess we're in? A lot of people are very angry at me and you.'

'Why me?' Kismet demanded in an age-old whine.

'Because you're my daughter, that's why,' snapped her mother.

'Lucky me,' said the girl. She was wearing a midriff top despite the cold, and tight black pants. Her childish figure still had the little tummy that she would soon lose.

'Why can't I?' The pouting snarl of thirteen. Cass almost remembered her own version of it. 'Why can't I go anywhere? This place sucks. Fucking nuns, for Christ sake.'

'Watch your language,' warned Loveday. 'This is Miss Meredith. She's the one I was telling you about. The investigation? The cassette I took to the press.' Kismet rolled her eyes towards heaven as if nothing could interest her less.

'What's to eat?'

'I don't know. Margaret and Carmel will be home soon. Margaret said she'd bring something.'

'Bloody nuns' food. I want some McDonald's. Something decent for a change. All that health food is making me sick.' The girl raised the cigarette to her lips and took a long appraising look at Cass. She came down to where her mother was standing; she was almost as tall. Then she went to the kitchen and returned with a scotch. Her mother lunged at it, trying to take it from her. 'No! I've told you, no alcohol.'

'If I can't see Leo I might as well get drunk. There's nothing to do around here.'

'There's your homework.'

'You stupid bitch. I wish you'd drop dead.'

The contempt in the girl's voice was arresting. Mother and daughter glared at each other.

'Put that booze down,' said her mother, hopelessly. 'You're too young.'

Kismet jerked herself away from Loveday's ill-timed grab.

'Too young for what?' she said.

She crushed the cigarette out in a saucer and ran upstairs again, but not before Cass noticed that her long eyes shone with tears. Loveday screamed after her.

Cass phoned a cab and let herself out the door, Loveday's abuse still echoing in the house. At the kerb Cass stood tall, unable to see her bodyguard, until the cab pulled over and she stepped into it.

LUKE DAVIES

'Problems with Detachable Heads: 1' from *Candy*

I watched her licking her ice cream and tried to imagine that it was my dick. But this was dangerous territory, since heroin and sex could so easily become confused.

'Me too,' I said. 'I don't really want to go home yet.'

'What should we do?'

I looked in her eyes for that flicker. We were circling each other, baiting, fishing. My gut started to roll and I knew without doubt what was going to happen.

I acted casual, like I was plucking random suggestions from the warm air. This was part of the game, so no one could ever say that fucking up was a deliberate act.

'There's not much to do around here,' I said. 'We could go up to the Cross and check the nightlife.'

'Are you sure?' She gave me a token admonishing look, but the edges of her lips were quivering.

'Hey, we're just going for a walk, we don't have to use!'

'That's the problem,' she frowned. 'I wouldn't mind some.'

The sweet dam had burst, the Dam of Relief which would bear us tumbling up William Street and into our own veins and home.

What was it about love? Coming down off heroin, it was so hard to think of anything but pain. When we were stoned we loved each other, we touched each other, we laughed a lot, it was us against the world. We spent every moment together, ambling through the musky days, aware only of the way our boundaries seemingly had dissolved, revelling in the sensation of submersion and inundation. But the future made me edgy. It would be good not to use drugs, I thought. I wanted us to live our lives, to laugh and touch and share things, but without hammer. I thought that surely must be a place you could get to. And yet here we were, six days down the track of another expedition into sobriety, jumping out of our fucking skin.

I could have said no. It was a moment in my life when I could have said no. But I grinned weakly and then looked away and then looked back at her, chewing my lip.

'I wouldn't mind some either.'

'Do you want to?' she asked. 'It's been a week. That's OK, isn't it?'

'Let's do it,' I said.

And we were off.

At this time of night there was nowhere to get syringes. We racked our brains about the situation at home. With good intentions of course you throw all that shit out. But had we put out the garbage in the last week? It was unlikely but possible. Anyway, we couldn't take that risk. And having made the decision to score, it was like hanging out again. That acidic anticipation in the gut.

We certainly couldn't buy some heroin now and wait until morning to use it. That was more than inconceivable. It was silly and absurd. Snorting it or chasing the dragon was on the very outer rims of the possible. Pussy stuff.

There was only one thing to do: we had to buy the dope, *and* somehow get hold of a pick or two. Hopefully unused.

We were OK for cash, we were six days healthy, we were feeling pretty cruisy. A nervous edge about the syringe situation, but we would work that out. Even when I lived in ratholes I was generally meticulous about the vein and hygiene factor. Occasionally, however, fate dictated that you had to take a chance.

We took a table at the Cockatoo Club, which was empty at this early hour, and ordered drinks. Yusef the manager came and chatted to us for a few minutes. Just then Ronny Radar walked past the window. I was out of my seat and moving.

'Just saw Ronny. Back in a minute.'

I caught up with him and we talked the talk. I gave him the money and told him where we were sitting.

'One thing, Ronny,' I added. 'I need a pick. Where can I get a clean one?'

Ronny looked at his watch.

'Buckley's chance, mate. Buckley's. There's nothing open now.'

'Haven't you got any?'

'I'll tell you what,' he said. 'I'll give you one that only I've used. All you have to do is give it a good clean. I'll go without until I get home later.'

A regular saint was Ronny. It would have to do.

'Thanks Ronny. You're a champion. Oh, and a spoon. Can you get me a spoon? The fucking teaspoons in the Cockatoo have got holes drilled in them.'

Ronny moved in too close to my face.

'Mate,' he hissed, 'I'm not a fucking supermarket. I'm a heroin dealer. Got it?'

'Sorry Ronny. It's just that . . . I've been away. I'll give you five bucks if it helps.'

He sighed deeply and held out his hand. I gave him five more dollars.

'Sometimes . . .' he said, shaking his head and letting the sentence trail away as he walked around the corner.

I went back into the Cockatoo and smiled at Candy. Yusef was over at the bar touching up the topless waitress. We finished our drinks and Ronny came in and sat down with us. I introduced him to Candy and all of a sudden he was a friendly suck-hole. He handed everything to me under the table and left.

We ordered another drink and I looked down and checked the syringe. Shit! It was a detachable head, two mils, a big awkward monstrous motherfucker. God I hated those things!

The thing about those detachable-head syringes was, they always seemed to collect a little blood, down in the neck area, where the replacement head and needle slipped tight over the plastic nozzle of the barrel. You could never fully empty them out into your vein, because the black rubber stopper on the end of the plunger couldn't get down into that bridging neck. This was dead space.

Sure enough, Ronny's syringe was this sleek clear plastic rocket with a band of dried crimson down near the point where the needle began. Not what I wanted to see. A very used syringe. I pointed this out to Candy. We discussed the pros and cons of going home or having a shot here in the Cockatoo toilets.

'I'll see how I go cleaning it,' I said.

I went into the Men's. There was a wash basin and a piss trough and four cubicles. My plan was to clean the pick thoroughly, then mix up and have a hit, then clean it again and fill it with a hit for Candy to take to the Ladies'.

I turned the tap on slightly and filled the spoon with water. I carried it into the end cubicle and placed it on the cistern. There was a window above the cistern, looking out over the back alley that ran behind the Cockatoo. The glass was broken but a security grille of iron bars covered the space. I hoped that if I flushed out the pick several times I could get rid of that blood.

Normally I'd suck up the water and squirt as hard as possible, to jiggle things around in there and dislodge the caked blood. It was a pretty automatic habit. But I forgot to account for the fact that I wasn't familiar with this type of syringe. If you were going to squirt hard, you had to hold the end on with your fingers.

I dipped the needle into the spoon and drew up water until the barrel was full. The window invited. I don't know, I just wasn't thinking. Maybe I was being neat, not spraying water on the walls of that filthy bog. I aimed towards the window and pushed the plunger hard.

The pressure was too great. The needle, like the pod of Saturn Five, came off from the main body at supersonic speed. By the time I heard the *pffft!* of its flight through the cubicle, it had sailed through the security bars, straight out the window and on into the night.

I looked down at the useless piece of plastic in my hand. A syringe without a needle was like a car without an accelerator. You could admire it or polish it but not get that glorious wind in your hair. I couldn't believe this had happened. I couldn't believe my stupidity.

I had to find that missing piece. I couldn't risk getting home to a flat devoid of syringes. I stood on the toilet bowl and hoisted myself up to the window.

The alley was dark. I tried to imagine trajectories, angles of entry, angles of descent. I figured it could only have come down in the mini-skip full of construction rubble that was opposite the window. Then again, it might have been in that huge pile of green garbage bags wedged hard up against the skip.

No question. I had to get out there.

I went back out into the club and explained the dire situation to Candy. I walked around the block and found the alley. I located the mini-skip and the pile of garbage bags, most of which had split open. The place stank of rotting vegetation.

I looked back to the window and figured the bags were the go, not the mini-skip. I trod on them gingerly, using the edge of the skip to keep my balance. Everything was spongy under my feet. Suddenly my right leg disappeared beneath me. I fell knee-deep into rotten tomatoes. A wet squelch filled my jeans. I heard the scurrying of panicked rats.

I pulled my leg out. My jeans and shoes were soaked. Now I stank. I stepped back cursing and shook my leg. From the corner of my eye I noticed movement.

Two figures were walking down the alley towards me. They were in silhouette, but I had no trouble making out the police hats and holsters. My heartbeat picked up a little. It was not cool to run. I could stay and pretend to be looking for something in the garbage. There was nothing wrong with that. For some reason I thought of a tennis ball. I would tell them I was looking for a tennis ball.

Then I remembered the dope. I had half a gram of heroin and half a syringe and a dessert spoon in my pocket. It was time to go. Just not my night.

I did the fast-casual walk. I didn't look back but I didn't hear their foot-steps pick up. I rounded the corner and ran the half block to the Cockatoo Club. A kind of high-speed limp, a *whoomp-slurp*, *whoomp-slurp* sound.

Candy was being chatted up by some young turks. Wide lapel types. Good luck to them.

'Big fuck-up, baby doll,' I said to her, nodding polite hellos to them. 'Let's get a taxi out of here.'

'Aw, where youse goin?' they shouted, but we were out the door already.

'Maybe Ronny's got AIDS,' mused Candy in the taxi on the way home. 'Maybe it was meant to happen.'

'That'll be a small fucking consolation if there are no syringes at home.' My stomach was doing somersaults by now. When you made the decision, you wanted to act fast.

We got home and Lex was there. At this time we were sharing a flat with Lex. Not the Leichhardt house, but a place of our own, the three of us. Now Lex had his own little problems, sometimes with heroin, sometimes with freebasing, off there on the sides of our lives. Sometimes our problems intersected, sometimes not. Usually only in cases of emergency. It must have been some Catholic guilt hangover bullshit thing. We generally liked to try to keep our problems separate and hidden.

It blew me out that he could fuck up so spectacularly, one year on heroin, the next on cocaine. I'm talking about solid blocks of dedication. How anyone could use cocaine for even an hour without wanting some hammer pretty quick smart was beyond me. But there you go. He was always an odd one, Lex. Off on his own obscure path.

Lex had recently done the get-healthy thing too. (I think this was a heroin period for him.) It might have been a week, maybe two, since he'd had a whack. So I'm sure he must have picked up the vibe when we walked in. The anticipation. You don't go to the movies, six days off the gear for God's sake, and come home abuzz with excitement about the late news coming up.

He was suspicious but it was a stand-off. If everyone was pretending to be clean, then everyone had to keep up the facade. We sat in front of the TV chatting idly. My pulse was racing and I couldn't concentrate. On anything but the fact that I had heroin: in my pocket and not in my body. But on the outside I was trying to be calm.

Lex asked about the bad smell coming from my pants. I told him I trod in a puddle and it must have had something awful in it. He told me it hadn't rained for three weeks. I told him it was a puddle next to a construction site.

The lounge room led into the kitchen. We couldn't search through the garbage bag while he was there, and we couldn't really carry it past him into our bedroom either. Finally he went to bed. Sulking a bit I think.

We sprang into action. I carried the garbage bag into the bedroom. It was putrid. That's what happens when you detox at home. You don't do normal things like take the garbage out. Everything is a touch difficult coming down off heroin.

I laid out some newspaper on the floor and tried to pick the least rank things out of the garbage bag, one at a time. If there were any syringes, they would be down the bottom. Finally I created enough room to tilt the bag sideways and shake it a bit. I spotted the orange lid of a Terumo 1 mil—my kind of pick, Mother Jesus we are home!—in an ashy sludge of wet cigarette butts. Then three more. Must have thrown out a handful.

I threw everything back in and took the bag back to the kitchen. I rinsed the ash off the syringes and washed my hands and arms. I went back to the bedroom and Candy already had a belt tied tight around her arm. There were times when I loved her enthusiasm.

I took the lids off and felt each needle for the two that were least barbed. These syringes had had a good run in the weeks before we stopped. I took the best two and scraped them backwards and forwards hard on the flint of a matchbox, to try and reduce the barbs. It would do.

We mixed up and had the blast and fell into each other's arms and told each other how very very much we loved each other. How we had such a bright future, all this abundant love, this intense thing, and how very stupid it would be to throw it all away and fuck up on dope. How we would stop again tomorrow. In that bliss, in that love, in that confidence, in that melting, you couldn't doubt it was true.

MERLINDA BOBIS

'Fruit Stall' from *White Turtle*

I am forty. Divorced. No children. I own a fruit stall in Kings Cross. And I am Filipina, but this is my secret. People ask, are you Spanish? Mexican? Italian? A big man, brushing his hairy arm against my waist, whispers in his beer-breath, aha, *Latina*! Cringing, I say, *si, si, si* to him, and to all of them. I am Filipina, but this is my secret.

I dyed my hair brown. It goes well with this pale skin from my Spanish grandfather whom I never saw. He owned the *hacienda* where my grand-mother served as housemaid. They sent her away when she grew a melon under her skirt.

Melons have their secret, too. No one knows how many seeds hide in their rose-flesh. Or who planted them there. Mother used to say, it is God, it is God who plants all things. I don't believe her now.

'Is this sweet?'

'Very sweet. And few seeds.' I pretend to know a secret.

But he's not interested. This man frowning at the melon sounds like a customer back home. He touches the fruit doubtingly, tentatively. His hand is smooth and white against the green rind.

'Want a taste?' I offer the last slice from a box labelled 'For Tasting'. I pretend I am a fruitseller at home where we let the buyer sample the merchandise before any business takes place.

Sample the merchandise. This is how the men, who go to my country to find themselves a nice, little brown girl, put it. They're great, these rice-ies. Give them a bowl of rice and they can fuck all night! An American serviceman said this once, grabbing me by the waist. I was twelve then. I remember I went home crying.

He gets it cheaply. He walks away with the melon now, the man with the smooth, white hand. More like the hands of my grandfather. Mine are white, too, but hard and rough.

So father said, papayas are good for your skin. Mash them well with your hands tonight, so they get soft and smooth when Jake arrives. Remember to be nice to him, ha? And fix that face—*Dios mio*, will you stop snivelling? Jake, the old Australian, whom my father had met in the city, became my husband. It must have been the papayas.

They're too small here and not as sweet. See these here? Too expensive, but not as good as the papayas back home. The tourists go gaga over our papayas there. They are sun-ripe, tree-ripe, we say. And cheap. Have dollar, no problem.

'How much for this?' Her hand on the papaya is very tanned, with fine golden hair. She's wearing a T-shirt with a coconut print. She looks happy. Good holiday. I want to ask, did you go to my country? But I keep my secret safe.

She frowns though, when I tell her the price. You see, papayas are expensive here. Go to my country. We sell them cheaply. I bite my tongue.

'And a kilo of grapes as well, please.'

My youngest brother ate himself sick with the grapes which Jake brought from Australia to our village. It was the first time my brothers tasted grapes. It was the first time our neighbours tasted grapes. Jake was very pleased with himself. He promised more grapes. A week before the wedding, my father strutted about, imagining himself the father-in-law of a grape-king. When I came here, I found out grapes are very cheap, especially in late summer.

It was getting cold when I arrived. Autumn is cold for me. Winter is freezing. Hardly any grapes by then. Jake said we were too greedy—why are you always sending something home? He must have suspected I sneaked in some grapes in my letters. He opened them. He frowned at my dialect on paper. What stories are you telling them, huh?

I can tell many stories about sweaty white hands running all over me in front of other men nodding over their beer. Guess where she's from? Oh, no, I didn't get myself an Asian with small tits. This is no Asian. Look at her melons. And they taste like plums—don't they, luv? He laughed until he was beetroot-red, while his fingers fumbled at my buttons, much to the joy of his clapping and stamping mates. My ex-husband was a fruitseller. I learned my trade from him, and I learned to say, si, I am Spanish. Or, Mexican by birth, Señorita. Or, Italian, Signore.

He reminded me of the pet monkey we had when I was young. My father gave it away, because it would wake up the whole house in the middle of the night with its crazed monkey-sounds. Jake did the same, chattering away about his great big white banana getting bigger and harder—turn over. On your belly, quick. He was very quick. Then he snored his way through a land of fruit. I imagined it had an overripe smell that made me sick. After a while, I learned how to doze off dry-eyed and dream of fruit-flies tracking down the smell, feeding on the smell, until each one dropped dead from too much sweetness.

I keep my stall clean and insect free. White people are particular about what they put in their bellies. Don't get me wrong. I don't say this is bad. I only say they're lucky, they have the choice to be particular. That's why I like it here. Actually, I liked it more after the divorce papers were signed. Oh, yes, I love it now, I do not wish to go home any more. Who would want to see a divorced woman there anyway? My mother with her strange God? My grape-less father? Never mind. I can have more than grapes here. I also have mangoes, pineapples, avocadoes, even guavas around me. I smell home each day.

'Kumusta.'

The woman with the red headband must have smelled what I smell. She smiles with the greeting I know so well. The blond man beside her is smiling, too, at her expectant face.

'Kumusta.' She is in earnest.

He shifts his gaze at me.

'You mean, como esta?' I pretend to look confused. 'Of course, of course—muy bien.'

'Told ya, yer wrong, hon.' He strokes her hair.

'But –' she searches my unsmiling face—'you're not Filipina?'

'You're Filipina.' I stare back.

'Yes, oh, yes,' she nods vigorously. 'Arrived two months ago with my husband here—your mangoes, very expensive—'

'From Queensland, that's why,' I shrug.

'May I?' She lifts a mango and smells it hungrily.

'Geez, isn't she pretty?' The husband runs his fingers through her hair again. The red band gets caught in his large, white hand.

'This one, please.' She lays the prized fruit on the weighing tray and quickly rearranges her band.

'Only one? Let's have a kilo—nah, two kilos, if you want, hon.' He winks at me, before proceeding to stroke her hair again. 'Ain't I lucky?'

'Where I lived, we have a yard of mangoes.'

I go for mangoes, too. Jake said we were not only grape-starved, but mango-greedy as well. I told him I would be asking for green mangoes if I were back home. He didn't understand what I meant until I started having fainting spells. He took me to the doctor 'to fix me up'. He did not want brown kids. I never told anyone.

'Let me tell ya, the Filipino *kumusta* comes from the Spanish *como esta*. The Philippines was once under Spain, y'see,' the husband lectures me on my ancestry.

'Spain very far . . .' Her sweeping gesture leaves an unfinished arc in the air. 'A long way?'

The other side of the world, honey.' He brings her hand to her side, then draws her closer.

'Hard for you, yes—?'

'One gets used to it—ten dollars for these, thanks.'

As they turn to go, I notice the blowfly, a big black seed dotting the last slice of melon for tasting. Must have been here for ages! All because of that bloody chatter—I roll a newspaper and get a good grip. Ay, my knuckles had never looked so white.

LORENZO MONTESINI

from *My Life and Other Misdemeanours*

Rob was now starting to fail; the blotches were spreading around his body, and he was becoming frail. He would look in the mirror and shudder.

His two remaining brothers, Neil and Alan (Gary had died several years ago), were coming from Melbourne to see Rob, to say goodbye, adieu. They had not seen each other for several years and this would be a kind of reconciliation. Rob had always said he could never forgive them for not accepting me. I smiled gently, of course. The plan was for 'the boys', as they were called in the family, to take a day off work and fly up especially.

Freud would have recognised the family romance at work, known only to themselves. Robert prepared carefully, it was a project for him, and he was going to give them their money's worth. They arrived, there was no offer to pick them up at the airport; it was implied that Rob was too ill to be left alone. I took them upstairs to the sunroom—they were nervous, expectant, we shook hands; I had been a part of their family for nearly thirty years and they were my in-laws. They seemed physically larger in close-up, so like Rob; the hands, the posture, the eyes.

The sunroom was empty. Rob was in the bathroom, waiting for them. He finally opened the door and stepped into the corridor wearing his terry-towelling bathrobe. They stood facing each other, from the same flesh and blood, inhabitants sharing experiences of that country we call childhood. A moment of hesitation on their part—they had expected a spectre, raddled meat, but here was Rob, a recognisable brother, his expression coy, head slightly to one side. The sigh of relief was almost audible.

Then Rob came in and said, 'I'll show you what an AIDS person looks like,' and dropped his robe to reveal his naked, emaciated body, covered in purple blotches.

The smiles vanished.

It was cruel and it was a magnificent performance, with Rob bravely taking the initiative. Ruthless control in a ruthless family romance. I just marvelled and respected them all, since they had all made each other the way they were, and they recognised it; these brothers were united not by a bond of saccharine tenderness but in this passion play, each acting his role and fitting in, a mystery to me, who had never experienced this as an only child.

The oldest brother, Neil, an accomplished landscape painter, had brought Rob a painting he had done especially for him; it was of the Blue Mountains, where Rob had been staying.

The brothers talked all day, joined by another childhood chum, Barry Billings, who is now an advocate in the Department of Veterans Affairs and was in Vietnam at the same time as we were. The edges blurred; they were children again, boys together, oldest, younger and youngest—the youngest had died; they were counting off. Then it was time to go, and Rob, suddenly well, was all for taking them to the airport, having a last drink and seeing them off on their flight south.

'Why couldn't they have brought the children?' he asked.

'Don't do this, it was a great day.' I drove on—by now Rob did not drive.

The sweats returned in force, three, sometimes four times a night. I got up, changed the sheets, bathed him, changed him and went back to bed.

I contracted the flu and one Sunday we called the doctor to visit—there we were, the two of us ill; it was almost funny, two for the price of one.

'I think we'd better give you a break and put Rob up at the hospice for a few days of R&R, the doctor said.

My heart sank—never, not there. But Rob was genuinely pleased.

'Don't be silly, it's a marvellous place; the staff are great. The problem is, will they take me?' he said. Rob knew the place, but for me it was a charnel house, the house of the dead. However, the arrangements were made and the next day we drove the short distance to Darlinghurst Road.

The Sacred Heart Hospice is more like a convalescent home attached to St Vincent's Hospital. Rob was still happy as they took him into a beautiful, sunny room with a small balcony overlooking the city. He made himself comfortable in his last home, as I brought in books and flowers, and rearranged the furniture; for me this place was just a small hiatus of rest before coming home again. Rob, however, knew he was home; he wanted to spare me any further work and he knew he was in very good hands. Best of all, Jason could come in with me and stay with Rob; the hospice administration welcomed animals, in fact they had two resident cats. We let the word out and the world came to see him, propped up in bed like a pasha, with me meeting and greeting, making coffee and tea for the visitors and then escorting them out to the lift, where I would be told how well he looked. Back in the room, Rob would immediately ask me what they said.

I read to him from The Iliad and The Odyssey; of course, Rob loved Odysseus and his cunning and wiles, they were twins in some sense. Odysseus was the first modern man—the cast of characters in The Iliad are really all puppets of the gods but Odysseus acts independently though in concert with the gods, often tricking them, using their words against them; he is one of us.

I also read from Virgil's Aeneid, that magnificent tract of propaganda written to prop up Augustus. Rob did not care about the background of the story but he was moved to tears by Dido's lament at the loss of Aeneas. I borrowed Purcell's Dido and Aeneas from a friend and we listened to the music in the dark.

All very well, but in my heart of hearts I think what I should have done is hired a spunky, blond ephebe to come to his room and do a dance of the seven veils—erotic and from the cavern of desire. That might have had a more restorative effect on him than all the Shakespeare and Virgil by making him feel himself again in what he did best.

At home, Rob's one great job had been to prepare the pills he had to take every day, about twenty or thirty—he would line them up, and send them on their way like little soldiers that were going in to fight the war of the virus for him. At the hospice, he no longer had to do that—at the appropriate time, gentle hands brought the medication required, and he gave up, gave in, relaxed, sighed. I started doing three-day trips—two nights away and then home to be with him; I was saving my sick leave and my holidays for when he came home and I would need to look after him full-time. I made arrangements for all sorts of aids that would be installed in the bathroom and bedroom when he came home. Rob knew better.

Barry Billings came and we arranged for his funeral; Rob wanted it all to be in order. It made him feel good, in control, to be able to plan every-thing. Barry and the veterans were planning a full military funeral—bugles, last post, flags, guard of honour, the works. We planned the music and who would sit where; there was no connection with reality for me during all this, but it made Rob happy.

More and more people came to see him and he enjoyed the visits but only for a little while, soon tiring of them and just wanting to sit in companionable silence with me. Another routine evolved: walk Jason, bring in flowers, walk him around the block again, morning visitors, lunch and then I would hurry out for my bit of bliss; a brisk swim at Bondi with Jason, where I would fall into the water and, as if by magic, all my cares were washed off. After this, I would shop, go home to attend to chores and return to be with Rob for the rest of the day, with more and more visitors arriving towards the evening. I served drinks for whoever was there at six so that Rob could have a drink with his friends and we could toast his health.

To get to Rob's room, I passed a dark room with a sad young man curled up in bed, always alone, his food untouched on the table, so different from us, who were always full of life. I formed the habit of bringing this young man, called Jonathan, a drink. He was, of course, dying of the virus; his parents had insisted that no one be told of his illness and his whereabouts, and those of his gay friends who came to see him were turned away. Jonathan died a week later, alone, without seeing anyone except his mother who was pleasant and caring but adamant that this was a great disgrace. When she sweetly came to thank me for giving her son a drink, there was nothing to say to her.

Robert said he was in pain and that he needed morphine to ease it; as a pagan, Rob had never believed in pain—none of this offering it up, as we Catholics were taught. The regulars were always there to help us: David Wansborough, the author of that great work *The Pillar of Salt*, wrote poems for Rob, even brought his children to see him; his Vietnam buddies came, all the cast; Julia Ross arrived one Sunday afternoon and insisted he must come to see her new house in Woollahra, and she packed us into her Porsche so that Rob, in dressing gown and slippers, made his last outside visit. He had a mild stroke on her stairs which no one noticed, it seemed like a dizzy spell.

The next day, I decided to take him on an outing in a wheelchair. He seemed happy about it and I turned it into a game, with Rob rugged up in his camel-hair coat, slippers and sunnies; down in the lift and out into Darlinghurst Road, right past the park where hustlers work in the early evenings and where junkies find their fixes, to the corner. Rob said he wanted to go across the road to St John's, where he had decided that his funeral service would be held. We waited for the lights and as we crossed, a bump in the road loosened a wheel, which scampered down the incline; Rob tipped forward as I tried to retrieve the wheel, Jason was halfway across the road, the wheelchair was leaning forward with Rob's weight, the lights were changing.

It was funny—we held up the traffic. I retrieved the wheel, called Jason back, repositioned Rob and we called it a day. It made for much laughter when friends came to see us that night.

I read to him from *Paradise Lost* and *Swann in Love*. What he enjoyed most were the sonnets of Shakespeare that I read to him, one after another. We both had our favourites. We were amazed to think that had Shakespeare just written the sonnets and nothing more, he would have been celebrated, but with all the rest of his output, you felt a shiver to be a member of the human race.

Rob fell in the bathroom and gashed his forehead; I cried in anguish, wanting to transfer all the pain to me. By now, I was staying nights with him.

The last night of our life was busy. I brought Jason back from his last walk of the evening in the hospice garden below, and I fussed around, changing the water in the vases, bringing crushed ice from the pantry to refresh

Rob's mouth, putting it just under his tongue. Rob had now slipped into a coma, but for me it was only a temporary condition; I always believed that Rob would give us the full Stations of the Cross.

My routine, a routine I thought would last forever: I placed fresh lavender that I had picked in the garden around his pillow and inside the covers, more ice crystals under his tongue as he had not ingested anything for several days now. I prepared my cot next to his bed, close to him so that I could touch him during the night. I lowered the blinds; opposite I could see St Vincent's Private, the procession of life and death, the tumult, the traffic below had eased, people were hurrying home to their burrows, to their deaths, oblivious to us as we had been to others.

The last visitors—David Wansborough. Julie Virtue, Tom Milligan— had long gone, and I tucked myself in next to Rob. He was breathing heavily, deep, long breaths, his chest heaving, his eyes half closed, his mouth slightly open. I held him, one arm around his head, the other touching his face. With the hospital curtain around the bed half drawn and the large door open, I could hear the murmur at the desk just outside, the changing of the guard, the afternoon shift handing over to the night shift.

A rattle, a little knock; it was Warwick, one of the staff, he appeared, shy, tentative, smiling, then one of the girls entered and then another.

'Come in,' I said, 'it's just us boys.'

'We wanted to say goodnight.' They all sweetly stood around.

'He's quiet, I said, and slowly I started to talk to them about Rob and me. They sat down, putting bags and backpacks on the floor; they encouraged me. I talked of our times together; I was proud of us. Jason whined, a little canine nightmare as he was curled up against Rob's legs; we all laughed. We looked at Rob, we all admired him. They said goodnight.

'I'll see you in the morning,' I said.

'Do you need anything?'

'No, thanks, go home, go.'

I was happy in my memories. They knew it was goodbye; I was smiling. They closed the door behind them as they tiptoed out.

The night shift was on, all visitors ashore, all was quiet. Jason was fast asleep again, my head was against Rob, my breathing matching his, my hand over his heart, one beat, one pulse.

I must have fallen asleep, like my mother holding her own mother on her last night in Egypt so long ago. A vigil that would transport us through the night, with me a guardian.

I awoke with a start—all was quiet, everything still; that's what woke me. Rob had stopped breathing; he was still, he was warm against me.

It was a white moment, a moment out of time; a crack in the fabric, a glimpse of eternity and a dawning realisation of the enormity of this. I looked at Rob, his face. It was just after midnight on 15 August. His mouth was closed.

The pain which followed made me aware of myself and of the terrible realisation that one being is separate from another, no matter how loved. Pain is our only possession, no one can hold us or them, the steaming entrails of self-hood revealed. We come to the gate and surrender them to some higher power, like my mother had surrendered me, her son, at my first day at school, but now I knew I could not ransom Rob any more. All was quiet. I gently rocked him as millions of generations before me had done; so dear to me, to so many, I was merely the caretaker. I moved away to see him better—Jason stirred, he sniffed the air, looked at me, his ears pricked back, he uncoiled himself, jumped off the bed, then went to the window corner and sat there, looking at me.

'It's all right, Jase,' I said, 'he's gone but he's here.' Jason knew something had happened, he weakly wagged his tail. I sat next to Rob, looking at him for a long time, willing myself to accept.

There had been too many tears, too much outpouring, too many scenes. I called the matron, an ample country lady who loved horses. She touched him.

'Darling, isn't it wonderful, he's gone without suffering, in your arms.' She looked at me, her hand on my cheek.

'But I didn't know it was going to be so soon.'

'He didn't suffer, he's at peace now. Do you want to have time with him?'

I packed up, I undid my cot, packed all his things. I took out some scissors and cut locks of his hair for his family and friends, and for me. His hair will outlive me. When all was done, I put cologne on his face, combed his hair, kissed him for all of us. I picked up the bags, Jason behind me.

I said goodbye to the matron, and I turned for one last look, across the desk lobby, into his room, where I left him, in his bed, there in peace at last. The security man opened the gates for me, Jason hopped into his seat in the back. I turned the key and to my surprise the engine came to life.

Alone, I drove onto Darlinghurst Road.

'Let's go home, boys,' I heard myself saying.

It started to rain.

LOUIS NOWRA

from *Red Nights*

Having made the phone call to Marion, Nelson decided he was tired of the bar and moved on deeper into the Cross. He passed thin young men dressed in black with their anorexic girlfriends, would-be models in their short black dresses, ghostly make-up and the perfect pout. There was no way he was going to have a drink surrounded by Sneering Ghosts and the Sulks. He wanted a different sort of a pub, something rougher and edgier, something that had the jingle-jangle to match his mood. And there was only one hotel that would do that.

When he arrived the place was crowded with drunks, druggies, standover men, drag queens, rough trade, huge Maoris, old timers and girls, barely eighteen with pupils the size of pin heads, tingling with pleasure as they mixed with the desperadoes and the haunted. Nelson felt at ease as he leant against the bar. He watched the TV screens hanging from the ceiling showing a game of hurling, and took in the pokies, the blaring dance music, the stench of cigarette smoke, the smell of booze, the cheerful chatter that could turn to anger at any moment as people slipped over that point between just enough drink and too much. It was like he was part of an opera, only this time he didn't have to pay a small fortune for a walk-on. He gratefully sipped his gin and tonic. It stopped him from grinding his teeth. Next to him were two men absorbed in a squalid tale of their own or repeating what happened to a friend. 'He said that cunt's not breathing. Well, in that case, you've got to put your missus out in the street.'

'So it looks like a hit and run,' said the other in a gloomy voice of experience.

'Absolute. She was like . . . the first thing a woman like her wants is something that allows her to be what she wants to be. So she wants it. And follows it. She craves it. You know what it's called?' The friend shook his head. 'Bad luck!' he said cheerfully.

Nelson hated talk of bad luck so he tuned out. A whirlwind of expressions and thoughts spun around in his head and he tried to stop them by concentrating on what he had to do. He thought of how men of poor beginnings cause empires to fall and although it was a truism it *was* true; and for some reason Mark appeared in his thoughts, pushing him, pushing him while they were on that ferry hoping he would break, but he hadn't. No, he knew his brother and even though Mark was mad there was a method in it. Quite simply he liked to get Steve upset and agitated so he could say, 'Not so cool now, Steve' but he had remained calm and Mark realised that if he sometimes pricked his brother, he did not bleed. The reason Nelson did not bleed was that he had separated himself from Mark. He knew he should have visited him more often, but in distancing himself he found a sense that he was not like his parents or Mark and that he was made of stronger stuff, which had been proved that night on the island over ten years before when he had had enough courage to take the risk. Mark wouldn't have taken the risk. He would take another risk and become a man of good fortune again.

Someone was shouting in his ear. 'Christ Almighty, Nelson, what are you doing in this dump?'

Nelson turned and saw a huge mottled face with wet blubbery lips. He pulled back instinctively. 'Reggie!'

'I like the fact you never forget a face.'

Recovering quickly from his surprise Nelson adopted his flippant demeanour. 'I could ask you the same question,' he said poking his finger in Reggie's marshmallow belly.

'When you get to my age only the dregs in a place like this will allow you to suck them off. Is that why you are here, Nelson? You have a secret life that likes rough trade?'

'I'm just filling in an hour or so.'

Reggie ordered a drink from the barman ('Irish whiskey, not fuckin' Scotch, you drongo') and then spoke *sotto voce* to Nelson: 'He's so ugly.' Nelson glanced at the barman. Indeed he was; but given Reggie's ruined body, he was the last person to talk. 'You know what I'm doing, Nelson?' he continued cheerfully. 'I'm drinking to forget Joe. This is a plague, a plague, Nelson. I can't keep up with the number of friends keeling over. Bring out your dead! Bring out your dead!' *I need something to eat. I've had nothing to eat. The lights are too bright. Reggie was always boring. Gossip columnists are the most boring . . . Has he got AIDS? No, he's too fat—*

'Not like the old days, Nelson. There's a sort of decay, terminal decay to this era, as if everyone is going through the motions. Nothing is new any more. Merely recycling. I remember going to France when everything was new and sparkling. I didn't know a word of French. You know the first words I learnt? "Shut up and suck". Now everything's decayed. Not that there aren't advantages. I can take out my false teeth and Howdy-do, Joffa Boy—bliss for the lucky ones.'

Nelson felt himself grinding his teeth again and ordered another drink.

'Having a night out without the wife, are we?'

'Got to see a man about a dingo,' Nelson wanted to say but he'd said that before. 'Your guess is as good as mine,' he replied instead and wondered why he had said that. He felt as if he were suffocating in the boozy heat. Instead of ceiling fans the hotel had Irish hurling. A curious set of standards.

'Yes, it is.'

Nelson paused before picking up his glass, wondering if he had actually made that comment to Reggie or had misheard himself. He smiled at Reggie as if he were on top of things and sipped his drink. The grinding stopped.

'You know, I've never seen you angry in real life.'

'Really?' said a pleased Nelson.

'Only in photographs.'

'Photographs?'

'On the front page of the papers. You know, behind the iron gates of The Dourantine, snarling at those process servers who wanted to get in.'

'I was protecting the Palace, dear boy. A siege requires a modicum of indignation towards your besiegers. Anyway, in a way I won.'

'You were kicked out.'

'I lost the battle but won the war. The Dourantine belongs to me now.'

'Don't get it.'

It was obvious that Reggie hadn't heard of the demolition yet and that pleased Nelson. 'Well, dear Reggie, you never will.'

A tall drag queen dressed conservatively in a white twin-set and pearls came in through the door to be greeted by a chorus of excited shrieks. 'Annabel,' said Reggie motioning towards her with his glass. 'You know who's her favourite customer? Griffin, the Leader of the Opposition. Yep, she reminds him of his wife. His wife hates sex but he has this thing about her appearance, so Annabel has to dress up in twin-set and pearls. Yet the idiot still hasn't worked out he's screwing a boy. The doggy style is fraught with ambiguity, Nelson. Dear, dear me, what are the morals of this city coming too?'

'Morals? It's morels they want,' said Nelson suddenly. 'I'm going to buy a restaurant. Spanish. No tapas, that's passé.' And in imagining the restaurant, one that was much more upmarket than the Catalan, he saw Sophie sitting at a table and she wasn't walking away, she was waiting for him and she wanted to make love to him and she wanted to give herself to him and she looked as gorgeous as ever in that she's-gonna-break-your-heart-Sonny Jim way. Then let's see what Len said about that! It would be a wrench to leave Marion but he needed new blood, he needed to plug into another electrical circuit and he didn't need a woman on her knees pleading hysterically to be whisked away to the country for some crazy, crazy reason. With new blood he would be reinvigorated and this transformation would need a new way of looking at things. 'No more Red Nights,' he exclaimed.

'I didn't think you were having any more.'

'Another colour.'

Reggie nodded unsurely as if not following. Two men behind Nelson were talking about hair, the best hairstyles in movies. One was saying it was Robert de Niro's mohawk in *Taxi Driver*, another Brad Pitt's stiff tidal wave in *Johnny Suede* and then there was ferocious disagreement about John Travolta's ponytail in *Pulp Fiction*. 'You see, the in people were hair-dressers in the seventies, waiters in the eighties, and now it's chefs in the nineties, so there's been some progress,' said Nelson to a puzzled Reggie.

'What colour?'

Nelson paused for a moment and remembered what he had been talking about. But when he came to think of it, what other colour for his Red Nights could there be? Red Nights were as closely associated with him as The Dourantine. 'Haven't decided yet.'

'So who are you going to get to replace Joe?'

'Joe's dead.'

'I know that,' said a testy Reggie.

'Well, I was just stating a fact,' said Nelson, puzzled by Reggie's reaction.

'Did you know he committed suicide?'

Nelson shook his head, believing Joe had died a natural death. If you could call dying of AIDS a natural death.

'He didn't want to end up in Saint Vinnie's hospice with all those other living dead, so he wrapped himself up in a kimono and cut his throat. Very dramatic, very sayonara, very drag queen.'

'He wasn't a drag queen.'

'The attitude. The fucking attitude, Nelson!'

'You laughed at my eulogy and by doing that you laughed at Joe.'

'Don't be ridiculous.'

'Anyway, that will be my weapon.'

'What weapon?'

'Why they can't touch me. I'm going to get that transvestite and parade her up and down outside Parliament House and tell everyone that the Premier is screwing a boy whore in twin-set and pearls. If anything her fashion sense should sink him.'

'It's Griffin.'

'Same diff, he's a politician,' said Nelson slapping the bar top with enthusiasm, not aware that the barman took that as a signal to get him another drink.

Reggie laughed. 'You know that cemetery this morning? Well, a lot of the headstone inscriptions are worn away. One took my fancy. It read, "He gave his life for King and Cuntry." Now was the letter O worn away or was it an accurate description of the fellow's behaviour?'

Nelson wasn't paying much attention and he shrugged. Then looking around for Annabel he saw that damn cowboy who had been at the memorial service and Bunker Bar. 'Who is that guy?' asked Nelson, pointing to him.

'Dunno,' said Reggie. 'Some outfit.'

'Stupid.'

'Maybe it's in. I don't know what's in or out anymore. Maybe that's why my column is going downhill rapidly.'

'They can't touch me, Reggie.'

'Who?'

'Cowboys and politicians. I'm back. The poltergeist has returned!'

'What poltergeist?'

'The one that's going to haunt The Dourantine and Parliament House and this fucking hotel. I want you to write me up in your column. Nelson's back from the Twilight Zone and is coming to haunt them. Have a picture of my back! A message to them, Reggie: it's not cute to play without a parachute.'

'Do you know what I liked about your Red Nights?'

'What?' yelled Nelson.

'Two things. The last Red Night when nobody would talk to that head shrinker, Ray McLynn, after he was debarred for his pethidine habit and you rostered people to go and talk to him every twenty minutes. One from the heart, Nelson. Very noble. And then there was the bravery. That's why the Red Nights were a success. The bravery. If you liked the husband but not the wife you would only invite the husband.'

'The point and fun of giving a party is about those you don't invite. I invited five people and made five thousand enemies.'

'God knows why you have enemies. People with the real stuff have enemies.'

'What are you jabbering on about?'

'What you don't understand, Nelson, is that you have no moral centre, actually no centre at all. You're just a willy-willy of wind, dust and temporary excitement. Nothing is inside you. You're all that you pick up in your whorl across this desert.' Reggie flinched, thinking that Nelson, with those dangerously gleaming eyes, was going to hit him. It excited Reggie to get a rise out of him.

'What kind of crap is that?'

'Hey, I know you, Nelson, because I'm like that myself.'

'We have no similarities, Reggie,' Nelson glared and turned away to see how the extras and the props were doing. A waiter with a 'We Don't Call Cops' T-shirt was shaking awake a customer asleep at a table.

Who was that cowboy? It was irritating to see someone smile at him and yet not know him.

Then there were the faces of the drag queens. They looked as ancient as Louise did in the church cemetery. Reggie looked bloated and crinkly, as if his face were a bowl of blotchy custard that had developed a wrinkled skin. His hands were sprinkled with liver spots and the skin was loose, like a shabby over-large pair of gloves. It would not be a surprise if Reggie just keeled over one day and carked it. Or maybe Reggie would reach a certain stage when his flesh would decay as he lived and it would slowly dissolve on him and the skin gradually separate itself from the skeleton, like those corpses Sulawesi villagers kept in their huts until they had enough money to give them a big funeral.

Although he had picked Sulawesi for a honeymoon and it was marvellous for most of the time, Nelson had been uneasy about their culture of death. It seemed wrong to celebrate death. Although he liked the feast of the dead, with the oxen slaughtered in front of the guests, a sudden sprinkle of warm blood on his face like primitive rain that included him in the ceremony, and the subtle dancing (not like the baroque Balinese style, but grave and solemn), he did not like those caves where the bones of the relatives were kept. A guide had taken the honeymooners to a cave and they had come upon another Australian couple. The man was blind and he was guided by his much younger wife. 'Let me feel one,' the man had said when his wife had told him that the ground was littered with skulls. It made Nelson's flesh crawl to see the middle-aged man stroke the skull while his pretty young wife stared at him quizzically as if she saw beneath her husband's aging flesh the smooth unwrinkled bony certainty of death. Marion had later remarked that she was merely bemused by the blind man feeling the skull, but Nelson had been profoundly disturbed, as if that were a relationship based not on life but on death. When they ran into the couple again in a Ujung Pandang restaurant, Nelson pretended he didn't recognise them, even though the woman smiled at him across the tables. He shivered at the thought that the wrinkled husband who had so lovingly stroked the skull would stroke her young flesh. A skeleton making love to a beautiful young woman.

Aggravated by the presence of that grinning cowboy in the bar, pushy Reggie and memories of the blind man and his young wife in Sulawesi, Nelson decided to leave. 'I'm going for a walk,' he laughed. 'I may be gone some time.' He was about to go when the barman plonked another glass of gin and tonic down on the bar.

'What about your drink?' said Reggie.

Nelson looked down at the fresh drink with its drifting ice cubes and bracing slice of lemon. 'Oh,' he murmured with surprise and picked it up.

GRAEME AITKEN

from *Vanity Fierce*

I took great pleasure in announcing to my mother soon after her threat to throw me out that I was moving out of my own accord to live in Kings Cross. On William Street.

Elisabeth was horrified. 'People don't live on William Street, surely?'

I assured her that they did.

'Well, I can't imagine how anyone could ever get any sleep. All that traffic noise. Cars driving up and down there all night, ogling the prostitutes.'

I pointed out that my flat didn't overlook William Street, it overlooked the lane behind it. 'Actually, there's a view of a church from my lounge room.'

'You can't afford to pay rent,' Elisabeth scoffed. 'You're going to be a student.'

But that was the reason I could afford to move out. I'd had a private conversation with my father and struck a gentleman's agreement, that Elisabeth was not to be privy to. He would pay my rent in full on the condition that I study Legal Institutions in my first year at uni. I was set to start a combination law degree, with English, History and Psychology. I knew the Legal I would be a drag but I figured I could fudge my way through it.

The flat I found was cheap, which was lucky; Elisabeth would have become suspicious had I moved into anywhere too grand. It didn't bother me that it was in the heart of William Street's sex for sale precinct. The girls literally operated from the doorstep of the building, sometimes even using the foyer as a place to freshen up their make-up or adjust their clothing. But to my mind the location was perfect: only a ten minute walk down the hill from the gay bars of Oxford Street. The building was one down from the corner of William Street and Forbes Street, above a car showroom. I was relieved to overlook the back lane. Those residents that faced onto William Street couldn't even open their windows, the traffic noise and fumes were so severe. Instead they left their front doors open onto the landing to let some air through. The apartments overlooking St Peters Lane were infinitely preferable. As well as being much quieter, they had French doors off the living room which opened out onto tiny Juliet balconies. The lane was named after St Peter's church which was situated on the corner intersecting Bourke Street, but there was another name for the lane. It had been scrawled on the wall beneath the official street sign in aerosol paint. I noticed it the first time I stood there at the balcony looking out at the view. Shame Lane.

There was a shameful side to Kings Cross and it was exemplified by the fact that in some instances the suburb did not even dare speak its own name. There was an amusing ambiguity over where I was actually living. I had presumed myself to be in Kings Cross but the mail I received was addressed otherwise and was completely contradictory. According to Telstra, I was living in East Sydney, while Sydney Electricity considered I was in Woolloomooloo. My bank said I was in Darlinghurst.

When I mentioned this to my new neighbour, Strauss, he roared with laughter. 'Darling, you're living in Betty Bay, didn't you know? Well, that's where my estate agent claims I'm living. When I came to look this place over, it was advertised as being "a penthouse apartment in Elizabeth Bay". *Elizabeth Bay?* The thing is, Kings Cross is considered so down-market in terms of real estate that it doesn't exist as an address. It's always Darlinghurst or Woolloomooloo or East Sydney, and in the fanciful imagination of some real estate agents it's Elizabeth Bay. I just adore telling people that I live on William Street, Elizabeth Bay.'

I invited Elisabeth to inspect the flat as soon as I'd moved in. I knew that otherwise she would turn up unannounced and that inevitably it would be at a bad moment. I arranged for her to visit during the day when there would be no prostitutes hanging about. She arrived with Uncle Vic. I could hear her complaining to him as she mounted the stairs that she hadn't seen any prostitutes. The first thing she asked me when I opened the door was, 'Where are they all?'

'They come out at night,' I explained.

'Well, that seems like a gap in the market. Why doesn't one of them do a day shift?'

'I think the idea is that they look their best by night.'

'Oh,' said Elisabeth. 'Yes, I see.'

Uncle Vic had wandered over to the French doors and was looking out at the view. 'It's quite pleasant by day,' he remarked.

His eyes told me he knew exactly what went on down below by night. I was grateful for his discretion. Elisabeth joined him at the doors. She glanced at the view. 'South facing,' she observed. 'It will be cold even at the height of summer.'

Then she strode into the kitchen and looked around it with distaste. I had invited her for lunch. 'Perhaps we'll go out for lunch,' she decided.

'I'm all organised to cook,' I said.

'We'll eat out,' she said in a voice that wouldn't tolerate any dissent.

The bathroom was off the bedroom and as she walked through to inspect it she made a point of averting her eyes from the unmade bed. 'If you'd make your bed, this place might not appear so much like the awful dosshouse that it is.'

Uncle Vic and I remained in the living room while my mother snorted her disapproval of the bathroom. Uncle Vic smiled sympathetically at me. 'She's putting on a bit of a show. Of course she'd like to keep you at home forever.'

Elisabeth emerged from the bathroom. 'Well, I can't imagine why anyone would want to live here, let alone pay to live here; however, I daresay you have your reasons. They're just not fit for a mother to hear.'

She fixed her eyes upon me, waiting to see if I'd respond. When I didn't, she declared herself ready for a Bloody Mary at the Bayswater Brasserie, her favourite restaurant. 'Because it's a proper restaurant,' she was always telling me. By which she meant lots of dark wood surfaces, attentive young men attired in black and white and dazzling white linen everywhere you looked. But in fact it was the attention she loved not the decor or the service. The staff all knew her and fawned over her whenever she turned up.

Elisabeth had hit the nail on the head with that remark. I *had* moved out of home so that I could have a sex life. It was basically impossible to manage when I was living with my parents at Wahroonga. I had been going out on the weekends to Oxford Street for some time, but it was hopeless. The bars only began to get lively around the same time that I had to leave if I wanted to catch the last train back to Wahroonga. If I stayed out in the hope of meeting someone, I was forced to be out for the entire night. The trains didn't start up again until five-thirty in the morning. A taxi was out of the question on my budget. But it was also embarrassing to have to admit to anyone I did get talking to that I still lived at home with my parents. Their interest in me always seemed to curdle soon after that point in the conversation.

For the first two weeks after moving into the William Street apartment I went out to Oxford Street almost every night. The girls working the street were always performing at full throttle by the time I made my way home and they soon got to know me and would enquire how my night had been. 'Not so good if you're coming home alone again,' the tallest and most attractive of them cackled.

However, when I did finally bring a boy back, the tall one, who called herself Sass, pounced on us and encouraged all her colleagues to join in her inspection. 'Stephen's finally got a fuck,' she announced loudly.

They crowded round us, tweaking the boy's face, asking his name, speculating loudly as to what would happen once we got inside and assuring him that I had been 'an absolute monk' for as long as they'd known me. When we did finally escape them, the boy was trembling so badly I had to help him climb the stairs. 'I'm sorry but I'll have to stay the night. There's no way I can face going back out there again. They're not still there in the morning, are they?'

I reassured him that they wouldn't be.

I quickly became friendly with the regular girls and got to know them by name. I call them girls—everyone called them girls—but of course they weren't. I was always curious as to how many of the louts who leered at them out of their car windows as they kerb-crawled down William Street actually realised. They fooled a lot of people, my father included. He called in on me after he'd finished work one night and encountered Sass as he entered the building. She was the leader of the William Street girls by virtue of her success. She was the most authentic-looking, the most glamorous, the most outrageous and undoubtedly the most financially successful. My father made little comment on the apartment. All he could talk about was Sass. 'I had no idea the prostitutes were so glamorous. She was like some sort of movie star.'

I couldn't be bothered explaining. Why ruin the illusion Sass put so much work into creating? But my father was right. Sass and the other girls were like movie stars. Everything about them was so big and glossy and provocative. The actual women prostitutes who operated further along the street towards the city seemed very drab, even grim, by comparison. Certainly they rarely smiled. Whereas outside my front door a party atmosphere prevailed. Sass was the wildest. She strutted, flounced and flirted. The pavement was her stage and her audience in their cars whooped, hollered and even applauded their appreciation. The highlight of her act incorporated the use of the council rubbish bin. She would daintily balance one stiletto-clad foot on top of the rubbish bin, the other on the brink of the gutter, and then thrust her pelvis in and out, tossing her long blonde hair about behind her as the cars slowly streamed down the hill towards her. She stopped traffic. Literally. Sass's performances were short-lived, however. She always got snapped up quickly by a punter.

I was puzzled that someone with Sass's looks and personality worked the street, and I said as much to her one night when we struck up our first real conversation. It was late, the early hours of Sunday morning. I was getting home from a night at the Shift. Sass, sitting out in the square, noticed me as I stumbled down the Chard Steps. 'No luck, honey?' she called out to me. 'It's been a slow night here too.'

She waved me over and insisted I sit down beside her. I drunkenly told her she could do better for herself. 'Honey, I hear that line so many times. All my johns tell me the same thing. But do they offer to look after me and keep me in the style that I'm accustomed to? No. The fact is that deep down most people regard me as some sort of freak and eventually that sentiment rises to the surface. You say I could do better for myself, and I used to feel the same way, but in fact I can't. I know because I've tried. There ain't many opportunities in the work line for a chick with a dick. I've tried to get conventional work—restaurants, reception—but once they realise I piss standing up, that's the end, I'm out. Even the gay places don't want girls like me. I project the wrong image. All those queens are trying desperately to be as butch as possible, while I'm doing the exact opposite. The only sort of job I can get is one that exploits what I am. Makes me out to be some sort of freak. On the stage at Les Girls, pulling my wig off at the end of the night. No, thank you. I won't do a job where I get laughed at by small-minded people. It's too humiliating. I want to be respected and, believe it or not, I can get more respect as a hooker.'

She paused for a moment. 'Sure I'd like not to have to work the street. It's a bitch in winter. But setting yourself up to work privately from home isn't easy either. It can be almost impossible getting an apartment. What do you write down as your occupation on the estate agent's form? You've got to prove you can pay the rent, but if you write down "escort", they'd never give you the place. So you lie on the form and if you're lucky you get the apartment. But even once you're signed up, there's no security. The neighbours always cause problems. You notice them sneaking looks at you in the lift, then they start to talk amongst themselves and watching who comes to visit you. Eventually you're accused of operating a brothel and get evicted. I was kicked out of one apartment, which was my home. I never worked from there. But my uncle came to visit me, the only member of my family who will have anything to do with me, and of course he was mistaken for a john. You just get so frustrated and discouraged after a while. Ultimately, this is the simplest way. Working the street. And I have to work to keep this up. It ain't cheap looking good.'

I was intrigued by Sass's accent. She had a pseudo-American way of speaking. She laughed when I asked. 'I grew up in Gympie, Queensland. But an American accent is sexier. The guys just love a Californian blonde. I've watched a helluva lot of porn videos trying to get the accent right. Actually, I do a lot of business in dirty talk. Some of those boys are just too damn nervous to be up to much else. Penises are fragile things. I'll be glad to get shot of mine once and for all. But I'll never do that if I sit here chit-chatting instead of working up a bit of business.'

With that, Sass sprang to her feet and prowled across the pavement to a car that had slowed down opposite us. 'Hey, butch,' I heard her say as I got to my feet and began to walk away.

There was a definite hierarchy amongst the girls who worked that particular segment of William Street, and Sass was at the pinnacle. She was very tall. Six foot two without heels. Yet she insisted on always wearing two-inch stilettos. Her hair could add a couple of inches as well, depending on which wig she wore and how she had it styled. Her height seemed to imbue her with an unassailable confidence. She towered over the majority of her clients and claimed most of them loved it that way. They 'all want me to dominate them. Seems like they never get it that way at home. Luckily it's something that just comes natural to me.'

Her rival, Jo-Jo, said Sass looked like Centrepoint in drag, she was so tall and skinny. Naturally enough, they hated one another. Once Jo-Jo had strutted her stuff on William Street and had been the most popular girl on the strip. But that was ten years ago. Now her 'surgical enhancements' were showing their age and as she wasn't pulling in the kind of money she once had, she couldn't afford to go for some 'reconditioning'.

'She's had every tooth in her mouth pulled out so that she can give better head, that's how desperate she is to attract clients,' jeered Sass, laughing as she unfolded Jo-Jo's tragedy, failing to consider she might conceivably share the same destiny one day. But Sass was young. 'I'm only twenty-four and much prettier than Jo-Jo ever was,' she gurgled.

These days Jo-Jo was forced to lurk down Shame Lane, where the light was less cruel and the clients not as discerning. She wouldn't even venture down to the little square below the Chard Steps to sit with some of her old mates and talk on a slow night. That was Sass's territory now and Jo-Jo steered clear of it. 'They're all louts from out west anyway, or country boys with no idea what they're cruising. They don't even know the back lane exists, where the real action is.'

But if Sass dared to venture up the stairs to the intersection of Forbes Street and Shame Lane, Jo-Jo would detonate, screaming at her, chasing her away, threatening to beat her up. Their fights were as regular as clock-work. 'I respect your patch, now you respect mine and fuck off back to where you came from,' Jo-Jo would screech.

'Just checking,' Sass would reply smoothly.

'Checking what?'

'Checking the merchandise and the prices of the rival business, like any competitive businesswoman would do.'

'You're no woman.'

'And you ain't got no business,' Sass would cackle, retreating back down the stairs, a string of expletives firing from Jo-Jo like a round of ammunition.

Sass delighted in stirring Jo-Jo. She'd venture up the Chard Steps most nights and would always act disappointed if Jo-Jo was with a john and not there to tell her to fuck off. They woke me and the rest of my neighbours up most nights, going off at one another. Finally, we had a residents' meeting about the problem. One evening when I got home from uni, I found a note in my mailbox. *Your attendance is requested at a residents' meeting 'chez Strauss' (Flat 9) to discuss the raucous behaviour of the trannies in the back lane after midnight. The main culprits will be in attendance.*

Sass actually apologised to me personally before the meeting. She rushed over when she saw me coming home one night. 'Oh, you poor darlings,' she gushed. 'Being woken up by that witch. She's got a voice like fingernails on a blackboard. Oh, I can imagine the agony she must've been causing you all. Strauss is organising a meeting, but in the meantime, you let me know if you have any more problems and I'll fix her good and proper. Stuff her wig down her filthy loud mouth.'

Sass winked and promenaded back to her spot, the car horns tooting as she walked.

It was at that meeting that I came to know Strauss and the other residents of the apartment block. I had seen Strauss on the stairs several times and we always exchanged greetings. I said hello. Strauss said, 'Ciao bello.' That was Strauss's style. I soon learnt that he always had to appear more exotic than everyone else: in his manner, his conversation and, above all, in his appearance. Every time I saw him he looked completely different. One day his hair was a cropped jet-black stubble, the next day an Andy Warhol white thatch. He was either dressed very stylishly and formally in something black and severe, or he would be wearing a completely ridiculous outfit such as a safari suit he had dyed canary yellow.

One evening he stopped me as I passed him on the stairs, placed a white-gloved hand upon my arm and looked at me through his cat's-eye sunglasses. 'We meet again upon the stairs. Are you a resident or merely the regular trade of one of my *lucky, lucky* neighbours?'

I didn't understand what he meant by trade. 'I live here.'

'Which apartment?'

'Number Seven.'

'Lovely. I know it well. I'm in the penthouse apartment, on the roof. I have that enchanting view of everyone's laundry on weekends. Thankfully, I'm generally asleep during the sunshine hours.'

With that, Strauss flounced down the stairs. I watched him descend, startled but impressed. It was the first time I'd encountered him close up. I was astonished to discover that he wore make-up.

The residents' meeting was more of a cocktail party than a meeting. Strauss opened the door wearing an ankle-length striped kaftan. Before I even had a chance to say hello he handed me a glass. 'I'm serving Orgasms,' he confided. 'I thought it was appropriate given our guests of honour tonight.'

No introductions were made. I said hello to Sass who was seated on the couch talking to a smartly dressed girl I hadn't seen before. Jo-Jo stood by the French doors, smoking a cigarette.

'Are there more people to come?' I asked.

'Oh, I scare the people who live in number four,' claimed Strauss. 'The Asian couple. Recent arrivals to our country, I believe. Every time I encounter the wife, she screams. I thought an invitation would only alarm her further.'

'Is Ant coming?' asked the girl.

'The delectable Antonio,' Strauss sighed. 'Yes. After he's been to the gym. He can't possibly miss a day's training. He will be arriving all flushed and sweaty at any moment, I imagine.'

I took the chair opposite the couch and the girl turned her attention to me. 'I'm Blair,' she said.

I introduced myself.

'How are you settling in?' she enquired.

'It's my first time out of home,' I admitted. 'So it's quite new and strange.'

'It doesn't get much stranger than round here,' cackled Sass. 'Jo-Jo, for Chrissake get away from that balcony and stop brooding over the business you're missing out on.'

There was a knock at the door.

'Entrez,' Strauss called out.

The door swung open and there he was. Ant. He had indeed come straight from the gym. He was wearing a pair of cut-down sweat pants and a black Bonds singlet. Strauss bounded over to welcome him and kissed him on both cheeks. Ant didn't exactly recoil, but his stance was stiff and awkward as he submitted to the greeting, drawing back as soon as it could safely be declared over. I felt a pang of disappointment. I liked the look of him but his reaction made me suspect that he was straight. Strauss had him clutched by the wrist and was gushingly unfolding some anecdote, his eyebrows arching, his smile twisting with flirtatious insinuations. Ant appeared to be listening intently, but his expression was inscrutable; there was no clue to whether he was interested or indifferent to what he was being told. While he was absorbed, I studied his profile.

The more I stared, the more his looks appealed to me. His face was quietly handsome. Not turn-your-head striking, but very masculine and steady looking. His hair was dark brown and cropped close to his head. His body was well displayed by what he wore. He was deeply tanned, so tanned he almost glowed, and he was very muscular. There was a great jut to his chest and his biceps looked rock-hard and ripe, like apples in his arms. And he was unshaven! Not his face, but his chest and legs. Dark hair sprouted from the scoop of his singlet. *This* was very exotic. Body hair was practically extinct on Oxford Street. All the muscle men I'd noticed and admired around the bars were all perfectly hairless. I wasn't so impressed by what he was wearing. It was a bit sloppy: his pants unhemmed and dangling threads, his singlet faded and thin. I would never be seen in such a state. But on him, I rather liked it. It was rough and careless, the way I imagined he might treat me in bed.

Strauss was laughing, in snorting ripples—his story had reached its climax. Ant gave a quick terse smile. His profile was so severe. But I liked that! Gruff not gushy. Then he turned to face the rest of us in the room and the conversation ground to a sudden halt. Someone gasped. Ant's right eye was a slit, the eyelid swollen and livid. He had a black eye.

Strauss was cooing over it but was being steadfastly ignored. Ant smiled and nodded at Blair and Sass, then his good eye settled on me. It was no cursory glance. This was a look that raked me over intensely and I knew at once that I had been mistaken about where his sexual interests lay. I felt borne up by his speculative gaze, light, giddy, as if I might float away out the French doors. Then, just as suddenly, that sensation crumpled and I was plummeted back to earth, shot down by a shocking spasm of nerves. Shocking because it was such an utterly alien feeling to me.

I'm *never* shy. My self-confidence and eloquence are my greatest gifts. It was inconvenient and highly frustrating that they should suddenly desert me at such a crucial moment. But they had. I was bereft. I cast about for an opening remark, something original and witty with a teasing undertone that would initiate our conversation with a stylish flourish, but found I could think of . . . *nothing*? Meanwhile Ant's gaze pressed upon me relentlessly. There was such an intensity to that one eye, perhaps because it was temporarily doing the work of two. I felt more and more unnerved and tongue-tied with every second that passed.

I tried to focus upon his other eye, the black eye, but found it too disturbing. I caught a glimpse of the iris, a sudden flash of movement and colour between the lids. Strangely, that made me feel more exposed than I had under the scrutiny of his good eye. I looked away, which immediately made me feel foolish and defensive, unequal to the challenge of his attention. I reached for my glass and drained it automatically, then wished I hadn't. The Cointreau burnt my throat and I gagged. I could feel myself blushing.

I was too embarrassed to look up again. I stared at the carpet instead. It was an offensive sight, being in dire need not only of a vacuum but also an intensive steam clean. Dark stains (red wine? rouge? blood?) adorned it in a pattern not unlike that of the Great Lakes across the continent of America. Upon these 'lakes' lay a litter of cockroach corpses, withered olives, cigarette butts, and a solitary false eyelash, jumbo size. When a Converse clad foot crushed one of the olives into the carpet, then halted there before me, I knew I had to look up. My eyes ran up his legs and instinctively paused at his crotch. It was unavoidable, being barely half a metre from my face, exactly at eye level, and looking remarkably prominent and promising, flattered by the cling of his cotton sweat pants. I jerked my eyes up to his face. Ant gazed down at me and offered his hand. 'You live here?' he asked, slightly puzzled.

I took his hand and nodded.

'I'm Anthony.'

Up close there was a slightly bewitched air to his stare. He gave a quick abashed flicker of a smile. 'You look a little like someone I know,' he said, as if in apology for staring. 'You could be his brother.'

He paused, expecting a reply, but I could think of nothing to say to that. I had no idea to whom I was being compared. If it was even a compliment. He cleared his throat. 'What . . . what's your name?'

I realised I had forgotten to introduce myself, yet I was still clutching his hand like a halfwit. I released it abruptly, apologising and blushing.

'Stephen. Stephen Spear.'

I could think of nothing, *nothing* more to say.

'You must be in number seven,' Ant finally remarked. 'Above me. I heard you moving in.'

'I hope I didn't disturb you,' I replied without thinking and then cursed the inanity of such a remark.

It was exactly what I did want to do—disturb him. Deeply. Captivate him. Seduce him. In the past I'd had no problem charming whomever I wanted. Usually the flirtatious banter rippled off my tongue as if it had been scripted. But Anthony—*Ant*—he was an entirely different proposition. Desire had never really been a motivation before. Now it was and its urgency danced through my veins. But instead of inspiring me into an imitation of Elisabeth at her finest, it rendered me useless, huddled in my chair, blushing and bumbling.

Ant reassured me that I hadn't been an intrusion. 'You get used to noise in these apartments,' he said with a sharp look at Jo-Jo.

He slid down and knelt on the carpet beside me. Our faces were at the same level. He rested his elbow on the arm of my chair. Neither of us spoke but the atmosphere between us was charged with expectation. Suddenly Strauss swooped down in a whirl of psychedelic kaftan and insinuated his body between us. '*Voilà*, Antonio,' he cried, presenting Ant's drink with a flourish, his other hand stealing up his arm to caress his bicep.

I wasn't sure whether I was more relieved or irritate by this invasion. Certainly Strauss commandeering the conversation filled the daunting silence between Ant and me and provided an opportunity for me to gather my wits, but that charge of intimacy between us had been lost. I'd had a sense that something profound and revealing might have occurred at any moment. Instead, we were obliged to listen to Strauss prattle on as he pried into the origin of Ant's injury.

'Now, darling, what have you been doing with yourself? How did you get that black eye? You brushed by me without a word of explanation but that won't do. I demand to know. And don't bother to think of a lie because I shall see straight through it. I have an instinct for distinguishing fact from fantasy.'

Ant said nothing. There was a frosty edge to his silence.

'Now don't get peevish,' Strauss continued. 'You know how overactive my imagination is. I will believe the worst of you if you don't tell me the truth. That you're dreadfully allergic to mascara or something ghastly like that.'

But even that couldn't coax a smile from Ant.

'I had a fight with someone,' he finally said stiffly.

'Hmm,' mused Strauss, arching his eyebrows. 'I believe I know with whom.'

'Yes, you do and let's leave it there.'

'Very well,' sighed Strauss. 'Perhaps you'll confide in me later when you're drunk. Or maybe Stephen can cajole the details out of you. I'll leave you two to get acquainted. Ant is about to flee to the Land of the Long White Cloud. Did he tell you?'

'What?' I was horrified that he was about to disappear before I'd had a chance to impress him. 'Where?'

'Neeeew Ziiiiland,' said Strauss in an exaggerated mockery of the accent. 'I like to refer to it by the English translation of the Maori name. It speaks so eloquently of the weather there.'

Strauss flitted back to the kitchen to mix some more drinks. Ant's face was flushed. He looked a little annoyed, or rather he looked as if he was trying to hide the fact that he was very annoyed.

'You're going away?' I asked, trying to keep the agitation I was feeling out of my voice.

'Just for a holiday to visit my family.'

I nodded, relieved. 'For long?' I asked.

'Five days. It's enough.'

I was so pleased that it wasn't for weeks that I forgot to continue the conversation. I became preoccupied planning how our romance might unfold upon his return. It took Strauss's announcement that he was putting a Nana Mouskouri record on the stereo to jerk me back to reality.

'He's a character,' I remarked for something to say.

'Yes,' said Ant with a twist to his voice. 'But the thing is you never know what character he's going to be. One day he looks like Sid Vicious, the next day he's got up like Liberace.'

'What does he do?'

'For work?' Ant frowned. 'He doesn't as far as I know. He runs a night-club one night a week, just down the road at Club 77. We should go along some time.'

I was so thrilled and surprised by his invitation that I found myself lost for words again. By the time I'd recovered myself, Ant had carried on the conversation, with me failing to indicate any interest in his proposition.

'I guess he's on the dole, although I don't know how he could possibly support his lifestyle on the dole. He goes out so much and he must spend a fortune on clothes. Maybe he disguises himself and claims the dole under a dozen different names.'

'I *would* like to go to his club,' I said abruptly. 'With you, I mean.'

The thread of that conversation had been lost and Ant seemed faintly startled by my belated eagerness. 'Okay,' he said, but there was no enthu-siasm to his voice, something I hoped was due to his irritation with Strauss, not to the prospect of my company.

Abruptly, Nana's voice, which had been in mid-chorus of 'Four and Twenty Hours', began to deepen and slow down, gradually winding down into silence. Jo-Jo had kicked the stereo's power point out of the wall. She stood by the French doors looking pleased with herself. 'Can we get cracking?' she demanded.

'That was a nasty thing to do to Nana,' Strauss protested.

Jo-Jo looked unrepentant.

'Very well,' said Strauss. 'I merely thought if everyone was made mellow by some strong drinks and some lovely music, we might be able to resolve this problem in friendly, casual fashion. However, Jo-Jo, if you prefer everyone to be sober and serious, businesslike and brutal, so be it. I call this meeting to order.'

He paused and stared with mock solemnity first at Jo-Jo and then at Sass. 'Now, it has been brought to my attention that you two ladies are indulging in Bette Davis theatricals every night after midnight and disturbing the residents of this building from their slumber.'

'If madame would stick to her patch, then there wouldn't be a problem,' said Jo-Jo moodily.

'You're always spying on me from the top of the stairs. I'm just doing the same,' Sass retaliated.

Jo-Jo's voice rose. 'Those stairs are off-limits to you . . .'

'Thank you, but no thank you, ladies,' Strauss interrupted Jo-Jo firmly. 'We don't need a demonstration of your animated conversation. But now I know what everyone's been complaining about. I'm never in at night so I've never heard you. That's why I've taken it upon myself to mediate some sort of agreement, as I'm not affected personally. Now, I believe the first step would be to agree upon some limits.'

'Hear, hear,' said Blair.

'I don't think it would be unreasonable for Sassparilla to restrict herself to making her nightly excursions up the stairs to Shame Lane before eleven o'clock on week nights, and before midnight on weekends. Does that sound fair?'

'Why arrange visiting hours for her when she's not welcome in the first place?' grumbled Jo-Jo.

'I don't come to visit *you*. I like the view from the top of the stairs.'

'Then why don't you gaze at the fucking harbour instead of down the alley to see who I'm busy with.'

'Ladies, ladies,' protested Strauss. 'It seems to me, Jo-Jo, that from your vantage point at the top of the stairs you can look down upon Sass whenever you please. It's probably only fair that Sass should be allowed to climb the stairs to look in on you occasionally.'

'That's true,' declared Sass jubilantly, and eventually Jo-Jo, after a good deal of moaning and mumbling, was forced to agree.

'Good. But, Sass, restricted hours of calling. Okay? Can I also point out that it does nothing to fuel your clients' delusions when they hear you two bellowing at one another like warring football fans. If you want to foster an atmosphere of allurement and enticement down there in the alley, I'd keep it strictly silent.'

Jo-Jo scowled, though she did look a little thoughtful, once the irritation had faded from her face.

'Now, I believe Jo-Jo has a complaint of her own to air. Jo-Jo?'

Sass leant forward with interest.

Jo-Jo turned a baleful eye upon each of us in turn. 'Someone from these apartments threw an egg at me,' she said slowly.

Sass shrieked her approval.

'Did they hit you?' enquired Strauss.

'No,' said Jo-Jo with a toothless smirk. 'They missed.'

'Well, I doubt very much it was anyone in this room. We all have a very good aim. Is anyone going to own up?'

No-one spoke.

'Any witnesses?'

'It may have been the guy next to me, in number two,' suggested Ant. 'He owns his place. He's always complaining about the prostitutes cheapening his investment.'

'Very likely,' said Strauss. 'He has also failed to turn up tonight, which seems to be a sure sign of guilt. I'll speak to him. Jo-Jo, you're not to go exacting revenge.'

I was relieved that a likely culprit had been identified. Jo-Jo had been making a frightful noise on one of my first nights in my new apartment. Finally, in exasperation, I had thrown one of the eggs I had intended to cook Elisabeth for lunch at her. I was surprised to learn I had missed. From the pandemonium that followed, I had assumed it was a direct hit.

Jo-Jo lurched across the room on her high heels. At the door she turned, hands on her hips, and glared at us all. 'Anyone throws anything at me, eggs, anything, I'll be after them for compensation. Disruption to business. Loss of income.'

'You'll get your lawyers onto them, won't you, Jo-Jo?' taunted Sass.

'Naw,' drawled Jo-Jo. 'I'll get Slash and Eddie onto them. They're more effective than any lawyers.'

Jo-Jo hauled herself out the door, chuckling.

Surprisingly, Sass came to Jo-Jo s defence once she'd gone. 'Don't throw eggs at the poor old tart. She has enough insults hurled her way without eggs to cap it off. Besides, her mates are bad news. You don't want to know about them.'

'Be warned,' Strauss added. 'I declare a cease-fire and that it's time for another round of drinks.'

I was surprised when Ant got to his feet and excused himself. 'You're going?'

'I have to eat,' he replied. 'And then I have to pack for going away. Nice to meet you.'

Strauss rushed over with more drinks. 'Ant, you can't leave!' he cried indignantly.

'Sorry,' he said without a trace of sincerity.

He strode across the room saying goodbye to Blair and Sass as he went. At the door he paused and glanced back across the room, but it was his right profile, his black eye, that was now turned towards me. It was impossible to discern anything—longing, curiosity, indifference—from that swollen slit. I couldn't even be sure if his attention was directed at me or at our host who stood next to me and was bemoaning Ant's premature exit in my ear.

ABOUT THE AUTHORS

GRAEME AITKEN was raised in Central Otago, New Zealand, but has lived for the past decade or so in Sydney. He is the author of two novels, *50 Ways of Saying Fabulous* and *Vanity Fierce*.

INEZ BARANAY Born in Italy, 1949, she came to Australia in the 1950s. She has worked as a journalist, school teacher, script writer and an Australian Volunteer Abroad in Papua New Guinea. Her novels are *Between Careers* (1989), *Pagan* (1990) and *The Edge of Bali* (1992). *The Saddest Pleasure*, a collection of short stories, was published in 1989.

BRUCE BEAVER was born in Manly, Sydney in 1928. Before settling on writing as a career he was a radio programmer, clerk and freelance journalist. He published his first volume of poetry, *Under the Bridge*, in 1961. His *New and Selected Poems* 1960-1990, reveal his considerable achievements as a poet.

MERLINDA BOBIS is the author of four poetry books, four plays and a collection of short stories, *White Turtle*. She has won major awards for her writing, including the internationally prestigious Prix Italia in 1998. She lectures in Creative Writing at the University of Wollongong.

JOHN CLARE was born in the Sydney beachside suburb of Maroubra in 1940. He is a freelance journalist who has written widely on jazz for various newspapers and periodicals. Clare is the author of *Bodgie Dada and The Cult of Cool* and the memoir *Low Rent*. Clare lived on Victoria Street, Kings Cross in the mid-1970s.

DYMPHNA CUSACK (1902-81). Born in Wyalong, NSW, she worked as a teacher before concentrating on her writing. She published twelve novels including *Say No to Death* (1951) and *Come in Spinner* (written in collaboration with Florence James in 1951). She also wrote children's books and plays. Her work was translated into numerous languages and was especially popular with the former socialist block.

ROBIN DALTON was brought up in Kings Cross and has lived in London since 1946. She has been a writer, television performer and intelligence agent. She has also been a literary agent and film producer. Her film credits include *Madame Souzatska* and *Oscar and Lucinda*.

LUKE DAVIES was born in Sydney in 1962. He has worked variously as a truck driver, teacher and journalist. He is the author of the novel *Candy* and a collection of poetry *Absolute Event Horizon*.

DULCIE DEAMER (1890-1972). She was at various times an actor, freelance journalist, playwright and novelist. Her most well-known book of poetry is *Messalina* (1932). A notorious figure in Sydney bohemian and literary circles in the 1920s and 1930s she is a key figure in Peter Kirkpatrick's *The Sea Coast of Bohemia* (1992).

PETER DOYLE grew up in Sydney's eastern suburbs in the 1950s. He has worked as a taxi driver, teacher and musician and now lives in Newtown. His first novel, *Get Rich Quick*, won the 1997 Ned Kelly Award for best first crime novel.

'M. BARNARD ELDERSHAW' was the pseudonym adopted by Flora Eldershaw and Marjorie Barnard for the works on which they collaborated, published 1929-47. Together they wrote histories, essays, short stories and five novels including *The House is Built* (1929) and *Tomorrow and Tomorrow* (1947), republished in its full, uncensored version as *Tomorrow and Tomorrow and Tomorrow* in 1983.

SUMNER LOCKE ELLIOTT (1917-1991). Raised in Sydney, he became an actor, a writer for radio and a playwright. His most important play is *Rusty Bugles*. In 1948 he went to live in the USA where he wrote his highly popular autobiographical novel, *Careful He Might Hear You* (1963). Other novels were *Eden's Lost* (1963) and *Water Under the Bridge* (1977). He last work was *Fairyland* (1990) a semi-autobiographical novel which gives a vivid picture of Sydney in the 1930s.

LYDIA GILL was born in Sydney in 1913, where she lived for most of her life. Orphaned at five, she grew up during the Depression and World War II. It was during this period she developed her intimate and comprehensive knowledge of Sydney streets and landmarks.

KATE GRENVILLE was born in Sydney in 1950. From the ages of 26-34 she lived in Europe and the USA. She has written a collection of short stories, *Bearded Ladies* (1994) and five novels including *Lilian's Story* (1985), *Joan Makes History* (1988) and *The Idea of Perfection* (1999).

BOB HERBERT (1923-1999). Born in Yea, Victoria, he worked in radio, television and theatre as actor, stage manager, director and playwright. His plays include *An Isolated Case of Heterochromia* (1970), *The Last Wake of Sheoak Creek* (1988). He is known best for *No Names . . . No Pack Drill* (1980) which was made into the film *Rebel*. He lived infrequently in the Cross.

BARRY HUMPHRIES was born in Melbourne, 1934, and is an actor, performer and writer. On stage he has created such memorable characters as *Edna Everage* and *Les Patterson*. He has also compiled such anthologies as *Bizarre* (1965) and *The Barry Humphries Book of Innocent Austral Verse* (1968). His autobiography *More Please* (1992) was a revealing self-portrait, followed by the novel *Women in the Background* (1995).

IVOR INDYK is the founding editor of the literary journal *HEAT*. A critic, essayist and reviewer he has written a monograph on David Malouf. He lectures on English and Australian Literature at the University of Sydney.

FLORENCE JAMES (1904-1993). Born in New Zealand she was a journalist in London and lived in Sydney from 1938 to 1947. She collaborated with Dymphna Cusack in writing *Come In Spinner* (1951). In 1988 (living once again in Sydney) she reassembled the original text for publication.

GEORGE HENRY JOHNSTON (1912-1970). Born in Melbourne, he was a journalist during the Second World War. He wrote several non-fiction books about Australians at war and from 1954 to 1964 he lived in Greece. His most well-known novels are *Clean Straw for Nothing* (1969) and *My Brother Jack*. In 1964 he returned to Australia and lived in Sydney until his death from tuberculosis. A prolific writer he also wrote short stories and plays for radio and television and several thrillers under a pseudonym.

YUSEF KOMUNYAKAA is a Professor of Creative Writing at Princeton University. He has published ten collections of poetry, including *Magic City* (1992), *Dien Cai Dau* (1998), the Pulitzer Prize-winning *Neon Vernacular* (1993), which also won the Kingsley Tufts Poetry Award. Komunyakaa lived in Kings Cross in the mid-1980s and frequently wrote poetry about the area, most of which is collected in *Thieves of Paradise* (1998).

GINA LENNOX is a writer and film maker. She worked as a film editor at the ABC and then became a freelance writer, researcher and producer-director. Over the years she has both lived and worked in the Cross.

JACK LINDSAY (1900-1990). He was the son of Norman Lindsay, and although born in Melbourne, was brought up in Brisbane. In 1926 he left for England and never returned to Australia. He was a poet, dramatist, editor, historian, translator, classical scholar, biographer, novelist and critic. His best work is probably his autobiographical trilogy, *Life Rarely Tells* (1958), *The Roaring Twenties* (1960), *and Fanfrolico and After* (1962).

GABRIELLE LORD was born in Sydney in 1946. She was a common-wealth employment officer for nine years, after which she became a full-time writer. Some of her fiction includes *Fortress* (1980), *Salt* (1990) and *Whipping Boy* (1992). She has also written for television and co-authored an account of her convent education, *Growing Up a Catholic* (1986).

RONALD McCUAIG (1908-1993) Born in Newcastle, NSW, he was a literary critic and magazine editor, short story writer, anthologist and essayist. An underrated poet, his first book of poetry *Vaudeville* (1938) is perhaps his best and certainly most influential.

KENNETH 'SEAFORTH' MACKENZIE (1913-1955). He moved to Sydney from Perth in 1934. His novels include *Chosen People* (1938), *Dead Men Rising* (1951) and *The Refuge* (1954). He also published four volumes of poetry. In 1955 he drowned in a creek.

LORENZO MONTESINI was born in Alexandria, Egypt. As an adolescent he settled in Melbourne. He spent two years in the Australian army, including twelve months on active service in Vietnam as an inter-preter. He now lives in Sydney and is employed as a steward with Qantas. Besides his autobiography, *My Life and Other Misdemeanours*, he has also written a novel entitled the *Cardboard Cantata*.

FRANK MOORHOUSE was born in Nowra in 1938, and was a journalist before becoming a full-time writer. The short story collection, *The Americans, Baby* (1972) established his reputation. Later collections included *The Everlasting Secret Family and Other Secrets* (1980) and *Lateshows* (1990). He has also edited several anthologies of short fiction and written the screenplays, *Between Wars* (1974) and *The Everlasting Secret Family* (1988).

LOUIS NOWRA is a novelist, playwright and screenwriter. His most recent book is his memoir, *The Twelfth of Never*. He was born in Melbourne and now lives in Kings Cross.

BETTY ROLAND (1903-1995). Born in Victoria, she started out as a journalist. Her first play was *The Touch of Silk* (1942). She spent over a year in Russia in 1934 and returned to Australia where she worked as a journalist, a playwright, screenwriter, novelist and travel writer. Her best work is probably her four autobiographies, especially, *Caviar for Breakfast* (1979) and *An Improbable Life* (1989).

JON ROSE is the author of *At the Cross* and *Peppercorn Days*. Born in Melbourne, he spent several years in Kings Cross before going to live in England.

FRANCES RUSH worked for several years in Kings Cross as an advocate and community development worker, primarily involved with people living a street-based lifestyle. She was involved with a number of projects in the early 1990s including coordinating the Kings Cross Mural, creative writing projects and literacy projects. Rush now thoroughly enjoys living in the Cross.

MANDY SAYER is the author of three novels. *Mood Indigo* (winner of the 1989 Vogel Award), *Blind Luck* and *The Cross*. Her memoir *Dreamtime Alice* was published in 1998, winning The National Biography Award and Australian Audio Book of the Year. It has since been published in the USA, the UK and translated into several European languages. Sayer lived in Kings Cross as a child and, after completing a BA and MA at Indiana University, returned to live and work there in 1994.

KENNETH SLESSOR (1901-1971). Born in Orange, NSW, he was a journalist, poet and essayist. His *One Hundred Poems* (1944) reveals him as one of Australia's greatest poets. He also wrote light verse, including *Darlinghurst Nights* (1932). His *War Diaries* and *War Despatches*, were published in 1985 and 1987 respectively. From 1944 until his death, he only wrote two more poems. Slessor lived in King Cross for several decades.

VIVIAN SMITH was born in Hobart in 1933, though he has spent many years in Sydney. He has published several volumes of verse including

An Island South (1967) and *Tide Country* (1982). He has edited several poetry anthologies and written monographs on such writers as James McAuley and Vance Palmer.

ROBERTA SYKES was raised in Queensland. She has written and lectured widely on race relations and has worked for Aboriginal medical and legal services. Non-fiction books include *Black Power in Australia* (1975) and *Black Majority* (1989). She has also published a collection of poems, *Love Poems and Other Revolutionary Actions* (1979). She achieved notoriety and success for her first autobiographical volume *Snake Dreaming*.

JOHN TRANTER was born in Cooma NSW in 1949. He has been a publisher, editor, literary reviewer and teacher. He is a prolific and significant poet. Some of his books of poetry are *Crying in Early Infancy* (1977), *Selected Poems* (1982) and *At the Florida* (1993). He has also edited several anthologies of poetry.

PATRICK WHITE (1912-1990). He was educated in NSW and then in England. His first novel was *Happy Valley* published in 1939. He was an intelligence officer during the Second World War in the Middle East. In 1948 he returned to live in Australia where he wrote such novels as *Voss* (1959), *The Eye of the Storm* (1973) and *The Twyborn Affair* (1979). He published two collections of short stories and several plays including *A Cheery Soul*. He wrote the script for the film, *The Night the Prowler* (1978) and received the Nobel Prize in 1973.

SELECT BIBLIOGRAPHY

Brewster, H.C. & Luther, Virginia. *Kings Cross Calling*. Liberty Press, Sydney, 1945.

Butel, Elizabeth & Thompson, Tom. *Kings Cross Album*. Atrand, Sydney, 1984.

Byrell, John. *Up the Cross*, Child and Henry, Brookvale, 1983.

Carmen. *Carmen: My Life: as told to Paul Martin*. Benton Ross, Auckland, 1988.

Clune, Frank. *Try Nothing Twice*. Angus & Robertson, Sydney, 1946.

Cockington, James & Carlotta. *He Did It Her Way: Carlotta, Legend of Les Girls*. Pan Macmillan, Sydney, 1994.

Coombs, Anne. *Sex and Anarchy: The Life and Death of the Sydney Push*. Penguin (Viking), Melbourne, 1996.

Dimond, Jill & Kirkpatrick, Peter. *Literary Sydney*. University of Queensland Press, St Lucia, 2000.

Drury, Nevill. *Pan's Daughter: The Strange World of Rosaleen Norton*. Collins, Sydney, 1988.

Ellis, Rennie & Stacey, Wesley. *Kings Cross Sydney: A Personal Look at the Cross*. Thomas Nelson, Sydney, 1971.

Farwell, George. *Requiem for Woolloomooloo*. New Century Press, Sydney, 1971.

Falkner, Heather. *Up All Night*. Collins Australia, Sydney, 1989.

Finey, George. *The Mangle Wheel: My Life*. Kangaroo, Sydney, 1981.

Furbank, B. *Kings Cross and the Idea of Urban Sin*. James Cook University, Cairns, 1999.

Harding, Alex. *Only Heaven Knows*. Currency Press, Sydney, 1989.

Hooton, Harry. *It is Great to Be Alive*. Twenty-First Century Art Group, 1961.

Jarratt, Phil. *Ted Noffs: Man of the Cross*. Pan Macmillan, Sydney, 1997.

Kelly, Max. *Faces of the Street, William Street, Sydney, 1916*. Doak Press, Paddington, 1982.

Kings Cross Community Aid and Information Service. *Kings Cross 1936-1946*, Potts Point, 1981.

Kirkpatrick, Peter. *The Sea Coast of Bohemia: Literary Life in Sydney's Roaring Twenties*. University of Queensland Press, St Lucia, 1992.

Koch, Christopher J. *The Doubleman*. Chatto & Windus, London, 1985.

London, Jack. 'Jack London's Article'. *Australian Star*, 7 January 1909:1.

MacDonnell, Freda. *Before Kings Cross*. Thomas Nelson (Australia), Sydney, 1967.

Mendelssohn, Joanna. *The Yellow House 1970-72*. Art Gallery of NSW Press, Sydney, 1990.

Norton, Rosaleen. *The Art of Rosaleen Norton*. Walter Glover, Sydney, 1952.

Perkins, Roberta. *The Drag Queen Scene: Transsexuals in Kings Cross*, Allen & Unwin, Sydney, 1983.

Pierce, Peter (ed). *The Oxford Literary Guide to Australia*. Oxford University Press, Melbourne, 1993.

Residents of Woolloomooloo Group. *Watch on the 'Loo, 1920-1980*. Sydney, 1983.

Slessor, Kenneth & Walker, Robert. *Life at The Cross*. Rigby, Sydney, 1965.

Spears, Steve J. *In Search of the Bodgie*. Collins Australia, Sydney, 1989.

Sprod, George. *Life on a Square-Wheeled Bike, the Saga of a Cartoonist*. Kangaroo Press, Kenthurst, 1983.

Sprod, George. *When I Survey the Wondrous Cross*, Quincunx Press, Dee Why, 1989.

Tench, Watkin. *Sydney's First Four Years: Being a Reprint of a Narrative of the Expedition to Botany Bay and A Complete Account of the Settlement at Port Jackson*. Angus & Robertson, Sydney, 1961.

Wilde, William H Joy Hooton & Andrews, Barry. *The Oxford Companion to Australian Literature*. Oxford University Press, Melbourne, 1988.

Wright, Judith. *Half a Lifetime*. The Text Publishing Company, Melbourne, 1999.

ACKNOWLEDGMENTS

Acknowledgments are due to the following authors, estates, publishers and agents for permission to include the extracts of stories, poems and memoirs which appear in this book.

The extract from *Vanity Fierce* by Graeme Aitken, Random House Australia, 1998, reprinted by permission of Graeme Aitken.

'Angel's Weather' from *New and Selected Poems 1960–1990: Bruce Beaver* by Bruce Beaver, University of Queensland Press, 1991, reprinted by permission of University of Queensland Press (UQP).

'The Great Rite: Sex Magick' from *Pagan* by Inez Baranay, Angus & Robertson, 1990, reprinted by permission of Inez Baranay.

'Fruit Stall' from *White Turtle* by Merlinda Bobis, Spinifex Press, 1999, reprinted by permission of Spinifex Press.

'El Rocco' from *Bodgie Dada & The Cult of Cool*, UNSW Press, 1995, reprinted by permission of John Clare.

'Sunday VI' from *Come In Spinner* by Dymphna Cusack and Florence James, first published 1951, reprinted by permission of HarperCollins Publishers Australia.

The extract from *Aunts Up the Cross* by Robin Dalton, Viking, 1998 (first published by Blond, London, 1965), reprinted by permission of Penguin Australia and Robin Dalton.

'Problems with Detachable Heads:1' from *Candy* by Luke Davies, first published by Allen and Unwin, 1988, reprinted by permission of Luke Davies.

The extract from *The Queen of Bohemia—The Autobiography of Dulcie Deamer* by Dulcie Deamer, UQP, 1998, reprinted by permission of the estate of Dulcie Deamer.

The extract from *Get Rich Quick* by Peter Doyle, Minerva, 1996, reprinted by permission of Peter Doyle.

'Morning' from *Tomorrow and Tomorrow and Tomorrow* by M. Barnard Eldershaw, Virago Press, 1983, reprinted by permission of Curtis Brown (Australia) Pty Ltd, on behalf of the authors.

The extracts from *Fairyland* by Sumner Locke Elliott, Pan, 1991, reprinted by permission of Sara Menguc on behalf of the estate of Sumner Locke Elliott.

'Kings Cross' from *My Town—Sydney in the 1930s* by Lydia Gill, State Library of NSW Press, 1993, reprinted by permission of the State Library of NSW Press.

The extract from *Lilian's Story* by Kate Grenville, first published by Allen & Unwin, 1986, reprinted by permission of Kate Grenville and Australian Literary Management.

The extract from *No Names . . . No Pack Drill* by Bob Herbert, Currency Press, 1980, reprinted by permission of Currency Press.

'The Silver Spade' reprinted by permission of Ivor Indyk.

'Sydney, 1946' from *Clean Straw for Nothing* by George Johnston, first published by Bodley Head, 1969, reprinted by permission of HarperCollins Publishers Australia.

'John Says', 'Message' and 'The Piccolo' from *Thieves of Paradise*, 1998, reprinted by permission of Yusef Komunyakaa and Wesleyan University of Press © 1998.

'Living the Piccolo Mondo: Vittorio Bianchi, maestro of the cappuccino machine' and 'The Tunnel: John Ibrahim, nightclub owner at nineteen' from *People of the Cross—True Stories from People Who Live and Work in Kings Cross* (oral histories based on interviews by Gina Lennox and Frances Rush), Simon and Schuster, 1993, reprinted by permission of Gina Lennox and Frances Rush.

The extract from *The Roaring Twenties: Literary Life in NSW in the Years 1921–6* by Jack Lindsay, first published by Bodley Head, 1960, reprinted by permission of Jack Lindsay and The Bodley Head Publishers.

The extract from *Whipping Boy* by Gabrielle Lord, Hodder Headline, 1998 (first published by McPhee Gribble 1992), reprinted by permission of Hodder Headline Australia.

The extract from *The Refuge* by Kenneth 'Seaforth' Mackenzie, first published by Angus & Robertson, 1954, reprinted by permission of ETT Imprint.

'The Razor', 'The Letter', 'Pretty Kid', 'They Also Serve Who Only Stand and Wait', and 'Music in the Air' from *Selected Poems: Ronald McCuaig*, Angus & Robertson, 1992, reprinted by permission of ETT Imprint.

The extract from *My Life and Other Misdemeanours* by Lorenzo Montesini, Penguin, 1999, reprinted by permission of Penguin Australia.

"The American, Paul Jonson' from *The Americans, Baby* by Frank Moorhouse, reprinted by permission of Pan Macmillan Australia Pty Ltd. Copyright © Frank Moorhouse 1972.

The extract from *Red Nights* by Louis Nowra reprinted by permission of Pan Macmillan Australia Pty Ltd. Copyright © Amanita Pty Ltd 1997.

The extract from *The Devious Being* by Betty Roland, Angus & Robertson, 1990, reprinted by permission of ETT Imprint, on behalf of the estate of Betty Roland.

The extract from *At the Cross* by Jon Rose, Andre Deutsch, 1961, reprinted by permission of Andre Deutsch.

"The Heiress" and "The Receptionist" from *The Cross* by Mandy Sayer, Angus & Robertson, 1995, reprinted by permission of Mandy Sayer.

'Life at the Cross', 'My King's Cross', 'Choker's Lane', 'Ticket in Tatts!', 'Up in Mabel's Room', 'Nocturne', 'King's Cross Gardens' by Kenneth Slessor reprinted by permission of Paul Slessor and ETT Imprint.

'Cannibal Street' from *Selected Poems: Kenneth Slessor* by Kenneth Slessor, Angus & Robertson, 1993, reprinted by permission of Harper Collins Publishers Australia.

'Twenty Years of Sydney' and 'A Few Words for Maxi' from *New Selected Poems* by Vivian Smith, Angus & Robertson, © Vivian Smith, 1995, reprinted by permission of Vivian Smith.

The extract from *Snake Dancing*, first published by Allen & Unwin, 1988, reprinted by permission of Roberta Sykes.

'Storm Over Sydney' from *At the Florida* by John Tranter, University of Queensland Press, 1993, reprinted by permission of John Tranter.

'At the Piccolo' from *Selected Poems* by John Tranter, Hale and Iremonger, 1982, reprinted by permission of Hale and Iremonger and John Tranter.

The extract from *Voss* by Patrick White, Jonathan Cape (first published 1957), reprinted by permission of Jonathan Cape and the estate of Patrick White.

Every effort has been made to identify copyright holders of extracts in this book. The publishers would be pleased to hear from any copyright holders who have not been acknowledged.